The Band
FAQ

The Band
FAQ

All That's Left to Know
About the Fathers
of Americana

Peter Aaron

Backbeat
Books

An Imprint of Hal Leonard LLC

Published in 2016 by Backbeat Books
An Imprint of Hal Leonard LLC
7777 West Bluemound Road
Milwaukee, WI 53213

Trade Book Division Editorial Offices
33 Plymouth St., Montclair, NJ 07042

The FAQ series was conceived by Robert Rodriguez and developed with Stuart Shea.

Every reasonable effort has been made to contact copyright holders and secure permission. Omissions can be remedied in future editions.

Printed in the United States of America

Book design by Snow Creative

Library of Congress Cataloging-in-Publication Data

ISBN 978-1-61713-613-9

www.backbeatbooks.com

For Mom, from the luckiest son in the world

Contents

Foreword

Out of the swirling, smoky kaleidoscope of mid-sixties psychedelia and misty-eyed flower power strode five no-nonsense men who appeared to come to us straight out of an old daguerreotype, with their beards, black hats, string ties, and boots. The only things missing from the picture were their trusty six-shooters, but they had their musical axes in hand and those did the trick just fine. The image they projected was unique in that time of tie-dye, velvet, and paisley—at once earthy, mysterious, and very real. What these players and singers brought to the forefront of the hippie-dominated music scene was a raw, roots-based North American music, honed during years of playing in rough-and-tumble roadhouses, fleabag bars, and smoky honky-tonks. Their no-nonsense sensibilities were informed by their working-class Canadian families and heavily flavored by Levon Helm's hardscrabble Arkansas farmer folks.

These days their music is mostly listed under the "Americana" label, but the Hawks—a.k.a. the Crackers, the Honkies, and finally, simply, The Band—knew virtually nothing about the ballads and acoustic guitar picking of the folk revival. When Levon Helm was initially approached about backing up Bob Dylan, he was reportedly derisive of playing behind a "strummer." Rather, their musical style grew out of the rockabilly of Jerry Lee Lewis, Buddy Holly, and the Everly Brothers; the blues of Muddy Waters, Otis Spann, and Howlin' Wolf; and the R&B of Little Richard, Ray Charles, and Fats Domino. Levon, of course, could trace his musical roots to the Delta blues of Sonny Boy Williamson and to the bluegrass and gospel of the Stanley Brothers and the Carter Family. They all knew everything there was to know about commercial country music and rock 'n' roll.

Their musical world gradually, inevitably expanded, initially through Dylan's wide-ranging knowledge of folk, Celtic, blues, and "high lonesome" Appalachian traditions. The Band—especially their most prolific songwriter, Robbie Robertson—eventually took to the more traditional elements of the music with growing respect, incorporating earthy folk ballads, dance tunes, and Civil War styles into their music. "Up on Cripple Creek," "Rag Mama Rag," and especially "The Night They Drove Old Dixie Down" were steeped in these traditions.

My first experience of hearing these musicians was at Bob Dylan's October 1, 1965, Carnegie Hall concert. Bob played the first half of the show exactly as we had come to expect—standing alone in a spotlight on the big stage, strumming his Gibson acoustic, and singing the songs that had stunned and mesmerized us as they seemingly poured out of him throughout the previous half-decade: "Mr. Tambourine Man," "Gates of Eden," "Desolation Row," "Love Minus Zero/No Limit" . . . The audience was rapt and utterly worshipful. After intermission he was back, but now there were drums, keyboards, and amps onstage and five additional players surrounding his slight, wraithlike figure. Of course, we had all heard about the debacle at the Newport Folk Festival just a couple of months before, so we were expecting the power and electricity. It was a shock to the system nonetheless as the first notes of "Maggie's Farm" blasted through the hallowed concert hall. Some in the audience walked out almost immediately, but most stayed to hear, and to cheer, for band versions of the likes of "Mr. Tambourine Man," "Just Like Tom Thumb's Blues," "Ballad of a Thin Man," and, of course, "Like a Rolling Stone."

Fast forward to 1967. My wife, Jane, and I had moved from New York City to Woodstock the year before and had made contact with Dylan, who had retreated to his home in Byrdcliffe following his motorcycle accident. Aside from our shared musical connections, we had kids who were roughly the same ages as his older children Maria and Jesse, so we spent quite a lot of family time together.

That Thanksgiving, we were invited to their rambling, rough-hewn old home, Hi Lo Ha, for what would be a most memorable dinner. At some point early in the evening there was a knock at the door and Sara, Bob's wife, said, "That must be the boys." In walked the five guys we had seen onstage a couple of years before. We had heard that they had been holed up at a pink ranch house in Saugerties and had been doing some recording there, but it was all just a rumor at that point. Now here they were, in all their Old West glory. My first impression was of Levon, bearded and grinning, who immediately swept up our two-year-old son, Adam, and started talking to him as if he were a fellow Arkansan. The four others followed, introducing themselves and joining the party. At some point in the evening Richard Manuel sat down at the piano, and he and Rick Danko brought the guests to silence as they sang a heart-stopping duet of "I Shall Be Released." It was the first time I had heard the song and it was a performance that I'll never forget.

Woodstock is a very small town, so it was inevitable that we would frequently run into these guys. We became friendly with each of them in varying degrees. Levon recounts in his book, *This Wheel's on Fire*, how Jane and I had him to our home for dinner that first year they were here and he never forgot our hospitality. We retained a warm friendship with Levon for the next forty-five years, and I played frequently as a "special guest" at his Midnight Rambles.

My late brother, Artie Traum, used to recount, onstage, how he met Rick and Robbie late at night "in the munchie aisle of the local Grand Union supermarket," and they taught him "Bessie Smith" (from *The Basement Tapes*) on the spot, amongst the Oreos and Mallomars. We later recorded it on our debut album for Capitol as "Going Down the Road to See Bessie," and it became one of our signature songs.

One night, Robbie invited Artie and me to his house to listen to the tapes of what would become *Music from Big Pink*. Garth Hudson was there too, and as the music filled the room we were thunderstruck. It was, of course, different from anything we had ever heard before: neither rock nor country, blues nor pop nor folk nor anything else we recognized, although it had elements of all of those genres and more. This was a true collaboration of five highly talented and passionate musicians—interchanging voices, swirling organ swells, pounding piano licks, incisive guitar solos, all grounded by the fantastic rhythm section of Rick and Levon. The songs, too, were unexpectedly complex, poetic, powerful.

Richard Manuel's friendship and musical generosity to me were brought to view when, in 1979, he agreed to help out in a recording session I was doing for a small folk label, Greenways Records. He spent the day with us in a funky little studio, adding electric piano and clavinet to the title track, "Bright Morning Stars," and even adding a piano part to my own version of "I Shall Be Released." What a thrill it was for me to have Richard add his astonishing musicianship, talent, and insights to my album, a gesture that stays with me to this day.

Robbie would move out of Woodstock for Hollywood to work on film music for Martin Scorsese and to pursue his own musical journey. Rick, Levon, Richard, and Garth, though, would live on and off, through ups and downs, in the Catskills for the rest of their lives. I feel incredibly fortunate to have known each of these artists as a friend and to have played with them at venues large and small through the years.

Happy Traum
Woodstock, New York

Singer and songwriter Happy Traum is an icon of American folk music. In 1967 he and his brother Artie formed a duo that Rolling Stone *said "defined the Northeast folk music style." Happy helped found the long-running Woodstock Mountains Revue musical collective. As a member of the New World Singers, he sang and played on the first recorded versions of Bob Dylan's "Blowin' in the Wind" and "Don't Think Twice, It's All Right." He has performed and recorded with Dylan, Levon Helm and other members of The Band, Paul Butterfield, Peter Tosh, and many others. Happy served as editor of* Sing Out! *magazine for three years and in 1967 co-established, with Jane Traum, the world-renowned musical instruction materials company Homespun Tapes. With a catalog of over five hundred DVDs, CDs, books, and downloads, Homespun offers lessons taught by top professional performing musicians covering a wide variety of instruments and styles.*

Acknowledgments

When I began this book, I was terrified. The Band was one of the most powerfully mythic, far-reachingly influential, and devoutly admired musical groups to ever exist. They were like the Mount Rushmore of rock 'n' roll. An act the big boys in the world of so-called rock critics ("critic" has always had a negative ring for me; I prefer, simply, "music journalist") had made their careers writing about. Beyond the basic story (Dylan, etc.) and their first few records, though, I honestly didn't know that much about them.

As a subject, The Band felt like towering mountains I could never climb. Miles of earth I'd never be able to shovel my way to the bottom of. Wide-open, Southwestern desert vistas that go on forever and that I'd never reach the end of, no matter how far and how long I trudged. But as a student of music I wanted to learn about them. And, I reasoned, the best way to learn about a subject is to write about it. No one gets to be an authority on something by waiting for someone else to come along and make them one. Plus, I was a music journalist who'd lived in the Hudson Valley—The Band's very home turf, for chrissakes—for more than a decade. I *had* to write about them. I had many frequently asked questions of my own.

So here we are. Along with the basic synopses of The Band's main albums for those who are just discovering their music, I've attempted to cover the basic facts about the group without retreading too much of what's already been written; to present lists of recommended and related recordings, books, and films; to point the way to other musical artists I feel fans of The Band would enjoy; and to unleash an avalanche of as much deep, finite, potentially esoteric, I-didn't-know-that minutiae as I could pack into these pages. I now know *a lot* more about The Band than I did when I began this expedition over a year ago. Hopefully, you'll find at least some of what I've learned useful, and it will inspire you to undertake your own expedition through the world of The Band and their incredible music.

But I didn't get here alone. For all of their help, my most sincere, undying thanks are due to the following fine people:

Happy Traum, for agreeing to write the beautiful foreword to this book, for making his own superlative music, and for continuing to preserve traditions with his Homespun Music label.

John Simon, for his incisive interviews, his ongoing input, and especially his role in shaping the recordings of The Band and other artists.

Elliott Landy, for his generous tales about photographing The Band and for creating some of the most arresting images in the iconography of music.

Jim Weider, for so eagerly providing answers to my questions about The Band's later years, and of course for playing guitar in the group.

Tim Moore, for being a forthcoming fount of details about his life as a Woodstock musician during The Band's heady heyday.

Harold Swart, for lending some of his rare images for use in the book and for his tales about seeing and meeting the group back in the day.

Barbara O'Brien, and everyone else at the Midnight Ramble, for being so nice and taking care of me whenever I've attended. Keep it goin'!

Mark Braunstein, for his vivid accounts as a fly on the wall during the making of *Stage Fright*.

Peter Viney, whose website, theband.hiof.no, was an indispensable resource.

Bob Cavano, for his sage tips and advice.

Sarah Perrotta, for providing transcripts of her talks with Garth Hudson. Make sure to check out Garth's playing on her sublime 2007 CD, *The Well*.

Bob Bert, for his remembrances of seeing The Band in the 1970s and for making music with me for so many years.

Bernadette Malavarca, my looooong-suffering and unduly patient editor.

My publicist, Wes Seeley, and everyone else at Backbeat for their faith and assistance.

My cats, Penelope and Kizzy. Daddy wasn't ignoring you. He was busy.

And, of course, my eternally supportive and superhumanly understanding family. "We carried you in our arms . . ."

Introduction

Music lovers, take a minute to thank whatever deity you pray to for thrift stores. I started hitting them in earnest when I was in my early twenties. They're where I've found so many of the records that have altered my musical consciousness. Maybe it was an album by someone I'd never heard of—but for a buck or less? If it looked interesting in the slightest, what the hell? Sometimes, though, the discs that came home with me were by acts whose names I at least knew somewhat, usually from having repeatedly seen them as a preadolescent on the covers of *Creem*, *Rolling Stone*, *Circus*, or one of the other big-kid rock magazines next to the comic books at 7-11. (I was born in 1964, the year the Beatles blitzed America, and mostly missed out on the 1960s rock revolution; punk rock was *my* Big Bang.) Or maybe it was a case of my being vaguely familiar with the hits, if there happened to be any, on these cast-off, hippie-era artifacts that were clogging the Salvation Army bins—I figured that at such a can't-go-wrong price I may as well check out the rest of the album. One of the LPs that made its way into my life in this manner, sometime in the mid-1980s, was a well-loved copy of The Band's 1968 debut, *Music from Big Pink*.

The songs were creaky. Strange. Ghostly. Anachronistic. About hangings, wheels on fire, and some crazy coot called Chester trying to give away his dog (who was named Jack, of all things). Honestly, some moments made for a bit of a musical double take about whether *Music from Big Pink* really even *was* a rock album. Sure, you had Robbie Robertson's charged electric guitar, which had a decidedly rock edge. And yet the sound was also very country—although it never went all-the-way country. There was a strong, bubbling funkiness underneath some of the songs, which was very much at odds with the country thing. But somehow this funkiness fit right alongside the country vibe, encouraging this strange meeting, saying, "Bring it, cowboy! Now how's about settin' yerself down with a big ol' plate of this greasy fatback?" Much of this quality came from Levon Helm's idiosyncratic beats, which were both funky and tough.

But at the same time as all that, the music felt so incredibly *antique*. Pre-rock, really, maybe even pre-country. Garth Hudson's churchy fills often came across more like a steam-powered calliope than the modern electric Lowrey Festival organ he played. And the alternating lead vocals of Helm, Richard Manuel, and Rick Danko were like the worry-filled, beaten-down voices of weary old men—dying men, maybe—whose souls had been eviscerated by lifetimes spent breaking their backs in the mines, fields, mountains, and plains of an America that no longer existed. Today, watching flickering 1930s newsreel footage of gray-bearded Confederate Civil War veterans coughing out the rebel yell *one last time, boys!* for their seventy-five-year reunion, I'm reminded of the mental imagery I had that first time I played *Music from Big Pink*. This is a rock band from the 1860s, not the 1960s, I thought. But as the record played I had to keep reminding myself, of course: There *were no* rock bands in the 1860s. The Band was *not* "retro"; retro implies an effort to simply mimic the past, and that's not what they were doing. Their sound took in *all* of America's music, past, present, and future. It felt like music that could have been made in 1968 or, indeed, one hundred years earlier. Or now, almost fifty years after that, in 2016. How were these guys able to pull off this trick of hovering between the centuries, between the electrified era of FM rock and the one long before rural electrification? Which was the flesh and which was the apparition? I listened more. I listened harder. I looked for clues.

The artwork on the cover fortified the mythos. No, not the abstract painting on the front by the group's famed erstwhile employer, Bob Dylan. No, past that pastel mess and inside the gatefold. In there was Elliott Landy's stark black-and-white portrait of the band members themselves, looking just as the music would have them appear. At a time when most rock bands looked like mystic gypsies with their heads in the clouds, these guys came across every bit the gang of earthy, grounded frontier homesteaders and itinerant prospectors evoked by their songs. Here they are, all duded up on a Saturday and about to ride into town, where they'll walk through the swingin' doors of its lone saloon, drink far more than their fill of rotgut, plant some sloppy kisses on the ladies, get in a few fistfights, be thrown out when the barkeep's lost his patience, and ultimately stagger back up the dirt road to the bunkhouse, where they'll pass out and wake up just in time for church—after which they'll write a song about the whole chain of events (what they remember of it, anyway) to yowl around the evening campfire like a pack of hungover hound dogs.

And then there was the larger, color image of the guys with their real-life extended families, gathered in front of a barn, looking like they were all about to sit down to a picnic dinner. What "cool" rocker worth his tight pants would want to be photographed next to Mom and Dad? And for the cover of his band's *debut album?!* Say goodbye to your street cred, Mr. Badass Rock God, the Rotary Club is this way . . .

But of course, in taking this seemingly kiss-of-death stance, The Band were not only being honest about who they were; they were also making a genius move in setting themselves far apart from the sensationalistic faux rebellion of so many of their peer acts, with a grand, metaphoric statement: "The rich traditions and music that inspire us are deeply and immovably rooted. And they will still be here long after the haze of all of this fluorescent psychedelic hoo-hah foolishness has evaporated."

So this was powerful brain fodder for me, a defiant young man—early twenties, about the same age the group's members were when they made *Big Pink*—who at that point hadn't lived away from home all that long and was still trying to carve out his own identity and sense of place. To me, *Big Pink* said not only that it was okay to love and not deny tradition and family, but also that you could do it while distancing yourself from the greater bullshit with which society was trying to crush you. You didn't have to forsake one team for the other. You could, in fact, be yourself and still play for both, which really made you your own man and thus *truly* cool. What's cool is what's honest. What's real. The Band's songs seemed like clear, honest extensions of the members' authentic love for the simple life, for the act of music making, and for music itself. Moving, ageless, and, hell yes, real. About as real as music can get. Exploring their other albums (especially the next one, the magisterial *The Band*, and the later gems *Stage Fright* and *Northern Lights—Southern Cross*) and seeing the group in full flight in *The Last Waltz* only cemented the sentiment.

Eventually, after years of busting my own ass as a so-called musician in New York City, I ended up here, in the Hudson Valley, where I felt privileged to see the late Levon Helm perform at his magical Midnight Ramble sessions in Woodstock and to catch Garth Hudson sitting in with various acts. Here, The Band's legend is inescapable. A natural, beautiful fact. Just like our stunning Catskill Mountains, which continue to reverberate with the group's music. But far beyond the woods of this region, one can easily hear the quintet's reverent-but-impressionistic roots fusion in the music of the 1960s and '70s hitmakers who had fallen under their spell, like the Beatles and Eric Clapton, '80s and '90s mainstays like the Jayhawks and the Waterboys, today's alt-Americana acts like Wilco and the Felice Brothers, and whatever new bearded-and-flannelled combo is whooping it up in Brooklyn tonight.

Without The Band, not only would the current roots rock and Americana genres very likely not exist, but much of our own great music might simply have been forgotten. The Band created a consciousness that says that the past is just as contemporary as the present. That any music, if it's true and real, *never* gets old. And ever since those five scruffy young men came to a quiet upstate New York town to find their own way of timeless music-making, generations of musicians have been inspired to follow a similar path. A path that sees them also discovering, exploring, preserving, and reinterpreting the music of earlier eras while adding their own voices to the eternal choir.

Peter Aaron
Hudson, New York, 2016

The Band
FAQ

Let Him Take It from the Top

A Primer on The Band's Five Original Members

Founded in 1960 as the Hawks, the backup band of rockabilly singer Ronnie Hawkins, the classic original lineup of The Band consisted of drummer, singer, mandolinist, and guitarist Levon Helm; lead guitarist and singer Robbie Robertson; bassist, singer, and fiddler Rick Danko; pianist, singer, and drummer Richard Manuel; and keyboardist and saxophonist Garth Hudson. After parting ways with Hawkins in 1963, the five continued as Levon and the Hawks until being hired by Bob Dylan to back him on his 1965 and 1966 tours. Following the Dylan tours, the quintet settled in Woodstock, New York, where they collaborated with Dylan on the music that appeared on the Basement Tapes and composed the songs heard on their 1968 debut, *Music from Big Pink*.

That album and its 1969 follow-up, *The Band*, altered the course of popular music in unassuming but deep ways, and the group went on to make five more studio albums, tour extensively, and work with Dylan again for 1974's *Planet Waves* and its supporting tour. The original members stayed with the band until their much-publicized farewell concert in 1976, which was filmed for the movie *The Last Waltz*. In 1983, The Band reunited without Robertson, whose position was first filled by brothers Earl and Ernie Cate and later

Recordings of the quintet's July 18, 1976, show at the Music Inn in Lenox, Massachusetts, make up the double CD *Plays On*.   *Author's collection* by Jim Weider. The resurrected Band continued after the 1986 death of Manuel and officially dissolved in 1999 with the passing of Danko.

This chapter focuses on the five members of The Band's best-known lineup; subsequent members and ancillary players are covered later in the book.

Levon Helm

(Mark Lavon "Levon" Helm; born May 26, 1940; died April 19, 2012) While The Band's four other original members were Canadians obsessed with American vernacular music, Levon Helm was their living link to the real stuff. Raised in the Elaine, Arkansas, hamlet of Turkey Scratch (near Marvell), Helm worked on his music-loving family's cotton farm as a boy. By the time he'd turned four, little Levon had been firmly bitten by the music bug.

Arkansas was a buzzing crossroads of the musical strains that converged to become rock 'n' roll, and Helm soaked them all in. He took up guitar at age eight in order to join in the family's weekend hootenannies, eventually learning harmonica, mandolin, and drums. The blues, in particular, coursed like blood through the region, and Helm was especially fascinated with that style. Also key were the local rent parties and the minstrel and medicine shows that frequented Elm Street, the Helena nightlife district catering to local African-Americans, where Robert Johnson and the young Howlin' Wolf had played. Levon's first stage appearances were at local talent shows as a solo singer and as a singer and guitarist in a duo with his sister Linda on washtub bass. By high school he'd formed a rockabilly trio, the Jungle Bush Beaters, in which he sang and played guitar. After catching early tour stops by Elvis Presley, Bo Diddley, Carl Perkins, and other rock 'n' roll pioneers, the seventeen-year-old Helm set out for Memphis, where he joined Ronnie Hawkins and the Hawks.

With the Hawks, Helm developed the instantly identifiable, uncluttered drumming style that flows like a mountain brook through The Band's music; producer John Simon dubbed his style "bayou folk." Besides being such a unique instrumentalist, Helm had one of the most idiosyncratic lead voices in rock, a drawling, dust-dry twang that brought an air of down-home authenticity unheard in the music of The Band's Southern-U.S.-roots-mining contemporaries—especially the ones from England—during the 1960s and '70s. During a May 2, 2012, concert at Newark's Prudential Center, Bruce Springsteen called it "one of the greatest, greatest voices in country, rockabilly, and rock 'n' roll" and dedicated an acoustic rendition of The Band's "The Weight" to the drummer.

Following the 1976 dissolution of The Band, Helm formed the RCO All-Stars, released solo albums, and had a successful side career as an actor. From 1983 to 1999 he performed and recorded with the re-formed Band before leading Levon Helm and the Barn Burners as well as the Levon Helm Band. In 1991 a fire destroyed the Barn, his beloved Woodstock home and recording studio, but he eventually rebuilt the structure and began holding his famed Midnight Ramble sessions there to offset the costs of his treatment for a 1996 throat cancer diagnosis. He released two final, Grammy-winning albums, 2007's *Dirt Farmer* and 2009's *Electric Dirt*, before the disease took him.

Robbie Robertson

(Jaime Royal Klagerman; born July 5, 1943) Toronto native Robbie Robertson was The Band's primary songwriter and penned, among many others, the group's three best-known songs: "The Weight," "The Night They Drove Old Dixie Down," and "Up on Cripple Creek." In addition to his compositional gifts, Robertson is a self-taught, virtuosic guitarist with a highly recognizable style marked by his distinctive use of trilling notes, sleight harmonics, string-bending, and dynamic manipulation of volume. Local Toronto players worshipped him (the rumor that he got his sound by soaking his guitar strings in turpentine led many to try it, unsuccessfully; he did use a banjo string in place of the low E string on his guitar, however), and Bob Dylan called him, according to Al Aronowitz's review of *Music from Big Pink* in the July 1968 issue of *Life* magazine, "the only mathematical guitar genius I've ever run into who doesn't offend my intestinal nervousness with his rearguard sound."

Born to Alexander Klagerman, a Jewish gangster who died before Robbie knew him (Barney Hoskyns's account says he was killed in a shootout; others say he was fatally struck by a car), and Rosemary "Dolly" Chrysler, a Mohawk Indian, he grew up a street kid in Toronto's rough-cut Cabbagetown neighborhood and took his last name from his stepfather, jeweler James Patrick Robertson. His initial exposure to music was via local street performers and the live country music he heard around his mother's childhood home, the nearby Six Nations Reservation. But it was his encountering rhythm and blues and early rock 'n' roll—Little Richard, Elvis Presley, Bo Diddley, Jimmy Reed, Link Wray, Fats Domino, the Drifters, and others—via the wild radio broadcasts emanating from the American stations to the south that really lit young Robbie's fuse. Before long, he was playing in a succession of local bands: Little Caesar and the Consuls, the Rhythm Chords, Robbie and the Robots, and Thumper and the Trambones [*sic*]. Like many Toronto rock 'n' roll fans, Robertson became a devotee of Ronnie Hawkins and the Hawks when they began packing local club the Le Coq d'Or in 1958. Two years later, the eager, fifteen-year-old Robertson had worked his way into the Hawks camp. After his time with Hawkins, and before The Band emerged as such, he played on Dylan's 1966 landmark *Blonde on Blonde*.

As it did for his musicianship, Robertson's bootstrapping background appears to have fueled his ambitious nature. As a singer, however, Robertson lagged far behind Helm, Manuel, and Danko. He only sings lead on three songs in The Band's official studio catalog: "To Kingdom Come," "Knockin' Lost John," and "Out of the Blue." In tandem with producer Martin Scorsese, he was instrumental in the making of *The Last Waltz* (1978), the gorgeous film of the original Band's 1976 final concert. After the breakup he moved into music production and film roles before concentrating on soundtrack work. Robertson has released five solo albums as of this writing.

Rick Danko

(Richard Clare Danko; born December 29, 1942; died December 10, 1999) For many, the first thing that hits them about Rick Danko is his voice. One of the most achingly plaintive in the classic rock canon, it can bring a dampness to the eye corners of the most hardened Hell's Angel. And as a bass player he was singular as well. When locked in with Helm's drumming, Danko's melodic, rubbery, and subtly expressive approach formed one of rock's greatest rhythm sections.

Like Helm, Danko grew up in a backwater farm community: Simcoe, Ontario, a tiny town populated by expatriate Southern U.S. farmers and mainly known for producing tobacco, arcane amphibious logging vessels called "alligator boats," and a steady crop of hockey players. Also like Helm, he came from a music-loving agricultural family (parents: Tom and Leola Danko) who whiled away their weekends listening to American country radio and playing at communal "musicales." Rick's younger brother, Terry Danko, is an acclaimed multi-instrumentalist who himself has worked with Ronnie Hawkins, as well as Eric Clapton, George Harrison, and the

Rolling Stones; their older sibling, Maurice "Junior" Danko, also played and was a musical mentor to Rick. The future Band man got his start in grade school, singing and accompanying himself on tenor banjo, and by the time he was thirteen he had formed (with Junior) the Rick Danko Band, which performed at area dances and weddings. Despite his local musical success, as a teenager Danko was on a career path that saw him cutting meat, not records; he worked as an apprentice butcher until he saw the Hawks perform, got to know the band, and was hired by Hawkins. Betraying his country-soul style, Danko named Hank Williams and Sam Cooke as his greatest early vocal and songwriting influences; as his bass heroes, he claimed jazzmen Ron Carter, Edgar Willis, and Chuck Rainey and Motown's James Jamerson, whose flowing, funky sound is most audible in Danko's own.

Danko coauthored "This Wheel's on Fire" with Bob Dylan, and he sings lead on that and two other *Music from Big Pink* tracks. In 1968, before The Band could tour in support of *Big Pink*, Danko was in a serious car accident that put him in traction for several months and would cause him pain for the rest of his life. He was the first of the members to release a solo album after The Band's split, and he remained in the Woodstock area, working with the later Band and the trio Danko/Fjeld/Andersen, recording live albums and touring on his own, and playing with other musicians like Paul Butterfield, Ringo Starr, Jorma Kaukonen, and Roger Waters. Danko's body finally succumbed to his hard-living ways just weeks before his fifty-sixth birthday.

Richard Manuel

(Richard George Manuel; born April 3, 1943; died March 4, 1986) As beautiful a singer and as troubled a soul as Danko was, he was arguably eclipsed in both those realms by the late singer, pianist, and drummer Richard Manuel. Blessed with a pronounced nose that earned him the nickname "Beak" and a haunting, vulnerable voice that could come only at the cost of an eternally wounded heart, Manuel is remembered by many as The Band's *true* lead singer. Despite their own stellar vocal contributions, this same view was held by both Danko and Helm themselves, the latter calling Manuel the best singer he'd ever heard. One listen to Manuel's quavering, devastatingly poignant delivery on *Music from Big Pink*'s debut of the Bob Dylan classic "I Shall Be Released" shows exactly what Helm was getting at.

Another Ontario boy, Manuel hailed from Stratford, where his father, Pierre "Ed" Manuel, worked as a mechanic at a Chrysler dealership and his mother taught school. Like his future Band-mates he heard country music early on, and he sang alongside his three brothers in the choir of their Baptist church. He started lessons on the family piano at age eight but soon

Glenn William Grainger's play *Manuel*, based on the troubled life of The Band's divinely talented pianist and singer, premiered in 2016.
Author's collection

abandoned them, thanks to a drill sergeant–like teacher, and proceeded to develop his own approach, which featured an innovative use of inverted chords. It was the blues and R&B that first set the young singer on fire— Jimmy Reed, Otis Rush, Bobby "Blue" Bland, and especially Ray Charles, whose gospel-steeped soul voice most clearly provided the model for his own. When he was fifteen Manuel formed a rock 'n' roll band, the Rockin' Revols, also known as, simply, the Revols.

MANUEL

WRITTEN BY GLENN WILLIAM GRAINGER

Presented by Pacheco Theatre and Blues Canvas Concert Productions, *Manuel* is a play about Richard Manuel, the deeply talented and enigmatic piano player and vocalist from the acclaimed musical group, THE BAND.

The play is told from the point of view of Richard's last remaining brother Al, who reflects back on thirty key years in his brother's turbulent and incredible life. Hailed as "the light of THE BAND" by his good friend Eric Clapton, Richard Manuel had a voice that could melt hearts, that was forged from another world... but so too was his sensitive spirit. This story by Glenn William Grainger chronicles the clash between the harsh external road of the musician's life, and one man's profound inner longing for peace and acceptance.

The play will be performed at the Paul Davenport Theatre in London, Ontario from April 26th to May 1st, 2016.

For tickets, please go to www.grandtheatre.com

Manuel's voice, on *Music from Big Pink*'s pleading "Tears of Rage," a tune he cowrote with Bob Dylan, is the very first voice heard on the album. Prior to *Big Pink*, during the Basement Tapes period, Manuel added the drums to his working resume. As with the keyboard, he was mainly self-taught behind the kit, and he developed a loose, jazzy technique he called upon when Helm switched to guitar or mandolin (see *The Band*'s "Rag Mama Rag" and "Jemima Surrender" and much of *Cahoots*); he also dabbled on baritone sax, harmonica, and lap steel guitar. As a composer, Manuel was talented if woefully underproductive. He's credited with writing or cowriting with Robertson only seven of the group's officially released songs, which is especially tragic considering that his *Big Pink* originals, "In a Station" and "Lonesome Suzie," are two of the highest points on an album wall-to-wall with high points.

Sadly, Manuel's lack of songwriting focus—along with his increased unreliability, loss of vocal range, personal and marital strife, and numerous automobile accidents—stemmed from a debilitating depressive condition compounded by his addiction to alcohol and hard drugs. In the years following the initial Band's breakup he entered rehab, briefly led the Pencils (a Los Angeles–area group), and toured with Danko in an acoustic duo. Shattered by manager Albert Grossman's January 1986 death, the relapsing Manuel hanged himself three months later in a Florida hotel room while on tour with the reunited Band.

Garth Hudson

(Eric Garth Hudson; born August 2, 1937) The Band's eldest member and resident musical mad scientist, Garth Hudson was born in the Canadian-American border city of Windsor, Ontario, and moved with his family to the province's nearby London three years later. His multihued, classically based organ style, a crucial signature component of The Band's sound, remains unique for rock.

Hudson's family was highly musical: His father, Fred, an entomologist/farm inspector and former World War I fighter pilot, was a brass band drummer who also played cornet, clarinet, flute, piano, and saxophone; his mother, Olive, sang and played piano and accordion. He began classical training at a very young age and played organ at his uncle's funeral parlor, a gig he admits did much to color his idiosyncratic technique. By twelve he'd begun writing songs and was playing in a local dance band, before eventually enrolling at the University of Western Ontario to study music.

While there he grew increasingly frustrated with the conservatory mentality and began gravitating more toward improvisation and the new rock 'n' roll and R&B he was hearing on Cleveland DJ Alan Freed's *Moondog Rock 'n' Roll Party*.

"I sang once professionally in 1957," he told musician Sarah Perrotta in 2015. "The band leader was Glenn Birkland from London, Ontario. I wrote out this arrangement for a jump tune . . . maybe it was [Lionel Hampton's] 'Hey! Ba-Ba-Re-Bop.' I wrote this arrangement they couldn't play. I wrote too many notes!" As a saxophonist Hudson worshipped New Orleans horn man Lee Allen, and he played the instrument in his first band, the Melodines. He next joined the Silhouettes, a group that played Windsor and Detroit clubs before mutating into Paul London and the Kapers.

The sight of the full-bearded Hudson, surrounded onstage by his fortress of keyboards with his head down as he plays, consumed by the music, provides some of the most unforgettable images in live footage of The Band. Likewise transcendent is his sax work, such as the soprano solo that closes "The Unfaithful Servant" and his baritone and tenor blowing on the *Cahoots* rocker "Volcano," and his flourishing accordion, as heard on standouts like *Stage Fright*'s "Strawberry Wine" and *Cahoots'* "When I Paint My Masterpiece." For the making of 1973's *Moondog Matinee* and 1975's *Northern Lights—Southern Cross*, the keyboardist added cutting-edge synthesizers to his arsenal. As a vocalist Hudson only appears on one commercially released track, a rare 1995 version of the Coasters hit "Young Blood."

Besides playing in the second-testament Band, Hudson has been extremely active as a session musician who has appeared on dozens of recordings by artists ranging from old friends Bob Dylan and Van Morrison to newer acts like the Lemonheads and Neko Case. An active local fixture into his late seventies, he has led the twelve-piece band the Best! and remained one of the most beloved musicians in the Hudson Valley.

I See My Life Before Me

A Brief History of The Band

They never sold as many records as the Beatles, but the Beatles worshipped them. They're not spoken of today as often as Eric Clapton is, but their arrival made Clapton quit his millions-selling band Cream and, after unsuccessfully trying to join their lineup, attempt to make music that sounded like theirs. They're not as iconic as Bob Dylan, but as his erstwhile collaborators and backing band they were instrumental in changing the course of his music—which, in turn, changed the course of popular music itself. As a performing unit they had more sheer talent than several superstar bands put together, possessing not just one but *three* incredible singers, and the innate knack for casually shuffling their musical roles to best fit whatever song they were playing. And they pioneered what came to be called Americana or roots rock, recording some of rock 'n' roll's greatest songs and leaving behind a catalog of such enduring quality that it continues to be rediscovered and influence younger generations of artists. They named themselves with equal parts unpretentiousness and unshakeable self-assurance: The Band.

To set the stage for the unfamiliar by providing some context for what's to follow, here's their basic, bare-bones story.

We're Gonna Rock It, Gonna Roll It

It begins with one man: Ronnie Hawkins, the flamboyant, Arkansas-born singer and leader of rockabilly outfit Ronnie Hawkins and the Hawks. Hawkins formed the Hawks in 1957, recruiting fellow razorback Levon Helm after the teenager sat in with an early version of the band. The following year, upon hearing that Canadian audiences were ripe for real American rock 'n' roll, Ronnie and his Hawks set up shop in Toronto, where they quickly became the biggest band in town and proceeded to set the rest of the province ablaze with their fiery live shows. The group had scored a deal with U.S. label Roulette and was just starting to make inroads into the charts back in the States when all of the members, save for Hawkins and Helm, began dropping out, to be replaced with local Canadian players. The first to join was Robbie Robertson, in early 1960. That same year, Rick Danko stepped in, to be followed in 1961 by Richard Manuel and Garth Hudson. This definitive edition of the Hawks would continue to back Hawkins until separating from him in 1963.

Gonna Turn You Loose Like an Old Caboose

Freed from Hawkins, the group eked out an existence in Canada and the honky-tonks of the American South, mainly under the name Levon and the Hawks. Following a relentless working trajectory toward becoming the tightest and best bar band in North America, they played nightly multiple sets of cover tunes to twisting throngs at one hole-in-the-wall joint after another. In those days it was common for bands to be booked for extended stints as opposed to one-nighters, and the Hawks' itinerary eventually landed them a summer residency in the beach town of Somers Point, New Jersey. But in August 1965, while the five musicians were ensconced in the sun, sand, and grinding five-hours-a-night performance schedule at the Jersey Shore, they would've had no idea they were about to be offered a much more fortuitous engagement, one that would drastically alter all of their lives—and forever reshape the face of rock 'n' roll.

Up the New Jersey coastline and across the Hudson River in Manhattan was the office of the powerful artist manager Albert Grossman. One of Grossman's clients was the heretofore mostly solo acoustic Bob Dylan, who was looking for a hot rock 'n' roll band to back him at shows that continued the boundary-shattering "electric" sound he'd begun exploring on his about-to-be-released *Highway 61 Revisited* album and in his controversial set at the previous July's Newport Folk Festival. After being dogged to check out the Hawks, Dylan did just that and sensed a perfect fit.

Accounts of how he snagged the band vary wildly. One version has Dylan seeing the group backing John Hammond Jr. at a Manhattan club and contacting them soon after. Another has Dylan meeting Robertson and offering his group the gig when Hammond took the guitarist to watch Dylan record his groundbreaking electric rock single "Like a Rolling Stone"; Helm's written account says Dylan called *him* with his offer not long after he and the Hawks had heard "Like a Rolling Stone" on the radio and depicts Robertson as being as unfamiliar with the song as his bandmates.

Like the best Dylan stories, we'll probably never know the exact truth. But the upshot was this: Dylan asked if the Hawks would be interested in

When it was released in 1975, *Northern Lights—Southern Cross* was hailed as a return to form by critics and fans.   *Author's collection*

playing the Forest Hills Tennis Stadium and the Hollywood Bowl with him. If the shows went well, perhaps there'd be more.

Came to Make Me a Deal

The Hawks balked. At first. They were only mildly aware of who this Bob Dylan guy was. While he'd been making his mark as the folk doyen of Carnegie Hall and elite college campuses, they'd been smashing out street-level, grits 'n' gravy rock 'n' roll in blue-collar barrooms and rural road-houses. But they also knew they weren't going anywhere special as long as they remained a bar band. They took the gig. Tentatively. For the two dates, Helm and Robertson tested the waters by augmenting Dylan's group, which included organist Al Kooper and bassist Harvey Brooks.

The Forest Hills show turned out to be a baptism by fire—and thrown fruit. The bulk of Dylan's folk-purist audience vocally and violently rejected his loud bridging of the gap between "their" music and that of the Rolling Stones and the Beatles. Kooper and Brooks bailed after the comparatively milder Hollywood show, making way for Manuel, Danko, and Hudson to join—at the insistence of Helm and Robertson—just in time for Dylan's impending 1965–1966 world tour. For the Hawks, the tour would prove an even more challenging experience than their toughest tours with Ronnie Hawkins. Dylan's new, confrontational, envelope-pushing direction was marked by his venomous sneer and the group's shrill, shuddering wall of distorted sound. At nearly every stop, after Dylan had opened with a per-functory solo acoustic set, he and his band were greeted with unrelenting booing peppered with open hostility as the crowds squared off against the perceptions that their presumably tradition-reverent golden boy had either sold out or was making "anti-music."

Undaunted, the leader, who over the course of the tour would regularly stay up for successive nights with Robertson on amphetamines to work up new songs, reacted to the audience abuse by giving it right back to them, egging on his other speed-gobbling sidemen to crank up the volume. The Hawks' years of playing in rough environments had prepared them for almost anything, but after four months of doing battle with the booers, Helm, raised on working to make the people happy and admittedly unsure of the music, had had enough. In late November 1965, he told the other Hawks he'd see them down the line and beat it south to drift around and work on an oil rig, leaving his stool to be filled by a succession of drummers: Bobby Gregg, ex-Hawk Sandy Konikoff, and Mickey Jones. In late July 1966, after they'd spent most of the year barnstorming North America, Europe, and Australia, the remaining original Hawks were in New York awaiting another leg of the tour when Grossman called with grim news. Dylan had been injured in a motorcycle accident near his upstate New York home of Woodstock. All his live appearances were cancelled until further notice.

I Picked Up My Bag, I Went Lookin' for a Place to Hide

Because Dylan, thus far, hasn't discussed the crash in detail and no public record of it has been produced, there are those who believe it was a ruse concocted to allow him to detox from the drug-addled insanity of the 1965–1966 tour and bond with his family as he hid out in Woodstock; however, the common consensus seems to be that there *was* some kind of accident, but that the severity of Dylan's injuries was likely exaggerated. Whatever the case, Dylan had been hiding out in Woodstock off and on since 1963, as the then quiet Catskills town was Grossman's home. By early 1967, the Helm-less Hawks had joined Dylan in Woodstock to collaborate on *Eat the Document*, a documentary using footage from their 1966 tour. Danko, Manuel, and Hudson moved into a nearby house nicknamed "Big Pink," where they met regularly with Robertson, who was living at Grossman's estate, and Dylan to work out the singer's newest ideas and have fun playing whatever random non-originals struck their collective mood. The homemade recordings from this period would later surface as the Basement Tapes.

Time to Kill

Throughout their shared Woodstock woodshedding, Dylan, out of admiration for their abilities, had been urging his cronies to step out on their own. With Grossman as their new manager, the group signed with Capitol and lured Helm up to rejoin them. The reborn quintet renamed themselves the Honkies, and then the Crackers, which was nixed after Capitol caught on to its derisive meaning. When the fivesome entered a New York studio in January 1968 to begin recording their debut, they were still nameless, but they arrived with three Dylan songs from the basement sessions—"I Shall Be Released," "This Wheel's on Fire," and "Tears of Rage," the latter two co-written with, respectively, Danko and Manuel—and a stack of startling originals. That month, the band took time off from recording to back Dylan at a Woody Guthrie tribute at Carnegie Hall and finished the album in Los Angeles.

Named for the humble house in which the songs were mostly composed, *Music from Big Pink* wasn't an immediate commercial smash, peaking at number thirty in the U.S. ("The Weight" was a number twenty-one hit single in the U.K. but only reached number sixty-three in the States). But it sounded like nothing else at the time. Quiet, confident, and rich in the imagery of old-time America but unmired in folkie-museum dust, it blew the music press away and sent a ripple through the rock world that pointed to coming broad changes. With its unpretentious songwriting, sparse sound, and scarcity of the day's de rigueur jams and solos, *Music from Big Pink* influenced acts from the Beatles on down to alter their own paths away from psychedelia and hard rock and into more reflective, rustic realms. Since the group had yet to decide on a collective name, the labels of the LP and its singles listed all five of the members' names as the recording artists. Pressed to come up with a serviceable moniker, they decide to capitalize, literally, on what the locals had been calling them: simply, "the band."

In early 1969 The Band left the Catskill Mountains for the Hollywood Hills to record their second album. If *Big Pink* had been written off by the unconvinced as a fluke collection of great songs cooked up by a faceless, lucky crew of Dylan's hired guns, those skeptics were decisively silenced by *The Band*. Released in September of 1969, the group's sophomore opus, also known as "the Brown Album," is commonly regarded as one of the greatest of all rock albums. Loosely a concept work about America's rural past—embodied by the Helm-sung hits "The Night They Drove Old Dixie Down" and "Up on Cripple Creek"—it showed that The Band had come fully into their own, and for many it put them on par with the Beatles and the Rolling Stones in terms of artistic importance.

The quintet's idiosyncratic brew of disparate American homegrown musics was by now fully defined, and their musicianship (Manuel now doubled on drums, allowing Helm to play mandolin and guitar) and studio performances were even more authoritative. But the former Hawks had yet to make their live debut as The Band. Finally, and with much attendant fanfare, the group played its first shows in April of that year at San Francisco's Winterland Ballroom and New York's Fillmore East, and performed at the historic Woodstock festival that August.

All La Glory

By 1970 The Band had become one of the day's most acclaimed festival acts, even making the cover of *Time* magazine ("The New Sound of Country

The Band found steady work in smaller concert halls, auditoriums, festivals, and clubs when they reunited in the early 1980s.   *Author's collection*

Rock," January 12, 1970). Initially, the group had resisted long tours, intending to remain primarily a studio band after years of slugging it out on the road as the Hawks. But the commercial success of *The Band* (it went Top Ten in December 1969) changed that plan, and the outfit soon embarked on the first of several headlining tours.

Stage Fright, the group's third LP, appeared that August and saw them taking a somewhat less rootsy path, with songs that were more contemporary-rock-leaning and darkly personal. The move reflected the growing fissures within the band as the others (primarily Helm) began to resent Robertson's increasing dominance as the main credited composer (the disc features Manuel's final two Band songwriting credits). The less-consistent *Cahoots* arrived in September 1971, preceding the December taping of *Rock of Ages*, a blowout, horn-section-augmented live double LP released in 1972. *Moondog Matinee*, a set of rock 'n' roll and R&B covers that came out the following year, found the group harkening back to their teeth-cutting days with Ronnie Hawkins. In 1973, Danko, Helm, Manuel, and Hudson followed Robertson to Malibu, California, then the home of Bob Dylan, to back their former collaborator in the studio for *Planet Waves*. Dylan and The Band toured in 1974 to support the album, and the following year brought The Band's *Northern Lights—Southern Cross*, which was praised by many as the group's best studio album since *The Band*.

Unfortunately, for Robertson, at least, it was too little too late. During a break period while Manuel recovered from injuries sustained in a boating accident, the guitarist, by now also managing the group as they'd parted ways with Grossman, declared The Band would cease performing live, blaming it on fatigue brought on by their sixteen years on the road. The news blindsided Helm and his bandmates, who all wanted to keep touring. Nevertheless, on Thanksgiving Day 1976 The Band performed its final concert at the same venue where it had played its first, the Winterland Ballroom in San Francisco. With the group backed by a full horn section and accompanying an all-star procession of guests that included Dylan, Van Morrison, Eric Clapton, Neil Young, Dr. John, Joni Mitchell, Muddy Waters, and others, the grand event was captured by director Martin Scorsese as the 1978 film *The Last Waltz.*

The Band released one more studio effort, 1977's *Islands*, which was mainly made up of outtake material from previous albums, and disintegrated that year. The plan was for the group to reconvene to work on new music, but it wasn't to be. Instead, everything drifted apart as Robertson went off to work in the movie industry while his former partners toiled away as session and solo players and occasionally in pairs or trios. Until 1983, that is—but we'll save that story for another chapter.

3

So I'm Going to Unpack All My Things

Elements That Made The Band Unique

The period stretching from the late 1960s to the early 1970s is viewed by many as the glory years of modern popular music. By then, thanks largely to the Beatles, rock 'n' roll had grown well beyond being a so-called youth fad of performers who sang songs assigned to them to one that was dominated by self-contained acts who wrote and performed their own material. It's an epoch now codified as classic rock, the halcyon days of the Fab Four and other lionized legends like the Rolling Stones, the Doors, the Who, the Grateful Dead—and The Band.

But although they're one of the vanguard acts of the era when rock 'n' roll "matured" to become, simply, rock, there are several aspects that set The Band far apart from the artists they shared charts and stages with. Gestating off the pop music grid, removed from the trends of the day as they were about to create new ones themselves, the group developed a style defined as much by their individual personalities as the music they made. This chapter zeroes in on some signature elements that have set The Band apart.

No Front Man

The Rolling Stones have Mick Jagger. Led Zeppelin had Robert Plant. The Doors had Jim Morrison. Rock bands generally have a front man (or front woman), a dedicated, charismatic lead singer who acts as the focal point of the group during performances. The Band, however, didn't. They were a level team, with the group's lead vocal duties mainly shared by its three amazing, highly individual singers: Richard Manuel, Levon Helm, and Rick Danko. Thus, unlike the rock juggernauts cited above, there was never the feeling that the group was just another case of the musicians being there just to back up a star vocalist. With The Band, the lead vocal role shifted from song to song, sometimes within the *same* song, making for an egalitarian experience that was uncommon in their day and remains so even now. In this way The Band was similar to the Beatles, but even within the Beatles the lead vocals weren't as equally shared; most of their songs were sung by either John Lennon or Paul McCartney, and by dint of his persona it was Lennon who generally won out among Beatles followers as the de facto front man.

In spite of his fleeting title as the Hawks' leader after their split with Ronnie Hawkins and his later leading his own bands, Helm was simply not the personality type to relish stepping all the way out front as the strutting center of attention. Nor was the unassuming Danko or, especially, the fragile Manuel, even though, as mentioned earlier, his own bandmates called him their *real* lead singer. So they freely passed the torch around, depending on who sounded the best on a given song. It was the *song* that was king, not the adulation of the spotlight.

Robertson's emergence as the outfit's compositional leader and spokesman aside, this original democratic slant to performing had been a conscious decision by the group. After playing behind the micromanaging Hawkins for years and the headline-garnering Bob Dylan for a lengthy, grueling tour after that, the five musicians wanted an all-for-one-and-one-for-all situation. And being incredible, telepathic players who by then could basically set their watches by each other's breathing patterns, they knew very well they could pull it off.

One Voice for All

Danko's sweet, loving tenor. Helm's gruff, honey-ladled grit. Manuel's heart-piercing gospel cry. Any band would swear off a tour bus full of groupies to have just *one* such voice in their ranks. Contrary to Helm's statement in *This Wheel's on Fire* that "the songs themselves dictated who would sing and who would play the supporting roles," Robertson likes to tell it that he was "casting" the lead parts for his tunes, writing lyrics with certain members in mind to sing them. "When Robbie wrote a song he would usually sing it to whomever was going to sing it on the record," recalls John Simon, producer of first two Band albums. "And in doing so, the singer couldn't help but pick up a lot of Robbie's inflections in the vocal melodies."

In the case of the American South–evoking songs that Helm sings, the Canadian-born Robertson's fascination with that region was largely fueled by Helm's own accounts of it. Yes, "The Night They Drove Old Dixie Down" has been covered by many others, but has anyone else ever come as close to embodying the broken, defiant veteran in the song as Helm does?

Besides each of The Band's singers being so notable individually, there's also the hugely innovative way they worked together as a vocal ensemble. Taking a cue from the gospel acts they all loved, The Band's three vocalists worked out a way of harmonically "stacking" their voices for maximum color and dimension. Although there were other groups at the time known for their vocal harmonies, like the Beach Boys and the Four Seasons, those groups' unison styles had a much tighter construction in which the voices were more uniformly pitched and closer together in tonal range. Not so The Band, whose organically unmatched blend of three distinct and dissimilar voices was rare in 1960s rock 'n' roll, a combination that would've delighted a country church pastor but driven easy listening choral acts like the Swingle Singers nuts. It's rough-edged at times, but down-to-earth, and beautiful in the way a flower growing out of a bluestone cliff is beautiful. The trio arrived at it through their experimentation in the basement of Big Pink: Helm's baritone on the bottom, Manuel's falsetto flying high above, and Danko's tenor in the middle tying it together. The choruses on "Rockin' Chair" come to mind as glorious examples of this sonic structuring.

Another aspect of The Band's unconventional vocal-ensemble practices is the "conversational" style of many of their songs. The members would alternate verses, and sometimes trade lines back and forth. "We Can Talk," off *Music from Big Pink*, is an entertaining instance of the latter, with Helm, Danko, and Manuel exchanging lyrics about life on the farm.

Arcane Influences

From *Music from Big Pink* through their 1976 departure, The Band were one of rock's most popular and critically exalted acts. Yet when they initially stepped out from behind Dylan their ascent was far from assured. True, their association with the Spokesman of a Generation had put them in the spotlight and helped get them a record deal. But until they came on the scene under their own steam, the greater public had yet to learn about their songwriting prowess, and the music they created and drew upon was very much at odds with what was all the rage at the time.

By the late 1960s the dominant trend in rock 'n' roll was one of lofty psychedelic pop and ear-splitting acid rock. Most rock fans at the time seemed to view the older genres The Band were obsessed with—country, gospel, Dixieland, bluegrass, even the blues and R&B the Beatles, Rolling

Stones, and other British Invaders had referenced just a few years before—as musty and cornpone. To them, rock was about reaching for rainbows, not digging in the dirt. But the way The Band channeled these heritage styles, in an organic, unselfconscious manner within a contemporary rock format coupled with incredible songwriting and musicianship, would soon hit many of these same listeners as a total revelation. Concurrent with The Band's emergence, the abundant legacy of America's homespun music was suddenly valid to a demographic that had spent the previous five years giddily singing "Yeah! Yeah! Yeah!" and swirling around in a purple haze.

But despite their unapologetic mining of earlier forms, The Band's music never felt dated or static. So how was it that the group steered clear of the pitfalls of passing fads while not becoming a nostalgia act? Theirs was a very particular trajectory. A tight-knit gang of five very young men who never let go of their shared love for the music that had first inspired them to play, they had existed outside both the mainstream *and* the counterculture for years before they arose as the act the world now knows. For roughly a decade beforehand they'd been sequestered under Ronnie Hawkins, playing nothing but rockabilly and R&B, largely oblivious to what was in the charts. When they did turn on the radio during those long drives between roadhouses, however, they weren't impressed by much of what they heard. They loved Motown, which they viewed as an evolution of 1950s R&B, but they scoffed at the Beatles, Beach Boys, et al., whose music they considered lightweight teenybopper fare. After their time with Hawkins, they were thrown into the fire of the 1965–1966 Dylan tour, playing music that was likewise a departure from the status quo, but from an entirely different angle. And once they were in Woodstock, they cocooned themselves in Big Pink's basement to come up with their own sound. For that, they took bits of deeper styles and injected them with their own personalities and the sensibility that came with being a young, searching person of the post–World War II era. All of this gave their music a wisdom not found in such concurrent acts as, say, Iron Butterfly.

Lyrical Bounty

In 1969, two of the top positions in the *Billboard* Hot 100 singles chart were occupied by songs from the hippie-patronizing Broadway musical *Hair*. One of them was "Aquarius/Let the Sunshine In," a medley performed by vocal group the Fifth Dimension with lyrics about Jupiter aligning with Mars and love steering the stars. Trite, passing, pseudo-psych fluff. No wonder

The Band preferred to hide out in the mountains. The Band's lyrics, mainly written by Robertson, tell their vivid stories like the plainspoken confessions of characters ripped straight from a movie screen or a Flannery O'Connor or Cormac McCarthy novel: the layabout frontier drunk in "Up on Cripple Creek," the bittersweetly departing domestic in "The Unfaithful Servant," the village oddball Crazy Chester in "The Weight." No surprise the guitarist, an admitted cineaste, would eventually go into film work.

"At one point Robbie and I were discussing lyrics and he said he'd never write a song in the first person, the inference being that it would be too personal," says John Simon. "Of course, he did write songs in the first person but the narrator in those songs would be a character he invented, not Robbie himself."

There are other artistically divergent lyrical aspects of Robertson's word-play. His use of cryptic folk and mythological/biblical imagery is something he picked up from Dylan and applied in a less random, more narrative-driven way. His signature practice, though, is his well-researched animation of specific historical events, such as the Civil War ("The Night They Drove Old Dixie Down"), the Great Depression ("Knockin' Lost John"), the eighteenth-century expulsion of Acadians from Canada ("Acadian Driftwood"), the early American farm labor movement ("King Harvest [Has Surely Come]"), immigration ("Shoot Out in Chinatown"), and industrialization ("Last of the Blacksmiths"). "The Night They Drove Old Dixie Down" and the colorful townsfolk and carnies in *Stage Fright*'s "The W.S. Walcott Medicine Show" were based largely on Robertson's interpretations of Helm's own remembrances of his Southern upbringing, in a sense making the drummer a kind of "indirect" lyricist, a muse. And it's conceivable that Helm's bandmates provided inspiration as well; Robertson has pointed out how all of The Band's members were themselves characters worthy of literature. Couched in the group's unfaddish instrumentation and down-home delivery, these narratives brought the common people of America's past vibrantly to life and were, in their own way, a far more eloquent Vietnam-era protest than the ham-fisted histrionics of Barry McGuire's topical hit "Eve of Destruction." "Who can write *songs* about all this garbage that's happening now, wars and revolution and killing?" Robertson told *Look* magazine in 1970. "I can't. Words for that stuff don't work right in songs."

But to say that Robertson was hung up on history or parable doesn't quite get it. Lonely towns, local eccentrics, and railroad tracks existed in the 1960s and they exist today, not only in picture books of the Old West, and some of his songs drop in contemporary totems like buses, telephones, and even Fender guitars ("Rag Mama Rag"). It's a delicate device, evoking a bygone era while not remaining confined within it, and one well off the trendy "Now Sound!" radar of the times. "There is a conviction here that every way of life practiced in America from the time of the Revolution on down still matters—not as nostalgia, but as the necessity of someone's daily life," wrote Greil Marcus in *Mystery Train*. "There is no feeling of being dragged into the past for a history lesson; if anything, the past catches up with us." The Band's songs remind listeners that they're part of something bigger, a story they themselves have a hand in, just as the ancestors brought to life in those songs do.

Another strikingly unconventional facet of Robertson's lyrical procedure then was the way he structured his lyrics. Instead of the customary ABAB blues scheme that rhymes the first and third or the second and fourth lines of a verse, or the epic, wordy, labyrinthine style Dylan then employed—piling up his image-rich lines and "saving up" his payoff rhymes until the last second—Robertson's rhyme scheme often seems to have a mind of its own. Sometimes he uses a fairly typical country/blues AABB pattern where the first and second and then third and fourth lines rhyme with each other; "Daniel and the Sacred Harp" is a good example of this. But in other instances, the rhymes happen in weird, choppy intervals that feel detached from the meter of the music behind them, sometimes occurring within the same line; see "Time to Kill." Without knowing Robertson wrote the music *and* the lyrics, a listener might understandably conclude that he was purely a poet and not a musician as well, a writer unaccustomed to how words flow with the natural grain of the music. But of course when he wrote these songs Robertson was not only extremely familiar with the songwriting styles of the acts his group had been covering; he had also made some early compositional attempts for the Hawks and directly absorbed the golden genius of Bob Dylan. So he'd been learning his craft, challenging himself as a writer as well as challenging the accepted way that songs were being written by other rock acts of the day.

It wasn't *all* Robertson's show with the word writing, though. Besides The Band's advantage of having Dylan himself as a contributor on *Music from Big Pink* and *Cahoots*, there was occasional input from Danko and Helm and the sadly slim contributions of Manuel, who was responsible for the picture-painting verbiage of jewels like "Lonesome Suzie" and "Whispering Pines." For the same group to have both a screenplay-worthy storyteller and a devastatingly romantic poet in residence is rare indeed.

The Canadian-American Factor

How is it that The Band had such an uncanny grip on America's musical soul and collective consciousness when most of the group's members weren't even from the U.S.? Two words: outside perspective.

For Robertson, Danko, Manuel, and Hudson, the broadcasts of early rock 'n' roll, rhythm and blues, and country music they heard beaming across the U.S.-Canadian border were electrifying transmissions from a land where larger-than-life personalities like Elvis Presley, Bo Diddley, and Jerry Lee Lewis reigned. While they were very young, the four became passionate students of American music, dissecting and assimilating the techniques of the musicians and songwriters they admired, eventually carrying this focused appreciation with them into the mid-1960s, when most of their peer players were obsessing over the music's English interpreters and oblivious to its sources. And even though the Rolling Stones, the Animals, and other hit-making British bands worshipped the same American artists as they did, these Britons did not possess the inside track these four savvy young Hawks had via Hawkins and Helm, two living, music-making veins of experiential country/folk grist. Later on, when the ex-Hawks hooked up with Dylan in the basement of Big Pink, they got a crash course that went even deeper into American music, excavating the arcane vernacular songs that had been hidden away in the hills and hollows of the nation's remotest regions.

Although they agreed with many of the 1960s protest movement's core ideals, especially in matters of race, much of the reason The Band didn't blindly hop on the countercultural bandwagon of their contemporaries is due to their outsider status. Like many immigrants who eschew the critiques of younger citizens, the four Canadians saw it as unseemly to bash the American establishment when it had afforded them such opportunities.

And then there was America itself. When Robertson boarded a bus bound for Fayetteville, Arkansas, to replace the Hawks' departing bassist Lefty Evans in the spring of 1960, it was a pilgrimage to the Holy Land for the sixteen-year-old. Already captivated by an imagined South he'd heard mythologized in the songs of his heroes, the wide-eyed Canuck, with Helm as his guide, soaked up everything around him—the people, the farms, the food, the folklore, the dialects, the music—and devoured the literature of Southern writers like William Faulkner and Tennessee Williams. He hung out in Memphis, where he visited the legendary Sun Studio and the blues hub of Beale Street, and continued to be an attentive observer as the Hawks rock 'n' rolled their way through America's backwoods and back roads. When he began writing songs for The Band, he drew on these experiences to create music that held a mirror up to America, reminding it—and the rest of the world—of its own forgotten essence.

Image/Mystique

In 1968 there was no band on a major label that looked quite like The Band. Since settling in the Catskills to begin carousing and collaborating with Dylan in Big Pink's basement, they'd ditched the matching Rat Pack mohair suits of their Hawks days and remade themselves as cheroot-smoking mountain men with mismatched Mennonite gear and scruffy beards. Remember, this was at a time when rock acts generally dressed like Carnaby Street mods or paisley-smeared, Nehru-jacketed sultans à la the Strawberry Alarm Clock. So it was actually shocking for kids to open up the cover of *Music from Big Pink* and see a gang of men staring back at them like who looked like their great-grandfathers in the pictures on the family mantelpiece. And the music sounded like the members looked: countrified and slightly old-timey, but with a touch of stately humility and a sense of worldliness that said these men weren't rednecks. (Prior to The Band there had been the Charlatans, a pioneering California unit who dressed like Wild West gunfighters and Victorian dandies and played jug-band-influenced music. But that group was little known outside the San Francisco area and didn't release an album until 1969, a year behind *Big Pink*.)

The new aesthetic, which they'd gradually shed over time in favor of a more contemporary but still unpretentious look, was emblematic of their desire to distance themselves from the gaudy glitz of the commercial pop scene, and it matched the "pioneer" vibe they felt in their hardscrabble upstate surroundings. "People said we dressed 'weird,'" says Robertson in the BBC documentary *Classic Albums: The Band.* "But we just thought we dressed normal. *Everybody else* dressed weird, with the polka dots and the psychedelia." By the time of the Brown Album's chart success, groups around the world were adopting a similar country-casual look.

The public perception was that The Band were this odd bunch of guys who'd once played with Dylan and were now hiding out in the mountains, making this strange, time-warped music when they weren't drinking moonshine, shooting empty cans, and eating venison. And such assumptions weren't too far off, as several of the guys actually did own firearms and there are tales of Hudson and Danko skinning deer (the jury's still out on the moonshine). This back-to-the-land imagery was captivating to a generation that had begun to see through the "plastic" hype of Madison Avenue and

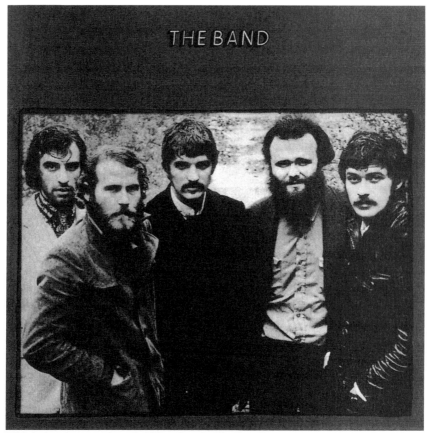

With its iconic cover photo by Elliott Landy, The Band's eponymous second album, from 1969, is a cornerstone of Americana and one of rock's greatest albums.   *Author's collection*

was seeking refuge from the insanity of Vietnam and other social unrest. Thus, the quintet became a much-imitated archetype, that of the rock band "getting it together in the country."

Initially, The Band were dead set against touring and planned only to make records. But with the buzz continuing to mount as listeners discovered *Music from Big Pink*, the offers became too good to pass up. Just as the group was set to capitalize on their newfound aura with a tour, however, Danko was in a severe car accident that put him in traction for several months. The ensuing silence, though, only heightened The Band's reputation as reclusive backwoods sages, something their notoriously savvy manager, Albert Grossman, seized on and used to his charges' advantage by having them refuse interviews and generally keep the press at bay—much as he'd done, to good effect, with Dylan. By April 1969, the month of their very first concerts as The Band, they were one of rock's biggest acts.

Swapping Instruments

Be they part of a symphony orchestra, a chamber group, a jazz combo, or, yes, a rock band, each member of a musical ensemble normally has a role assigned to them based on their expertise on a given instrument. While there were existing bands with musicians who dabbled on other instruments in the studio—the Beatles, the Rolling Stones, the Byrds, the Who—onstage those players tended to keep the program streamlined and not deviate from the position they were most identified with. And that's still generally the case today. The guitarist plays the guitar. The drummer plays the drums. The keyboardist plays the keyboards. And so on.

The Band, however, whose members could play seventeen instruments between them, famously shattered this constricting mold, on record and right before the eyes and ears of their audiences. The steadiest configuration was Helm on drums, Danko on bass, Manuel on piano, Hudson on organ, and Robertson (always) on guitar, with Manuel, Helm, and Danko taking turns on the lead vocals. But after playing drums on, say, "Don't Do It," Helm might turn the kit over to Manuel and grab his mandolin while Danko swapped his bass for a fiddle to play "Rag Mama Rag." Next, the three might resume their previous places for, say, "The Unfaithful Servant," on which Hudson would step out from behind his organ and clavinet to blow some soprano sax. And for the following numbers, the positions could shuffle yet again.

Instead of becoming a momentum killer, as it might have been for other groups, The Band's instrument swapping gave their shows an informal, back-porch quality that fans found refreshing. But of course this, if you will, musical-chairs methodology wasn't designed as a gimmick to impress concertgoers. It was the natural byproduct of a gang of musicians on an eternal search for ways to best express the music pumping through their brains and their veins, several of whom had already been playing numerous instruments since a very young age. They used these multiple abilities to serve the song, not some preordained idea of what a particular rock musician's function is. Keeping the songs loose and sonically unpredictable—a mandolin here, an accordion, clavinet, or even a synthesizer there, maybe producer John Simon on a horn over here—just enhanced the tunes and made everything sound that much more extraordinary.

"We would try different players on different songs and take things as far as they could go," explained Helm in *This Wheel's on Fire* about the group's basement experimentation. "'What would this part sound like with this person singing, or this person playing this?'" This freewheeling adaptability was another strength that made The Band the envy of other groups and further defined them as musical craftsmen. Blessed with an even distribution of talent that trumps even that of the Beatles, the members of The Band actually inspired each other with their skills, and the artistically egoless approach to music they showed at their height is novel even now.

Minimal Soloing

Speaking of egos, if there's ever an opportunity for one of those to run a little too rampant, it's when a rock musician decides to take a solo. And the late 1960s were the dawning of the age in which rock musicians began playing more and more solos. Guitar solos. Drum solos. Bass solos. Tambourine solos. Hell, many of them would've soloed on their headbands and love beads if they could've figured out how (no doubt it was attempted). The problem was that not every musician was a Jimi Hendrix or a John Bonham, artists who actually had something to *say* on their instruments. And there seemed to be an ever-growing legion of say-nothing players who took the innovations of the day's inspired musicians as a license to broadcast their own vapidity via hour upon hour of stoned, aimless noodling. Like, far out, man.

Concurrent with their M.O. of turning down the volume, simplifying life, and rebelling against the rebellion, The Band kept the solos to a minimum on their first two LPs. This was a big step, especially for Robertson, whose unhinged lead work had been a calling card of the Hawks. But he, like the other Band members during their time in that Saugerties basement with Dylan, had turned the lens away from showmanship and back onto the songs themselves; once again, it was about *serving the song.* On *Big Pink*, there's just one solo, by Robertson, on "To Kingdom Come" (unless you count Hudson's unaccompanied intro to "Chest Fever"). On *The Band*, there's a total of four; the tender turns by Robertson and Hudson on "The Unfaithful Servant" and the scorchers by Robertson on "Jawbone" and "King Harvest (Has Surely Come)."

Although The Band's employment of solos would never approach that of, say, their buddies the Grateful Dead, it did grow measurably during their remaining Robertson years—in hindsight, their subsequent move away from the earlier, strict ensemble arrangements and increased incorporation of comparatively self-indulgent solos can be seen as a reflection of their unraveling comradery. But thanks to the democratic musical template of those first two albums, many longwinded players who heard them suddenly felt the need to rein it in and shut the heck up. Thankfully.

A Singing Drummer

They're rare today and were even more so in the 1960s: drummers who are also lead singers. Back then, other than Levon Helm, who was there? The most visible was Ringo Starr. But in concert films of the Beatles his occasional turns with the mic, great as they are, come across as novelties programmed in to break up the dominant singing of his charismatic band-mates. There have been a few other notable singing drummers, but ask most classic rock fans to name one and it's usually Helm they cite first (drummer Phil Collins, who became Genesis's lead singer when original front man Peter Gabriel left in 1975, is mainly identified with his group's post–classic rock 1980s period). Even now, listeners are still more used to stand-alone lead vocalists or lead-singing guitarists, keyboardists, and bassists, and most find it mind-boggling that someone can sing and keep the beat at the same time, let alone do both so well as Helm did.

One could say Helm's skills for vocal/rhythmic multitasking were the fruits of his having grown up down on the farm. Many of his very first gigs were at the local childhood talent contests sponsored by the Arkansas branch of the 4-H Club, the 1902-founded, U.S. Department of Agriculture–sponsored youth organization that stresses "Head, Heart, Hands, and Health." At these early performances/competitions—which he usually won—Helm sang while accompanying himself on body-slapping "hambone" percussion. So when the young rock 'n' roller eventually picked up the sticks and sat behind a real drum kit, layering his voice over what his hands and feet were playing was for him a natural evolution, something he'd already been doing since before the age of ten. "People give me good credit, and I appreciate it," said a typically modest Helm about his distinctive technique in *Classic Albums: The Band*. "They think it's harder to play when you sing. But it's actually easier, because you play along and you leave holes where you sing and that's where you sing. So [while playing] you can actually 'punch' your voice on the 'punch lines' of a song." He certainly made it *look* easy, at least, and in doing so further helped The Band stand apart from the other musical groups of their time.

Organ-Piano Combination

Thanks to digital technology, keyboards have become as portable as electric guitars only recently. Presumably, this is why the standard template for most rock bands of the last fifty years includes a second guitarist before it includes a keyboardist. If a band does have a keyboardist, it tends to have either an organist *or* a pianist, not both. In many cases, they have one player who alternates between the two instruments—a concept that, once again, likely stems from issues of equipment portability; toting around a piano *and* an organ is a daunting prospect. Whatever the genesis of this trend, instances are rare in rock music of performing units having the organ-piano blend that Hudson and Manuel made such a hallmark of The Band's sound. Some may point out that the British band Procol Harum, another act with a piano-organ pairing, had hit the charts a year before *Music from Big Pink* with 1967's "A Whiter Shade of Pale." But by then the musicians in The Band had already been utilizing the piano-organ format for seven years; Hudson had joined Manuel in the Hawks in 1961.

The piano-organ concept was a staple of other genres long before it was adopted by rock 'n' rollers. It was commonplace in the gospel music that begat so many of the soul and R&B artists who influenced The Band, and, before that, in the sphere of classical music; Mozart and other composers had famously written duets for the two instruments. At the start of rock 'n' roll, in the 1950s, the piano was integral—see Little Richard, Jerry Lee Lewis, Fats Domino, or Chuck Berry sideman Johnnie Johnson—but by the mid-1960s garage rock epoch it had been largely supplanted by the portable electric organ, such as those made by Farfisa and Vox. So in a way The Band's inclusion of both piano and organ represents a bridge between eras, much as their music itself does. And the link is audibly distinctive, with Manuel's chiming ivories hovering above and scuttling beneath Hudson's swells and sustained chords. A fine example of this characteristic coupling in action is "Stage Fright," in which Manuel hammers hard on the downbeat against Hudson's bluesy slurs in the choruses and comps behind his brief but animated solo. Add to the mix other keyboard instruments like accordion or synthesizer by Hudson or clavinet by Hudson or Manuel, or have Hudson move to piano while Manuel assumes the drum throne, and the palette morphs even further.

Garth Hudson: Secret Weapon

"To get Garth Hudson [in the Hawks], that was a big day because nobody could play like Garth anywhere," says Helm in the liner notes to The Band's 2005 box set *A Musical History*. "He could play anything and play it better than anybody you knew. Once we had a musician of Garth's caliber, we started sounding professional."

If Manuel was the heart of The Band, Robertson its conceptualist, and Helm its soul, then Hudson was its brains. (Danko? The loose cannon, of course. Every great band has one.) Much chuckling occurs over the story of Hudson's placating his worrisome parents by agreeing to join the Hawks if he would be guaranteed extra income as the band's in-house music teacher. But he really did fulfill that role, frequently breaking down the nuts and bolts of musical theory for his bandmates; this was, after all, someone who'd taken apart and rebuilt his family's antique pump organ as a young boy. Having Hudson as a member was like having the minds of Charlie Parker, Johann Sebastian Bach, and John Cage all in the same band. And thanks to his uncanny dexterity, it was also like having an extra keyboardist: How many other groups had a guy who could simultaneously play one melody on organ with his right hand, manipulate the pitch with his foot pedals, and play an entirely different melody with his left hand on clavinet?

More than anything, though, it was Hudson who made The Band *sound* different. Without his painterly and highly idiosyncratic colorations weaving in and out—most other rock organists simply followed the base melody and took an occasional solo—sonically, at least, the quintet wouldn't have stood out as much as they did among the Savoy Browns and the Ten Years Afters. "Garth was different, he heard all sorts of weird sounds in his head and he played like the Phantom of the Opera," Ronnie Hawkins remembered in his 1989 autobiography, *Last of the Good Ol' Boys*. "He wasn't a rock 'n' roll person at all, but it fitted."

Constantly searching for new sounds, Hudson reveled in modifying his Lowrey organ. According to engineer Shelly Yakus, during the *Big Pink* sessions he created a "staggered" sound by running the instrument's signal through an antique telegraph key salvaged from an army surplus store. While on tour he combed through pawn shops, looking for vintage horns and other odd instruments to add to his growing collection and broaden the group's tonal spectrum. "The distinctive horn sound of The Band was mostly Garth's brainchild," says John Simon. "He encouraged us both to moan our parts, he on the soprano sax and me on the baritone horn."

The genius, Jew's harp–like effect he got from piping his clavinet through a wah-wah pedal on "Up on Cripple Creek" is one of the most instantly recognizable sounds in popular music, while his use of cutting-edge synthesizers on *Northern Lights—Southern Cross* was still radical for rock 'n' roll in 1975. There's no denying the quantum leap in overall musicality that Hudson brought to the group, giving them a level of complexity and a sonic arsenal other acts—especially their fellow below-the-belt bar bands— would never have dreamed of.

Adventurous Arrangements

That musicality made Hudson crucial when it came to The Band's working out their musical arrangements (in layman's terms: the organization of the different parts of a song). "If I was trying to do a song that was on the verge of being a little more sophisticated than what we normally did," Robertson admits in *Across the Great Divide*, "Garth would help me with the chord structures."

While The Band can be called the ultimate roots rock outfit, let's face it: To many the term "roots rock" connotes basic cowboy chords and standard twelve-bar blues. And while those elements do help form the backbone of The Band's music, the five men who made that music were never content to be entrapped by them—indeed, their yearning desire to experiment had much to do with their leaving Ronnie Hawkins, whose view about his Hawks' comfortable bar-band status was "If it ain't broke, don't fix it." Hawkins more or less liked to keep the rockabilly party train barreling straight down the track. His fiery young protégés, however, had reached a point where, yeah, they still liked that, too, a lot, but they also liked to spike the ride here and there with an unexpected melodic or structural turn—to keep the music interesting for them as well as the listener, to do something that made the older music they loved their own and not just some slavish imitation.

There was never any danger of The Band venturing into the convoluted realm of the day's prog-rock/jazz-fusion showoff acts. But still, a good number of their songs do have strikingly odd, deceptively clever arrangements that belie any perceived images of the players simply being a bunch of musty traditionalists. *Music from Big Pink* offers glimpses of this (such as the bizarre, oddly placed Salvation Army band interlude in "Chest Fever"), but *The Band* bears the full early fruit when it comes to audacious arrangements. The plum, if you will, is "King Harvest (Has Surely Come)," a segmented wonder whose distinct, interlocking parts work together kinetically like some Rube Goldberg mobile. Meanwhile, the rambling-but-hooky "When

You Awake" demonstrates the group's singular technique for creating songs that are easily followed but don't rely on the standard linear verse/chorus/verse-with-a-middle-eight approach, which most other rock bands still adhered to in 1968.

Funky Country

Although The Band were harbingers of what came to be called country rock, they also helped spawn a whole crossover school called, oddly enough, country funk—yet another iconoclastic concept the quintet carried with them when they stepped out of the Woodstock tree line. On paper and in the narrow minds of naysayers it would've seemed incongruous: the fusion of high-lonesome-hillbilly/country-folk melodies with deep-down, rump-rolling soul rhythms. But just as the country-and-R&B-merging rock 'n' roll pioneers who'd originally inspired them had shown, such seemingly disparate white and black styles weren't that far apart at all. The Band's inimitable "mountain funk" blend felt effortless and natural, like the best roots music always does.

The kernel of this sound is its distinctive, lazy cadence—somewhere between a shuffle and a waltz—that pumps through many of The Band's songs. Think of "The Weight," with its steady, stoic stagger, or "Don't Do It," their version of the Marvin Gaye hit "Baby Don't You Do It," which eases back the clip of the original just enough to bring the fatback funk further to the fore, making the tune slinkier and sexier than even the Motown love god himself could have fantasized. Or, of course, "Up on Cripple Creek," whose name slyly references a lily-white bluegrass standard while its rhythm is steeped in pitch-black Southern funk. All of these examples boast the sound of Helm's (in producer John Simon's words) "bayou folk" drumming rubbing up against Danko's bubbling bass—it's where the clear highland creek meets the murky, boggy swamp. A signature element of The Band's approach, this device informed the music of later acts like Little Feat and today's jam bands. But in the late 1960s it really wasn't common in rock 'n' roll.

Record Thyself

Also not common in rock 'n' roll, or any music in the 1960s, was the notion of making commercial records outside of a traditional recording studio. Informal "field recording" was viewed by most record labels as the province of figures like John and Alan Lomax, Library of Congress anthropologists/

engineers dispatched into the wild to document folk bluesmen and Navajo chanters in their natural environments—not something you did if you wanted to produce radio hits.

For that, there was no alternative to the controlled, laboratory-like conditions of state-of-the-art facilities like A&R Studios in New York and Gold Star Studios in Los Angeles, where The Band had recorded *Music from Big Pink*. But even though the sessions for that album yielded stunning results, they were hard-wrought for the players. To prevent microphone bleed (the sound of outside instruments "leaking" onto a track meant for a single instrument), the method of most professional studios then dictated that during recordings the musicians play while isolated from each other behind sound-deadening baffles and wear headphones to hear each other—a blind-man's-bluff-like situation not at all representative of the way bands play in rehearsal or onstage. So, after giving it a go to humor their Capitol overseers, the group elected to take off the "cans" and set up in a tight circle in the middle of the room, just as they were used to doing in the cellar of Big Pink. It helped tremendously, as we hear on the record, but the band was still "on the clock" and missed the relaxed atmosphere that had produced the Basement Tapes.

By the time it came to record the second album, in Los Angeles, they knew what they had to do. "We didn't wanna go back into studios and use engineers and union people," said Danko in *Across the Great Divide.* "We'd get engineers who'd had hits for people so they'd wanna take you on *their* trip." And so, with a budget from the label, they rented a mansion in West Hollywood, brought in recording equipment, and converted its pool house into a makeshift recording studio. There, with John Simon engineering, the five lived and worked in a "clubhouse" setting, completing the bulk of the tracks for *The Band*. They kept the self-recording practice going with *Stage Fright*, taping that set in the basement of a playhouse in Woodstock, once again using rented gear. After making *Cahoots* and most of *Moondog Matinee* nearby at their manager Albert Grossman's newly opened Bearsville Sound Studios (with admittedly mixed results), The Band ultimately opened their own private studio in California: Shangri-La, where they recorded *Northern Lights—Southern Cross* and parts of *Islands*.

In the 1960s, an artist or band taking control of the process for recording their own music—with the idea that they, first and foremost, would know best how it should sound—was largely unprecedented in the major-label world. In doing so, The Band helped establish a core practice of successive generations of "D.I.Y." musicians.

4

When I Paint My Masterpiece

The Band's Greatest Tracks

For a Band fanatic, narrowing down the track listings of the group's vanguard albums to a list of their greatest songs is a gut-wrenching, guilt-ridden process. Sure, there are some inarguably obvious choices—you can probably think of two or three right now—that few Band buffs would beat your brains out for including. But beyond those, it's a difficult dilemma. Which soul-baring Danko- or Manuel-sung heartbreaker makes the cut, and which does not? Which raw-boned, Helm-helmed rocker remains on the raft, and which must return to the muddy Mississippi bank, becoming a shrinking dot on the horizon until the next mixtape comes along? Here are one Band lover's personal picks.

"The Weight"

"I pulled into Nazareth, was feelin' about half past dead." Think back to the first time you heard "The Weight." Helm's cracked-leather voice bearing those weary words of woe. Danko relaying the ramblings of Crazy Chester. Laid atop the song's stoic gospel lope and couched in the group's unfaddish instrumentation, Robertson's words put the taste of the hot, dry dust of that lonely, biblically named town right in your mouth.

Turns out Crazy Chester was a real person, one Helm had told Robertson about, a happy-go-lucky Fayetteville eccentric who wore cap guns on his hips and thought himself the local keeper of the peace. The character of Luke was a nod to early Hawks guitarist Jimmy Ray "Luke" Paulman, Young Anna Lee was a girl from Turkey Scratch, and ("take a load off") Fanny, Miss Moses, and Carmen and the Devil just fit the rest of the parable. The location seemingly references the home of Jesus, but Robertson admits it was inspired by Nazareth, Pennsylvania, the site of the Martin guitar factory.

And believe it or not, what's probably The Band's best-known song—about "the impossibility of sainthood," a motif explored in *Nazarin* and other films by one of Robertson's favorite directors, Luis Buñuel—was recorded for *Music from Big Pink* as an extra track that almost didn't make the album. "'The Weight' was, like, 'Okay, this doesn't have a very complicated chord progression, it's just kind of traditional,'" recalled Robertson in *Across the Great Divide*, "'so we'll cut that when we get stuck for a song.'" Thankfully they did, and decided it sounded "kind of effective."

"King Harvest (Has Surely Come)"

Besides being one of The Band's signature LP cuts, "King Harvest (Has Surely Come)" is unlike anything else in their catalog—or, for that matter, the catalogs of other rock bands of their day. Written by Robertson and affectingly sung by Manuel, the song is about a struggling dust-bowl farmer and his relationship with the local agricultural union, and it reflects the rural theme of the album's original working title, *Harvest*. Who else was taking on such topics at the time? Certainly not the Archies or the Strawberry Alarm Clock.

But perhaps more than the subject matter, what makes "King Harvest" stand out is the arrangement. After a Robertson intro lick that recalls (the coincidentally named, given the topic) Steve Cropper of Booker T. & the MG's, in come Helm and Manuel's hushed, ill-omened voices ("Corn in the fields / Listen to the rice when the wind blows 'cross the water") portending a season rife with burning barns and failing crops. Manuel leans into this sharecropper's hardship confessional and soon, without warning, the band shifts to a higher gear, Hudson's organ hovering overhead as a funk pulse flows beneath it. The coda's volatile, hot-wire solo is largely out of character for Robertson during this phase of the group. But it sure works well.

"The Night They Drove Old Dixie Down"

A given, both here and in the high pantheon of rock itself. In a mere three minutes and thirty-three seconds, this heroic song conjures the same level of Civil War tragedy and defiant Southern grit that *Gone with the Wind* takes almost four hours to put forth. With battle-beaten Confederate soldier Virgil Caine as the narrator, the piece, recorded during the throes of the 1960s civil rights protest period, paints a vivid picture of the complicated feelings and existence of white Southerners during the decades that followed the most devastating event to ever take place on American soil.

According to Robertson, the seed for the song was planted in his brain when Helm's father offhandedly remarked to him, "The South's gonna rise again." "At one point when I heard it I thought it was kind of a funny statement and then I heard it another time and I was really touched by it," Robertson recalled to Rob Bowman for the box set *A Musical History*. "I thought, 'God, because I keep hearing this there's pain here, there is a sadness here.'"

Naturally, Helm, the direct conduit to the down-home Americana with which The Band is so identified, was indispensable to Robertson during the writing of "The Night They Drove Old Dixie Down." His advice on the geographical particulars and his cultural counseling were vital to Robertson's keeping the lyrics in line with the Southern experience. And of course there was no one better suited to sing this affecting opus than Helm himself. Sadly, he refused to sing it after the Last Waltz, feeling, apparently, like the violated vessel of Robertson's Reconstruction-era fetishism.

"I Shall Be Released"

Written by Bob Dylan during the Basement Tapes phase in Woodstock, "I Shall Be Released" is one of the most beloved songs of both Dylan's and The Band's repertoires, a hymn of redemption to rival the civil rights anthem "We Shall Overcome." Although "I Shall Be Released" would later be recorded by many others, its official unveiling on *Music from Big Pink*, so elegantly sung by Manuel, will always be the model others strive for but never match; indeed, Dylan himself didn't even try, taking the tune in a more upbeat country-rock direction for his 1971 *Greatest Hits, Vol. 2*.

Since Manuel's passing, some have come to view the song as analogous to the troubled musician's finally being "released" from the hellhounds who drove his addictions. But while there's some sense in that angle, one also gets the impression that the introverted Manuel would've preferred the spotlight not be on him, and to instead let the song be a balm to others. On the *Big Pink* version, his gossamer-fragile falsetto hovers, yes, high above the wall behind which the prisoner/narrator is so cruelly confined, its ascension a strength-giving allegory of the unconquerable human spirit. "You can lock me up behind the thickest, tallest stone walls," it implies, "but here within, in my heart, I will always be free."

"Rag Mama Rag"

In 2013, when Robbie Robertson was asked which song he was most proud of having written, the guitarist answered without hesitation: "Rag Mama Rag." Great answer—*great* song. And according to the guitarist, like "The Weight," it was initially considered a throwaway and recorded as "an extra one."

In a way that no other Band track does, "Rag Mama Rag" rolls together nearly all the disparate musical styles that influenced the group: Helm on bluegrass mandolin, Manuel on loose-limbed bebop drums, Danko on keening country fiddle, Hudson on barrelhouse piano, and John Simon guesting on jug-band-sounding tuba. Interestingly, besides having written

A rare Yugoslavian picture sleeve for the single of "Rag Mama Rag."   *Author's collection*

it, Robertson doesn't do much on "Rag Mama Rag"; he plays the chords, but the solo goes to Hudson, whose honky-tonk-whorehouse tinkling, combined with Simon's second-line blurting, evokes the New Orleans ragtime jazz of Jelly Roll Morton. Robertson's critics can accuse him of megalomania, but, in light of the above, his choice of this song as his favorite feels egoless.

The song made the Top Twenty in the U.K. but stalled at number fifty-seven in the U.S. "I really thought it was gonna be a radio song," recalls Helm in *Classic Albums: The Band.* "It had all the elements a song like 'Blue Suede Shoes' had. It swung real good and didn't take a whole lotta time." One can only agree, shake one's head in disbelief at the song's lack of American airplay, and listen as Helm twangs out tales of railroad tracks and rosined bows on this Brown Album highlight.

As it did in the U.S. and other countries, "The Unfaithful Servant" appeared as the B-side of "Rag Mama Rag" in Yugoslavia.   *Author's collection*

"Chest Fever"

This groaning beast is about as close as The Band ever got to straight-up hard rock. The anomalous bruiser on *Music from Big Pink*, "Chest Fever" (originally called "The Tracker") begins with a wicked, cathedral-filling solo that Hudson would stretch and improvise to ever-expanding realms in concert as "The Genetic Method." At the 2:33 mark on the studio version, the drums drop out, and what sounds like a drunken Salvation Army band—Manuel singing, Danko on violin, Hudson on tenor sax, and John Simon on baritone horn—stumbles by before Helms kicks it all back in with the line "Very much longer!" The crunching main riff lurches along with heaving unison vocals by Helm, Manuel, and Danko, who somehow make Robertson's bizarre lyrics sound meaningful.

According to Robertson, the lines were originally "dummy words" he intended to swap out for "real" ones later. But he never did, and they stuck. Eventually he admitted that, yeah, the words really didn't make any sense. Helm maintained that it's not the lyrics but the organ, anyway, that makes "Chest Fever" so memorable, and he continued to sing it with the new Band and his own groups.

"It Makes No Difference"

Danko's finest hour. One of *Northern Lights—Southern Cross*'s many delights, this dawn-breaking, down-on-my-knees plea for a lover's return spells out why The Band is as exalted for their beautifully down-tempo performances as they are for their upbeat dance numbers. It was rare for Robertson to write something outside his usual rural/historical/mythological concerns— especially a straight-ahead love song. With a few wrong turns, things could have veered treacherously close to the maudlin neighborhood of Eric Carmen's "All by Myself," which was released the same year, 1975. Instead, the song's haunting blues melody and novel, irregularly rhyming wordplay combine with the biting cry of Robertson's guitar and Hudson's soothing soprano sax solo to make it a true stunner. But really, this is Danko's show. Calling on his deep country/soul upbringing—think Hank Williams meets Otis Redding—the bassist yearns in vain with a heart that will never heal, his trembling, breaking falsetto leaving no doubt he's feeling every lonesome word. At six and a half minutes, it's one of The Band's longest songs. But its sweet, abandoned ache has you hoping it will never end.

"In a Station"

And then there's this longingly poignant Richard Manuel song off *Music from Big Pink*. Manuel considered it a "George Harrison–type song," and you can hear what he was getting at; the watery atmosphere of the track hints at "Within You Without You" and certain other songs by the Quiet Beatle. (Helm believed the comparison was due to the song's peaceful spirituality, a quality felt in much of Harrison's work.) The pianist composed it in honor of Woodstock's Overlook Mountain, which for him had come to embody the long-needed tranquility the group was feeling in their new home after so many crazy years on the road as the Hawks. With its Baroque opening, hazy, dreamy clavinet and organ by Hudson, arcing slide by Robertson, and soft drums by Helm, it brings to mind sun-dappled afternoons at Big Pink, the singer half-dozing with his girl on a blanket in the backyard, nuzzling to taste her hair and listening to the chirps of the birds. If only we all could stay like this. Right here. Forever.

"Up on Cripple Creek"

"Up on Cripple Creek" is the yarn of a happy-go-lucky vagabond—most Band scholars seem to agree he's a truck driver—with a girl in every hick town he passes through. Seems there's this one lady named Bessie, in Lake Charles, Louisiana, who really treats him well. And he's determined to visit her again, as soon as he gets down off the gad-danged mountain he's driving over. Or maybe he's not a trucker, but is instead a failed prospector in the real-life Gold Rush town of Cripple Creek, in the Colorado Rockies. Whoever he is, Helm portrays this wily road dog as no other vocalist ever could; you can visualize the flea-bitten drifter sitting in a steaming claw-foot bathtub, with a contented grin across his face and little Bessie scrubbing his tired back.

The title was most likely inspired by the traditional "Cripple Creek," a song recorded by Band favorites the Stanley Brothers, Charlie Poole, and Mainer's Mountaineers. But Kripplebush Creek, located just south of Woodstock, may have been a mental trigger as well. The song's recurring sonic signature is Hudson's burbling, Jew's-harp sound, achieved by running his Hohner clavinet through a wah-wah pedal—a pioneering, now ubiquitous funk effect predating Stevie Wonder's "Superstition" by years.

"The Unfaithful Servant"

Another cut from the second LP, and another heart-melting showcase for Danko. The song, a vaguely country/Southern Gothic tale of a servant banished from his master's house for an unnamed misdeed, was written by Robertson during the trip he and John Simon took to Hawaii just prior to the recording of the album and features an odd, descending chord progression that's more reminiscent of the jazzy compositions on Simon's own first album from 1971 than the bulk of The Band's work (apparently, the chords came out of a new tuning the guitarist had been experimenting with).

On *The Band*, "The Unfaithful Servant" (other album appearances of the tune omit the "The" in the track listings) works on another level by providing a tender interlude during the play list. The song also really shines on the live versions. Take the one on *Rock of Ages*, which juxtaposes Danko's soaring lamentations against Allen Toussaint's sympathetic horn chart and includes piercing guitar by Robertson and a consoling sax solo by Hudson. The studio version also came out on the B-side of "Rag Mama Rag."

"The Shape I'm In"

Also an album track and B-side (of "Time to Kill") is this *Stage Fright* slammer. Sung with frantic, frayed-nerve desperation by Manuel, it's clear that the juice-jonesing, gutter-bound gent in Robertson's lyrics is really a stand-in for the troubled pianist himself. Looking at the bigger picture, though, some critics have pontificated that the song is a metaphor for the inner turmoil of The Band itself, which was really starting to fester around the time the album was being made in Woodstock. In classic Band style, the narrative draws on the Old West (the line "I just spent sixty days in the jailhouse" calls to mind a frontier hoosegow) and biblical imagery (the "peace in the valley" bit). The track was a live showstopper and frequently positioned at or near the top of the group's set lists.

"Tears of Rage"

As the slow, sad opening cut on *Music from Big Pink*, "Tears of Rage" marks the point where many Band fans first came in. Manuel had written the song with Bob Dylan during the Basement Tapes doings a year before. Moving at a mournful, unwavering pace, it starts with Robertson's guitar, which has been fed through one of the mysterious "black boxes" that Hudson built, giving the track an underwater sound similar to the effect produced by a rotating Leslie organ speaker. Rising through the murk is Manuel's voice, with a delivery that sounds emotionally defeated. These are the words of a brokenhearted father to the daughter who has spurned him and his family. Like the situation with the domestic and the lady in "The Unfaithful Servant," the listener can't tell why or how this transgression took place, but we feel the storyteller's pain nonetheless.

Complementing Elliott Landy's "Next of Kin" photo on the album cover, "Tears of Rage" makes a powerfully sympathetic statement about the group's pro-family stance during the height of youth rebellion. In what would become a trademark Band device, Helm halves the tempo on his dampened drums, while Hudson's funereal chords and a tambourine play up the song's liturgical air.

"Jemima Surrender"

This gritty killer off *The Band* rules the rocking roost. Sung by Helm, it's a rare instance of him on guitar, and given the wonderfully rough, choppy chords he lays down, it's such a shame he didn't record more with the instrument. Credited to him and Robertson as the writers, the track has Manuel on drums, Hudson on piano, and Danko and Robertson in their usual, respective, bass and lead guitar slots; Hudson also contributes baritone sax. The recurring, stuttering riff is irresistible, and the weird section where it momentarily slips into a burlesque bump 'n' grind is a clever curveball. Said to be a lusty ode to a woman of color (like Ronnie Hawkins's similarly themed "Odessa"), the song builds upon the amorous hubris of the same album's "Rag Mama Rag" but takes the sexual energy several notches up. Helm bellows like a whiskey-soaked ranch hand kicking open the swinging saloon doors on a night of whoring and debauchery, begging the lady in question to let him give it straight to her: "I hand you my rod and you hand me that line." Now how could lil' ol' Jemima say no to that?

"Whispering Pines"

Once again, Beak gets bleak. And oh, how beautiful the sound. Continuing with the Brown Album, this ultimate Manuel tearjerker finds his heart-melting falsetto in full effect, arguably surpassing even the awesome ballad feel of his hero Ray Charles. According to Robertson, Manuel had the chords already mapped out when he came to him for help on the lyrics. The lines the guitarist wrote fit the music's unbearably deserted mood, and the singer's sensitive delivery and delicate personality, with uncanny perfection. Although the song was born in Woodstock—picture the lyric's "empty house in the cold, cold sun," which could easily be the secluded Bellows Lane home where Manuel composed the autumnal melody—its desolate scenes play out next to the ocean. The shattered protagonist's much-missed lover has been lost at sea or has left on a ship, to return he knows not when, if ever ("pines," indeed). The lost-at-sea trope is certainly symbolic of the isolation felt by an increasingly introverted soul such as Manuel. Listen late at night, when the sting of loneliness is sweet. And keep your handkerchief close.

"This Wheel's on Fire"

"This Wheel's on Fire," like the two other Bob Dylan–associated songs on *Music from Big Pink*, had evolved during the Basement Tapes sessions. Dylan cowrote it with Danko, who here sings the lead with Manuel's high harmonies buffering the "Best notify my next of kin" refrain (perhaps this line helped inspire the title of the album cover's "Next of Kin" photo?). Danko had been teaching himself piano when Dylan presented him with the surreal verses, which somehow fit the music he'd been tinkering with. In interviews, the bass player explained how he worked on the song's melody and phrasing himself before completing the chorus with Dylan.

The common view is that The Band distanced themselves completely from psychedelia, and by and large they surely did. But the *Big Pink* version of "This Wheel's on Fire" represents a rare psych gesture by these hypothetically hermitic woodsmen. Triggered by Hudson's avant-electronic blips at the opening, it bursts into the kind of darkly lysergic mood that permeates the first Country Joe and the Fish album. Also psych-tinged are the song's baffling, quasi-mythic words, which appear more concerned with mood than meaning. It feels like the dialogue of a modern-day Odysseus—a rock 'n' roll musician—living life on the edge, rolling down the road, about to explode.

"The Rumor"

A biting but low-key exposé of the local social/music scene that members of The Band were finding increasingly stifling in the wake of fame, "The Rumor" is emblematic of the blacker tone that permeates *Stage Fright*. Despite its Utopia-in-the-mountains identity, Woodstock was, after all, a tiny town, and its gossip mill had grown quickly and disproportionately with the sudden influx of Band/Dylan-peeping interlopers. "The Rumor" addresses this, tracing the trail of some scathing scuttlebutt as it slithers from door to door, ruining reputations and leaving deep scars along the way.

The track is also one of the best examples of the group's singular technique of vocal interplay. Over a slinky, around-the-top-of-the-kit drum pattern that sounds like Manuel but is in fact Helm, Danko sings the first line, about the rumor coming to town. Helm picks it up from there ("it grows and grows . . .") and the two pass the lyric back and forth, with the choruses going to a growly, low-registered Manuel. The song retains its circular motion, each voice coming back around, just as a rumor does. As in "The Gossips," Norman Rockwell's painting of small-town blabbermouths, there's a life lesson here.

"Acadian Driftwood"

This lengthy *Northern Lights—Southern Cross* cut is the bookend to The Band's other historical magnum opus, "The Night They Drove Old Dixie Down." Inspired by a TV documentary that Robertson stumbled upon, "Acadian Driftwood" tells the tale of the French Canadians who were forced out by the English in the mid-eighteenth century and ended up in Louisiana. In composing it, the guitarist also referenced Henry Wadsworth Longfellow's epic poem about the Acadians' bitter plight, "Evangeline" (which also informed the so-named tune the group performs with Emmylou Harris in *The Last Waltz*), alluding in its title to the driftwood that came from the ships of those who didn't survive the journey.

Like "Dixie Down," the track starts with a pronouncement by Robertson's acoustic, but it takes a vastly different aural path, adding accordion, piccolo, and bagpipe chanter by Hudson to lend the lilting melody the perfect sea-chantey air—you can almost hear the gulls crying overhead. That the lead vocals are traded, in typical Band fashion, between two Canadians and a Southerner underscores the saga's cross-cultural exchange, and the fiddle lines of guest Byron Berline (Country Gazette, the Dillards) suggest the musical traditions of the Maritimes.

The Band rarely performed "Acadian Driftwood" live; perhaps they felt its sustained subtlety worked best on record. Canadians Neil Young and Joni Mitchell sang it with them at the Last Waltz, but that version was deemed unworthy of release.

5

All Kinds of People You Might Want to Know

Notable Figures in Bandland

In their early Woodstock days, The Band's perceived persona painted them out as a cloistered collective of backwoods basement pickers who kept to themselves, living only for their music. But while there was certainly some truth to this during their early Catskills days, that image was largely embellished. By the time the Hawks became The Band, the five musicians had already been playing together for years, and along the way they had built up a formidable list of friends, associates, and other outside personalities who contributed to the group's history, and they met still more during the latter phases of their trajectory. Below are introductions to some key figures who remain deeply stitched into Band lore. Major players Ronnie Hawkins, Elliott Landy, and John Simon are covered elsewhere in the book.

Howard Alk

It was this Chicago-based filmmaker who introduced the Hawks-cum-Band to John Simon, the producer and recording engineer who would be such a key part of their first two albums. Alk had met the group (sans Helm) during their 1965 U.K. shows with Bob Dylan, while he was working on D. A. Pennebaker's tour documentary *Dont Look Back*. He'd come to Woodstock with his brother, Jones Alk, to assist Dylan with the editing of that film's surreal sequel about the singer's 1966 U.K. tour, *Eat the Document*. While in Woodstock, Howard was involved in yet another bizarre counterculture movie, *You Are What You Eat*, which was the brainchild of local folksinger

Peter Yarrow of Peter, Paul and Mary and starred novelty singer Tiny Tim. Alk hired the Hawks to back Tiny Tim on some songs for the soundtrack, Simon hit it off with the group, and the rest is rock 'n' roll history. A long-time heroin addict, Alk died in 1982.

Al Aronowitz

Journalist and short-serving Bob Dylan road manager Al Aronowitz is best remembered for two things: (1) introducing Dylan to the Beatles, and (2) introducing the Beatles to marijuana (both meetings allegedly took place on August 28, 1964, in a New York hotel room). But in addition to chronicling the Beat writers and being a biographer of Dylan, Bobby Darin, Mick Jagger, and Miles Davis, Aronowitz was also an early champion of The Band, covering their 1969 Woodstock Festival appearance in a piece for the *New York Post* and penning one of *Music from Big Pink*'s first reviews, for *Life* magazine. Unfortunately, the scribe, who himself struggled with addiction, also got a personal taste of The Band's dark side when he caught the drug money–seeking Richard Manuel and the pianist's then-girlfriend robbing his Woodstock house. Aronowitz, the original manager of the Velvet Underground, once brought Robbie Robertson to see the proto-punk icons perform (the guitarist was unimpressed). He died of cancer in 2005 at age seventy-seven.

Bill Avis

Born just outside Toronto, Bill Avis worked as the road manager of Ronnie Hawkins and the Hawks before going on to do the same for Levon and the Hawks and then The Band. Avis also road-managed Canadian group the Female Beatles, who were sharing the bill with Levon and the Hawks at the New Jersey club they were playing when they met Dylan. Avis had quit the road in 1970, shortly after he met his wife-to-be, and was considering Albert Grossman's request that he work with Janis Joplin when the troubled chanteuse died that year. He was back on board for The Band's farewell concert in 1976, and then once more in the 1980s for a U.S./Canadian/Japanese tour by the reunited group. Avis and Helm were especially close: The drummer was best man at Avis's wedding and the godfather of his son Jerome, with whom the elder Avis has staged several Band/Helm tribute concerts.

Dan Bass

A talent scout for Toronto indie label Quality Records, Dan Bass caught Ronnie Hawkins and the Hawks in action at the local club Le Coq d'Or and promptly signed them to record a single. Two of the tracks from the date, an early attempt at the Hawks' signature "Bo Diddley" and the ballad "Love Me Like You Can," would compose their now-rare debut single. Besides being the Hawks' first waxing, the disc is generally considered the first true rock 'n' roll record made in Canada; it's also Levon Helm's first appearance on record.

Larry Bennett

In the spring of 1959, this jazz-bandleader-turned-booking-agent at the New York–based Associated Booking Corporation procured Hawkins and the Hawks a residency in the Jersey Shore town of Wildwood. With their unhinged stage show, the group began to do sellout business in the resort mecca, and Bennett urged the powerful record executive Morris Levy to check them out. This led to the successful audition that saw them sign to Levy's Roulette Records and the beginning of a hot string of classic rockabilly hits.

Roy Buchanan

Though he remains, as the title of a 1971 PBS documentary would have it, *The Best Unknown Guitarist in the World*—or certainly one of them, at least—Roy Buchanan is still worshipped by legions of blues-rock guitar players for his lyrical lines and searingly expressive solos. One of his most devout devotees is Robbie Robertson, who learned directly from Buchanan when the genius musician was briefly a member of the Hawks.

Born in rural California, Buchanan entered the Los Angeles blues/R&B scene under the tutelage of bandleader Johnny Otis before backing rockabilly great Dale Hawkins (Ronnie's cousin). Presumably this was how, in 1960, Ronnie Hawkins came to hire Buchanan, who proceeded to teach the young Robertson, then on bass, his pioneering use of pinch harmonics and other guitar tricks. "For a while there, I was looking at having two lead guitars, using Roy alongside [Hawks guitarist] Fred [Carter Jr.]," recalled Ronnie Hawkins in *Last of the Good Ol' Boys*, although by most accounts Carter had left before this pairing could occur.

The intense, oddball Buchanan, who talked about being half man and half wolf and eschewed his boss's insistence on showbiz theatrics, didn't last long in the band and left after only a few months (coincidentally, he would be the hired session bassist on Robertson's first studio dates, the 1961 recordings that produced Hawkins's signature "Who Do You Love"). Unfortunately, Buchanan also didn't last long on earth. In 1988, after recording several exquisite but commercially unsuccessful albums and allegedly turning down an offer to join the Rolling Stones, the alcohol-plagued guitarist hanged himself in a Virginia jail cell while under arrest for public intoxication. He was forty-eight.

Thurlow Brown

The electric guitarist in Helm's duo with his sister Linda and his later high school rockabilly band the Jungle Bush Beaters, Thurlow Brown was an exceptional player who greatly influenced Helm's musical sensibility and a friend and jamming partner of legendary blues guitarist Robert Nighthawk. Brown also backed rockabilly singer Mack Self on the sessions for a 1957 Sun Records single ("Easy to Love" b/w "Everyday"), but little else is known about him.

Jimmy Carter

The Band met the future thirty-ninth president of the United States on their 1974 tour with Bob Dylan, when the then governor of Georgia had the entourage over for breakfast at his mansion after his kids had attended their Atlanta concert. In honor of Carter's 1976 presidential election run, The Band released its studio version of the Hoagy Carmichael standard "Georgia on My Mind" as a single with, oddly perhaps, given its title, "The Night They Drove Old Dixie Down" as the B-side ("Georgia" later appeared on 1977's *Islands*). Coincidentally—or not—Carter beat out the incumbent Gerald Ford just days after The Band's October 30, 1976, performance of the Hoagy Carmichael–penned classic on *Saturday Night Live*.

Bill Clinton

In 1979, Band fan Bill Clinton invited Helm to perform at the "Diamonds and Denim Gala" commemorating his first gubernatorial win in the drummer's home state of Arkansas. Helm would also speak alongside the future forty-second U.S. president at the May 1990 dedication of the Delta Cultural Center in Helena, later recalling it as one of the proudest honors of his life—along with the evening the reactivated Band headlined the "Blue Jean Bash" dinner at Clinton's 1993 presidential inauguration.

"I was saddened to learn of the death of my fellow Arkansan, Levon Helm," said Clinton in a press release upon the occasion of Helm's 2012 passing. "Levon was one of America's great musicians. His music, with the Hawks, The Band, and throughout his career, and his standout performance in *Coal Miner's Daughter*, touched a chord with me and with many Americans. He never forgot his roots. I was always grateful that he helped the annual Delta Blues Festival get off the ground. He will be deeply missed."

Bob Dylan

Arguably the most important and influential songwriter in the last sixty years of Western popular music, Bob Dylan (born in Duluth, Minnesota, in 1941) and his ineradicable ties to The Band are touched on elsewhere in this book. But of course no list of Band associates could exist without his name.

Dylan grew up as Robert Allen Zimmerman in the tiny western Minnesota mining town of Hibbing, and via Southern radio broadcasts, he was drawn to much of the same blues and country music that the members of The Band were inspired by when they were younger. In his high school years, at the same time that Ronnie Hawkins and the Hawks were establishing themselves in Toronto, he played Little Richard and Elvis Presley songs in rock 'n' roll cover bands. In 1959, the year Hawkins's first singles (of which Dylan was a fan) began appearing on Roulette, he briefly played piano for Bobby Vee and the Shadows before enrolling at the University of Minnesota in Minneapolis. He soon dropped out, changed his name to Bob Dylan (after the writer Dylan Thomas), and shifted his focus to folk, writing and performing songs in the style of his early idol, Woody Guthrie.

In 1961 he moved to New York, where he made his name in the Greenwich Village coffeehouses and clubs and signed to Columbia Records. Albert Grossman became his manager in 1962, and although his covers-dominated, self-titled debut album wasn't a big seller, 1963's *The Freewheelin' Bob Dylan* greatly impacted the folk scene; the Grossman-managed folk trio Peter, Paul and Mary had a huge hit with *Freewheelin's* "Blowin' in the Wind," and Joan Baez (briefly Dylan's romantic partner) and other artists began recording his songs. Suddenly, it seemed that Bob Dylan was a household name. In 1964, the still-acoustic artist hit with the social commentary of *The Times They Are A-Changin'* and the image-driven poetry of *Another Side of Bob Dylan*.

By March of 1965, inspired by the British Invasion and electrified versions of his songs (that year's hit adaptation of "Mr. Tambourine Man" by the Byrds), the shapeshifting Dylan had recorded *Bringing It All Back Home*, which features him backed by an electric rock 'n' roll band on one LP side. His "electric" performance with members of the Paul Butterfield Blues Band at the Newport Folk Festival that July was a landmark musical event, garnering a hostile reaction from the mainly folk-purist audience. But Dylan remained defiant, further ushering in the folk rock sound with the fully electric *Highway 61 Revisited*.

It was at this point in 1965, just before *Highway 61*'s release and while its advance single "Like a Rolling Stone" was in the Top Ten, that Dylan hired Robertson and Helm for the band that backed him for concerts at Forest Hills Stadium (a divisive event discussed elsewhere in this book) and the Hollywood Bowl. The other Hawks soon met up with Robertson, Helm, and Dylan for a six-month tour of the U.S. and Canada, which was followed by the sessions for 1966's *Blonde on Blonde*, on which Robertson is the only Hawk to appear. Next came the controversial '66 Dylan/Hawks tour of the U.K. and Australia, followed by Dylan's motorcycle crash and the Hawks' joining him in Woodstock for the 1967 Basement Tapes era, which presaged their rebirth as The Band. Although they would again back him at a 1968 Woody Guthrie memorial concert at Carnegie Hall, in an August 1969 set at the Isle of Wight, and for 1974's *Planet Waves* and its subsequent tour, the original Band's formal collaborations with Dylan ended with the 1976 Last Waltz concert, at which he performed as a guest. In 1992, the reunited Band performed with him at Madison Square Garden for the Bob Dylan 30th Anniversary Concert Celebration.

Rob Fraboni

After working with Dylan and The Band on *Planet Waves* and as a sound consultant for that year's Dylan/Band tour, this acclaimed producer and engineer built and designed The Band's Shangri-La studios in Zuma Beach, California. Prior to his associations with Dylan and The Band, Fraboni had worked with John Lennon, the Beach Boys, the Rolling Stones, the Raspberries, and others. At Shangri-La, he engineered and mixed *Northern Lights—Southern Cross*; he produced Eric Clapton's 1976 LP *No Reason to Cry*, on which the members of The Band and Dylan appear; he coproduced Rick Danko's eponymous 1977 debut; and, in tandem with Robertson and John Simon, he produced the *Last Waltz* soundtrack album. In the 1980s he served as corporate vice president of Island Records; worked with John Martyn, Buckwheat Zydeco, Bonnie Raitt, and Etta James; he later remastered recordings by U2 and Bob Marley. The list of artists Fraboni worked with in the 1990s and 2000s includes Phoebe Snow, Alvin Lee, Ivan Neville, Hubert Sumlin, Melissa Etheridge, and others. In 2002, he won a Grammy for his production of Keith Richards's track on the Hank Williams tribute album *Timeless*.

David Geffen

The Band's relationship with this future billionaire media mogul began in the summer of 1973, when Dylan terminated his contract with Columbia Records and signed with Geffen's Asylum label to make *Planet Waves* with The Band. In partnership with promoter Bill Graham, David Geffen also organized The Band's 1974 tour with Dylan, which produced the Asylum-released live album *Before the Flood*. The activity around *Planet Waves* and the 1974 tour necessitated The Band's moving to California, as at the time Dylan was living in Malibu and the six musicians needed to be in close proximity to rehearse. So, in a way, Geffen was instrumental in the original group's shifting their base away from Woodstock and establishing Shangri-La studios on the West Coast. A commercial powerhouse in the 1970s, Asylum never released an official Band album but did feature many acts associated with and/or influenced by The Band, such as Joni Mitchell, the Eagles, Jackson Browne, Linda Ronstadt, Tom Waits, Warren Zevon, and J. D. Souther.

In 1980 Geffen founded Geffen Records, which in addition to big sellers by John Lennon (his final album, that year's *Double Fantasy*), Neil Young, Elton John, Peter Gabriel, Nirvana, Guns N' Roses, Aerosmith, and others, released Robertson's first two solo albums, 1987's *Robbie Robertson* and 1991's *Storyville*.

Ralph J. Gleason

Like the above-mentioned Al Aronowitz, San Francisco's Ralph J. Gleason was an influential music journalist who, early on, understood what made The Band important, unique, and great. Writing in *Rolling Stone*—the magazine Gleason himself cofounded in 1967 with Jann Wenner—about the group's second performance of their three-night April 1969 coming-out at the Winterland Ballroom, Gleason said, "it was instantly clear that this was no Hollywood studio group in buckskin and beads playing what they'd learned off Carter Family records."

Gleason is perhaps most equated with jazz (he penned liner notes for Frank Sinatra and cofounded the Monterey Jazz Festival), but he viewed other styles as equally valid and was one of the first critics to review jazz, folk, rock, and pop records and concerts with a level of attention previously reserved only for classical music. Born in New York, he worked for the Office of War Information during World War II and landed in the Bay Area after the war to write for the *San Francisco Chronicle*. During the San Francisco Renaissance of the 1950s and '60s, he crossed paths with and interviewed Beat writers and envelope-pushing comedian Lenny Bruce, and he wrote supportively about the city's pioneering psychedelic rock acts at a time when other critics were yet to understand them. Gleason dispatched articles and syndicated weekly columns for newspapers and magazines across the U.S., authored books about jazz and the San Francisco rock scene, served as an associate editor and contributor to *Down Beat* for twelve years, and hosted the Emmy-nominated TV program *Jazz Casual* from 1961 to 1968. He died in 1975.

Henry Glover

It's unpardonable that as of the writing of this book Henry Glover, who died in 1991, has yet to be inducted into the Rock and Roll Hall of Fame. Born in 1921 in Hot Springs, Arkansas (about three hours from where Helm grew up), Glover was one of the most important behind-the-scenes figures in American music and one of the first successful black executives in the business. Over the course of his Zelig-like, nearly fifty-year career, he worked as a producer, arranger, talent scout, A&R rep, musician, studio designer, and songwriter whose credits include such hits as "Honky Tonk" (Bill Doggett), "Drown in My Own Tears" (Ray Charles), "California Sun" (the Rivieras), and "Peppermint Twist" (Joey Dee and the Starliters).

After playing trumpet in the big bands of Buddy Johnson and Lucky Millinder in the 1940s, Glover was hired by King Records. At the Cincinnati label he signed and produced white country artists like the Delmore Brothers, Moon Mullican, Hawkshaw Hawkins, Cowboy Copas, Grandpa Jones, and the York Brothers alongside black jazz, jump blues, and R&B

greats like James Brown, Hank Ballard and the Midnighters, Wynonie Harris, Little Willie John, Bull Moose Jackson, Tiny Bradshaw, and many other artists beloved of The Band members as young listeners. In 1958 Glover joined Roulette Records, where he worked with Sarah Vaughan, Dinah Washington, and Ronnie Hawkins and the Hawks, whose early hits he produced.

From the start, Glover saw something in Hawkins's backing players, and he told them so. After a session with Hawkins, Glover produced the group's first-ever track without the front man—appropriately, a version of Bobby "Blue" Bland's "Further On Up the Road" with Helm on vocals. Once they'd split from Hawkins, Glover oversaw the lone single they made as the Canadian Squires and their 1965 recordings as Levon and the Hawks. He remained a friend to the Hawks long after they'd become The Band, advising them on contractual matters and helping with horn arrangements and production at the Last Waltz concert. In 1975 Glover and Helm founded RCO Productions (the acronym stood for "Our Company"), which oversaw albums by the drummer's RCO All-Stars and Muddy Waters.

Bill Graham

As the presenter of the original Band's first and last concerts, this most prominent promoter in rock history was there at both official ends of the group's glorious story. Graham was born Wulf Wolodia Grajonca in Berlin, Germany, in 1931, and in 1941 he fled Europe to escape Nazi persecution (his mother, one of his five sisters, and many others in his Jewish family perished in the Holocaust). He settled in the Bronx before serving in the Army during the Korean War, during which he was awarded the Bronze Star and the Purple Heart.

In the early 1960s he lit out for San Francisco, where he befriended the political-satirist San Francisco Mime Troupe. When the group's leader was jailed on an obscenity charge in 1965, Graham organized a series of successful benefit concerts to raise defense funds. Having found his calling, the charismatic organizer began booking early shows by the Grateful Dead, the Jefferson Airplane, Big Brother and the Holding Company, and other local and touring acts at the city's Fillmore Auditorium (the operation would be relocated across town and renamed the Fillmore West) and eventually opened the Fillmore East in New York. Graham also ran San Francisco's Winterland Ballroom, where he presented The Band's debut concerts in 1969 and, six years later, the original group's farewell Last Waltz performance (glimpses of Graham in the wings can be seen in the 1978 concert film). The promoter organized The Band's famed 1973 Watkins Glen, New York, concert with the Allman Brothers Band and the Grateful Dead and their epic 1974 tour with Bob Dylan, as well as stadium concerts by Led Zeppelin, the Rolling Stones' 1981 U.S. tour, and 1982's U.S. Festival. He was killed in a helicopter crash in 1991.

Emmett Grogan

New York–born Emmett Grogan, a writer (1972's *Ringolevio*) and a friend to both The Band and Dylan, founded the Diggers, a legendary group of radical community advocates and improvisational actors based in San Francisco's hippie haven, the Haight-Ashbury district. The Diggers (named for a similarly progressive seventeenth-century English group) organized protests, distributed free food to the homeless, ran a series of "Free Stores" that offered clothing and other goods without charge, and helped AWOL servicemen hide from the authorities. Grogan dated Helm's longtime partner Libby Titus before she and the drummer got together, and he helped dramatically with the Last Waltz concert, acting as a gofer during The Band's epic rehearsals for the show, booking several of his fellow poets to appear that night, and reading one of his own poems onstage. With Rick Danko, he cowrote the majority of the songs on the bassist's 1977 solo debut. In 1978, Grogan, a longtime junkie, was found dead on a New York subway car of an apparent overdose.

Albert Grossman

People called him the Bear. The Baron of Bearsville. The Grey Cloud. Known for his stout stature, aspirations as a real estate developer, pure gray hair, and dour demeanor, Albert Bernard Grossman was the famously uncompromising manager of Bob Dylan, The Band, Janis Joplin, Todd Rundgren, Odetta, Peter, Paul and Mary, and other folk and rock acts.

Born in Chicago to working-class Russian Jewish immigrants in 1926, he entered the music world by opening the folk club the Gate of Horn there in 1956. Grossman was a paradox in the music industry, especially during the 1950s and '60s: a discriminating champion of pure, authentic art, extremely protective of his clients, and at the same time a merciless businessman (one of his legendary techniques was to make his opposing negotiators uncomfortable by remaining silent until they gave in to his demands).

Albert Grossman was already well known in the music business as the manager of Bob Dylan and Peter, Paul, and Mary when he became The Band's overseer and secured them a contract with Capitol Records in 1967. Grossman's other clients included Janis Joplin and Todd Rundgren, and his local Bearsville Records offices and recording studio helped make the Woodstock, New York, area a music industry hub for decades. *Photofest*

After cofounding the Newport Folk Festival with jazz promoter George Wein in 1959, he sensed the greater commercial potential of folk music and in 1961 brought together Peter Yarrow, Noel Paul Stookey, and Mary Travers to form the millions-selling Peter, Paul and Mary.

He became Dylan's manager the following year and helped foment his new client's reputation as the most important new songwriter of the era by getting other acts to record his songs (e.g., Peter, Paul and Mary's hits with "Blowin' in the Wind," "Don't Think Twice, It's All Right," and other Dylan tunes). Grossman has been credited with recasting performers as "artists" in the public consciousness, popularizing the use of the word "concert" for live rock and folk performances (previously, it was reserved for classical events), and orchestrating deals that let his acts retain creative control, which had been unheard of prior.

Through Dylan he came to know the Hawks, and after prodding from his wife, Sally (see below), he took them on as clients when they broke from the singer to begin looking for a record deal of their own. He increased their cachet as an artistic entity, supporting their adoption of the "anonymous" name The Band and cultivating an air of mystery around them by keeping the press at bay.

A lover of fine cuisine, he erected the Bear Café restaurant in 1971 outside Woodstock, followed by his Bearsville recording studio and record label offices. The Band remained with Grossman until defecting to David Geffen in 1973. He died of a heart attack in 1986 while flying to England.

Sally Grossman

Introduced to the pop world through her posing decadently behind Bob Dylan on the cover of 1965's *Bringing It All Back Home*, Sally Grossman, the spouse of Dylan/Band manager Albert Grossman, was no mere trophy wife. The cultured socialite and college literature major was vital when it came to The Band's stepping out from the long shadow of her husband's chief client.

When Dylan took his indeterminate break from touring in July 1966, his band was ever-eager to establish themselves under their own identity. Albert, though, was skeptical as to whether they'd mean anything without their more famous erstwhile front man. But Sally, who loved the music the five were making, lobbied her husband hard on their behalf, and once Dylan made it clear the following year that he had no plans to tour in the near future, she helped convince Albert to manage the group. After he died in 1986, she managed Albert's Bearsville Records label and his recording studio/theater/restaurant complex.

John Hammond Jr.

The son of famed record producer and talent scout John H. Hammond (who discovered and worked with Billie Holiday, Benny Goodman, Bob Dylan, Bruce Springsteen, and many others), John Hammond Jr., also known as John P. Hammond, is one of the foremost modern interpreters of traditional blues. He was gigging in Toronto in 1964 when he caught the Levon-led Hawks, and he jammed with them on his frequent returns to the Canadian city. The following year, when the band was doing its fateful pre-Dylan residency at the New Jersey Shore, the singer and guitarist engaged Hudson, Helm, and Robertson to appear on his fourth album for the Vanguard label, *So Many Roads* (leftover tunes from these sessions would appear on 1967's *Mirrors*; Hammond would again enlist Robertson and Danko for 1967's *I Can Tell*). Hammond maintains that it was around the time of the *So Many Roads* recordings that Dylan first saw the Hawks perform, with him, in a casual set at a Manhattan nightclub.

Glyn Johns

A 2012 Rock and Roll Hall of Fame inductee, this veteran English studio engineer and producer was enlisted to mix *Stage Fright*, which The Band recorded with Todd Rundgren engineering. In the end, though, only three of the tracks he mixed appeared on the original album (the rest were Rundgren's). Glyn is the brother of another famed producer-engineer, the late Andy Johns, and the father of producer-musician Ethan Johns.

Al Kooper

Al Kooper isn't as celebrated as other artists of the 1960s generation, but he's a rock 'n' roll legend nonetheless. After playing guitar with early rockers the Royal Teens ("Short Shorts"), Kooper turned to studio work and songwriting, co-penning Gary Lewis and the Playboys' 1965 hit "This Diamond Ring"; coincidentally, he met Levon and the Hawks in New York that year when they were briefly considering signing with Lewis's manager.

During Bob Dylan's June 1965 session for *Highway 61 Revisited*, Kooper talked producer Tom Wilson into allowing him to sit in on organ, even though he had little keyboard experience. The resulting track, on "Like a Rolling Stone," became the song's signature instrumental element and one of the most famous organ performances in rock music. Kooper backed Dylan, alongside Robertson, Helm, and bassist Harvey Brooks, the following August and September when the singer debuted his new electric songs at Forest Hills Tennis Stadium and the Hollywood Bowl. But after the engagements Kooper and Brooks had had enough of the abuse from Dylan's confused folkie audiences and stepped aside to let the rest of the Hawks join the singer for his upcoming tour.

Kooper next made two albums with the Blues Project, before forming and briefly fronting Blood, Sweat & Tears and cutting 1968's *Super Session* with Mike Bloomfield and Stephen Stills. Writing for *Rolling Stone* in 1968,

Kooper gave *Music from Big Pink* one of its first rave reviews, calling it his album of the year. As a producer, session player, and A&R rep, he's worked with the Rolling Stones, Jimi Hendrix, the Who, Cream, B.B. King, Alice Cooper, the Zombies, and Lynyrd Skynyrd.

Harold Kudlets

Called "the man who brought rock 'n' roll to Canada" by music fans and "the Colonel" by the Hawks (after Elvis Presley's manager, Colonel Tom Parker), the Scotland-born Harold Kudlets got his start in the music promotion business in the late 1940s, booking American big-band and jazz acts like Duke Ellington and Louis Armstrong in his native Hamilton, Ontario. He transitioned to rock 'n' roll in the late 1950s when he took over the bookings for Arkansas's Conway Twitty, whose rambunctious rockabilly had gotten his band tossed out of their original local residency at a stuffy area hotel. Booked into the right rooms by Kudlets, Twitty soon became a hit with the American–rock 'n' roll–starved Canadian crowds.

The impresario soon set Hawkins and the Hawks up with a run at Hamilton's Brass Rail Tavern in 1958, and from there he proceeded to build them up in Toronto and the rest of the country and handle their U.S. bookings as well. When the Hawks decided to split from Hawkins in 1963, Kudlets agreed to continue as their booking agent and kept them working north and south of the border. After the group signed with Albert Grossman, Kudlets kept busy in the entertainment business, booking other touring acts and serving as the talent buyer for venues in several U.S. cities. When The Band restarted in 1983, he returned to the fold to help with their bookings. In 2015, the ninety-eight-year-old Kudlets was living on a pension in a Hamilton retirement village, fondly reminiscing about his days with the Hawks and The Band.

Morris Levy

The founder and president of Roulette Records, home to Ronnie Hawkins and the Hawks, among other 1950s and '60s acts, Morris "Moishe" Levy was one of the most powerful behind-the-scenes figures in the early days of rock 'n' roll—and one of the most notorious. Levy was known as "the Octopus" for his omnipresent reach throughout the record industry and "the Godfather" for his mafia ties and unscrupulous business practices. Among other unsavory activities, he engaged in payola, added his own name to songwriting credits to collect partial royalties, and leveraged airplay from influential DJ Alan Freed, a compulsive gambler, by helping to cover his debts.

Levy could be either an indispensable ally or a fearsome enemy to the artists and industry associates he came in contact with. Luckily for the Hawks, he took a shine to them, wooing the band to Roulette in April 1959 with visions of Hawkins becoming the new Elvis Presley. Eventually, Hawkins's decision to concentrate on performing in his band's lucrative Canadian home base instead of Roulette's American market saw him part ways with the label.

Levy, who had entered the business via his ownership of New York's legendary Birdland jazz club and other venues, also owned and operated nearly twenty other labels and the Strawberries record store chain. He died in 1990, two years after being sentenced to a decade in prison for extortion. Despite his disreputable standing, Levy, who also regularly donated to several charities, was well liked by the Hawks.

Mary Martin

By most accounts, it's this humble former secretary we have to thank for introducing Bob Dylan to the Hawks. After having gotten to know the Hawks as a regular attendee of their gigs in her hometown of Toronto, Martin got a job as Albert Grossman's receptionist in New York. While working there in 1965 she learned that her boss's top act wanted an electric band to back him onstage. Knowing that Dylan had sensed the burgeoning folk-rock movement inspired by the Byrds' hit version of his "Mr. Tambourine Man," she suggested to the singer that he visit the bars of Toronto to check out the Hawks. But as it turned out, Dylan didn't have to go that far to find the Hawks, who at the time were doing their summer residency at the Jersey Shore. Thanks to Martin's playing them an advance copy of *Bringing It All Back Home*—and the presence of "Like a Rolling Stone" in the Top Forty—the Hawks were passingly familiar with Dylan's music when he phoned with his offer to play Forest Hills and the Hollywood Bowl.

Martin went on to become a leading music industry executive, signing Leonard Cohen to his first management deal, orchestrating Emmylou Harris's and Vince Gill's first record contracts, and managing Van Morrison and Rodney Crowell.

Phil Ramone

This Grammy-winning producer was one of the first studio engineers to work with the post–Ronnie Hawkins–era Hawks, manning the mixing board during the Henry Glover–produced sessions for the group's 1965 Atco single as Levon and the Hawks. Three years later, the group would again come into contact with the South African–born Ramone when they began cutting *Music from Big Pink* at A&R Recording, the New York studio he and his business partner Jack Arnold (the moniker came from their last names) opened in 1959. And when The Band needed some sharp recording expertise for the taping of the 1971 *Rock of Ages* concerts, it was Ramone (and fellow engineer Mark Harman, who worked on *Cahoots* and *Moondog Matinee*) they called upon. He died in 2013.

Martin Scorsese

Born in Queens, New York, in 1942, the director, producer, screenwriter, actor, and film historian Martin Scorsese directed *The Last Waltz* (1978), the dreamlike document of the original Band's final concert. He's also one of history's most influential moviemakers and the winner of multiple cinematic awards: Among his best-known films are *Mean Streets* (1973), *Alice Doesn't Live Here Anymore* (1974), *Taxi Driver* (1976), *Raging Bull* (1980), and *Goodfellas* (1990).

It was The Band's erstwhile road-manager-turned-movie-producer, Jonathan Taplin, who recommended Scorsese (whose *Mean Streets* screenplay Taplin had recently produced) when Robertson brought up the idea of filming The Band's 1976 farewell show. A Band fanatic himself, Scorsese had also worked as an editor on the 1970 concert film *Woodstock*, making him well suited for the job. Robertson, a passionate lover of film who was soon to try his hand at screen acting, became fast friends with Scorsese during the making of *The Last Waltz*. Since forging their relationship in 1976, Scorsese over the years has frequently enlisted Robertson as a film music consultant, producer, and soundtrack artist.

Cathy Smith

Born Cathy Evelyn Smith in Ontario, this notorious groupie/drug dealer will be forever known for her role in the overdose death of comedian John

Belushi. But when she was sixteen, long before she and Belushi met, Smith was involved with the Hawks, dating Manuel before next taking up with Danko and then Helm.

According to Smith, she was in bed one night with Danko at the city's Seahorse Inn, but the bassist left when she told him she wasn't on the pill, leaving Helm to take his place. Six weeks later, she learned she was pregnant. Manuel offered to marry her but she declined, eventually giving birth to the child, who because of the indeterminate paternity became known as, simply, "the band baby." At one point, when the Hawks had been busted for pot possession and were facing charges brought by a particularly obstinate police officer, Smith gave the cop in question a blow job, afterward telling him she was only fourteen and "convincing" him to drop his charges against the group. After a volatile romance with local folksinger Gordon Lightfoot (his hit "Sundown" was written about her), Smith entered a lengthy relationship with Helm. As the 1970s wore on, she occasionally served as a backup singer to various acts, got deeper into heroin abuse, and began dealing drugs herself.

On March 5, 1982, while partying with the wild-living Belushi at the Sunset Strip's high temple of inequity, the Chateau Marmont hotel, Smith injected the *Saturday Night Live* star eleven times with the potent cocaine-heroin cocktail known as a speedball before leaving the scene. When Belushi was found dead in the morning, she fled to Toronto. She returned to the U.S. in 1986 to accept a plea bargain on manslaughter and drug charges and serve a fifteen-month prison term.

Jonathan Taplin

The Band's tireless tour manager from 1969 to 1971, Taplin has enjoyed multiple careers: road manager to other acts, writer, film producer, businessman, and journalism professor. He had been touring with folksinger Judy Collins when her manager, Harold Leventhal, hired him to assist with the January 1968 Carnegie Hall Woody Guthrie tribute concert at which Dylan and the Hawks performed. When *Music from Big Pink* began to take off, Albert Grossman tapped Taplin to head The Band's road team. In 1971, George Harrison asked him to help with the staging of the famous Concert for Bangladesh at Madison Square Garden. Eventually, Taplin swapped music work for a long career in the movie business, starting with his role as the producer of Martin Scorsese's 1973 crime epic *Mean Streets*. He returned briefly to the Band/Dylan fold to help set up their 1974 tour, and two years later was back again to work alongside Scorsese as the executive producer of *The Last Waltz*.

Allen Toussaint

This New Orleans legend heavily impacted The Band's music in two ways. First, as the author of literally dozens of early R&B's most enduring tunes, Toussaint was responsible for a wide swath of the music The Band was inspired by. Second, and more directly, he injected his Southern genius straight into The Band's music when they hired him to write some of his innovative horn arrangements for their songs, starting with *Cahoots*' "Life Is a Carnival" and following that with the brass accompaniments for *Rock of Ages* and *The Last Waltz*.

Born in 1938, the pianist, singer, arranger, and producer was originally inspired by local keyboard kings Professor Longhair, Fats Domino, and Huey "Piano" Smith. As a teenager he worked with blues greats Snooks Eaglin and Earl King before becoming a session player with R&B producer/composer/performer Dave Bartholomew. In 1960 he cemented his name as a hot producer with Jessie Hill's national smash "Ooh Poo Pah Doo," which opened the gates for a long run of Toussaint-penned hits that exemplify 1960s New Orleans R&B: Ernie K-Doe's "Mother-in-Law"; Benny Spellman's "Fortune Teller" and "Lipstick Traces (on a Cigarette)"; Irma Thomas's "Ruler of My Heart"; Lee Dorsey's "Ya Ya," "Ride Your Pony," "Working in the Coal Mine," and "Holy Cow" (the last covered by The Band on *Moondog Matinee*); and many more. Toussaint released his first solo album, *The Wild Sound of New Orleans*, in 1958 and opened Sea-Saint Studios with composer/producer Marshall Sehorn in the mid-1960s.

Paul Simon, Sandy Denny, Little Feat, and The Band all hired him for his colorful horn arrangements. Toussaint wrote Three Dog Night's Band-esque single "Play Something Sweet (Brickyard Blues)" (1974) and produced Dr. John's "Right Place, Wrong Time" (1973) and Labelle's "Lady Marmalade" (1975). On top of having his songs covered by Glen Campbell (1977's number one "Southern Nights"), Bonnie Raitt, Boz Scaggs, Devo, Robert Palmer, the Judds, and others, he collaborated on albums with Elvis Costello, Joe Cocker, Etta James, and Albert King. Toussaint died in 2015.

Conway Twitty

Singer Conway Twitty (born Harold Jenkins, 1933; died 1993) is best known for his 1958 number one single "It's Only Make Believe." But before hitting with that ballad and going on to an illustrious career in country music— he held the record for most number-one country hits until 2006—the Mississippi-born Twitty, as Harold Jenkins, was a rockabilly sensation on the same Arkansas circuit from which Levon Helm and Ronnie Hawkins had sprung. Jenkins's band, the Rockhousers, included early Hawks guitarist Jimmy Ray "Luke" Paulman and were a marked influence on Helm's high school band, the Jungle Bush Beaters (the teenaged drummer was in high heaven one night when he sat in with his hero).

It was Twitty, just returned from a hugely successful stint in rock 'n' roll–crazed Toronto, who suggested Hawkins give manager Harold Kudlets (see above) a call about getting his band into Canada. And so it was in 1958 that Ronnie Hawkins and the Hawks, with Helm newly installed on the drum stool, set out to take their red-hot rockabilly blowtorch up north, where they would soon recruit Robertson, Danko, Manuel, and Hudson.

6

They Gave This Plowboy His Fortune and Fame

The Musical Genres That Forged The Band's Sound

With the breakthrough of The Band, many listeners who would've been dismissive, or simply unaware, of older music were now hearing things differently. They wanted to know more about this stuff, where it all came from. Many of them even wanted to play it themselves, or at least to play it filtered through the way The Band played it. In a way that no prior rock act had done, The Band assimilated, remade, and contagiously celebrated the diverse strains that make up the rich fabric of American vernacular music. Blues, country, jazz, folk, gospel, rock 'n' roll, soul, ragtime—with a dash of classical or a sprinkle of polka or gypsy music by way of Europe—the members absorbed all of it, distilling what they heard into their own timeless brew. And it was this vibrant concoction that reshaped rock music, basically creating what's now called roots rock or Americana. Here, we'll hit on the essential ingredients.

The Blues/Rhythm and Blues

"To me," Levon Helm said when I interviewed him in 2008, "the blues are the ABCs of music." And, at least when it comes to Western popular music, that view is as square on the beat as the drummer's own unshakable playing style. The blues is a musical genre with a shared tradition of lyrics that are sometimes topical but customarily focus on universal themes like romantic, economic, and social hardship, although sometimes they're humorous or contain sexual innuendo. At the same time, the blues is also the name of the musical form itself, a given, malleable system of rhythms and notes (specific chord progressions, i.e., the twelve-bar blues) that serves as its nuts and bolts; many of the structural tropes of the blues have been adapted for use by other genres. And then, of course, the blues is also what we call the intangible *feeling* that runs through much music, whether it's blues-based or not.

With audible roots in the ancient African tribal chants and social music brought to America's Deep South by slaves, as well as the field hollers, spirituals, work songs, and ring shouts they developed and the white country-folk music they learned to play, the blues is the foundation of all modern American popular music: rock 'n' roll, soul, jazz, funk, rhythm & blues (the last term is often used interchangeably with the blues, but there is some distinction, which we'll get to below), and everything that has come after. None of these styles—not to mention later ones like contemporary pop, disco, hip-hop, or even the most mechanized electronic dance music—could exist without the signature blues elements that form their very backbones: the call-and-response patterns, trance-like rhythms, cycling chord progressions, and use of "blue notes" (notes sung or played below the major pitch for dramatic effect).

Broadly speaking, in terms of specific influence The Band's music tends to downplay the blues' darker, more emotionally fatalistic qualities in favor of its more aggressive, cathartic, wistful, and at times celebratory sides. Helm, Robertson, and the group were more closely influenced by the rocking heft of Muddy Waters and Elmore James and the melancholy reassurance of Mississippi John Hurt than the stark, stygian abyss-plunging of Blind Willie Johnson.

The blues started as a raw, rural vocal and instrumental music sung and played by black folk musicians mainly on guitar or banjo and sometimes fiddle, harmonica ("mouth harp"), mandolin, or the crude "diddley bow" made by nailing taut lengths of wire to the side of a barn. Composer W. C. Handy was inspired to write 1912's "The Memphis Blues" after stumbling across a street performance by an itinerant bluesman in Mississippi. While Handy's piece was much more of a novelty song than a strict blues, it became a sizeable hit that saw the "blues" suffix affixed to dozens of similar songs written by Tin Pan Alley pop composers. This in turn led to the blues form being adapted for an urban audience via an early-1920s wave of piano- and jazz band–backed female black vaudeville circuit singers like Mamie Smith (her 1920 "Crazy Blues" is the first recorded vocal blues by an African-American artist), Ma Rainey, Victoria Spivey, and, arguably the greatest of them all, Bessie Smith, who would be honored directly in song by The Band.

The blues craze of the day helped demonstrate to the record industry that there was an untapped market among newly urbanized blacks for the authentic country blues they knew from their former surroundings. In the 1920s and '30s labels began sending engineers to cut "race records" by local players in hotbed regions like the Mississippi Delta, the Piedmont area of North Carolina, and various locations in Texas, Tennessee, Georgia, and Louisiana. It's to this effort we owe the discovery of dozens of enormously influential legends, such as singer-guitarists Robert Johnson, Charley Patton, Blind Lemon Jefferson, Skip James, Blind Willie Johnson, Mississippi John Hurt, Son House, Blind Willie McTell, and Furry Lewis. (Bob Dylan wrote a song in honor of McTell, which The Band cut for 1993's *Jericho*; Joni Mitchell plays her "Furry Sings the Blues" with The Band and Neil Young in *The Last Waltz*.)

As Southern blacks made the first Great Migration north to cities like Chicago and New York, boogie-woogie and jazz-crossover "stride" piano players Cow Cow Davenport, Clarence "Pine Top" Smith, Jimmy Yancey, Albert Ammons, and Pete Johnson became popular; other urban artists, like guitarists Big Bill Broonzy and Tampa Red, worked with small groups featuring bass and washboard players to establish an upbeat "hokum" approach. The blues became increasingly citified, fusing with jazz horns to become jump blues, which was mainly a late-1940s West Coast phenomenon dominated by Louis Jordan and white bandleader Johnny Otis, and rhythm and blues (R&B), which retained the stomping backbeat of jump blues—the "rhythm"—but with sparser instrumentation. (The term "rhythm and blues," coined as a euphemism for the offensive "race music," would later be applied to the soul and funk music of the 1960s and 1970s; "contemporary R&B" refers to today's more polished soul-based pop.) In the years just after World War II, the blues was electrified, figuratively and literally, with amplification by figures like Elmore James, B.B. King, Howlin' Wolf, Sonny Boy Williamson, Little Walter, and Muddy Waters.

Rock 'n' Roll

Initially, "rock 'n' roll" was just a marketing term. At the dawn of the 1950s, when the Chicago electric blues innovators were plugging in, the rhythm and blues charts were at the same time being ruled by black singers like

Ray Charles, Ruth Brown, Etta James, and Faye Adams and vocal harmony groups like the Ravens, the Flamingos, and the Dominoes. Cleveland DJ Alan "Moondog" Freed became aware that although the music was becoming increasingly popular with white teenagers, during the pre–civil rights era its "race music" stigma was problematic. He began using the term "rock 'n' roll" for the R&B records he played on his WJW radio show, his listenership grew, and he jumped to WINS in the massive New York market as other DJs across the U.S. began following his programming lead.

Through Freed rock 'n' roll had become a catchall name for the music of the above generation of acts and that of a transitional wave of African-American artists playing a more stripped-down, hopped-up take on R&B: Chuck Berry, Fats Domino, Little Richard, Bo Diddley, and others. Also under the rock 'n' roll banner came concurrent subgenres of black, white, Hispanic, and racially mixed vocal groups (doo-wop) and white artists who were crossing their country music roots with blues and R&B (e.g., Bill Haley and His Comets, who started out playing western swing, and the rockabilly rebels erupting from the South).

The cultural and social impact of this phenomenon cannot be overstated: Rock 'n' roll was music that could be played, shared, and enjoyed by everybody, no matter what their background. This is the epoch during which the members of The Band came of age and first climbed aboard the musical mystery train.

Rockabilly

Rockabilly was The Band's true launchpad. It's the Southern-born sound of crazed white juvenile delinquents raised on honky-tonk country and newly jacked up on black R&B and jump blues, a sound that quivers hysterically with jittery vocals and train-track rhythms. The elemental format of rockabilly, whose name derives from the fusion of "rock 'n' roll" and "hillbilly," consists of a singer, electric guitar, upright acoustic "slap" bass (later swapped for electric bass), sometimes piano, and minimal drums (early on, rockabilly groups followed the percussion-less bluegrass group template; drums were soon added to match the volume punch of the electric guitar). Along with lusty braggadocio inspired by hard-edged bluesmen like Junior Parker and Arthur Crudup, rockabilly lyrics often focused on novelty Atomic Age themes pulled from science fiction movies (see "Flying Saucers Rock 'n' Roll" by Billy Lee Riley and His Little Green Men).

Run by producer Sam Phillips, Memphis's Sun Records codified the music, capturing the raw early energy of Elvis Presley, Jerry Lee Lewis, Carl Perkins, Johnny Cash, Roy Orbison, Charlie Feathers, and other Southerners, accenting their attack via vocals soaked in "slap-back" reverb and guitar leads laden with outer-space-sounding tape echo. But many of the best rockabilly artists were on other labels: The Rock and Roll Trio, featuring brothers Johnny and Dorsey Burnette and influential guitarist Paul Burlison, were Memphis boys signed to Coral; Capitol's Gene Vincent and His Blue Caps, with another monster guitarist, James Burton, originated in Virginia; Eddie Cochran grew up in California and recorded for Liberty; and another Coral artist, Buddy Holly, was from Texas. Then there were Arkansans Dale Hawkins, who cut the 1957 swamp rock classic "Susie Q" for Chess Records, and his cousin, The Band's mentor, Ronnie Hawkins.

By the late 1950s, rockabilly had been diluted and drowned in America by the rise of corporate teen idol singers like Frankie Avalon and Fabian. But in a sense this loss was another gain: The continuing demand in Canada for authentic rockabilly was what brought Ronnie Hawkins and Levon Helm northward to eventually link up with Robertson, Danko, Manuel, and Hudson. Rockabilly went dormant with the dawn of the 1960s but experienced a revival in the late 1970s and early 1980s. Producer John Simon remarked that Levon Helm was The Band's strongest link to rockabilly, a theory substantiated by his Sun-soaked vocals on twangin' tracks like "Strawberry Wine" and "Jemima Surrender."

Doo-Wop

A dominant genre of early rock 'n' roll and R&B, doo-wop is named for the nonsense syllables archetypally sung behind the lead tenor in a vocal harmony group. Rooted in gospel music and in 1930s and '40s pop vocal groups like the Mills Brothers and the Ink Spots, doo-wop was developed toward the end of the 1940s by the African-American a cappella groups who sang on urban East Coast street corners. Although in its essential form doo-wop is vocals-only, backing instrumentation was added when it began making its way onto records. First-generation doo-woppers include many groups named for cars (the Edsels, the Cadillacs, Little Anthony and the Imperials) and birds (the Ravens, the Penguins, the Flamingos; perhaps the Hawks' handle was a partial nod to this). Next came more black groups, like the Drifters, the Moonglows, and Frankie Lymon and the Teenagers); white groups that included the Skyliners, the Diamonds, the Mello-Kings, and Italian-American combos such as Dion and the Belmonts, the Capris, and the Del-Satins; and racially integrated outfits like the Crests, the Del-Vikings, the Impalas.

The Band were certainly doo-wop appreciators, as shown by their covers of the Rays' "Silhouettes" with Dylan during the Basement Tapes period, the Platters' "The Great Pretender" (on *Moondog Matinee*), and, in their later years, the Coasters' "Young Blood." But although The Band was known for having multiple singers who harmonized beautifully, their approach owes more to raw gospel/bluegrass-style harmonies than the operatic, high-tenor-floating-over-onomatopoeic-backups technique commonly identified with doo-wop. More apparent in the group's own music is doo-wop's penchant for torchy, regal arrangements, especially the ones crowned with Manuel's wounded voice ("Sleeping," "The Moon Struck One").

Country

To many, country music is the most stereotypically "American" music there is. But like America itself, it actually descends from many outside traditions. Born from the ballads and shanties of the English and Scots-Irish settlers of the Southern Appalachian Mountains and the cowboy singers of the American West (hence the lengthier and now rarely used term *country and western*), country began as story-based social and dance music sung and played primarily by solo and harmony singers accompanied by banjo, fiddle, guitar, harmonica, or small string bands. Over time, country has intermingled with and was influenced by the blues, whose melodies and lyrical themes make it country's clear cousin, as well as Celtic, European, Hawaiian, and Mexican music, jazz, pop, and other styles.

With the blossoming of the commercial recording industry in the early 1920s, record labels looking for a way to capitalize on the emerging working-class phonograph market began sending recordists into the field in search of local talent. Many early country recording artists signed in this way were authentic, straight-off-the-farm players or moonlighting mill workers (especially in recording hubs like Virginia, Georgia, and the Carolinas) who made only a handful of "old-time" or "hillbilly" records, as they were marketed, before disappearing. But there also were those who became the genre's initial stars, such as the "father of country music," Jimmie Rodgers (not be confused with the identically named 1950s pop singer), Vernon Dalhart ("Wreck of the Old 97"), and confirmed Band favorites the Carter Family and Charlie Poole.

The Great Depression of the 1930s saw a decrease in record sales and the rise of radio listenership among the country audience, especially for WSM's live musical variety show *Grand Ole Opry*, which has been broadcast from Nashville since 1925. The weekly program helped further popularize country music, making household names of artists like Uncle Dave Macon, Roy Acuff, Eddie Arnold, Patsy Cline, Hank Williams, Kitty Wells, Johnny Cash, and the Louvin Brothers, among many others, and even today, for any working country act an appearance on "the Opry" is an affirmation of their arrival. The show was a regular highlight of life on the family farm for Levon Helm when he was a boy, and the making of his 2011 live album, *Ramble at the Ryman*, recorded at the show's longest-running home, the Ryman Auditorium, must've been a heartwarming homecoming for the drummer. "I'd always wanted to go to Nashville to be a cowboy singer," Rick Danko recalled for *Rolling Stone* in 1968. "From the time I was five, I'd listened to 'the Grand Ole Opry,' the blues and country stations." Hudson, who played accordion in a country band when he was twelve, remembered his father "used to find all the hoedown stations" on the radio.

Garth Hudson played on this 1959 single by country singer Don Crawford.
Author's collection

The 1930s brought duos like the Delmore Brothers and the Blue Sky Boys and cowboy movie singers like Gene Autry and Roy Rogers (the latter formerly of the Sons of the Pioneers, whose hit "Cool Water" was recorded by Bob Dylan and The Band during the Basement Tapes sessions), along with western swing, which is marked by snappy, big-band-jazz-influenced cadences that directly informed the rockabilly beat. The "Kings of Western Swing" were Bob Wills and His Texas Playboys; flashes of Wills's sound can be heard in Danko's sweeping fiddle as it kicks off "Rag Mama Rag."

In the 1940s, honky-tonk, a heavily blues-inflected style with touches of Mexican *rancheras*, scaled the larger western swing band format down for dancing in smaller saloons. Its sprightly tempos and lyrical themes—drinking, love gone wrong, lonesomeness, depression—struck a common chord, making it the day's most popular form of country music. The giants of honky-tonk, whose instrumentation brought steel guitar and barrelhouse piano to the fore, include Ernest Tubb, Floyd Tillman, and, far above all others, Hank Williams. In the early 1950s honky-tonk entered its golden age with artists like Webb Pierce, Hank Locklin, George Jones, and Lefty Frizzell. For the young Robbie Robertson, absorbing the Williams and Frizzell songs his relatives played was an influential highlight of visits with his mother's family.

By the late 1960s country was generally seen by young rock 'n' roll listeners as backward, conservative stuff. So when The Band reclaimed the humble genre to pioneer country rock, it was a powerful revelation to a new, young generation seeking grounding in a turbulent time.

Bluegrass

Bluegrass is a later substream of country music, one that's of the mother genre yet at the same time distinctly separate from it, representing a return to country's acoustic folk roots, but with added flavoring. Like the Appalachian music that came before it, bluegrass descends from traditional English, Scottish, Irish, and Welsh music (ancient ballads like "Pretty Polly" and "The Cuckoo Bird" are in the bluegrass canon). But unlike early country, bluegrass places a greater emphasis on harmony singing and bears a strong jazz influence via virtuosic solo improvisations during fast instrumental passages called breakdowns. The father of bluegrass is Kentucky-born singer and mandolinist Bill Monroe, who recorded more standard old-timey music the 1930s and fully developed the bluegrass sound in the mid-1940s with the additions of firebrand banjo player Earl Scruggs and guitarist Lester Flatt to his band, the Blue Grass Boys (for whom the genre is named). Monroe inspired Elvis Presley, whose first single was a rocked-up cover of his 1946 waltz "Blue Moon of Kentucky."

Flatt and Scruggs further advanced the bluegrass style when they left Monroe to form their own Foggy Mountain Boys; Scruggs performs alongside Helm and others on 1989's all-star roots album *Will the Circle Be Unbroken: Volume Two*. The most influential bluegrass act after Monroe is the Stanley Brothers, Ralph (vocals, banjo) and Carter (vocals, guitar), whose version of Charlie Poole's "If I Lose" The Band would record as a *Big Pink* outtake. Other significant first-generation bluegrass artists include Jim and Jesse, Doc Watson, Mac Wiseman, the Osborne Brothers ("Rocky Top"), Reno and Smiley, Jimmy Martin, and fiddler Vassar Clements, who appears on The Band's *Jericho*.

Cahoots' opening track, "Life Is a Carnival," which features horn arrangements by Allen Toussaint, has strong elements of Dixieland jazz. Released as a single, it went to number twenty-five in Canada but peaked at seventy-two in America.   *Author's collection*

Jazz

Jazz stands as one of America's legitimately original art forms, a musical genre that couldn't have come from anywhere else. Born in African-American communities during the late nineteenth and early twentieth centuries, jazz at its root is the synthesis of African-derived rhythms and expressive, improvisational sensibilities with European harmonies and instrumentation (brass band instruments and piano). Elemental to jazz are the blues foundation that serves as its lingua franca, its "swing" feel, and its emphasis on improvisation; ragtime, which we'll get to below, gave early jazz it its syncopation.

The acknowledged crucible of jazz is New Orleans, long a melting pot of African, European, Creole, and Caribbean cultures (the last responsible for the so-called "Spanish tinge" of early jazz), where the euphoric style now called Dixieland was originally performed in brothels, bars, and dancehalls and, as it still is, by street-marching bands for funerals. The major architects of early New Orleans jazz, all black artists, are trumpeter and singer Louis Armstrong, pianist Jelly Roll Morton, and clarinetist and saxophonist Sidney Bechet; the first jazz records were made by the Original Dixieland Jass Band, a white New Orleans outfit. This era of jazz is strongly detectable in The Band's more effervescent, horn-accompanied songs like "Ophelia" and "Life Is a Carnival." But the best example is "Rag Mama Rag," on which a tuba, played by John Simon, fulfills the bass role—a characteristic approach necessitated by the mobility issues and low recording volume of an acoustic double bass in the days before microphones and amplifiers.

From New Orleans, jazz spread north and northeast to be further developed by both black and white musicians (influential trumpeter Bix Beiderbecke being among the latter) in Chicago, Kansas City, and New York. By the 1930s and '40s the collective improvisation that had exemplified small-group "hot jazz" had given way to the big band swing of Duke Ellington, Count Basie, Benny Goodman, and others, which favored more precise arrangements with integrated solos. The Band's use of a large horn section for the *Rock of Ages* and Last Waltz concerts connects them to big band music.

The late 1940s saw the evolution of bebop, a harmonically complex and rhythmically challenging style forged by saxophonist Charlie Parker, trumpeter Dizzy Gillespie, pianists Thelonious Monk and Bud Powell, and other trailblazers. Bebop was beloved of the brainy Hudson but wasn't a major part of his band's initial M.O. "We were trying to maintain a straight-ahead, traditional approach to the notes played, so we didn't play any bebop," he recalled in a 2012 interview for Prism Films. "Maybe a little swing in 'Rag Mama Rag,' but no bebop."

By "swing" Hudson is referring not only to the horn work of the big bands, but also to the trait that gives that subgenre its name: the "swing" feel itself, which comes from playing with a relaxed groove emphasizing the offbeat. More than any other major rock band of the 1960s or '70s, The Band *swung*. And, like the best veteran jazz musicians, they swung with the confidence, control, and capacity to relish their places as moving parts within a bigger apparatus, the cumulative collective gift of their years on the road. There are many examples of The Band's deadliness as a swingin' machine, but among the best are "Just Another Whistle Stop" and "Caledonia Mission," whose loping, pendulum-esque cadences flow like water from a tap.

When the group was Hawk-ing it up in Toronto, they loved checking out visiting jazzers like Oscar Peterson, Charles Mingus, and Cannonball Adderley. As mentioned elsewhere in these pages, there are some documented pre-Band jazz-crossover efforts by members: Helm and Danko's session with Lenny Breau, and Robertson's appearance on Charles Lloyd's *Of Course, Of Course.*

Soul

Soul music evolved out of rhythm and blues in the 1950s and reached its full flower in the 1960s, bringing the impassioned, testifying fervor of R&B's foundations in black gospel music to the fore. Indeed, many of the founders of soul music were erstwhile gospel artists who'd "crossed over" by reappropriating the songs they'd sung in church for a secular audience—Ray Charles's 1954 smash "I Got a Woman," for example, is based on the spiritual "I Got a Savior"—which created controversy among the black religious population. In addition to Manuel's idol Ray Charles, the list of soul performers who went from the steeple to the stage includes Otis Redding, Jackie Wilson, Aretha Franklin, Ben E. King, Solomon Burke, Bobby Womack, Al Green, Marvin Gaye, Sam Cooke, and many more. "The Godfather of Soul," however, was James Brown, whose musical trajectory stretches from the R&B sound of his earliest hits to those in the style known as funk, the soul genre that he's credited with creating. What The Band mainly gleaned from soul music were its heart-baring, gospel-reared vocal style and funky, deep-in-the-groove rhythms.

While soul was on the rise in the early 1960s, Ronnie Hawkins staunchly adhered to his rockabilly-with-a-dash-of-R&B model. But tellingly, he wasn't on the same page with his band, who were about to leave him and were going crazy over the soul singles they heard on the radio. By the time they'd ventured out as Levon and the Hawks, tunes by James Brown, the Isley Brothers, and other soul greats were staples of their live sets.

Without question, the foremost soul record labels of the sixties were Motown, Atlantic, and Stax. Motown, based in Detroit, was home to the Supremes, the Miracles, the Temptations, Martha and the Vandellas, the Four Tops, Stevie Wonder, Junior Walker and the All-Stars, and Marvin Gaye. With a trademark crossover pop sound, Motown had a crew of exceptional songwriters that included Norman Whitfield and the team of Lamont Dozier and brothers Brian and Eddie Holland (Holland-Dozier-Holland) and a crack, rotating studio band known as the Funk Brothers, who included bassist James Jamerson, a key influence on Rick Danko.

New York firm Atlantic, founded in 1947 as a jazz and R&B label, ushered in the soul era with Ray Charles in the 1950s and helped solidify it in the 1960s with Wilson Pickett, Solomon Burke, Doris Troy, Percy Sledge, and the "Queen of Soul," Aretha Franklin. Distributed by Atlantic was Memphis's Stax imprint, the flagship of deep, gritty Southern soul and the residence of Otis Redding, Sam and Dave, Eddie Floyd, Rufus Thomas, Carla Thomas, and Isaac Hayes. These acts were backed on record and onstage by Stax's house bands the Mar-Keys, Booker T. & the MG's, and the Bar-Kays, all of whom had hit careers in their own right. The horn section of the Bar-Kays is recognizable in the brass embellishments of several Band songs; the opening of the *Rock of Ages*/*Last Waltz* version of "The Night They Drove Old Dixie Down" hints at the somber start of Otis Redding's "Try a Little Tenderness."

Folk

The term folk music can be applied to the indigenous, orally learned music of any region of the world. But in the West today, it most commonly refers to the traditional, anonymously composed Anglo-Scots-Irish music brought to North America by settlers from those areas and the mainly acoustic music that descends from it: ballads, sea chanteys, cowboy songs, work songs, railroad songs, spirituals, instrumental dance pieces (especially for fiddle), and other variants. Considered the fathers of contemporary folk are singer-guitarist Woody Guthrie and singer-banjoist Pete Seeger, who cofounded the popular, politically outspoken Almanac Singers in the 1940s. When that group broke up, Seeger formed the Weavers, an act that helped promote the preservation of folk traditions in general and greatly informed the folk music revival of the early 1960s.

Brewed in the coffeehouses of Greenwich Village and Cambridge, Massachusetts (and Yorkville in Toronto; it also occurred in England), and on college campuses, the folk revival was initially the exclusive domain of artists who concentrated on traditional material, like Ramblin' Jack Elliott, Cisco Houston, Dave Van Ronk, Joan Baez, and a young Guthrie disciple named Bob Dylan. But on Dylan's second album, 1963's *The Freewheelin' Bob Dylan*, the singer changed the game by demonstrating how it was possible to write original songs with contemporary lyrics within a folk context. This fostered a move to writing original material and a new generation of more cerebral folksingers that included Phil Ochs, Tom Paxton, Tom Rush, Fred Neil, Judy Henske, Eric Von Schmidt, and Gordon Lightfoot.

It's mainly through Dylan that The Band, during their shared Basement Tapes incubation period, picked up the folk sensibilities in their music. Before sitting down with Dylan at Big Pink and learning to appreciate it in a new light, they'd been largely ambivalent about folk music. As hard-core rockers, they'd been put off by the rise of clean-cut folk groups like the Kingston Trio, the Limeliters, and Peter, Paul and Mary (ironic, given that they'd soon share that trio's manager and befriend them and Woodstock folk artists Happy and Artie Traum and Eric Andersen). In addition to the incorporation of acoustic instruments, it's the ballad/story-song aspects of folk that left their mark on The Band's music; not for nothing were dyed-in-the-wool folkies like Joan Baez moved to record their songs (see "The Night They Drove Old Dixie Down"). "The Unfaithful Servant" certainly hints at the English ballad tradition, while "Acadian Driftwood" pairs epic, sea-chantey-saga lyrics with French Canadian fiddle styles.

Gospel

"Gospel" can mean various styles of Christian music, but usually it refers to music rooted in the African-American Christian church. This form, sometimes called black gospel, can be traced to the era of slavery, when most African-Americans were forbidden to sing or play the music or practice the religions of their homelands. Having thus adopted Christianity, they created a new type of sacred music that mixed the African tribal traditions of call-and-response vocals and harmonies and rhythmic playing with traditional European harmonies and instrumentation and lyrics addressing Christian subjects. Gospel singing offered rare instances in which African-Americans could come together to express themselves musically and feel a sense of community, functions that it continues to fulfill today for many. "It is impossible to 'have church' without good music," wrote Pedrito Maynard-Reed, a professor of theology at Walla Walla University, in *Diverse Worship: African-American, Caribbean & Hispanic Perspectives.* "In the African-American community, music is to worship as breathing is to life."

After emancipation, church choirs became increasingly dominant, and in the late 1800s and early 1900s gospel was spread—in Old English, "the gospel" literally means "the good news" of the coming of the Kingdom of God—via the traveling revivals and "camp meetings" of popular ministers in the South. Using cheap, portable instruments (guitars, banjos, fiddles), black folk musicians began setting secular lyrics to the basic, easily learned gospel songs and techniques they'd picked up in church, creating the blues, which led to ragtime and jazz. Many early blues artists, like Blind Willie Johnson, Charley Patton, Blind Willie McTell, Skip James, and Blind Lemon Jefferson recorded both gospel and secular blues.

By the early twentieth century, many of the songs and melodies of black gospel had been embraced by whites, influencing their own church music and the country gospel and bluegrass gospel genres. Much of gospel's cross-racial popularity came via touring a cappella ensembles like the Fisk Jubilee Singers, who performed in formal settings for white audiences and included Stephen Foster tunes and other popular songs in their repertoire along with gospel pieces.

Although the Fisks set the stage for the explosion of long-running black gospel a cappella groups who recorded and appeared on radio in the 1930s—the Dixie Hummingbirds, the Swan Silvertones, the Five Blind Boys of Alabama, the Fairfield Four, the Soul Stirrers, and the Golden Gate Quartet were a few—the figure remembered as the father of gospel music is Thomas A. Dorsey. A former blues pianist under the name Georgia Tom, he'd once sung double-entendre ditties such as "It's Tight Like That" but was reborn as the composer of dozens of standards that reclaimed gospel's musical bastard son, the blues. Songs written by Dorsey include "Take My Hand, Precious Lord" and "Peace in the Valley"; the latter was performed by gospel disciples Johnny Cash and Elvis Presley (Presley sang with the exceptional white gospel groups the Jordanaires and the Blackwood Brothers). Major personalities of post–World War II gospel include singer Mahalia Jackson, singer and composer James Cleveland, and fireball singer and guitarist Sister Rosetta Tharpe.

Besides the use of "blue" or "worried" notes that are inherent to both gospel and the blues, The Band also gleaned from gospel its ensemble vocal style and the noble "churchy" chords that bolster its feeling of soul-baring emotional depth.

Christian Liturgical Music

When we talk about gospel's "churchy" chords we're talking about the profoundly reflective, minor-note-dominated music that comes originally from the European Christian church. It might not be the first musical genre that comes to mind when thinking about The Band's influences, but Christian liturgical music is nevertheless part of the mix; the concepts of multihued voicings initially developed by cathedral choirs and Gregorian-chanting monks were, over the centuries, adapted to the systems of notation used by organists and instrumental ensembles.

Richard Manuel credited the choir training he received as a boy in his family's Baptist church with informing his supernatural knack for vocal harmonies. The Band's Anglo-Christian musical expert, however, was Garth Hudson. As a child, Hudson had worked as the house organist of his uncle's funeral parlor, playing classic high-church Baptist and Anglican hymns. His swells behind Dylan on the Basement Tapes cut "Sign on the Cross" offer vivid, if you will, testament to his sacred youth.

Hudson has frequently remarked about how Anglican hymns, which utilize many countermelodies and are generally composed for choir (soprano, alto or countertenor, tenor, and bass) with or without organ accompaniment, were key for him. The folksy "Sacred Harp" shape-note singing of rural white American churches, which descends from Protestant vocal music, is also evident in The Band's oeuvre; "I Shall Be Released," all lulling redemption and endearingly creaking voices, evokes this tradition.

Classical

Moving from the cathedral to the conservatory, Bach, Haydn, Messiaen, and many other classical composers wrote sacred as well as secular Western art music—a parallel to the links between gospel and soul/blues explored above. Classical music's presence in the sound of The Band isn't overt—blues, soul, country, and rock 'n' roll remain the backbone—but it's there nonetheless, in ways that are apparent to varying degrees: the grand melodies in epic tracks like "The Night They Drove Old Dixie Down" and "It Makes No Difference," and Garth Hudson's Baroque-harpsichord-ish shades on "In a Station" and "The Genetic Method," his prelude to "Chest Fever" (performing Baroque-era organists themselves improvised during live preludes). As one might expect, the classically trained Hudson is known as The Band's chief proponent of this, the original "longhair" music.

Classical music, of course, spans centuries and is difficult to distill down to a couple of cursory paragraphs in a single chapter of a book. It incorporates everything from music for symphony orchestras and chamber ensembles to operas, choral works, solo pieces, the avant-garde, and film music. The history of classical music begins with the Medieval period (roughly 500–1400; prior to the advent of most written notation) and Renaissance (1400–1600; major composers include Dufay, Palestrina, and Byrd) and continues with the Baroque (1600–1750; Bach, Handel, Vivaldi), Classical (1750–1820; Beethoven, Mozart, Haydn, Schubert), Romantic (1804–1910; Chopin, Liszt, Wagner, Brahms, Tchaikovsky), and Twentieth Century/Contemporary (1901–present; Debussy, Mahler, Stravinsky, Ives, Schoenberg, Cage, Stockhausen) eras.

Parallels can be seen between the everyman outlook of The Band and those of composers like Antonín Dvořák and Béla Bartók, who referenced European and American folk music in their compositions, and Woodstock resident Aaron Copland, who drew on "hillbilly" and cowboy songs for his ballets *Appalachian Spring*, *Billy the Kid*, and *Rodeo*. In the early 1970s Robbie Robertson developed a fascination with Polish avant-garde composer Krzysztof Penderecki, which inspired *Works*, a symphonic project that remains uncompleted.

Minstrel Music

Music was a major element of the minstrel shows that toured the U.S. beginning in the 1830s and featured comedic skits, dancing, and other acts. These revues, regrettably, lampooned black people via racist stereotype-perpetuating performances featuring either white or African-American performers in blackface; however, as a positive byproduct, their popularity subversively helped bring an interest in real black American music and culture to the global stage during the lead-up to the Civil War.

Minstrelsy made its way to the grand theaters of Broadway by the 1840s to become the most prevalent form of entertainment in America, and was popular as well in England, mainland Europe, and Australia. Come the early twentieth century, however, minstrelsy was eclipsed by the rise of vaudeville and the mounting erosion of stereotypes and largely fell out of favor. The performance aspects of minstrelsy greatly influenced the traveling medicine shows that rolled through the South as late as the 1950s, fueling the performance aspirations of a young Levon Helm.

Musically, minstrel songs are in a light, proto-ragtime, folk-song-inspired style traditionally played using fiddle and/or banjo. Among the genre's best-known songs are "Buffalo Gals," "Jimmy Crack Corn" a.k.a. "Blue Tail Fly," Stephen Foster's black-influenced "Oh! Susanna" and "Camptown Races," and "Dixie." Although "The Night They Drove Old Dixie Down" alludes to "Dixie" in its title, the former song itself paints a picture of the Southern landscape that's far more sobering—and reality-based—than the idyllic, antebellum plantation owner's fantasy in the latter. Another Brown Album track, "Rockin' Chair," with its nostalgic, easygoing, back-porch ambience, hints sonically at the minstrel style.

Ragtime

Ragtime originated in the 1890s and peaked in popularity with the rise of jazz toward the end of World War I. Born in the African-American red light districts of St. Louis, its key characteristic is the syncopated or "ragged" rhythm that gives it its name. Pioneered by both black and white composers, ragtime fused European classical music with the popular marches of bandleader John Philip Sousa, spicing the whole mixture up with the daring polyrhythms of African music. Black stage entertainer Ernest Hogan is credited with the first written publication of a ragtime piece (1895's "La Pas Ma La"), and white Kentucky composer Ben Harney is cited as introducing ragtime to the mainstream (his "You've Been a Good Old Wagon but You Done Broke Down" was famously sung by Bessie Smith).

While "rags" were sometimes played by orchestras and brass bands, they were mainly performed by solitary piano and banjo players and often found their way into American parlors via top-selling sheet music. Ragtime's rhythmically busy modes were also picked up by the fingerstyle guitarists in the Southeast who created what became known as Piedmont blues (Blind Blake, Blind Willie McTell, the Rev. Gary Davis). But the best-known and most important figure in ragtime is undoubtedly Texas-born composer and pianist Scott Joplin, who authored a ragtime ballet and two operas as well as a roster of nearly fifty shorter works that includes the style's biggest and most influential hits, "Maple Leaf Rag" and "The Entertainer" (the latter was redone as the theme of the 1973 movie *The Sting*). Ragtime was an essential ingredient of early jazz and was resuscitated in the 1940s by Dixieland revival jazz bands and again in the 1950s at the hands of nostalgic novelty piano players with names like Crazy Otto and Knuckles O'Toole.

While "Rag Mama Rag" pays homage to ragtime via its title, the song itself is more reminiscent of rockabilly and early jazz (see above). A more tangible display of The Band's ragtime DNA is "When You Awake," with its jaunty, cakewalking cadence and sprightly melodies.

Cajun

The ebullient music of the Acadiana area of Louisiana, Cajun music is rooted in the ballads of the French-speaking white Acadians who immigrated to the region from Northeastern Canada in the 1760s; those ballads, in turn, descend from the folk songs of North America's original French settlers. The principal instruments of traditional Cajun music are the diatonic accordion, fiddle, and triangle, although over the years its players have in some cases added piano, guitar, bass, and drums as the style has broadened via the influences of country, blues, swing, R&B, and rock 'n' roll. Conversely, Cajun music has itself influenced these styles, most obviously country (Hank Williams's 1952 hit "Jambalaya") and rock 'n' roll (the regional swamp pop sound of the late 1950s and early 1960s). Some major early figures of Cajun music are Joe Falcon and Cleoma Breaux, Amédé Ardoin (a black creole), Leo Soileau, the Breaux Brothers (the first to record the perennial "Jolie Blon"), the Hackberry Ramblers, Harry Choates, Nathan Abshire, and the Balfa Brothers; more recent artists include Doug Kershaw ("Louisiana Man"), Wayne Toups, Zachary Richard, and BeauSoleil.

Cajun music is primarily social dance music. Its lively jigs, two-steps, and waltzes, commonly played at a *bal de maison* (all-night house dance) or *fais do-do* (public dance), are embodied in the performance of Bobby Charles's "Down South in New Orleans" on the *Last Waltz* soundtrack. But its seeds are the unaccompanied ballads of romantic hardship and harsh existence that form the moving basis of The Band's topically related "Acadian Driftwood."

Tin Pan Alley/Brill Building Pop

These two New York–spawned schools represent the chronological book-ends of what many consider the glory years of American popular song. Although it would become shorthand for an entire school of popular and musical theater songwriters, the name Tin Pan Alley originally referred to the block of West Twenty-Eighth Street between Fifth and Sixth Avenues where the leading Great American Songbook composers plied their trade from the 1890s through the 1930s. (The name allegedly derives from the collective din made by the staff writers of the block's many sheet music publishers working at their office pianos.) Legendary Tin Pan Alley tunesmiths include George and Ira Gershwin, Cole Porter, Jerome Kern, Harold Arlen, Yip Harburg, Johnny Mercer, and Hoagy Carmichael. Carmichael authored 1930's "Georgia on My Mind" (Manuel's version was openly based on his idol Ray Charles's immortal recording of the song). The painterly melodies and poetic wordplay of standards like his "Stardust," Harburg's "Brother, Can You Spare a Dime?," and Arlen and Harburg's "Over the Rainbow" are traceable in such Band songs as "Twilight," "Whispering Pines," and "Lonesome Suzie."

From the late 1950s to the early 1960s, the Brill Building, at 1619 Broadway and Forty-Ninth Street, was known as the center of American pop songwriting. In those years, the eleven-story site (activity also took place at 1650 Broadway) housed numerous music publishers whose staff writers included Otis Blackwell; the teams of Doc Pomus and Mort Shuman, Jerry Leiber and Mike Stoller, Burt Bacharach and Hal David, Barry Mann and Cynthia Weil, and Ellie Greenwich and Jeff Barry; future producers Phil Spector and Shadow Morton; and writers who went on to become recording artists in their own right, like Neil Sedaka, Paul Simon, Laura Nyro, Carole King, Sonny Bono, and Neil Diamond. The Band-influencing hits that came out of this seemingly fathomless hive of creativity are legion: Elvis Presley's "Hound Dog" (first sung by Big Mama Thornton) and "Jailhouse Rock," Ben E. King's "Stand By Me" and "Spanish Harlem," Aretha Franklin's "(You Make Me Feel Like a) Natural Woman," the Drifters' "There Goes My Baby," Wilbert Harrison's "Kansas City," the Coasters' "Young Blood," and LaVern Baker's "Saved" (the last three were covered by the group) are a few.

The star-struck teenage Robbie Robertson met several Brill Building songwriting icons when he visited the facility in the fall of 1960 with Ronnie Hawkins. Sixteen years later, in tribute to the Brill Building, he cast Neil Diamond in the Last Waltz, which also featured Van Morrison's version of

Tin Pan Alley writer James Royce Shannon's "Tura Lura Lural (That's an Irish Lullaby)."

European Folk

Also seasoning The Band's bouillabaisse are various strands of European folk music, another aspect that's easily overshadowed by their American roots influences. Perhaps the first such example that comes to mind is *Moondog Matinee*'s coolly playful "Third Man Theme." Originally recorded by Austrian zitherist Anton Karas for the so-named film noir, it was a massive international hit in 1949 and conjures the mysterious streets and cafés in the movie. "Third Man Theme" was clearly the basis for "Theme from the Last Waltz," which similarly hints of Viennese waltzes, traditional Eastern European gypsy music, and the gypsy jazz of Belgian-born guitar genius Django Reinhardt.

The accordion-oriented French style known as musette can also be glimpsed in certain Band tracks. Hudson's accordion in "When I Paint My Masterpiece" lends the song a distinctly Old World flair. Polka music was also beloved of Hudson, who cited the Grammy-nominated Gene Mendalski and the G-Men as favorites.

7

King Harvest (Has Surely Come)

The Band's Studio Albums (1968–1977)

F or an act that's had such an enormous and lasting effect on con-temporary music, it's easy to forget that the original Band didn't really make that many studio albums. From 1968's *Music from Big Pink* to 1977's *Islands*, a span of nine years, they released seven of them. Between 1963 and 1966—three years—the Beatles released as many studio albums as The Band did during their entire first-lineup run; between 1964 and 1966, the Rolling Stones released six. And between 1965 and 1966, the same two frantic years during which he was battling booers and baiters on the road with the Hawks, the song-hemorrhaging Bob Dylan waxed the holy electric trilogy of *Highway 61 Revisited*, *Bringing It All Back Home*, and *Blonde on Blonde*, the latter a double LP.

These days, artists routinely take three to five years between albums. But such was not the case for most acts in the 1960s and '70s. Back then, artists were commonly expected by their labels, as well as their fans, to deliver an album a *year* at minimum, sometimes more, and to do it between touring, making TV appearances, showing up at press conferences, writing songs for the next album, rehearsing, and, oh yeah, being a human being. This was just the accepted nature of the game.

True to their unhurried, slow-cooked image, though, The Band gener-ally took their time recording. Admittedly, however, the long lapses between their 1970s studio albums were also sometimes due to mounting internal dysfunction and shortages of songs. But as Al Kooper said about *Music from Big Pink*, when he gave it a rave review in *Rolling Stone*—and this can certainly be said of *The Band* as well—"There are people who will work their lives away and not touch it." For most fans, the sheer quality of the music on those two records offsets any shortcomings of their later work. And yet while

The Band's studio legacy will always rest mainly on those insurmountable first two late-1960s albums, there's still an abundance of exceptional music to be found on the five that followed in the next decade.

Music from Big Pink

It starts out slow and sad and pulls you in. And after all your wandering and feeling alone in this cold, cold world, you feel as though at last you're home. Really, really home. "Tears of Rage" is like meeting a grieving stranger who instantly bares his heart to you, rather than the balls-to-the-wall rocker most groups would have stuck up front. Its placement as the first track was the opening manifestation of the group's stance of "rebelling against the rebellion" to immediately differentiate themselves from their acid rock competitors. For the song, Helm created the distinctive "moaning" sound of his tom-toms by tightening two of the lug nuts that were directly opposite each other while leaving the others slack. This would become a signature element of the album and would almost immediately be picked up by other drummers to become one of the most widely imitated sounds in rock music.

"Tears of Rage," "We Can Talk," "Chest Fever," and "This Wheel's on Fire" were the first songs the group—operating as the Crackers at that point—recorded for 1968's *Music from Big Pink* in what was supposed to be a demo session for Capitol; both the label and artists liked the results so much that they were flagged as keepers. The January 10, 1968, session with John Simon at New York's A&R Studios began at 7:00 p.m. and got off to an awkward start. The engineers tried to impose the standard industry recording method of isolating the musicians behind baffles for the tracking. But after their months of casual playing at Big Pink, this approach felt completely unnatural to the group and they quickly rejected it. Most of the barriers were taken away as the players rearranged themselves and their gear into a more open, intimate setting. For those first four songs, the lead vocals, tambourine, and Hudson and John Simon's horn parts were overdubbed, but everything else, including the backup vocals, was recorded live in A&R's barn-shaped room on a four-track machine.

Garth's gospel chords give "We Can Talk" an old-time-religious flavor, and the group's circular, conversational vocals are aurally embodied by its line of "echoing along the hall." Robertson has admitted he dashed off the nonsensical lyrics to "Chest Fever," an organ tour de force that began as a simple groove workout, to counter the profound themes of "The Weight." "This Wheel's on Fire" bubbles with the weird sounds Hudson got from a cheap Roxochord keyboard, its electronic squiggles and Robertson's fuzzy lines fleshing out the ominous mood.

Capitol flew the band to Los Angeles to complete the album on eight-track. Like true Woodstockers, they spent much of the winter kicking back before getting around to finishing the record. The up-tempo, vaguely biblical "To Kingdom Come," which would be the album's second track, is a scarce Robertson-sung piece the guitarist came up with during the sessions. "In a Station" is one of Manuel's crowning achievements, a wistful, painfully romantic treasure that hints at what might have been had the singer continued to evolve as a songwriter in the years ahead. The same can be said about his other *Big Pink* solo composition, the aching spinster yarn "Lonesome Suzie." Simon plays guest piano on "Caledonia Mission," a buoyant, Danko-voiced country-funker whose lyrics, Helm believed, referenced the run-ins with the law the group had experienced in Arkansas. Closing side one is "The Weight," the little ditty that almost didn't get recorded (see chapter 4) and today stands as one of the best-known, most beloved songs of all time. It also represents a rare role reversal for Hudson and Manuel (Hudson's on piano and Manuel's on organ). Aptly, it's cowboy crooner Danko who handles the lead on the group's desolate cover of country king Lefty Frizzell's 1959 hit "Long Black Veil." The album ends on a redemptive note with the unforgettable first official airing of "I Shall Be Released."

"The Leslie sound on the electric guitar was exactly that, a nondescript box that had a [rotating] Leslie speaker inside that we simply called 'the black box,'" Simon says about "I Shall Be Released." "At the time, Garth was playing a Lowrey organ that had a button he could push with the ball of his foot in order to slide the pitch down one note. That's how he got a sound sort of like a steel guitar at times."

"For the snare drum sound on 'I Shall Be Released,' I was hearing in my head something vaguely military," says Simon, who mixed the L.A. tracks with the group back in New York at A&R Studios. "I ended up suggesting to Levon that he flip his snare over and run his finger across the actual snares for the backbeat. It was always important to consider the arrangements from the bottom up—that is, the bass drum and the snare, whether the backbeat is on two and four or at half that speed on the third beat. After that, we'd make sure the chords that the guitar and the keyboards were playing made sense, all the while bearing in mind that all of the instruments were supporting a vocal, the most important element. So often we'd set it up so that each section had its own pattern or feel under the vocal. Because only Garth read music, sometimes I'd become a living page of music paper, signaling the guys when a new section was coming up. That was really the case with Levon. Countless times while we were recording I'd lean on the gobos [baffles] in front of the drums and point to different drums or cymbals to help him remember what was coming up next, taking that concern off his mind so that he could simply get into the music. It was a good arrangement—in both senses of the word."

The 2000 CD remaster has nine bonus tracks, including alternate versions of "Tears of Rage" and "Lonesome Suzie."

The Band

As amazing as *Music from Big Pink* is, many view its self-titled follow-up as even better. With a characteristic, hand-hewn sound, 1969's *The Band* is among rock's most perfect albums. For all its idiosyncratic wonders, *Big Pink* has the feel of a group still discovering what it is they do, their sound unfolding right before them. But *The Band* (also known as "the Brown Album") sees that sound nailed down tight. Bolstered by the critical breakthrough of *Big Pink*, but still with something to prove, the group sounds more decisive and less detached.

The Band's twelve songs consistently evoke the imagery of a simpler, older America—buttressed by Elliott Landy's sepia-toned portraits of the players—making it appear to be a concept album. Robertson has maintained that this wasn't a conscious intention during the writing process, although the realization that there was a common thread among these songs did cause him to later say the title could just as easily have been *America*. Actually, the makers originally planned to call it *Harvest* (which Neil Young would, perhaps not so coincidentally, name one of his albums). But in the end they opted for a title that finally made it clear what the outfit's moniker really was; no more simply listing the five members' names as the "group" name, as had been done on *Big Pink*.

With winter returning to Woodstock, the band wanted to get back to sunny L.A. to record. But they didn't want to return to one of the city's expensive, antiseptic studios. Instead, they sought to recreate the live/work "clubhouse" setting that had done so well for them at Big Pink. So in March 1968 they rented an estate owned by entertainer Sammy Davis Jr. at 8850 Evanview Drive in West Hollywood and began converting the property's pool house into a makeshift studio, trucking in recording gear and soundproofing the windows with blankets.

Once again John Simon was involved, this time contributing tuba, electric piano, and various horns as well as producing. After Simon and Robertson had enjoyed a songwriting sojourn in Hawaii, they joined the others in Hollywood to commence recording. For the sessions, they brought in two instruments that would dramatically shape the album's sound: an antique, wooden-rimmed drum set purchased by Helm for $130 in a nearby pawn shop, and an old upright piano that Manuel would alter to mimic the out-of-tune model he'd gotten used to playing back on Bellows Lane in Woodstock.

"It would generally take us two days to record a song," Simon explains. "The first day was experimentation and then, once we arrived at something we were happy with, we'd repeat it over and over again to get comfortable with it and then crash. The next day, we'd come back and pick up where we left off until we eventually got a take. We took great care with every instrument to make it sound different for every song and appropriate for every song." Not all of the album was recorded in Hollywood, however; the group took a break to play their debut concerts before completing the sessions at the Hit Factory in New York.

The Band opens with a tremulous gospel invocation by Manuel that launches into "Across the Great Divide." Perhaps because it's overshadowed by the set's other "big" numbers, this one doesn't get mentioned enough among fans. Its springy cadence and bright melody is good mood incarnate, its lyrics' mountain-man images set the tone for the rest of the album, and it features a rare trombone track by Danko. The barrelhouse-boogieing monster "Rag Mama Rag" is up next. "I had never played a tuba before," recalls Simon about his debut on the big horn via the song. "It took so much wind I got dizzy a couple of times and started to see stars."

"The Night They Drove Old Dixie Down" is the album's centerpiece, an expansive epic branded with Helm's bloodied-but-unbowed vocal, Hudson's melodica and bugle touches, and Robertson's lyrics of wounded Southern pride. After its consuming catharsis, the whimsical "When You Awake" makes the perfect palate cleanser. One of three cuts cowritten by Manuel and Robertson (the others are "Whispering Pines" and "Jawbone"), it has Manuel on drums, Helm on second guitar, and Hudson on organ; the country-boyhood-themed lyrics are delivered by Danko with harmonies by the other singers. Following it are two tunes taped in New York, "Up on Cripple Creek" and "Whispering Pines." The funky former took a couple of attempts to record, the group reworking the arrangement along the way. But it became The Band's highest-charting U.S. single, reaching number twenty-five in 1969 (number ten in Canada). The painfully lonesome "Whispering Pines," maybe Manuel's greatest moment, finishes out side one.

Side two kicks in with Helm's libidinous turn on "Jemima Surrender" before quieting things back down with the mainly acoustic "Rockin' Chair." A sweet bluegrass performance concerning an aged sailor retiring to reunite with his lost friend, it finds Manuel singing lead and harmonizing with Helm (on mandolin) and Danko atop Hudson's high-seas accordion. "Look Out Cleveland" has some torrid Robertson licks and Danko wailing the words about an impending storm—a clear metaphor for the social unrest of the times. "Jawbone" is an admonishment by Manuel of a ne'er-do-well inspired by the nefarious rounders of the Hawks' Toronto days, and it is marked by odd time signatures that are out of step with the group's other work. Danko returns to the spotlight with the melancholy, horn-laced "The Unfaithful Servant" before Simon takes the piano bench on "King Harvest (Has Surely Come)," freeing up Manuel to concentrate on his impassioned lead vocal as this organic opus comes to a close. Robertson is fond of saying that listeners can "feel the wood" on this record. As you lift the needle off, you can smell the sawdust as well.

The 2000 CD remaster's seven bonus tracks include outtakes and alternate performances and mixes. Beware of Capitol's 1980 vinyl reissue, which bizarrely omits "When You Awake" and "King Harvest (Has Surely Come)."

Stage Fright

"After *The Band*, I thought this thing was being taken too seriously," Robertson said for the liner notes of the 2000 CD reissue of 1970's *Stage Fright*. "I thought, 'Let's do more of just a good-time kind of record.'" Things didn't quite work out that way.

Because several of its songs have darker themes, reflective of the inner tensions that were about to envelop them, *Stage Fright* gets signposted as "the beginning of the end" for the group. If you're listening and know some of the behind-the-scenes story, there are clear reasons why it's called *Stage Fright*. After a decade on the road The Band was reeling from the mayhem of "sudden" success. Interior rivalry had reared its ugly head, and the first two albums had raised the critical bar, along with the stakes, to an intimidating level. They wanted solitude while they worked, but now their hometown was a magnet for overzealous fans and freaks. Mostly gone were the group vocals, in favor of more unaccompanied singing and instrumental solos, as

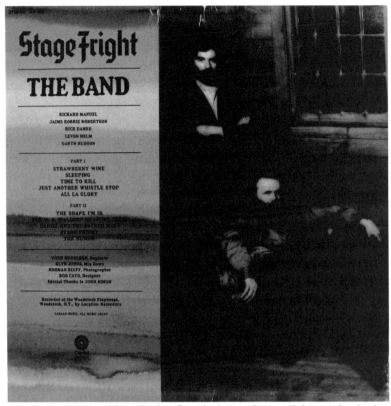

The darker themes of *Stage Fright* reflect the internal turmoil that was beginning to plague The Band by 1970. This rare Taiwanese pressing of the LP features alternate cover art.   *Author's collection*

personal fractures set in. And on top of all this, three-fifths of the group—Manuel, Danko, and Helm—were in the throes of addiction. But sometimes darkness and drama make for great art. And so they did for *Stage Fright*, a great album that contains some of The Band's best songs.

The logistical difficulties began before the June 1970 sessions. Deciding to produce the album themselves, the group elected not to rehire John Simon—although he would earn a "special thanks" on the cover for his dropping by the tapings to offer advice—and appointed their new neighbor Todd Rundgren as engineer. The Band's original plan was to record the set as a live concert album at the Woodstock Playhouse, but that idea was scuttled when the town council got wind of the project and strongly objected, fearful their community would be overrun by the group's out-of-town followers. So the playhouse was secured as a closed shop for the two-week span it took to record the album between summer-stock plays.

The Band cut the tracks on the theater's stage to an empty house, with Rundgren manning mobile mixing gear in the backstage scenery shop. What set it off remains unclear, but the Hermit of Mink Hollow and Helm did not get along; during one disagreement, the drummer threatened Rundgren and chased him around the theater. In contrast to all of this, however, Mark Braunstein, who worked for the playhouse at the time, recalls the scene being light and opulent. "I remember the guys playing football in the parking lot between takes," he says. "Robbie Robertson had a brand new, emerald green BMW, Garth had a new Mercedes, and I think Rick Danko was driving a Corvette. There was definitely money around." Rundgren and English producer Glyn Johns each mixed different tracks, although, inexplicably, Rundgren is credited only for engineering.

Starting things off with steam is "Strawberry Wine," a Helm/Robertson-cowritten rocker reminiscent of Sonny Boy Williamson's "Don't Start Me Talkin'." Outwardly, it's an upbeat dance number spiced up by Hudson's Cajun accordion and Danko's bass line, which doubles Helm's scatting. But beneath the shine there's an ornery standoffishness in Helm's delivery and in the lyrics, which have the narrator basically telling his woman to get lost and let him stay drunk. Maybe not the best subject for radio play. Second comes the exquisite "Sleeping," Manuel's thinly veiled confessional (cowritten with Robertson) about a recluse who finds solace in slumber à la local literary figure Rip Van Winkle. Also referencing the region, with its mention of the local town of Catskill, is "Time to Kill." Sung by Danko, its misleadingly sunny sound and lyrics mask the irony of the title and the inherent dangers of inactivity for some members of the group (himself included). The catchy "Just Another Whistle Stop" is another Manuel/Robertson piece sung by the pianist; perhaps inspired by news of the upcoming Festival Express train tour, it compares life on the road and the societal growing pains of the Vietnam era. "All La Glory," with a lead vocal by Helm, Hudson's soothing accordion, and Robertson's soft, watery chords, is the album's rare respite of innocence, a tribute by the guitarist to his firstborn daughter (the pidgin French title is a nod to her Quebecois birthplace).

Side two opens with the romping "The Shape I'm In." Fittingly sung by the tortured Manuel, about whom Robertson clearly wrote it, the song is a desperate confessional of a character who's hit rock bottom. "The W.S. Walcott Medicine Show," Robertson's celebratory impression of Helm's accounts of the miracle-cure-peddling troupes of his youth—and an alle-gory for the music business as well—is the first of the three lone tracks that retain the group's conversational singing style. In it, Helm and Danko swap verses, and Hudson's molasses-thick sax solo hints at the Allen Toussaint horn chart that would later do the song full justice on *Rock of Ages*. Further symbolic of the existential crisis Robertson was experiencing as a com-mercial artist is the understated "Daniel and the Sacred Harp." Here, Hudson's hymnal pump organ sets up the biblical fable of a musician who trades his soul for success. Helm and Manuel portray, respectively, the storyteller and Daniel. Similar similes are explored with the title track, an upbeat gospel-soul song. With a superb, trembling vocal performance by Danko, it's likely rooted in Robertson's first-night nerves at the group's 1969 Winterland debut. But on a larger level, it also stands as a cry for help, an open-hearted admission of vulnerability beneath the prying lights of fame. The disc ends with "The Rumor," a welcome reprise of the three-part Danko/Helm/Manuel vocal method leavened by a foreboding commentary on the destructive small-town talk that comes with fame.

The 2000 CD remaster includes alternate takes and mixes of "Daniel and the Sacred Harp," "Time to Kill," and "The W.S. Walcott Medicine Show," and a radio commercial for the album.

Cahoots

If the detrimental changes to the group weren't obvious to the fans who bought *Stage Fright*, they certainly should have been with the arrival of 1971's *Cahoots*. Criticized as being comparatively flat in terms of the songwriting, the album also feels like the musicians are holding back. With its formulaic themes of blacksmiths and rivers, it sounds at times like The Band are self-conscious and forced, doing what was expected of them. For the box set *A Musical History*, Hudson commented on how the songs had grown same-y, making it difficult for him to come up with distinctive parts for each of them.

Given the circumstances, it's not too hard to see how this happened. Despite the LP's unity-espousing title (from the line "young brothers join in cahoots" in the album's "Smoke Signal"), the group was far from united in their focus. The withdrawn and addicted Manuel had totally relinquished his spot as the group's other main songwriter, leaving Robertson to assume the dominant compositional role. Some of the others were also caught up in their addictions, often showing up late to recording sessions or even blowing them off. Now a father flitting back and forth between Woodstock and his new family's other home in Montreal, and further distracted by his classical *Works* project, Robertson was churning out songs in a vacuum without much quality control. The self-producing group was also the first act to record in Albert Grossman's new Bearsville studio, and was thus getting accustomed to the room as they worked out technical glitches and song arrangements. Shooting the group with their eyes closed for the back cover was photographer Richard Avedon's idea, but to them at the time it must have reflected the exhaustion they were feeling.

Despite the above, though, the severity of *Cahoots'* bad rap is still largely undeserved. Because for all its shortcomings, it's redeemed by some genuinely great songs, ones that stand among the most essential in The Band's catalog. No, *Cahoots* is not a perfect album, but it's still a good one. And it certainly beats *Islands* (we'll get to that).

The boisterous lead track, "Life Is a Carnival," is an album anomaly in several ways. Most strikingly, it represents the The Band's magnificent first encounter with Allen Toussaint's horn arranging, and as such, it is the seed of their later collaborations with him for the *Rock of Ages* and Last Waltz concerts. Toussaint's jabbing, contrapuntal lines bring an added layer of bubbling bop to this already supremely funky tune (when they first saw his charts, the hired session horn players scoffed at Toussaint's deliberately quirky notation—but they became instant believers after the first run-through). One of the group's by-now increasingly rare ensemble-sung efforts, it's also the sole song on which Robertson shares writing credit with his bandmates, in this case Danko and Helm, who took five days to create their parts (in *This Wheel's on Fire*, Helm says Manuel contributed the "two bits a shot" lyric). And it's the only *Cahoots* cut that became a consistent live staple for the group.

The premiere of the Bob Dylan gem "When I Paint My Masterpiece," the tale of an American artist living abroad who misses his homeland but won't return until he's made his name, was certainly a coup. It's sung here with great longing by Helm, the deep American lonesomeness in his accent juxtaposed against Hudson's Old-Europe accordion. "Last of the Blacksmiths," Robertson's unintentionally Band-self-parodying paean to the dying arts of metalworking and other technology-supplanted handicrafts, its lyrics rendered by Manuel, is most notable for Hudson's woozy, off-octave doubled saxophones. Similarly, the familiar topic of a vanishing America is explored in the Danko-sung "Where Do We Go from Here?" (the title was briefly considered as the name of the album), which mourns the demise of the railroad and the wild buffalo. The song's arm-waving title refrain feels like a maudlin rehash of "The Night They Drove Old Dixie Down," but Helm's subtle drumming is great, as is the line "You sure do miss the silence when it's gone" (some longing for those Big Pink days). A visit by Van Morrison resulted in "4% Pantomime," a mind-blowing spontaneous soul-blues duet between the Irishman and Manuel, who play the parts of a couple of drunk, down-on-their-luck musicians stranded in L.A. The title alludes to the difference in proof between Johnny Walker Red and Johnny Walker Black whiskey and to the physically animated performances the two singers gave in the studio (it's been said that both were in "research mode" at the time).

With Danko and Manuel harmonizing on the verses and Helm chiming in on the chorus, "Shoot Out in Chinatown" is another of Robertson's history-mining ditties, this one set in turn-of-the-century San Francisco Chinatown. Some may find its racially hackneyed imagery ("They came in undercover / To the laundry's back room") and cheesy oriental guitar motif annoying, but the group liked the composition enough to feature it on their 1971 tour. A mellow Manuel gives one of his best and most tender performances on "The Moon Struck One," a story of childhood friends that hovers dreamily somewhere between "Sleeping" and "When You Awake." "Thinkin' Out Loud" is a passably pleasant potboiler with a lead vocal by Danko, fleet piano by Hudson, Manuel on drums, and Helm in a rare bass slot. The record's two, er, fieriest cuts, "Smoke Signal" and "Volcano," come near the end. Helm sings the hard-rocking former, whose Native American–oriented lyrics foretell the subject matter of much of Robertson's later solo work; the latter, an innuendo-laced sexual come-on sung by Danko, has blasting big band/Stax saxes by Hudson. The group brings it all home, gospel-style, with "The River Hymn," which finds Hudson well within his churchy element and Helm in wonderfully oaken lead voice; the drummer's then girlfriend, Libby Titus, joins Danko and Manuel on backup vocals.

The 2000 CD remaster's five bonus cuts include alternate takes, outtakes, and a *Cahoots* radio ad.

Moondog Matinee

The Band's status may have been unsteady when they made *Cahoots*, but when it came time to make their next studio album things were even more tenuous. Although *Cahoots* had spawned a successful tour culminating with a sold-out, four-night run in New York (recorded for *Rock of Ages*), the album was savaged by critics and sold weakly. Morale in Band camp was low from its poor reception and the tensions resulting from a recently implemented royalty-disbursement agreement that Helm, at least, considered lopsided.

By early 1972, the members were all doing different things outside the group. Robertson was dallying with his ultimately unrealized *Works*, and Danko was coproducing Bobby Charles's self-titled album, whose sessions also utilized Hudson, Helm, and Manuel. Helm even enrolled at Boston's Berklee College of Music to sharpen his drumming skills. *Rock of Ages* came out in the summer of 1972 to great acclaim and sales (number six on the charts for six months), buying the group some time while they were scattered. They all knew they had to get back into the studio and cut a new album. There was one problem, though: Other than the lone original

The group revisited their bar-band roots with 1973's covers album *Moondog Matinee*.

Author's collection

"Endless Highway," they didn't have the material. Yet for the sake of their self-preservation they needed to make a record—and for the sake of their sanity, they needed to have *fun* while they were making it. Then someone brought up the idea of replicating one of the sets they used to do in their nightclub days as the Hawks. In the text accompanying *A Musical History*, Robertson maintains that the idea of "pay[ing] respect to some great songs and great songwriters" was his.

Whatever its genesis, 1973's *Moondog Matinee*, recorded from March to June 1973 at Bearsville Studios and Capitol Studios, is simply one of the strongest covers albums ever released—although, interestingly, it's been pointed out that only *one* of its tracks, Bobby "Blue" Bland's "Share Your Love with Me" (listed as "Share Your Love"), actually appears on extant early Hawks set lists. Apocryphal selections notwithstanding, the sessions seemed to reenergize the atmosphere within the group. And the original pressing's wraparound poster-sleeve with Edward Kasper's rendering of the group hanging out at a stylized juke joint is fun just to look at.

Hopping out of the gate first is Southern swamp popper Clarence "Frogman" Henry's 1956 debut hit "Ain't Got No Home," sung in full snarl by Helm—complete with the croaking spoken-word part as in the original (achieved by his grunting through a primitive "squawk box" devised by Hudson). Hudson blows honking Big Easy tenor, and both he and Manuel contribute piano (the shaky intro sounds like Manuel). Helm has said he played bass on the track, attributing the NOLA backbeat to Woodstock resident and Mothers of Invention drummer Billy Mundi (which makes it unclear what, or even if, Danko played on it). Another New Orleans vocalist, the Allen Toussaint protégé Lee Dorsey, had a hit in 1966 with "Holy Cow." The Band's take, warbled wearily back and forth by Manuel and Danko, with backups by Helm, is just slightly lazier than Dorsey's, glazing its rump-rolling rhythm with an extra layer of sensual humidity. The aforementioned "Share Your Love," the first of two beautiful ballads Manuel sings on the album, is heart-stoppingly gorgeous, with him taking ownership of the song by wringing forth a depth of pathos not even present on his idol Bland's version. The high-energy quotient is back on track with "Mystery Train," the Little Junior Parker song made famous by Elvis Presley. Helm sings this off-the-rails classic, which sees Hudson reprising the funk clavinet of "Up on Cripple Creek" and a newly written verse from Robertson. According to Robertson, both Manuel and Helm drum on the track, although some sources say it was Manuel and Billy Mundi drumming and credit Helm with stand-up bass. It *is* agreed, however, that Helm was away and Manuel played

Edward Kasper's artwork for the wraparound sleeve that came with original pressings of *Moondog Matinee* captured the nostalgic feel of the album.   *Author's collection*

drums when the group cut the instrumental "Third Man Theme," Anton Karas's title tune from the great Orson Welles film noir—an oddball choice for an album of mainly R&B nuggets. But besides satisfying Robertson's film-buff obsessions, it works brilliantly as a scene change at the end of the LP's first side, with Hudson's synth, organ, and clavinet reveling in its mischievous, gypsy-café cadence.

"Promised Land," one of two Levon-sung Chuck Berry favorites the quintet laid down during the sessions ("Going Back to Memphis" was left off), is emblematic of the rock 'n' roll spirit The Band sought to recapture with *Moondog Matinee*. But instead of merely aping Berry's buzz-burner, they take it with the tiniest hint of funk, thanks to Manuel's loose backbeat and Hudson's harmonica-sounding clavinet (Helm plays guitar). The Platters ballad "The Great Pretender" was a natural choice for Manuel, as it dates from his pre-Hawks repertoire with the Revols. Its stately tempo offers the perfect setting for his soulful voice, and its lyric of painfully unrequited longing fits his personality like no other cover he sang with The Band. The New Orleans lineage comes back around with Fats Domino's "I'm Ready," which is propelled by Hudson's pumping piano and both Helm (its barking singer) and Manuel on drums. Hudson also overdubbed all of the sax parts, which include a couple of apropos, greasy-gumbo solos. "Saved" is a gospel pastiche penned by the Brill Building's Jerry Leiber and Mike Stoller for LaVern Baker. Sung with born-again fervor by Manuel, it's one of the few songs here that The Band later played live. Danko's only solo lead vocal comes at the album's end with a beautifully touching rendition of Sam Cooke's "A Change Is Gonna Come," which has the singer on acoustic guitar and Helm on electric bass.

The 2001 CD remaster comes loaded with six previously unreleased performances.

Northern Lights—Southern Cross

During the making of *Moondog Matinee*, as fun as that was, it was becoming clear that Woodstock was turning into a drag. The town had been overrun by vampiric drug dealers, and its long winters had, for the moment at least, lost their novelty. Maybe a change of scenery would help. Why not relocate to the more temperate climes of California? After all, that was where the music business, with its growing crop of Band-influenced acts, was centered now. And besides, that was where Bob Dylan was moving, and if it was good enough for him, well, then, it was good enough for his longtime buddies.

Robertson moved out first, to Malibu, and by October 1973 the others had followed, settling in nearby Zuma Beach, where the group also opened their new Shangri-La studio. During the move, *Moondog Matinee* was released. Frustratingly, though, it didn't sell, charting even lower than *Cahoots*. The Band's collaboration with Dylan for 1974's *Planet Waves* and its subsequent tour added up to a prestigious (and financial) shot in the arm. But even through that triumph, detractors were grumbling that the group couldn't come up with good songs anymore, that they were just treading water with cover tunes and live albums of old material. They needed to get back down to business and prove these naysayers wrong.

And with their sixth studio album, 1975's *Northern Lights—Southern Cross*, that's exactly what they did. A solid return to form, to many aficionados it was The Band's best effort since the Brown Album. Although it fared no better on the charts than *Cahoots* or *Moondog Matinee*, it's a tight collection of refreshingly strong songs that blend the group's established style with new sonic possibilities. For its makers, *Northern Lights—Southern Cross* was both a critical comeback and a final burst of glory before the following year's flameout. As exemplified by its title, the album's core theme loosely centers on the duality of the group's Canadian/Cotton Belt heritage.

Northern Lights—Southern Cross has only eight songs, but they're longer, and several are highlighted with tasteful Robertson solos that harken back to the kind he played with Ronnie Hawkins.

The first is "Forbidden Fruit," a subversively danceable self-critique about the dangers of the drug abuse that had begun engulfing The Band in earnest before they left Woodstock. Helm handles the lead vocal on this one, which struts with Danko's smooth, fretless bass and Hudson's organ and synthesizer embellishments and sports Manuel on clavinet. Tom Waits must have loved "Hobo Jungle," dominated as it is by Manuel's beautifully sad vocals and forlorn cocktail piano. Decorated as well with Hudson's haunting keys and accordion, its somber, burn-barrel tale about the funeral of a boxcar-bound rounder echoes the album cover photo of the group huddled around a beachfront campfire. But the mood is brightened next, like the spirits-raising return parade of a jazz funeral, with the New Orleans–flavored dancer "Ophelia." An instant classic that became an audience fave for both incarnations of The Band as well as the groups led by Helm, its custom-cast Southern-accented singer. Robertson lays out some great bluesy licks on this song; Manuel adds Hammond organ and Hudson plays all of the brass parts, including the coda's "(I Wish I Was in) Dixie" quote. The South is once again the focus on "Acadian Driftwood," the album's grand centerpiece about the seafaring saga of the displaced French Canadians in Louisiana.

"Ring Your Bell," another funk-fueled track, has Helm, Danko, and Manuel on shared lead and harmony vocals that recall their examples on *Big Pink* and *The Band*. Robertson contributes hard rock guitar chords on the song's intro and doubles on piano with Manuel, Hudson squeezes out a colorful, squiggly synth solo, and the lyrics maintain the set's Far North/Deep South concept ("Run that rebel across the tracks / with the Mounties on his trail"). Danko delivers, arguably, the most moving performance of his career with the heart-crushing "It Makes No Difference," perhaps the most shockingly great track on this fine record—there's nary a dry eye around the hi-fi once the stylus has traversed its six and a half minutes.

"Ophelia" was released as a single in 1975 with "Hobo Jungle" as the B-side. Both tracks also appear on *Northern Lights—Southern Cross*.

Author's collection

The album's only really weak cut is "Jupiter Hollow," a light, melodic pop-funk track instrumentally reminiscent of Stevie Wonder's work at the time. One of the first rock recordings to utilize a drum machine, it's also the only officially released Band song with no guitars on it (Robertson plays clavinet instead). Unlike the bulk of *Northern Lights—Southern Cross*, "Jupiter Hollow" began as a basic track the group had been fooling around with at Bearsville Studios two years prior. With Hudson's synth fills, Robertson's questionable, mythology-inspired lyrics (a unicorn is mentioned), and Manuel and Helm (the latter on lead vocals) playing drums along with and around the mechanized beats, it's at best an experiment showing how aurally adventurous the group had become since their rockabilly days.

The album's closer, "Rags and Bones," was inspired lyrically by family stories of Robertson's rag-merchant grandfather and the guitarist's half-remembered sounds of his childhood streets. Manuel voices this sentimental number and plays electric piano and overdubbed congas, while Robertson's jazzy, George Benson-esque solo completes its laid-back 1970s vibe. Like "Jupiter Hollow" its melody doesn't really stick in the ear. But the lyrics are especially vivid, and the song does make for a calming conclusion to an album that explores some weighty themes.

The 2001 CD remaster's bonus tracks are demo versions of *Islands'* "Christmas Must Be Tonight" and the non-LP "Twilight."

Islands

The name of The Band's final album was a fitting bit of commentary on the group itself, but in a completely different way than that of *Northern Lights—Southern Cross*. While the title and the cover, a photo montage of the members' profiles set against a coastal sunset, suggest lives of carefree rock-star luxury, in actuality the group had drifted apart, each member isolated on his own emotional island. Or, perhaps more accurately, Robertson, who wanted the group to stop performing, was on one island and the others were on another.

In the early fall of 1976, Robertson had announced the news of their impending retirement from the road and their plan to continue as a studio-only act. Warner Bros.' president, Mo Ostin, had put up the money for the filming of *The Last Waltz* in exchange for his label's being able to release its soundtrack. But the group still owed Capitol one more studio album before they could sign to Warners. Hence 1977's *Islands*, a thrown-together contract-fulfiller essentially assembled from demos the group had been working on at Shangri-La. Although the intention may have been for the group to reconvene later to make more albums, that never happened, and the half-baked, phoned-in effort became their underwhelming swan song. Radio and fans responded accordingly: After struggling to get to number sixty-four on the *Billboard* album chart, the lowest of any of the original Band's albums, *Islands* sank with barely a trace. Capitol should have marketed it more honestly, like Robertson has pointed out, as "a record of B-sides and outtakes," instead of the way the label did, as a regular Band album—not that that would have necessarily translated into hits or higher sales. But, still being a Band album, even *Islands* has its gratifying moments.

Largely assembled from demos the group had been working on shortly before their split, 1977's *Islands* was The Band's last studio album—and its lowest-charting one. *Author's collection*

"Right as Rain," the introductory cut, isn't one of them. Manuel's voice is as beautiful as expected, and there are some evocative lines ("The dance-hall is deserted, where lonely worlds collide"), but the tune itself is utterly innocuous, its lush, airbrushed style closer to the sun-seeking soft rock of contemporary macramé-makers like Exile and Ambrosia. *Music from Big Pink* had begun with a quiet song, too; but while "Tears of Rage" opens like the creaking door of a confessional booth, letting us in for glimpses of ghosts and lives we're astonished to discover, "Right as Rain" feels like the leisure-suited square who desperately wants to be liked and allowed into the cool kids' party. Artie Fufkin in *This Is Spinal Tap*.

Danko takes his first turn at the mic for the similarly pedestrian "Street Walker," a prostitute's lament he cowrote with Robertson. Perhaps they thought they were once again giving voice to the marginalized here—a noble effort, although no one could have been fooling themselves with dreams of major airplay for such a song. Its highlight is Robertson's squealing, pinched-harmonic solo, which arrives near the end, after the lyrics have run out. Manuel is back up front for "Let the Night Fall," yet another bland ballad that's in no hurry to jostle the yacht-rock boat. Looking back, though, Robertson has expressed his feeling that more could have been done with the song, that this metaphorical commentary on the group's nocturnal lifestyle could have been taken in a more "haunting" direction. After listening repeatedly to the nondescript track with this in mind, it's admittedly difficult to visualize what he means.

The M.O.R. spell is broken at last by Helm with a piston-popping version of Memphis soul man Homer Banks's 1966 hit "Ain't That a Lot of Love," followed by Danko singing one of the album's most memorable tracks, "Christmas Must Be Tonight." Written by Robertson in honor of the birth of his son in July 1975, it was briefly pondered as a Christmas single and sits alongside Big Star's "Jesus Christ" as one of rock's holiday hits that should have been. Danko's lead vocal is as sweet as mulled cider, and Hudson's crystalline synthesizer and organ lend it an appropriately peaceful, reverent air.

"Islands" began as "Dr. Medicine Song," a sketch by Danko and Hudson in late 1976. Robertson never wrote lyrics for this mind-numbingly saccharine rhythm machine exercise, so it remained an instrumental. It's hard to fathom why this theme from an imaginary 1970s sitcom was ever released—let alone as the LP's title track. The Danko vehicle "The Saga of Pepote Rouge" is built on a descending gospel melody and typically full-bodied Helm/Manuel backup vocals. Robertson's Buñuel-esque lyrics concern the title figure, a mythic diva with a golden spaceship. For the last minute or so, the band simply rides out the main riff, making it clear they were still getting a feel for the song when it was cut. Manuel's trademark heart-melting reading of "Georgia on My Mind" at last makes it to wax via *Islands*, and "Knockin' Lost John" is Robertson's first lead vocal (doubled by Danko) since *Big Pink*'s "To Kingdom Come." It's upbeat, but nothing special, save for Robertson's detuned guitar solos and Hudson's accordion work, which is some of his best. "Livin' in a Dream" ends the album, and the original Band's studio career, on a deceptively happy note, with its singer, Helm, whistling cheerily away on the outro. The lines "Life goes 'round like a wheel / You never know if it's real" ring home.

The 2001 CD remaster's two bonus tracks include an alternate take of "Georgia on My Mind," which is interesting for its false start and slightly different synthesizer sound, and the great ballad "Twilight," a non-LP single from 1976.

8

Come On Baby, Let's Take a Little Walk

Ronnie Hawkins and the Hawks

I t's racket time!"

Ladies and gentlemen, meet Ronnie Hawkins.

With that battle cry, or some variation thereof, Hawkins—a.k.a. "Rompin' Ronnie Hawkins" or simply "the Hawk"—would kick off yet another set with the Hawks, his late-1950s/early-1960s band of rockabilly hellions, at yet another beat-'em-up Southern roadhouse or hole-in-the-wall Canadian club. An irrepressible character, Hawkins was legendary for performances that were powerful, ferocious, and oozing with base, crotch-grinding sexuality—essential traits of the best rock 'n' roll.

"The Hawk had been to college and could quote Shakespeare when he was in the mood," wrote Levon Helm in *This Wheel's on Fire.* "He was also the most vulgar and outrageous rockabilly character I've ever met in my life. He'd say and do anything to shock you."

In his American homeland, Ronnie Hawkins's profile has been eclipsed by those of Elvis Presley, Buddy Holly, Jerry Lee Lewis, and other rock 'n' roll pioneers. But in Canada he is the music's Big Bang personified: the rockabilly savior who, with seventeen-year-old drummer Helm in tow, brought the wild new sound to the Great White North, inspiring a generation of the region's native kids to make similar sounds of their own. And among that generation were Robbie Robertson, Rick Danko, Richard Manuel, and Garth Hudson, four young men who would learn the craft straight from Hawkins, as Helm had, when they themselves became Hawks. They would go on to perfect this craft when they became The Band.

The Fire's Burnin', the Wheels Are Turnin'

Born on January 10, 1935, in Huntsville, Arkansas, about a four-and-a-half-hour drive from where Helm grew up, Ronald Cornett "Ronnie" Hawkins is one of the most colorful characters in the colorful history of the music called rock 'n' roll. Until they moved to the comparatively bustling Fayetteville, when Ronnie was nine, his family lived in the cornpone hamlet of Hawkins Holler, a farming homestead his great-grandfather had settled in the 1870s. Although his parents weren't musicians—his hellraising-redneck father, Jasper, was a barber and laborer, and his religious mother, Flora, was a teacher—music was nevertheless omnipresent at familial gatherings. One of Ronnie's uncles, Delmar "Skipper" Hawkins, was a successful country fiddle player, and when he visited his brother's family in Hawkins Holler his sharp clothes and brand-new Cadillac captivated his young nephew. Later on, the Hawkins musical genes would also surface via Delmar's son, Dale Hawkins, Ronnie's fellow rockabilly legend.

Another decisive encounter came when Ronnie met Ralph "Buddy" Hayes, a blues musician who worked shining shoes in Jasper Hawkins's barbershop. Hayes led a New Orleans–style blues/jazz band and would rehearse at the shop with a piano player named Little Joe. Through these musical gatekeepers, Ronnie came under the ever-deepening spell of the blues. He made pilgrimages to Beale Street in Memphis to buy records by Muddy Waters, Howlin' Wolf, B.B. King, and John Lee Hooker; he listened to the gospel singers at local black churches; and he snuck down to Sherman's Tavern, Irene's Café, and other spots where black musicians hung out.

"Even back then I knew that every important white cat—Al Jolson, Stephen Foster—they all did it by copying blacks," Hawkins said in *Last of the Good Ol' Boys.* "Even Hank Williams learned all the stuff he had from those black cats in Alabama. That's all Elvis did. That's all I did. That's all those cats in Memphis were trying to do: Take those blues songs and copy them and make them commercial."

As with Helm, another powerful indigenous influence on Hawkins was the steady stream of medicine and minstrel shows that came through Arkansas. When rock 'n' roll began exploding across the South in the early 1950s, Hawkins wasted little time in getting involved, hopping onstage to sing with pickup groups and "whatever bands came through town," such as those of Roy Orbison and Conway Twitty. Just after graduating high school he put together a band with guitarists Harold Pinkerton and Bobby Keene, bassist Claude Chambers, and drummer Herman Tuck. There was no question as to what the combo would be called. "Right from the start we were the Hawks," wrote the singer. "*All* my bands have been the Hawks."

The early Hawks played the area honky-tonks the Shamrock, the Tee Table, and the Rockwood Club—all of which the teenage Hawkins, with promoter Dayton Stratton fronting, came to own at different points, thanks to the massive amounts of money he was making by running illegal booze into then still-dry Oklahoma. With visions of her bootlegger son ending up in prison, Flora Hawkins pushed him to enroll at the University of Arkansas in 1952. There, he studied physical education, which certainly helped his mastery of stage gymnastics, and played campus frat parties with the Hawks. He dropped out of college in 1957 to join the army, which would be an unexpectedly fortuitous move for his music career.

While stationed at Fort Sill in Oklahoma, Hawkins began playing with a group of black R&B musicians he met when he talked his way into singing with them at a nearby Amvets Club. After six months his army stint was up and the band—cleverly christened the Blackhawks, a partial reference to a popular DC Comics title—was performing throughout the region, though not without the controversy one would expect around a racially integrated band in the 1950s American South. "It was safe for mixed bands on army bases," says Hawkins in *Across the Great Divide.* "But when we left the base we got into trouble." Scary trouble. According to the singer, he and the band were shot at and physically attacked on more than one occasion.

Somehow they lived through it all, only to break up at the height of their game when constant poverty and racial hassles finally became too much. Hawkins's time with the Blackhawks was crucial, however, as their blend of blues and rockabilly helped him hone the fusion he'd been hearing in his head—a fusion, it turned out, that others had been hearing about and wanted a piece of.

We're Gonna Rock and Roll All Night Long

When Hawkins returned to Fayetteville in late 1957, he got a call from Memphis guitarist Jimmy Ray "Luke" Paulman asking him if he wanted to front a new band that would be recording for Sun Records. This was, as Hawkins himself might have said, big time. Paulman had played with regional greats Conway Twitty and the Rock Housers and Billy Lee Riley and His Little Green Men, and of course Sun was home to Elvis Presley, Carl Perkins, Jerry Lee Lewis, Howlin' Wolf, and so many other rockabilly and blues greats. The Hawk swooped down to Memphis as fast as he could, but by the time he got there the band had broken up in a dispute over who would be the leader.

So Hawkins followed Paulman to his home of West Helena, where the pair began putting together a new edition of the Hawks. George Paulman, the guitarist's brother, came in on upright bass and their cross-eyed cousin, Willard "Pop" Jones, was added on, as Levon Helm would later describe it, "kamikaze rockabilly piano." And it was Jones who suggested Helm, the Marvell kid he'd jammed with on occasion, as drummer. "Right from the start, Levon played more drums with less licks than any drummer in the world," said Hawkins in his autobiography. "And he could make it sound right. He liked what I liked in music . . . Hell, he might have been the best guitar player I ever had, too. He was better than Robbie Robertson was early on." Everything was in place, but there were two significant problems: The band had nowhere to rehearse, and Helm didn't own any drums.

Enter "Uncle" Charlie Halbert. A native razorback, Halbert worked as a stand-in for movie star Buster Crabbe and ran a successful trucking business in California before returning to Arkansas to become the owner of a local ferry service (Floyd Jenkins, the father of Halbert's godson, Conway Twitty, was one of the ferry pilots). A music fanatic, Halbert often lent money to struggling musicians (Elvis Presley included) and owned West Helena's popular Delta Supper Club, where Helm first performed with the Hawks; he also built and ran the Rainbow Inn motel and restaurant, where he allowed musicians to stay for free. He set the Hawks up with free rehearsal time in the basement of local radio station KFFA, and he loaned the group the cash for a drum kit and other gear, as well as the funds Helm needed to join the musicians' union. (Much later, when the newly recruited Robbie Robertson came down to rehearse with the Hawks, who'd returned from Canada to do some Southern shows, Halbert let them jam in the living room of his regal mansion. No wonder the guitarist called him a "patron of the rockabilly arts.")

The Sun deal never came to be, but the Hawks didn't let that stop them. With ex–Conway Twitty/Billy Lee Riley bassist Jimmy "Lefty" Evans taking over from George Paulman, the band quickly became a top draw on the circuit of tough bars that ran from North Central Arkansas up into Southern Missouri. But at the same time it was apparent that beyond the Hawks' stomping ground, rock 'n' roll's popularity in the U.S. was being eroded by the rise of the Fabians, the Bobby Rydells, and their prefab-pop, pretty-boy peers. On one early 1958 day, Hawkins bumped into Conway Twitty, who'd just returned from a wildly successful stretch in Canada. Twitty raved about the big money to be made from the rock 'n' roll–starved audiences north of the border and suggested Hawkins give booking agent Harold Kudlets a call. To the Hawk, that sounded like a good idea.

I'm Gonna Leave This One-Horse Town

Kudlets booked the Hawks into the Golden Rail in Hamilton for a week in the spring of 1958. At first, things looked grim for their Canadian debut. No one had heard of the band, and the rock 'n' roll–hating bartenders all threatened to quit when they heard the group rehearsing. But with a few phone calls Hawkins's local songwriter friend Dallas Harms ("Paper Roses") got about sixty people down for the opening night, and from there the Hawks began to soar as word spread about this wild gang of real-deal, Southern-American rockabillies. The steelworkers looking to blow off steam after work and the Coke-drinking kids at the all-ages matinees had simply never seen anything like them: the feral, energy-packed, acrobatic, dirty-jokester Hawkins backed by the loud, untamed, off-the-rails rocking of the Hawks.

The remaining nights at the Golden Rail sold out, and from there the group began packing other Ontario venues like the Brass Rail in London and the Le Coq d'Or in Toronto; the latter soon became their "home" club. Dan Bass of Quality Records caught the band in action and booked a four-song session at a local garage-cum-studio. Unveiled in late 1958 under the name the Ron Hawkins Quartet (Kudlets's idea), their debut single "Hey Bo Diddley" b/w "Love Me Like You Can" was flawed; the tape had stretched at some point in the process, making the vocals sound like the novelty act the Chipmunks. Nevertheless, the group now had the prestige of having a record out, and as their sets got wilder, the crowds—and the money—only got bigger.

After the Hawks had conquered Eastern Canada, Kudlets started to work on some American bookings. He got them a spring 1959 residency in the Jersey Shore town of Wildwood that attracted the attention of several New York–based major labels. The infamous Roulette Records chief Morris "Mo" Levy was so blown away when the quartet auditioned for him in 1959 that he signed them on the spot and had them in the studio that very night. Their first Roulette single, the catchy "Forty Days," an unabashed rewrite of Chuck Berry's "Thirty Days," hit the *Billboard* Top Fifty, landing the Hawks a spot on *American Bandstand* (see YouTube). The group's first album, *Ronnie Hawkins*, appeared that year, a rockabilly/doo-wop blowout highlighted by a slinky, sleazy version of R&B singer Young Jessie's "Mary Lou." The latter was a song Roy Orbison had suggested to Hawkins—only to wish he'd done it himself when Hawkins's version hit both the R&B and Top Forty charts.

But despite the group's ascension Jones and Paulman were growing homesick and resentful of Hawkins's increasing dominance as the star and highest-paid member. By late 1959 both had quit, although Paulman stuck around long enough to record a shelved, Henry Glover–produced session alongside his replacement, ex–Dale Hawkins guitarist Fred Carter Jr.

Ronnie Hawkins met sixteen-year-old Robbie Robertson in the fall of 1959, when one of the Hawks-worshipping guitarist's early bands, the Suedes, was opening for his idols. Fascinated by the musicianship and "very fast and very violent" music of Hawkins's band, Robertson decided then

Ronnie Hawkins and the Hawks hit the R&B and Top Forty charts with 1959's "Mary Lou."
Author's collection

and there he "wanted to find a way into that world." And soon enough he did, although initially just as a band gofer. Before long, though, Robertson was appointed "song consultant" and, ultimately, a songwriter for the band, when Hawkins decided to record two numbers the kid had written with Suedes pianist Scott Cushnie, who replaced Jones in the Hawks in early 1960: the quirky rhumba "Hey Boba Lou" and the ballad "Someone Like You," which appear on *Mr. Dynamo*, Hawkins's sophomore LP of that year. When Lefty Evans quit during a return run in Arkansas, Hawkins sent word up to Toronto for Robertson to come down and assume the bass slot. The teenager pawned his Stratocaster and boarded a southbound train, still wearing his heavy Canadian-winter coat as he marveled at the Dixie scenery en route.

But the game changed almost as soon as he arrived. With Hawkins and Helm about to fly out on a promotional U.K. tour, Fred Carter Jr. announced he'd be leaving the band that spring. When Robertson pleaded to become Carter's replacement, Hawkins gave him $100 and told him to learn as much as he could from the senior guitarist while Hawkins was away. The departing Carter couldn't be bothered, so Robertson spent his entire stipend on blues LPs at Beale Street's Home of the Blues record store, studied the riffs of the masters, and practiced with devout fervor. When Hawkins returned, he was stunned by Robertson's supernatural progress but still held off on appointing him guitarist. The Hawks snagged ace new keyboardist Stan Szelest (supplanting Cushnie) and bassist Rebel Payne from the Buffalo, New York, band the Tremblers and resumed their hectic performing grind.

Back Where You Belong

The Hawks flew back to Toronto. Before Robertson was fully instated as the group's guitarist, he shared Carter's old slot with Roy Buchanan (see chapter 5) as Hawkins decided which axeman he favored. The rivalry culminated with a fabled duel between the two players in Grand Bend, Ontario (see chapter 9), and when the smoke cleared Robertson at last had the job. Saxophonist Jerry Penfound was also added, giving the Hawks some authentic R&B heft. With acts like the Limeliters and the Kingston Trio coming into vogue at the dawn of the new decade, the band's leader took a shot at the folk market with 1960's *The Folk Ballads of Ronnie Hawkins*, a lukewarm affair that was dominated by session players and sold poorly; other than having Helm on drums, the same description can be applied to

ROULETTE
DYNAMIC HIGH FIDELITY

"MR. DYNAMO"
Ronnie
Hawkins
and the Hawks

R-25102

Robbie Robertson is credited with cowriting two songs for *Mr. Dynamo*, the 1960 debut album by Ronnie Hawkins and the Hawks, although he'd yet to join as the group's guitarist when it was recorded. The album features the young Levon Helm on drums.
Author's collection

1961's follow-up, *Ronnie Hawkins Sings the Songs of Hank Williams*. But in the Ontario clubs the Hawks were still the kings, and they lived like it.

There were, alas, *some* limits imposed on their lifestyles. One of Hawkins's ground rules—a decree he would eventually violate himself—was that his musicians were not to have steady girlfriends, much less wives. After all, good-looking single musicians brought the girls to the clubs, which in turn brought in the guys. So when Payne got engaged in early 1961 his days were numbered (reportedly, his drinking had also become an issue), and Hawkins began looking around for a new bassist.

In Simcoe, Ontario, Rick Danko, then seventeen and heading his own band, Ricky and the Rhythm Notes, on lead vocals and guitar, was a huge Hawks fan. He booked his group as the opener when the Hawks came through Simcoe that May. Impressed mainly by Danko's pure tenor voice, Hawkins hired him to play rhythm guitar while learning bass ahead of Payne's departure; Szelest was the next Hawk to leave the nest, joining former Elvis Presley bassist Bill Black's Combo. With producer Henry Glover in September 1961, this piano-less lineup of Hawkins's band cut scorching versions of two blues chestnuts sung by Helm: Bobby "Blue" Bland's "Further On Up the Road" and, with Buchanan on rhythm guitar, Muddy Waters's "Nineteen Years Old." Although the tracks wouldn't be released until 1963, on the non-U.S. album *Mojo Man*, the session notably precedes any recordings by the Rolling Stones, the Animals, and most other white electric blues rockers by three years. Also released in 1963 (but not in the U.S.) was the confusingly titled *The Best of Ronnie Hawkins*, a disc composed not of previous recordings but of new material.

Richard Manuel was eighteen in the summer of 1961 when his band the Revols played one of their first shows, opening for Hawkins and the Hawks, in Port Dover. He astounded the headliners with his voice, and when the two bands next shared a bill, at the Stratford Coliseum, Manuel's staggering performance of "Georgia on My Mind" (a trademark even then) nearly upstaged the Hawks. Rather than compete with such formidable upstarts on the same Canadian circuit, Hawkins became their manager and put them on the road. When Szelest left, the piano chair was opened to Manuel. "Richard wasn't a great piano player, but he had *the throat*," Hawkins told Barney Hoskyns. "He could sing the black stuff way better'n I could."

After crossing paths in clubland with the musically advanced Garth Hudson, the Hawks were eager to add him to their lineup. While Hudson wasn't a rock 'n' roll pounder à la Szelest or Pop Jones, Hawkins knew his deep, conservatory-bred knowledge of the inner workings of music would be a tremendous asset. Additionally, the organ/piano combination would give the group a unique sound and diminish any misgivings about Manuel's shortcomings as a pianist. In December 1961 Hudson agreed to join— though not without conditions. To placate his non–rock 'n' roll–friendly parents, the multi-instrumentalist stipulated that he be hired as the band's music teacher and get paid $10 a week from each of the junior members; he also wanted a new Lowrey organ. Hawkins consented, and the collective that would later become better known as The Band was now in place.

Ain't Yonge Street Lucky

For the next three years, this edition of the Hawks continued their reign as the terrors of Toronto, bashing out tough rockabilly for sweaty, ecstatic, sold-out audiences at the city's Yonge Street clubs and beyond. For reasons unclear, Hudson sat out, Buchanan played bass, and Danko played rhythm guitar on the January 1963 session for Hawkins and the Hawks' showstopping version of Bo Diddley's "Who Do You Love." Released as a single soon after, it stands as one of the most volatile rock 'n' roll tracks ever waxed, with Helm hammering a relentlessly propulsive backbeat as Hawkins leers menacingly and Robertson's leads lash like live wires. Ancillary singer Bruce Bruno came on board to front the band for the early sets; the Hawk, now married himself, often showed up late.

When they weren't rocking the room—or partying like Roman gods—the group was being whipped into shape by their insatiable leader via lengthy, near-constant rehearsals to become an impeccably honed, battle-ready rock 'n' roll machine. But as Hawkins ultimately learned, this pursuit of perfection would be to his detriment when the young players broke away from him late that year. "[Hawkins] shot himself in the foot, really, bless his heart," recalled Robertson in the November 2000 issue of *MOJO* magazine, "by sharpening us into such a crackerjack band that we had to go on out into the world. Because we knew what his vision was for himself, and we were all younger and more ambitious musically." Things came to a head between Hawkins and the group when Danko was fined for bringing a girlfriend to a gig, and the whole ensemble, including Penfound and Bruno, quit. Out into the world they went, with Helm as their new leader.

In the ensuing decades Hawkins drew on a steady stream of star-struck native musicians to keep the Ronnie Hawkins and the Hawks name flying in his adoptive homeland, although most agree that no version flew higher or hotter than the Helm/Robertson/Danko/Manuel/Hudson edition. Subsequent Hawks lineups have included bassist Terry Danko, Rick's brother; Janis Joplin guitarist John Till and pianist Richard Bell (the latter joined the reunited Band in 1991); hard rock guitarist Pat Travers; and many others. Hawkins made world news in 1969 when fan John Lennon and his wife, Yoko Ono, stayed at his suburban Toronto estate during the height of their peace protest period. Besides turning in a barnstorming performance with The Band for *The Last Waltz*, he acted in Bob Dylan's 1978 film *Renaldo and Clara* and the 1980 western *Heaven's Gate*. Over the years, he's further explored country music and battled pancreatic cancer. The recipient of a star on the country's Walk of Fame, he remains eternally beloved as the father of Canadian rock 'n' roll.

"There isn't a Canadian musician or performer anywhere who doesn't owe a debt of gratitude to Ronnie Hawkins," said folksinger Sylvia Tyson, according to Canadian magazine *Forever Young Information.* "Because without him being who he was at the time, without his talent and effort and dedication to the cause of developing Canadians for stardom on their own, we probably wouldn't be where we are today."

9

They Call My Home the Land of Snow

Band Landmarks in the Toronto Area

When Ronnie Hawkins, Levon Helm, and the rest of the original Hawks got to Canada in the spring of 1958, they quickly found out how right Conway Twitty had been with his recommendation they check it out—the country was wide open and waiting for rock 'n' roll. There were expatriate Americans, like Curley Bridges and Mouse Johnson, playing blues, jazz, and R&B in small Toronto clubs, while native vocal groups the Four Lads, the Crew-Cuts, and the Diamonds had had early-1950s hits with tamed-down versions of black American doo-wop songs. And in 1957 Elvis Presley had played sold-out shows at Vancouver's Empire Stadium and Toronto's Maple Leaf Gardens. But most Canadians had never seen or heard unhinged, undistilled rockabilly—the kind that came straight from the corn-liquor-swillin', fistfight-on-a-Saturday-night-havin' American South—up close. The kind that could only be played by flashy former farm boys who spoke with an exotic drawl, carried on like carnies offstage, and tore it up live like a pack of rabid mountain lions in a tornado.

And no part of Canada was more ready, willing, and able to rock 'n' roll all night than Toronto's Yonge Street. A former settlers' trail, Yonge was home to "the Strip," a neon-pulsing span stretching roughly ten blocks from Bloor Street to Queen Street and lined with seedy, rowdy nightclubs, greasy lunch counters, and stores selling garish goods. Since the 1950s it had been the sin-infested domain of gangsters, drunks, hookers, pimps, drug dealers, hard-partying factory workers, and the passing, tightly locked cars of the suburbanites who came to gawk it all. As young rock 'n' rollers barely off the farm and in search of adventure, the Hawks loved Toronto—and it loved them back. By the time they'd settled in for good at the Le Coq d'Or, Ronnie Hawkins and the Hawks had pretty much become the house band for all of Yonge Street, with Ronnie himself as the Strip's underground mayor.

Bordering Yonge Street to the northwest was Yorkville, the bohemian district that eventually became the center of the Toronto scene as live music on Yonge was steadily supplanted by nude dancing ("the Strip," indeed). With more of an artsy, intellectual bent, Yorkville was haven to coffeehouses, folk music, and jazz clubs, and it became the local breeding ground for the coming wave of psychedelic rock. Yorkville's clubs included the Riverboat, the Penny Farthing, the Mousehole, and dozens more.

This chapter delves into the vibrant geography of Hawks-era Ontario in the years before the five young musicians signed on with Bob Dylan en route to becoming The Band.

Cabbagetown

Although Robbie Robertson spent formative time with his mother's family on the Six Nations Reserve where she had grown up, it was in the Toronto slum of Cabbagetown that he lived most of his childhood. Located on the east side of the city's downtown, the area was originally a separate village called Don Vale, which was absorbed into Toronto proper in the late nineteenth century. Dominated by Victorian architecture, it became known as Cabbagetown when impoverished Irish immigrants began settling there and planting cabbage in their front yards. When Robertson was growing up there, it was much the same tough, colorful, working-class neighborhood chronicled in Hugh Garner's Great Depression–set 1950 novel *Cabbagetown* (a likely source of inspiration for The Band's history-fueled chief song-writer). *Northern Lights—Southern Cross*'s "Rags and Bones" came from family accounts of Robertson's great-grandfather, an Israeli immigrant scholar who became a neighborhood rag trader. An affluent quarter today, the area is referenced in the name of the juke joint ("The Cabbagetown Café") depicted in the original artwork of *Moondog Matinee*.

Golden Rail

Situated near the corner of King and John streets in the steel-manufacturing town of Hamilton, Ontario (about an hour and fifteen minutes south of Toronto by car), this humble tavern was the site of the first Canadian performance by Ronnie Hawkins and the Hawks—then working as the Ron Hawkins Quartet—in the early spring of 1958. The band had been booked there for a one-week residency, which almost didn't happen: When they were rehearsing at the bar the afternoon they arrived, the volume and intensity of the music drove the customers out and drove the bartenders to threaten to quit unless the band was fired. But the Hawks prevailed, quickly winning over the small but hungry contingent of local rock 'n' rollers and the regular clientele of hard-drinking steel workers. In fact, they were held over for a week.

Steak N'Burger Room
in the
BRASS RAIL TAVERN
657 Dundas St., East,
LONDON, Ontario.

Specializing in **Char-Broiled Steaks**; the Nautical Room for **Sea Foods**; for relaxation and comfort visit our unique **Sharks Lounge**; and for entertainment nightly (Monday to Saturday) in our **Pump Room**.

Canadian Post Card Co. Ltd., Toronto 3

The Brass Rail in London, Ontario, was the site of Ronnie Hawkins and the Hawks' second Canadian residency, in 1958.   *Author's collection*

Brass Rail

The Hawks' next stop in their quest to conquer Canada was this tavern and eatery, located at 657 Dundas Street East in London, Ontario. The band stayed for three weeks and made $550 per week before heading on to "the Big Smoke" of Toronto. To reflect the cuisine (steaks, seafood), the establishment was decorated in both western and nautical motifs. Ronnie and the boys must have felt right comfortable in the Sharks Lounge.

Concord Tavern

Once described by the local *Globe Magazine* as "a grim tavern," the Concord, at 925 Bloor Street West, was the site of Ronnie Hawkins's first Toronto gig, in 1958. Owned by Jack Fisher, who helped pay Levon and the Hawks' bail when they were busted for pot possession in 1965, the club held non-alcoholic matinees for teenagers on Saturdays from 3:00 to 5:00 p.m. These events, which served Coca Cola and French fries, were crucial in fomenting rock 'n' roll among the upcoming generation of Canadian kids, many of whom met at the Concord and other clubs where the Hawks played matinees; several went on to form their own bands and in some cases play with Hawkins themselves. Although the club is gone, the same address is now a Long & McQuade musical instruments store, part of a national chain that started in 1957 with a Yonge Street location that would certainly have been familiar to the Hawks.

Le Coq d'Or Tavern

Although the Hawks played many other venues in Toronto and beyond, the Le Coq d'Or Tavern, at 333 Yonge Street, was their true home, the residence where Hawkins and the group indelibly established their name. With the big advance buzz in the air from the group's recent gigs at the Concord Tavern and in Hamilton and London, club manager Gordon Josie—who'd fronted the club's old house band, country outfit Hank Gordon and the Melody Ramblers—was willing to pony up the $700 the group wanted per week. The gamble paid off quickly, and handsomely, for all parties: Word of the back-flipping Rompin' Ronnie and his wild rockabilly henchmen swiftly spread, luring block-long lines to every show. The Hawks did six nights a week, with a matinee on Saturday and Sundays off for out-of-town gigs, and they were soon Yonge Street's biggest attraction.

Hawkins remained at the Le Coq d'Or for nearly a decade, leading new Hawks lineups long after Helm and the others had left and using the second floor of the building as a rehearsal space and a den for legendarily debauched, orgiastic parties; the third floor eventually became the singer's office and private gym complete with a boxing ring. In 1964, Hawkins opened the Hawk's Nest, an upstairs teen dance club at 331 Yonge (the same building as the Le Coq) that presented the Kinks and other name acts until it closed in the mid-1970s. The entire site was torn down in 1991 and rebuilt as the 35,000-square-foot HMV Superstore, which until recent downsizing was the largest retail music store in Canada.

Grange Tavern

Another Hamilton venue rocked by the early Hawks was this one, at 25-27 King Street West in the so-called Ambitious City. The group played the four-story tavern for two weeks in April 1964, making $1,300 per week. "You had to stop [playing] Saturday night at 11:30 p.m., but the Grange could stay open longer 'cause it had dining," Hawkins told the *Hamilton Spectator* in 1995. "We got very drunk for the last set. [We were] sitting there eating those honey garlic ribs and puking all over the floor. Ah, the big time." It was here that the Hawks first met the infamous groupie Cathy Smith (see chapter 5).

Warwick Hotel

"ENTERTAINERS WELCOME," its sign said. This rundown hotel at the corner of Dundas and Jarvis streets, blocks away from the Le Coq d'Or, was home to prostitutes, strippers, and struggling creative types like author Hugh Garner (see above), who early on wrote pulp novels under the clever pseudonym Jarvis Warwick. The hotel also housed many musicians, such as the Hawks, who lived here when they first came to Toronto. The shady Warwick name was not exactly impressive to the girls they met. "That address ended a lot of dates for us before they even started," remembered Helm in *This Wheel's on Fire*.

CHUM Hi-Fi Club

Starting in the late 1950s, for several years Coca-Cola partnered with radio stations across North America to sponsor the teen-targeted Hi-Fi Clubs. As a local Coca-Cola affiliate, Toronto radio powerhouse CHUM held its Hi-Fi

Club events at a space on Merton Street. It was here, in the fall of 1959, that Robbie Robertson met his idol Ronnie Hawkins when Robertson's band the Suedes performed. Hawkins sang a couple of tunes with the kids and was duly impressed by Robertson's playing and the songs he'd written for the group. In need of material for his upcoming *Mr. Dynamo* album, Hawkins soon called upon Robertson, giving the young guitarist his entree into the Hawks.

Friar's Tavern

Just a couple blocks south of Hawkins's home base at the Le Coq d'Or was this smaller club, which also sponsored afternoon matinees for the underage set. In the summer of 1964, John Hammond Jr., in town to play at Yorkville's Purple Onion, first saw Levon and the Hawks perform at one of the Friar's afternoon shows. Mesmerized, he kept in touch and eventually hired them for his *So Many Roads* album at the time they were doing their summer 1965 Jersey Shore residency. Once the Hawks had agreed to do the '65–'66 tour with Bob Dylan, they still had to complete a few weeks of contracted shows at the Friar's. So on September 15, after he'd done the Forest Hills and Hollywood Bowl shows with Robertson and Helm, Dylan flew to Toronto to spend three nights rehearsing upstairs with the full band, following their obligatory sets, at this Yonge Street bar. Thus, one could say it was here that the radical new sound of Dylan and the Hawks really got off the ground. Today the building is a Hard Rock Café.

Lou Myles Tailor Shop

Amid the Friar's Tavern rehearsals the Hawks took Dylan to their tailor, Lou Myles, whose shop was located on Yonge Street across from the Le Coq d'Or. There, the singer had Myles make him the iconic houndstooth suit that he wore on the 1965–1966 tour. Myles had been the Hawks' official outfitter since the group first set foot in Toronto, creating the sharp mohair suits they wore onstage and in press shots. "Once Lou made your suit, you were officially a Hawk," said Helm in his autobiography.

Edison Hotel

Right next door to the Le Coq d'Or, at 335 Yonge Street, was the Edison Hotel, built in 1888. Another early Toronto rock 'n' roll hub, it sported a towering neon sign announcing "DANCING NIGHTLY" and was one of the first area venues to welcome visiting African American artists. The Edison hosted evening and all-ages matinee shows by Ronnie and the Hawks, Bill Haley and His Comets, Bo Diddley, Carl Perkins, and innumerable other acts in the 1950s and '60s.

Steele's Tavern

On the same Yonge Street block as the Le Coq and the Edison, crammed between music shops Sam the Record Man and A&A Records, was this bar and restaurant. It was best known as the venue where folksinger and Band friend Gordon Lightfoot made his name.

Club Blue Note

"Of all the innovative clubs for R&B and soul, the Blue Note was the place to go," Five Rogues/Mandala singer George Olliver told the *Toronto National Post* in 2011. "So many of the hit artists who used to work at the Maple Leaf Gardens came here after hours—people like Stevie Wonder, the Righteous Brothers. It was all mohair suits and flash and silk. And the girls used to dress up with gowns onstage." One memorable spring night in 1964 found the chart-topping Supremes surprising the seventy-seat club's clientele with an unannounced set.

Embassy Club

In the spring of 1964, Levon and the Hawks did a three-week stint at this Bellair Street tavern. In the audience for these shows was Mary Martin, the Hawks' future advocate to Bob Dylan (see chapter 5). This Embassy shouldn't be confused with the nearby Bohemian Embassy coffeehouse, which, according to Nicholas Jennings's book *Before the Gold Rush*, in 1962 wouldn't let a visiting Dylan read his poems because "the guy who ran the poetry night didn't know who the hell he was."

Massey Hall

The most prestigious and historic performance arts theater in Toronto, the stately Massey Hall was built in 1894 as a space for choral and classical recitals. Among the famous names who've graced its stage are Enrico Caruso,

Winston Churchill, George Gershwin, Vladimir Horowitz, Maria Callas, and Arturo Toscanini. Band hero Ray Charles played here, as did the all-star "The Quintet" featuring Dizzy Gillespie, Charlie Parker, Bud Powell, Charles Mingus, and Max Roach (their 1953 concert was released as *Jazz at Massey Hall*). Neil Young's January 19, 1971, appearance was also recorded for a live album released in 2007, and his fellow local boys Rush taped 1976's *All the World's a Stage* at the venue. Massey Hall figures most prominently into Band lore as the site of the Dylan-led Hawks' poorly received 1965 homecoming concert.

Frontenac Arms

Along with the above-mentioned Warwick Hotel, this ten-story Art Deco building on Jarvis Street was constructed as an apartment tower in 1930. It eventually became the Frontenac Arms hotel, which by the early 1960s, when the Hawks were living there, had become another "budget" establishment. In 1963, Helm and Robertson were sharing a two-bedroom suite at the Frontenac when they and their bandmates gave Hawkins their two weeks' notice and prepared to strike out on their own. Today, the structure is a Ramada Inn.

Hotel Imperial

The Lake Huron resort town of Grand Bend, Ontario, has long been a summer getaway spot for Torontonians. In the summer of 1961, the bar of this small hotel, which was built in 1905 at 62 Main Street, was the site of the fabled "showdown" between Roy Buchanan and Robbie Robertson during the brief period when both were playing guitar in the Hawks. By most accounts, the meteorically rising Robertson, as Hawkins himself put it, "blew Roy into next year." The duel was a pivotal moment that cemented Robertson's role as the band's lead guitarist. Lakeview Casino, on Main Street as well, also booked Ronnie and the Hawks on occasion.

Pop Ivey's Ballroom

This venue in Port Dover, a weekenders' mecca on Lake Erie in South Ontario, was another hotspot for the Hawks, both with Ronnie Hawkins and in 1964, when they were Levon and the Hawks. Managed by the genial Don

"Pop" Ivey, the ballroom hosted the latter lineup on Sunday nights, paying them $250 a gig. Ivey also ran the Summer Gardens, a covered outdoor performance space that Ronnie and the guys reportedly considered their second home during the warmer months of the early 1960s.

The Frontenac Arms Hotel provided low-rent lodgings to the Hawks during their Toronto years. *Author's collection*

10

I Got My Own Thing Goin'

The Band's Garage Rock Days (1964–1965)

W e never played no fruit rock, no punk rock," Levon Helm told *Rolling Stone* about The Band in a 1977 interview. By "fruit rock," he likely meant the glitter rock that had been all the rage a few years earlier—and no, his group never went anywhere near the gender-bending getups and glammy production of David Bowie or Roxy Music. But in a sense, his band *had* played punk rock—early versions of it, that is. The whooping, unbridled aggression of raw rockabilly like the kind the Hawks had played with Ronnie Hawkins was a definite touchstone for many punks, while the confrontational, abrasive music of their 1965–1966 tour with Bob Dylan likewise foreshadowed the coming of bands like the Clash a decade later. And between those two periods, in the clubs of Canada and the U.S., Levon and the Hawks had played tight, tough, blues-based songs with an unpretentious approach and a spirit akin to the 1960s garage bands who influenced the punk musicians of the late 1970s.

True, the Hawks had far deeper musical roots; they got their blues right from the source, not via some Rolling Stones cover of a Muddy Waters song, as most 1960s garage bands had. And yes, they could play rings around those cruder bands, whose audacity often outstripped their ability; the Hawks weren't a bunch of guys who, as Robbie Robertson put it in a 2016 *Rock Cellar Magazine* interview, "got guitars for Christmas and decided to start a band." But while the Hawks were never a garage band *per se*, the unpretentious approach and hard edge they brought to their music made them garage rock's wiser, more experienced cousins. A bar band, arguably the greatest bar band ever, but a *garage* bar band, not some group just trying to blend in and inoffensively regurgitate the hits of the day. This is why

I've elected to call this forgotten and fleeting "in-between" era The Band's garage rock period.

It Was Just a Childish Thing to Do: What Is Garage Rock and What Does It Have to Do with The Band?

The term garage rock was coined retroactively by early-1970s music journalists to refer to the wave of young North American rock 'n' roll bands that began at about the same time Levon and the boys left Ronnie Hawkins. Such bands were an unconscious response to the rise of the other teen idols who'd usurped the limelight of the original rock 'n' rollers, and many were amateurish teenagers who rehearsed in their parents' suburban garages, hence the name. Some of them graduated to the level of highly experienced, jobbing professional acts who played at over-twenty-one venues, such as the early R&B-ish incarnation of the Standells, who at the beginning sounded very similar to Levon and the Hawks. (See the Standells' 1964 debut, *In Person at P.J.'s.*)

Garage rock's earliest period encompasses frat rock, a subgenre largely made up of white groups, often with a saxophone in their ranks, who played covers of R&B songs for drunken fraternity students at campus parties, as the name suggests. The archetypal frat rock record is the Kingsmen's 1963 version of Richard Berry's "Louie, Louie," and typical frat-set fodder also included numbers like the Isley Brothers' "Twist and Shout," Tommy Tucker's "Hi-Heel Sneakers," Barrett Strong's "Money," and any number of Ray Charles, Bo Diddley, or Chuck Berry tunes—exactly what the Hawks were dishing out at the same time, although their Toronto audience was more "wise guy" than frat boy.

Of course, this was also the same music that inspired the Beatles and their British brethren, who crossed the Atlantic in 1964 and kicked garage rock into its second phase. Suddenly, young American and Canadian bands were starting up, sprouting bowl haircuts, and adding fuzz guitar to their sound. Except for the Hawks. They saw this abrupt Anglophilia, with its mop-top-mod trappings, as a passing fad. Still entrenched in Yonge Street's saloons and America's roadhouses, they stuck with their short hair, their mohair suits, and the same R&B and rock 'n' roll they'd always been playing, fashionable or not. The garage rock eon peaked in 1968, giving way to psychedelic rock and then, ironically perhaps, the more serious rock consciousness The Band helped usher in. But during their post-Hawkins/

pre-Dylan days the Hawks recorded three rare singles (discussed below) that would sound right at home on any *Nuggets*-type garage compilation.

He Gets to Sing Just Like a Bird: Levon and the Hawks' First Recordings

Once Helm, Robertson, Danko, Manuel, Hudson, saxophonist/flutist Jerry Penfound, and singer Bruce Bruno had left Ronnie Hawkins, they hooked up with his recently fired manager Harold Kudlets and began performing as Levon and the Hawks. Bruno soon quit for the married life, and the group briefly billed themselves as the Levon Helm Sextet before reverting to Levon and the Hawks. In the fall of 1964 the remaining members went into Toronto's Hallmark Studio to do some recordings financed by local DJ Cliff Roman. For the sessions they cut a few covers (James Brown's "Please, Please, Please") along with a handful of band originals that included "Biscuits and Taters," "Bacon Fat," and "Robbie's Blues." "Biscuits and Taters" remains unheard, but the latter two numbers appear on the 2005 box set *A Musical History*. "Bacon Fat," with a gritty vocal by Manuel, is a mid-tempo grinder that drips with all the requisite grease of its title. "Robbie's Blues" is a showpiece for Robertson, a slow instrumental the group would jam to epic lengths at gigs (one bootleg version, from a June 5, 1965, show in Dallas, runs to nearly ten minutes). The '64 studio iteration clocks in at 3:37, and besides Robertson's simmering leadwork, it boasts moody solos by Hudson on organ and Penfound on flute. Nothing would come of the session at the time, and the group, having forced Penfound out for economic reasons—after all, Hudson could double on sax and organ—once again headed out on the road.

Don't Tell Me What to Do: The Canadian Squires

In the spring of 1965 the band met up in New York with Henry Glover, their studio overseer from Hawkins's Roulette days, to cut a single for the producer's new Ware label. Glover implored the quintet to put their blues reverence aside and come up with something more "commercial." The resulting seven-inch was released on Ware in the U.S. and Apex in Canada under the name the Canadian Squires and comprises two Robertson-penned songs in the de rigueur Rolling Stones/Them/Animals–modeled vein. The A-side, "Leave Me Alone," is the standout: an ace, fist-in-the-face punker à la the Stones' "Satisfaction" with galloping drums, biting guitar, and Helm bellowing warnings like "Bad men, don't come around / or I'm gonna put your body down." The flip side is "Uh Uh Uh," which features prominent harmonica by Robertson and unison vocals by Helm and Manuel that brag of stealing the hearts of girls in various cities.

The group was reportedly unhappy with the thin sound, but it seems it was the new moniker that really killed the record—right or wrong, at that point most radio DJs on both sides of the border considered Canadian rock 'n' roll bands inauthentic by nature and wouldn't play them.

He Will Know Which Way to Go: The Atco Singles

The group reverted to the Levon and the Hawks handle for another New York studio date, this one in September of 1965. Under the loose supervision of Eddie Heller, an employee of the now-forgotten production company that fronted the costs, they recorded three songs: the Impressions-inspired garage soul workout "He Don't Love You (And He'll Break Your Heart)," the gospel-based "The Stones I Throw (Will Free All Men)," and a fast rock 'n' roll adaptation of the folk standard "Little Liza Jane." "He Don't Love You" and "The Stones I Throw," both sung by Manuel, were released as a single by Atlantic's Atco subsidiary later that year.

"He Don't Love You," which has a great fatback drum track by Helm and finds Manuel doing his best Brother Ray, is a lost Northern Soul gem. With its melody and Hudson's churchy organ, "The Stones I Throw" sounds much like the template for "We Can Talk" from *Music from Big Pink*. Robertson admits that the vaguely civil rights–themed song came out of his love of the Staple Singers. "It was out of context for us to do 'The Stones I Throw,'" he told Rob Bowman for the liner notes of *A Musical History*. "But if you imagine the Staple Singers doing it, it's right in context." Unfortunately, however, most radio programmers apparently lacked such imagination, and neither it nor "He Don't Love You" garnered much airplay. In another market, though, Australian singer Normie Rowe had a 1966 hit with "The Stones I Throw."

In 1968, after The Band had moved onto Capitol and was enjoying success, Atco released "Little Liza Jane"—for some reason retitled "Go Go Liza Jane"—with "He Don't Love You" as the B-side. "Little Liza Jane" had been an audience favorite, but the group thought the studio version paled in comparison (bootlegs bear this out). Still, it has a certain catchy, hand-clapping momentum, and the way that Manuel, Danko, and Helm hand off the verses to each other foreshadows The Band's multi-vocal arrangements.

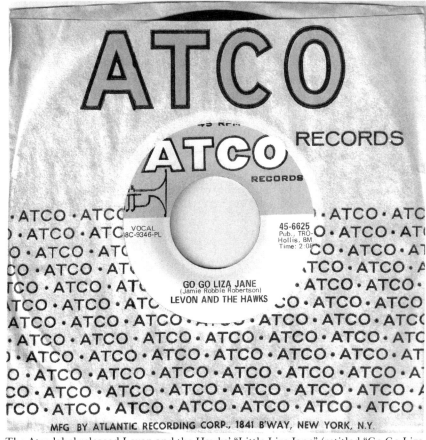

The Atco label released Levon and the Hawks' "Little Liza Jane" (retitled "Go Go Liza Jane") as a single in 1968.   *Author's collection*

They Came In Undercover: Bootleg Recordings of Levon and the Hawks

Amazingly, a few bootleg recordings actually exist of the Hawks live in the wild during this primal period, although the quality tends to be very rough. The earliest to surface thus far, if the bootlegger is to be trusted, are the five audience-taped songs from a 1964 Valentine's Day date in London, Ontario, that appear on *Old Shoes* (2000, Pontiac). Among these is an eight-minute jam on "Who Do You Love" spiked with squealing female attendees and Robertson's lethal crunch and lacerating leads. Before a version of Howlin' Wolf's "Howlin' for My Baby" (retitled simply "Howlin'"), it sure sounds like Ronnie Hawkins's Southern accent bantering with the audience and calling

Nineteen-sixty-five's "He Don't Love You (And He'll Break Your Heart)" was reissued as the B-side of "Go Go Liza Jane."   *Author's collection*

the girls "Levon's little hors d'oeuvres." But of course the Hawks had left him by then, so perhaps this was a rare guest return. Also on *Old Shoes* is live, studio, and TV material by The Band and three tracks from a 1964 Port Dover show.

These cuts mentioned above also crop up on the double-CD *Port Dover 1964* (2000, Qpro), culled from a two-track tape of one of the band's gigs at Pop Ivey's Ballroom in the titular town (the group is known to have played Pop Ivey's on April 14 and July 12 of that year, but no exact date is given on this release). The tape, which Helm mentions in *This Wheel's on Fire*, opens with him singing and drumming on a raw version of Buddy Holly's "Not Fade Away" and contains further curios like a version of Henry Mancini's "Peter Gunn" theme; the raunchy instrumental stroll "Hoochey John Blues," a saxophone showcase for Penfound and Hudson; and a rollicking romp through soul singer Tony Clarke's "Woman, Love, and a Man" (the poor fidelity makes it hard to tell if it's Helm or Manuel singing lead on this one).

Rougher in quality are the two iterations of Levon and the Hawks' August 15, 1964, show at Toronto's Crang Plaza. *Crang Plaza 1964* (2000, Qpro) is unique in having a (incomplete) version of the Dovells' "You Can't Sit Down," but it lacks the versions of "Georgia on My Mind," Huey Piano Smith's "Rockin' Pneumonia and the Boogie Woogie Flu," and Chuck Berry's "No Particular Place to Go" found on *Crang Plaza, Toronto* (no label).

Live in Dallas Texas (no label) captures a June 5, 1965, set at what's presumably the Jack Ruby–owned nightclub Robertson mentions in *The Last Waltz*. This one's for brave archaeologists only, as the muffled recording is quite the tolerance-tester. But the rewards are certainly there, among them the extended "Robbie's Blues" mentioned above, an early version of "Bacon Fat," and Manuel wailing away on the Cannonball Adderley/Oscar Brown warhorse "The Work Song" and the racy Charles Calhoun/Ray Charles gem "Smack Dab in the Middle." YouTube bears a boisterous version of "Go Go Liza Jane" at Oklahoma City's Onyx Club in 1966 with decent sound. The source claims to have the whole set and that it includes a version of "Chain Gang" (sung by Danko, one guesses).

Also still under wraps as of this writing is *From Bacon Fat to Judgement Day*, an eight-CD/one-DVD box set credited to Levon and the Hawks that documents the group's evolution from the pre-Hawkins bands of the late '50s to the Basement Tapes "and everything in between." The set, which has been in the works since 1997, is scheduled to be released by Other People's Music, the Canadian reissue label run by Jan Haust, who worked with Garth Hudson on restoring the recordings for 2014's *The Basement Tapes Complete*. The DVD is said to feature interviews with Hudson.

But I'd Rather Be Burned in Canada

The Toronto-Area Music Scene (1959–1965)

Levon Helm often said that in the late 1950s and early 1960s Toronto was the best place in the world for live music outside of the country-and-blues crossroads of Memphis. And much of the credit for making it even better is due to him and his bandmates. The Hawks are cited for crystalizing the "Toronto Sound"—hard, blue-eyed R&B played by young guys in matching tailored suits with Fender Telecaster and Precision Bass guitars, an electric organ, a honking sax here and there, and New Orleans–style drumming. Whether they were checking out the hard-rocking competition on rowdy Yonge Street, digging visiting jazz greats, or enjoying the sparser acoustic sounds of Yorkville's folk houses, the budding Band paid close attention to what they heard. They soaked all of this music in, jamming and making friends with the musicians whose paths they crossed.

So who were some of the other acts who were making the scene while the Hawks were ruling the roost? Examined in this chapter are some of the more recognizable names (and several that may be less familiar) with whom the group shared the region's pulsating nightlife landscape. Let's start where The Band's native Canadian members themselves started: with the bands they played in before joining Ronnie Hawkins's organization.

Rags, Bones, and Old City Songs: Pre-Hawks Groups

Prior to becoming Hawks, Robbie Robertson, Rick Danko, Richard Manuel, and Garth Hudson took their first steps on the rock 'n' roll road with these local teen bands.

Little Caesar and the Consuls and Other Early Robbie Robertson Bands

Little Caesar and the Consuls were one of the first R&B groups in Toronto and the first band Robbie Robertson played in. Although they wouldn't wax anything until after he'd moved on, they were the only one of his early bands to make records. Formed in 1956 as, simply, the Consuls, the group altered its name after audiences began saying their singer, Bruce Morshead, resembled Edward G. Robinson's character in the 1931 gangster film *Little Caesar.* It was in 1957 that the teenage Robertson joined the band, which only played the hits of the day (at one point its lineup included Gene MacLellan, later the composer of Anne Murray's 1970 smash "Snowbird" and other big sellers). Robertson remained with the group for just under a year before moving on to start his own bands (see below). Little Caesar and the Consuls enjoyed several Top Ten hits in Canada, including 1965's number one version of the Miracles' "You've Really Got a Hold on Me," and have occasionally reunited since officially breaking up in 1971.

Little Caesar and the Consuls were Robbie Robertson's first band. In 1965, after Robertson had moved on to the Hawks, the group had a number one hit in Canada with "You've Really Got a Hold on Me."
Author's collection

After leaving the Consuls, Robertson started the Rhythm Chords (a.k.a. Robbie and the Robots) and Thumper and the Trambones, both of which included bassist Peter "Thumper" Traynor, who would later head the Traynor amplifier company. In 1959 Robertson, Traynor, and pianist Scott Cushnie formed the Suedes, who Ronnie Hawkins saw perform that October. Hawkins sat in with the Suedes for a few tunes and was mightily impressed—especially by Cushnie, whom he would soon summon to replace the departing Will "Pop" Jones. Cushnie attempted to play the "all-for-one/one-for-all" card by demanding that Robertson and Traynor be added with him, but the Hawk wasn't having it. Eventually, though, the piano man's pressure would lead to the fifteen-year-old Robertson's entree into the group to (temporarily) assume the bass slot when Lefty Evans quit. (Suedes drummer Peter Deremigis would later cofound Kelly Jay and the Jamies with future Ronnie Hawkins/Crowbar pianist Jay and Revols guitarist John Till.) No recordings of these early Robertson bands are known to exist.

Kelly Jay and the Jamies featured drummer Peter Deremigis, who had played in the Suedes, one of Robbie Robertson's early bands.

Author's collection

The Revols/Rockin' Revols

This Stratford, Ontario, teenage group was Richard Manuel's first outfit. The pianist formed the band in 1957 with bassist Ken Kalmusky, guitarist John Till (later replaced by Garth Picot), vocalist Doug Rhodes, and drummer Jim Winkler. The five began as the Rebels but altered their name to the Rockin' Revols to avoid confusion with guitar-twanger Duane Eddy's group ("Revols" was short for "Revolutions"). Eventually known simply as the Revols, they were signed by Hawkins to his booking/management company and set up with a residency at his Rockwood Supper Club in Fayetteville, Arkansas (the teens ended up spending a night in jail when some Arkie cops assumed they'd stolen the white 1959 Cadillac they were driving; it actually belonged to Hawkins). Before Manuel joined the Hawks in 1964, the Revols made an unreleased demo composed of a rocked-up version of Franz Liszt's "Liebestraum" and two early Manuel songs, "Promise Yourself" and "My Eternal Love," the latter cowritten with Till. Kalmusky and Till next started a group called the Fab Four, who for a time had a weekly Toronto television show, before becoming Hawks themselves. Till went on to play with Janis Joplin's Full Tilt Boogie Band, and Kalmusky joined Band tour mates Great Speckled Bird. In 1984, Manuel, Till, and Kalmusky (who died of cancer in 2005) reunited as the Revols and opened for the re-formed Band in Stratford.

Paul London and the Capers

After playing in a couple of jazz combos and a rockabilly band called the Melodines in high school, Garth Hudson joined the Silhouettes, another rockabilly crew who toured clubs between Southern Ontario and Detroit. When vocalist Paul Hutchins came aboard in 1959, they became Paul London and the Capers, the singer's suave stage name a tribute the group's hometown. On top of doing their own dates, the Capers (sometimes spelled Kapers) backed up touring stars like the Everly Brothers, Bill Haley, and Johnny Cash and released two 1961 singles with Hudson on sax and piano: a version of R&B greats the Mello-Tones' "Rosie Lee" (backed with the storming "Real Gone Lover") and "Sugar Baby" (the latter disc was recorded in Chicago at Chess Studio and released on the iconic blues label's Checkmate subsidiary). Hudson's big-picture musical talents, as well as his instrumental skills, were apparent even early on: He arranged the music on both Capers discs and coproduced a 1959 single by pop country singer Don Crawford ("Sleeping Beauty" b/w "Beauty and the Beast").

Unfortunately, it appears that no recordings survive by Ricky and the Rhythm Notes (alternately known as Rick Danko and the Starliners or Rick and the Roxatones), the band Rick Danko led before he joined the Hawks.

Here on the Street: The Hawks' Contemporary Toronto Artists

The Hawks may have been known as the city's hottest live band, but within Toronto's explosive early-1960s music scene they were surrounded by dozens of other exceptional acts. Here are some of the notable groups and solo artists they shared the clubs with.

The Beau-Marks

The Beau-Marks were actually from Montreal, not Toronto, but they nevertheless have some connections to the Hawks. Besides being one of the earliest Canadian rockabilly bands to pop up in the wake of Ronnie Hawkins's arrival, they made a live album at his home base: 1961's *In Person! Recorded on Location at Le Coq d'Or.* Assembled in 1958, the bass-less quartet hit number one in Canada and Australia with the 1960 stomper "Clap Your Hands," from that year's rollicking *The High Flying Beau-Marks.* The group disintegrated after their self-titled third album in 1962.

Lenny Breau

Maine-born guitarist Lenny Breau was one of the leading lights on the early Toronto jazz scene. The son of popular Winnipeg country and western performers Hal "Lone Pine" Breau and Betty Cody, he formed the trio Three with singer-actor Don Francks and bassist Eon Henstridge, which toured widely and appeared on television in the U.S. and Canada (he had his own show on Winnipeg TV in the mid-'60s). Among his admirers were guitar greats Randy Bachman (the Guess Who, Bachman-Turner Overdrive), George Benson, Pat Metheny, Leonard Cohen—and the Hawks, whose Levon Helm and Rick Danko backed him on a November 1961 studio date. (The tracks eventually surfaced on 2003's *The Hallmark Sessions.*)

David Clayton-Thomas

A regular Yonge Street denizen, vocalist David Clayton-Thomas was one of the local kids who were moved by the Hawks to enter the rock 'n' roll field. Born in England and estranged from his parents after the family had immigrated to Toronto, Clayton-Thomas did time in jail for petty crimes and lived on the streets as a teenager. While fronting the second Canadian version of the Hawks, Ronnie Hawkins took note of this curious urchin's powerful, mile-wide baritone and would occasionally let him sing a couple of songs at gigs. Soon he was fronting David Clayton-Thomas and the Fabulous Shays, who also featured guitarist Fred Keeler, one of the Strip's better Robbie Robertson emulators. The band hit in 1964 with a raw version of John Lee Hooker's "Boom, Boom" and the following year with "Walk That Walk," which won them a slot on NBC-TV's *Hullabaloo.* Clayton-Thomas next formed the Bossmen, whose fuzzed-out 1966 Vietnam protest anthem "Brainwashed" is a garage punk gem. The singer would find much broader worldwide fame when he replaced Al Kooper in Blood, Sweat & Tears in 1968.

The Dirty Shames

An extremely popular Yorkville folk act (they packed the Riverboat in 1965 on the same night the Beatles played Maple Leaf Gardens), the Dirty Shames played hokum-style music reminiscent of the early Lovin' Spoonful and the Jim Kweskin Jug Band. The quartet is best remembered for guitarist Amos Garrett, who went on to Ian & Sylvia's Great Speckled Bird before moving to Woodstock to work with the Kweskin band's Maria and Geoff Muldaur, Paul Butterfield's Better Days, and Hungry Chuck. It was Garrett and the Shames' percussionist, Chick Roberts, who took John Hammond Jr. to see Levon and the Hawks at the Friar's Tavern in 1964. That outing led to the Hawks playing on Hammond's *So Many Roads* LP and helped put them on Bob Dylan's radar.

The Five Rogues/Mandala

After a couple of name changes, this erstwhile Blue Note Club house band would become better known as one of the most dynamic live bands in Canada. Formed as the Rogues in 1964, the group soon became the Five Rogues, and with the additions of lead guitarist Domenic Troiano (ex–Robbie Lane and the Disciples; see below) and unhinged singer George

Olliver, they began burning up the Hawk's Nest and other clubs with their high-energy soul rock. In 1966, after their manager rechristened them Mandala and made them over with a new image that included pinstripe gangster suits and strobe lights, the quintet really hit the stratosphere. In 1967, they performed with the Who, Cream, and Wilson Pickett in New York, and their single "Opportunity" reached number three on the CHUM Chart. Alas, an unstable lineup and flop album doomed Mandala, who played their final show, at the Hawk's Nest, in January 1969. Troiano and Olliver's replacement, Roy Kenner, later played with the James Gang. Troiano, an acknowledged Canadian guitar hero, died in 2005.

The Halifax Three

Originally from Nova Scotia, the folk outfit the Halifax Three featured future Mamas and Papas singer Denny Doherty and Lovin' Spoonful guitarist Zal Yanovsky. Upon making their name in Toronto at the same time the Hawks were peaking there, the group relocated to New York to record two albums for Epic Records before disintegrating in 1964. Afterward, Doherty and Yanovksy cofounded the short-lived Mugwumps before finding greater fame with the above-mentioned acts.

Ian & Sylvia

Considered the most influential male-female duo of the early-1960s folk revival, Ian and Sylvia Tyson (née Fricker) met in Toronto in 1958, the year the original Hawks made their loud landing on Yonge Street. The couple began performing together in 1959, fast becoming a top draw thanks to their haunting tandem vocals and strong repertoire of English ballads, traditional Canadian folk songs, blues, and originals. Among the latter were Ian's "Four Strong Winds" (a massive 1964 Canadian hit covered by Dylan and The Band during the Basement Tapes sessions, along with their original "The French Girl") and Sylvia's "You Were on My Mind" (a 1965 hit for We Five).

Although they would eventually return to Toronto, the couple moved to New York in the fall of 1961 and were picked up by Albert Grossman and signed to Vanguard Records. From 1962 to 1968 the husband and wife released nine albums—1968's *Nashville* includes versions of "This Wheel's on Fire" and its fellow Basement Tapes song "The Mighty Quinn"—and they were consistent favorites in the folk sphere, especially on college campuses.

By 1969, however, the pair were feeling the strong winds of change brought on by *Music from Big Pink*, and they duly formed the pioneering country rock band Great Speckled Bird. The couple split in 1975 but still perform individually.

Jack London and the Sparrows

The first Canadian rock band signed to a major label—Capitol, like The Band—this Beatles-esque group is notable for another reason: Within a few short years, they would morph into the kings of biker rock. The band, whose "bird" name was an homage to the Hawks, was formed in 1964 by faux-Englishman Jack London (a.k.a. Dave Marden; lead vocals), brothers Jerry (drums) and Dennis Edmonton (guitar), and Bruce Palmer (bass). Palmer left early on to join future Band friend Neil Young in the Mynah Birds (and eventually in the Buffalo Springfield; see below), whose previous bassist, Nick St. Nicholas, took Palmer's place in the Sparrows. The group had some Top Ten singles and made an album before London left to go solo in 1967. The remaining members added front man John Kay and keyboardist Goldy McJohn, Edmonton changed his name to Mars Bonfire, and the band was rechristened the Sparrow. After cutting one single for Columbia under that moniker, they relocated to California and renamed themselves, yet again, as Steppenwolf. "Born to Be Wild," "Magic Carpet Ride," and thousands of revving Harley-Davidsons were right around the bend.

Jon and Lee & the Checkmates

Fronted by lead singers John "Jon" Finley and Michael "Lee" Jackson, this soul/R&B band burned up Toronto's mid-sixties scene until a series of heartbreaking setbacks brought it all to an end. Specializing in many of the soul covers Levon and the Hawks also played (James Brown, Junior Walker, Isley Brothers), Jon and Lee & the Checkmates were known for the gospel-testifying vibe of their live shows, much like their close rivals Mandala (see above). The six-to-seven-piece group worked at the Avenue Road Club, the Friar's Tavern, and the Hawk's Nest, opened for the Rolling Stones, and in September 1965 sparked a riot at a concert for the opening of Toronto's new city hall. The buzz led to gigs in New York (the Peppermint Lounge, where the latter-day Hawks once played) and flirtation from U.S. labels. The sole single by the band (now called the Jon-Lee Group), "Bring It Down Front," did nothing in the States but charted in Canada on the

Sparton label in 1967. By then, however, Finley and Jackson, beaten down by industry red tape and disappointing studio sessions, checked out, leaving the Checkmates to briefly back David Clayton-Thomas under the hopeful name the Phoenix. Finley, drummer Jim Fonfara, and guitarist Larry Leishman later played in the much-hyped Rhinoceros.

Larry Lee and the Leesures

Interviewed for Helm's autobiography, Band road manager Bill Avis cites this outfit (erroneously spelled "Larry Lee and Leisures") as being one of the new crop of local bands who copied the Hawks' sound and look. But as has often been said, imitation is the sincerest form of flattery. And even if they couldn't touch their heroes musically, their existence just reaffirmed the greatness of the Hawks' mysterious mojo. Larry Lee was born Lawrence Milton Broderick in London, Ontario, and his group, which briefly included John Till (see above) on guitar, released one album and enjoyed some moderate hit singles in the early 1960s. The R&B-ish, un-Hawkins-like "Boot and Soul" is a favorite.

Gordon Lightfoot

Although Ian & Sylvia stand among Canada's leading folk exports, they are eclipsed in notoriety by Gordon Lightfoot, one of the most popular singer-songwriters of the 1960s and '70s. His Top Ten hits include "If You Could Read My Mind" (1970), "Sundown," "Carefree Highway" (both 1974), and "The Wreck of the Edmund Fitzgerald" (1976), and his songs have been recorded by Elvis Presley, Bob Dylan, Johnny Cash, Eric Clapton, Neil Young, and many others.

Born in Orillia, the site of the venerated Mariposa Folk Festival, Lightfoot sang advertising jingles, played drums in a jazz revue, performed in the folk duo the Two Tones, and served as a TV variety show singer-dancer and emcee before pursuing a solo career. Inspired by Dylan, he began singing his own songs at Yorkville's coffeehouses in 1964 and was soon selling out shows. Among Lightfoot's Toronto fans and friends were the Hawks; he wrote the humorous "Silver Cloud Talking Blues" about Ronnie Hawkins, and Robbie Robertson once called him "a national treasure." Another admirer was Albert Grossman's partner John Court, who in 1965 signed Lightfoot to the pair's firm, which placed his songs with some of their other acts ("For Lovin' Me" was a hit that year for Peter, Paul and Mary). Lightfoot hooked up with Band producer John Simon for 1968's *Did She Mention My Name?*. He's survived several health scares over the years, but he continues to tour and record.

Joni Mitchell

If Gordon Lightfoot is the king of Toronto-identified singer-songwriters, then Joni Mitchell is most assuredly the queen, in addition to having been one of the world's most popular artists during the 1970s. Her watercolor voice, jazz touches, and innovative guitar tunings make her recordings instantly recognizable, and her inward-looking, seemingly free-associative lyrics define her as the decade's archetypal female songsmith. Among Mitchell's best-known compositions are "Both Sides Now," "Chelsea Morning," "Urge for Going," and "Big Yellow Taxi."

Born Roberta Joan Anderson in 1943, Mitchell spent much of her early childhood in Saskatchewan, recovering from polio. At a very young age she gravitated toward music, primarily country and early rock 'n' roll, and began singing in Saskatoon and Calgary coffeehouses before heading to Toronto in 1964. Her name change came via a brief marriage to folksinger Chuck Mitchell; when the couple split up, she moved to New York. Tom Rush, Judy Collins, Dave Van Ronk, Buffy Sainte-Marie, and others she met on the Greenwich Village folk circuit began recording her songs, and she signed to Reprise Records in 1968, moving to Los Angeles concurrently. Crosby, Stills, Nash & Young's 1970 Top Forty version of Mitchell's "Woodstock" defined an era, and her 1971 album *Blue* is a benchmark of the confessional singer-songwriter genre. In 2015 she suffered a brain aneurysm that limited her mobility.

The Mynah Birds

Perhaps the musical equivalent of somebody's fantasy football team, the Mynah Birds were fronted by future funk singer Rick James ("Super Freak") and at points featured Band friend Neil Young, his future Buffalo Springfield cohort bassist Bruce Palmer, and future Steppenwolf keyboardist Goldy McJohn and bassist Nick St. Nicholas.

Besides sharing a bit of the same time and space with Levon and the Hawks, according to James the group has another, more serendipitous connection to the eventual Band. Not long after he'd joined the U.S. Naval

Reserve at age fifteen, the Buffalo-bred James (born James Johnson) came to Toronto in 1964 to escape the draft. That August, the AWOL serviceman was rescued from a street fight by none other than Levon Helm and Garth Hudson, who took him to a nearby bar to decompress. There, he joined the house band for a few raucously delivered songs and was recruited as their new singer. The group soon acquired a manager in the person of mynah bird merchant Colin Kerr, who, seeking to boost his day business, dubbed them the Mynah Birds and had them dress to resemble the namesake creature: matching black leather jackets and pants, yellow Beatle boots and turtlenecks.

With Johnson/James by now hiding out as Ricky Matthews, the group made one unsuccessful single for Columbia in 1965, "The Mynah Bird Hop." In 1966, just after Young and Palmer had joined, the group was working on an album for Motown when the law caught up with James and the Mynah Birds scattered. After a year in prison, James briefly re-formed the act before beginning his solo Motown career. The James/Young/Palmer lineup cut several great garage/folk rock tracks that have since surfaced on bootlegs and reissues.

The Paupers

It's somewhat surprising that Levon Helm mentions this band when talking about the Toronto scene in *This Wheel's on Fire*: The Paupers are most strongly identified with the psychedelic movement that The Band had distanced themselves from. But there are a few parallels between the quartet and his own band that Helm must've appreciated. Like the post–Ronnie Hawkins/pre–Bob Dylan Hawks, the Paupers were led by a revered drummer: Skip Prokop, who also played with Mike Bloomfield, Peter, Paul and Mary, Richie Havens, and Lighthouse. Also like the Hawks, the Paupers were known for being professional and well rehearsed and were at one point managed by Albert Grossman. And as with many Toronto mid-sixties bands, they started out paying homage to both the British Invaders and their hometown hero Ronnie Hawkins. The Paupers famously blew the Jefferson Airplane offstage in New York in early 1967—and just as famously blew their big shot that summer at the Monterey Pop festival, thanks largely to their LSD ingestion. The band drew and charted well in Canada and released two albums before splitting up: 1967's psych classic *Magic People* and 1968's *Ellis Island*.

Richie Knight and the Mid-Knights

Despite the live popularity of Ronnie Hawkins and the Hawks, their singles never got higher than number eight on radio in the Greater Toronto Area. This group of local teenagers, however, hit number one on CHUM and CKEY with their very first single. Started in the late 1950s by singer Richie Knight (a.k.a. Richard Hubbard) and guitarist George Semkiw, the band played area dances and backed up visiting R&B stars like Jimmy Reed and Barbara George before recording the sax-wailing "Charlena" for the tiny Arc label in 1963. The song rose quickly on the airwaves, leading to a place on one of Dick Clark's Caravan of Stars shows at Maple Leaf Gardens, opening slots for the Rolling Stones, and more singles. The success of "Charlena" was pivotal for Toronto rock 'n' roll, as it inspired other young bands to cut their own records. Later iterations of the Mid-Knights featured two future Ronnie Hawkins sidemen, singer/blues harpist Richard "King Biscuit Boy" Newell and pianist Richard Bell, who would join The Band in 1991.

Robbie Lane and the Disciples

When the Hawks left Ronnie Hawkins in 1963, the businesslike showman didn't have to look far for replacements. Locals Robbie Lane and the Disciples became the new Hawks. Hawkins had been keeping close tabs on the aptly named teen group, who were clearly modeled on the Hawks, having installed them as the resident band upstairs at the Le Coq d'Or in his Hawk's Nest club (he would run up and down the house stairs between their sets and those by his own band to sing with both combos).

The Disciples were formed at the dawn of the 1960s and initially boasted the greatest of Robbie Robertson's young Toronto guitar imitators: the scorching Domenic Troiano (see above). They began releasing singles on Hawkins's own Hawk label in 1964, scoring a sizeable hit with the frantic stormer "Fannie Mae" (produced by former Hawks pianist Scott Cushnie; the follow-up, "Ain't Love a Funny Thing," was produced by ex-Hawks guitarist Fred Carter Jr.). Though Troiano soon went on to the Five Rogues, singer Lane and his group backed Hawkins until 1965 while maintaining their own, separate identity. They were the house band for CTV's *It's Happening* and released a few singles on Capitol before breaking up in 1969. A 1996 reunion album, *Ain't Dead Yet*, includes their version of "The Shape I'm In."

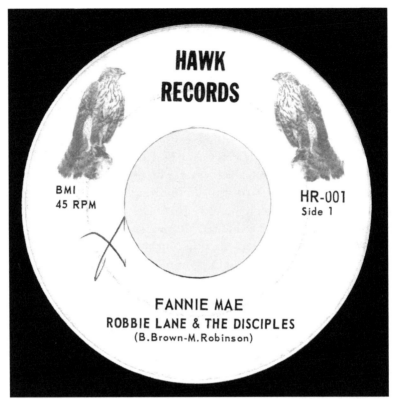

When Helm, Robertson, Danko, Manuel, and Hudson decided to go out on their own in 1963, Robbie Lane and the Disciples became Ronnie Hawkins's new backing band.   *Author's collection*

Buffy Sainte-Marie

Further testament to the richness of the 1960s Toronto musical culture in which the embryonic Band thrived was the graceful presence of singer-songwriter Buffy Sainte-Marie, who like Robertson is of indigenous North American descent. Sainte-Marie was born on the Cree First Nation Reserve in Saskatchewan and began performing at coffeehouses while she attended college in New England. By the early 1960s she'd made her mark on the Greenwich Village scene (Bob Dylan, Joni Mitchell, Neil Young, and Leonard Cohen were all early supporters) and had signed to Vanguard Records. With her high, haunting voice, Sainte-Marie was a favored head-liner at Yorkville clubs. In the basement of Yorkville's Purple Onion in 1964, she wrote her much-covered antiwar piece "Universal Soldier." Other signature Sainte-Marie songs include "Cod'ine," "Until It's Time for You to Go," and "My Country 'Tis of Thy People You're Dying." Her music has been performed by Elvis Presley, Janis Joplin, Donovan, Gram Parsons, and many others.

Jackie Shane

Jackie Shane was easily one of the most unique figures on the Toronto scene, especially for the early 1960s. A cross-dressing, unapologetically gay R&B vocalist from Nashville, Tennessee, who once sang backup for Little Richard, Shane was a top attraction on the Yonge Street Strip. He made a clutch of singles for the seminal soul label Sue, one of which, 1963's heart-stopping ballad "Any Other Way," went to number two in Canada. Backed by trumpeter Frank Motley's crack crew the Hitchhikers at his main haunt, the Sapphire Tavern, Shane recorded a storming 1968 live album that includes versions of many of the same R&B/soul staples covered by the Hawks and The Band ("Money," "Hi-Heel Sneakers," "Knock on Wood"). After 1970, he toured with blues legends Charles Brown and Amos Milburn before drifting out of the music world and into obscurity. For years Shane was rumored to have died violently in Los Angeles, but he was eventually found living and retired in Nashville.

12

We Are Gathered Here to Give a Little Thanks

Artists Who Influenced The Band

Duke Ellington, to whom Robbie Robertson is sometimes compared for his method of composing musical parts with specific players in mind, once put it like this: "There are two kinds of music. Good music, and the other kind." The Band was all about the good stuff. Lefty Frizzell? Motown? Both, please. And throw in some Bach as well. Within their catholic tastes, Helm, Robertson, Hudson, Danko, and Manuel gravitated toward specific figures, artists whose highly idiosyncratic work transcends their given idioms. In this chapter we'll meet several, with recommended anthologies of their music.

Hank Williams

Singer-songwriter and guitarist Hank Williams (1923–1953) is the most influential country musician of all time. His forlorn, nasal voice, his straightforward, slice-of-life lyrics, and his alternately shuffling or loping song tempos together provide the framework for contemporary country.

Williams was born in Alabama and as a child took guitar lessons from black street musician Rufus "Tee Tot" Payne, who greatly influenced his bluesy style. A reckless liver who wrecked his liver, Williams died from the effects of alcohol and drug abuse. His deceptively simple songs tended to be about universally understood topics like heartbreak ("Cold, Cold Heart," "Your Cheatin' Heart"), romance ("Hey Good Lookin'"), partying ("Settin' the Woods on Fire"), or loneliness ("Ramblin' Man," "I'm So Lonesome I Could Cry") and were popular with rural and urbanized-rural working class audiences. Williams's songs were easy to learn and play, making them

Considered the most influential musician of the genre, Hank Williams defined modern country music with his "lonesome" voice and songs about heartbreak and hell-raising. His songs were among the earliest ones that Levon Helm, Rick Danko, and Robbie Robertson learned to play.   *Photofest*

perfect fodder for musically inclined boys—especially the ones who happened to be named Levon Helm, Robbie Robertson, and Rick Danko. Recommended: *40 Greatest Hits.*

Sonny Boy Williamson

One of Helm's most direct early inspirations was Mississippi-born Sonny Boy Williamson (1912–1965; a.k.a. Rice Miller, Alec Miller, or Sonny Boy Williamson II; he took his name from rival bluesman John Lee "Sonny Boy" Williamson). Every weekday afternoon from 1941 to 1947, the vocalist/harmonica great and the King Biscuit Entertainers—guitarist Robert Junior Lockwood (an actual student of Robert Johnson and, like Helm, a Turkey Scratch native), pianist Pinetop Perkins, and drummer James Peck Curtis—played live on Helena, Arkansas, radio station KFFA's *King Biscuit Time* broadcast. Helm would often skip off to the KFFA studio to watch them. An eccentric figure with a gruff voice and an expressive instrumental style, Williamson toured the U.K. with native bands the Yardbirds and the Animals. In the spring of 1965, not long after Williamson had returned to *King Biscuit Time*, the Hawks almost became the next bunch of white boys to back him, after a mutually enjoyable post-gig jam session while they were in West Helena. Unfortunately, Williamson, spitting blood into a can between huffs on his harp, had contracted tuberculosis and died weeks later. Recommended: *The Essential Sonny Boy Williamson.*

Elvis Presley

At the dawn of rock 'n' roll, when all five members of The Band were forming their own first groups, there was simply no way *not* to be influenced to some degree by the man who would be called King. Rising up out of the South like a runaway rocket, Elvis Aaron Presley (1935–1977), to a far greater degree than any of his contemporaries, fired the collective imagination of a new generation, embodying a music and culture that (at last) belonged to *them* and not their parents. And beyond the phenomenon of fandom, Presley infected legions of aspiring teenagers with an urge that wouldn't be satisfied unless they, too, became rock 'n' roll musicians. His initial rockabilly sides for Sun Records and his early RCA material are essential foundation blocks of The Band's music, and without the world those songs created it's highly unlikely Ronnie Hawkins would have had the career that in turn begat their own. On The Band's version of "Mystery

Train" they channel Elvis as well as his fellow Sun artist Little Junior Parker, the song's originator. Recommended: *The Sun Sessions.*

Ray Charles

The impact of Ray Charles (1930–2001) on The Band is undeniably audible in the soulful singing of Richard Manuel, who was always forthcoming about modeling his style on that of the R&B genius. Singer and pianist Charles was born in Augusta, Georgia, and was blind from age six due to glaucoma. His classic early-1950s proto-soul hits include "Hallelujah I Love Her So," "Night Time Is the Right Time," and 1959's epochal "What'd I Say" (according to Band scholar Peter Viney, Helm once said Milt Turner, the drummer on the rhumba-spiked last track, was his greatest percussion influence). In the late 1950s Charles's music took on an easy-listening sheen, but his voice remained just as moving as ever.

The Band paid tribute to him with the unreleased early-1990s outtake "Nobody Sings 'Em Like Ray," and over the years, together and separately, they covered many songs associated with him, most notably the Manuel-sung version of the Hoagy Carmichael standard "Georgia on My Mind." Charles returned the favor, recording their "Ophelia" for 1980's *Brother Ray Is at It Again.* Recommended: *Anthology* and *The Birth of Soul.*

Hoagy Carmichael

Speaking of Howard Hoagland "Hoagy" Carmichael (1899–1981), the Indiana-raised composer whose tunes fill many a page of the Great American Songbook, is another figure whose music affected The Band's. Besides "Georgia on My Mind," the pianist and vocalist wrote or cowrote such immortal Tin Pan Alley classics as "Stardust," "Up a Lazy River," "Heart and Soul," and "The Nearness of You." His songs are known for their strong melodies and jazzy sophistication, the latter quality a byproduct of his early years performing in jazz bands with his college friend, the legendary cornetist Bix Beiderbecke. These qualities made Carmichael's songs incredibly popular via their hit interpretations during the swing and big band eras, so much so that he became a star himself, appearing in Hollywood movies like *To Have and Have Not* and *Young Man with a Horn.* Carmichael's influence is clear in several Band songs, and sometimes the titles alone tell the tale: "Jawbone" is musically and lyrically reminiscent of his "Lazy Bones," while "Rockin' Chair" recalls his identically named tune. Recommended: *Stardust Melody.*

Called "the Genius," soulful R&B icon Ray Charles was Richard Manuel's single greatest influence. Manuel's heart-stopping rendition of "Georgia on My Mind" with The Band was inspired by Charles's 1960 hit recording of the Hoagy Carmichael song.   *Photofest*

Louis Armstrong

Carmichael's "Rockin' Chair" was one of many hits for this universally known figure, perhaps the most influential musician America has produced. During his lifetime, along with being the leading proponent of the jazz music born in his New Orleans hometown, trumpeter and singer

Louis Armstrong (1901–1971) forever shaped jazz and popular music. His groundbreaking 1920s recordings altered jazz's focus away from its original collective improvisational style to emphasize solo performance: Not only was Armstrong a jaw-droppingly deft, endlessly inventive instrumentalist, he was equally a game changer when it came to singing. With his characteristic gravelly voice, he pioneered scat singing, the expressive technique that mirrors instrumental improvisation through the bending of sung notes and lyrical phrases. "Has there ever been a voice more unusual and more lovable than Louis 'Pops' Armstrong?" Robertson asks in the book *Legends, Icons and Rebels.* "Short answer, no." Any music with a Dixieland flavor has some "Satchmo" in it, and "Ophelia" and "Life Is a Carnival" are two of The Band's best examples of this rule. Recommended: *The Best of Louis Armstrong: The Hot Five and Hot Seven Recordings* and *Verve Jazz Masters, Vol. 1.*

Chuck Berry

Ask anyone with an awareness of music history to name the archetypal rock 'n' roll song, and for many, it can only be "Johnny B. Goode" by Chuck Berry (born 1926). Integral as Elvis Presley's early music is to rock 'n' roll, Berry's is arguably even more essential. As a musician, he created the elemental riffs and licks that make up the basic vocabulary of rock guitar. As an arranger, he retooled the galloping gait of rockabilly into the more easily danced-to 4/4 rhythm of straight-up rock 'n' roll. As a lyricist, he codified a checklist of all the signifying, teen-targeted tropes of the idiom: fast cars, hot girls, cool guys, mean teachers, boring school, and the liberating, life-giving beat of the music itself. The artists who learned to play and write their own songs through covering his—like "Maybellene," "Roll Over Beethoven," "Rock and Roll Music," and many others—include the Beatles, the Beach Boys, the Rolling Stones, and The Band (remember: Ronnie Hawkins and the Hawks' first hit was a rewrite of Berry's "Thirty Days"). Recommended: *The Great Twenty-Eight.*

Johann Sebastian Bach

Chuck Berry may have been on Beethoven to roll over and give Tchaikovsky the news about rock 'n' roll, but he left Bach alone. Perhaps he heard in Johann Sebastian Bach's (1685–1750) music certain unique qualities he admired, such as its innovative use of counterpoint, harmonic and

"Forty Days," a rewrite of Chuck Berry's "Thirty Days," was Ronnie Hawkins and the Hawks' 1959 debut single for Roulette Records.   *Author's collection*

motivic organization, and incorporation of styles from outside Bach's native Germany. Or maybe Berry just ran out of verses.

Whatever the story, Bach is to many the greatest classical composer of all time, and certainly the most prominent of the Baroque period. An incredibly prolific writer, he composed over one thousand works, among the best known being the *Goldberg Variations*, the *Well-Tempered Klavier*, and the *Brandenberg Concertos*. His tonally complex, highly ornamented approach influenced numerous later classical composers and even jazz artists. It also found its way into rock, most famously via the Beatles in the mid-1960s. It's no surprise Bach's music fascinated his fellow virtuoso organist Garth Hudson, who borrowed his *Toccata and Fugue in D Minor* for the intro to "Chest Fever." Recommended: *J. S. Bach: Great Organ Works* by Peter Hurford.

Little Richard

"Wop-bom-a-loo-mop, a-lop-bomp-bomp!" In 1955, Little Richard (Richard Penniman; born 1935) kicked off the atomic-bomb-as-45-rpm-single known as "Tutti Frutti," igniting the imaginations of millions of would-be rock 'n' roll shouters in the aftermath. Born in Macon, Georgia, the unstoppable piano-pounder had by far the loudest, hardest voice of rock's first wave, a blowtorch wail that's instantly identifiable. For all of the future Band members, life was never the same once they'd tuned into American radio and encountered "Tutti Frutti" and other high-octane Little Richard singles like "Good Golly, Miss Molly," "Rip It Up," "Lucille," "Long Tall Sally," and "Slippin' and Slidin'" (the last three became staples for the group). In *This Wheel's on Fire*, Helm recalled first hearing the explosive "Keep A-Knockin'" on his truck's radio in 1957. "I almost drove off the road to Turkey Scratch," he said, "because I was beating on the steering wheel so hard." Recommended: *Here's Little Richard*.

Bill Monroe

When Levon Helm was four, his father took him to see pioneering bluegrass singer and mandolinist Bill Monroe (1911–1996) and his band the Blue Grass Boys, an outing Helm said inspired him to become a musician. So it was likely also largely because of Monroe that Helm picked up the mandolin, a signature element of The Band's sound. Born in Kentucky, Bill began his career with his siblings Birch and Charlie in the Monroe Brothers; in the late 1930s, after that group had dissolved, he formed the Blue Grass Boys, who across their sixty-plus years included guitarist Lester Flatt, banjoist Earl Scruggs, fiddler Chubby Wise, guitarist Peter Rowan, Woodstock Mountains Revue banjo player Bill Keith, and fiddler and Band collaborator Vassar Clements. Others began copying Monroe's group during their 1940s heyday, giving rise to the bluegrass genre. His high, haunting vocals and fleet musicianship found a second wind during the 1960s and '70s folk revivals. Recommended: *The Father of Bluegrass: The Early Years, 1940–1947*.

Curtis Mayfield

Chicago soul king Curtis Mayfield (1942–1999) influenced The Band via his work as a solo artist and a member of the vocal group the Impressions, whose hits included "Keep On Pushing," "Gypsy Woman," "People Get Ready," and, as Jerry Butler and the Impressions, "He Will Break Your Heart" (beyond its title, Levon and the Hawks' "He Don't Love You [And He'll Break Your Heart]" has several audible similarities to the last tune). The Impressions' vocal style—Mayfield and his co-vocalists' practice of taking turns singing lead and harmonizing behind each other—informed The Band's multivoiced approach. But the more tangible evidence of Mayfield's effect on the group was his distinctive guitar style, which was liquid in feel and, shall we say, impressionistic. An avowed fan, Robbie Robertson has repeatedly cited his debts to Mayfield as a favorite guitarist, and the watery sound he sometimes dips into (see the beginning of "The Shape I'm In," especially) bears this out. Recommended: *The Anthology: 1961–1977.*

Bo Diddley

Another Chicago innovator who irrevocably altered the course of modern music and shaped The Band's methodology was this Mississippi-born rhythmic revolutionary. Guitarist, vocalist, and songwriter Bo Diddley (1928–2008; born Ellas Otha Bates a.k.a. Ellas McDaniel) pioneered the propulsive tribal rhythm known as the Bo Diddley beat. A version of his "Who Do You Love" was the Hawks' breakthrough single with Ronnie Hawkins, and with Hawkins they also cut Diddley's "Bo Diddley," "Hey! Bo Diddley," and "Bossman." Those and other driving, maracas-fueled 1950s Diddley rockers like "Mona," "Pretty Thing," "Road Runner," "You Can't Judge a Book by the Cover," "I'm a Man," and "Diddy Wah Diddy" were similarly inspirational for Elvis Presley, Buddy Holly, Jimi Hendrix, and most British Invasion bands, while the Hawks' John Hammond Jr. and Basement Tapes sessions likewise featured some of his tunes. Diddley's guitar style, a crunching, train-like technique using a minimum of chords, palpably affected Robertson's. Recommended: *His Best: The Chess 50th Anniversary Collection.*

Stephen Foster

Stephen Foster (1826–1864) was the most famous songwriter of his time and the author of many of the most recognized songs of the last 150 years. His more than two hundred compositions include "Oh! Susanna," "Beautiful Dreamer," "My Old Kentucky Home," "Jeanie with the Light Brown Hair," "Old Folks at Home" (a.k.a. "Swanee River"), and "Camptown Races," which today are mistakenly thought by many to be traditional folk songs— ironically so, given that Foster's music was itself influenced by folk music (as well as classical and popular styles). It's the wonderfully wistful, melodic sensibility of Foster's proto-pop-folk songs that's perceptible in The Band's music. Foster's period feel was also a natural fit for the Civil War–era aesthetic the group embraced early on. Recommended: *Beautiful Dreamer: The Songs of Stephen Foster.*

Muddy Waters

There were other giants who towered over the Chicago blues landscape—Howlin' Wolf, Little Walter, Willie Dixon, Otis Spann—but Muddy Waters (1913–1983; born McKinley Morganfield) is generally seen as the scene's top man and, to many, the most important artist of the entire postwar blues era. Another figure from the fertile state of Mississippi, the bombastic singer and guitarist was among the major early proponents of adapting the electric guitar to blues music, acting as a conduit, literally, between the acoustic Delta style and the modern age. His commanding voice and persona and scorching slide guitar made him an arresting performer and musician, and his rocking 1950s Chess records, such as "Mannish Boy," "Hoochie Coochie Man," and "I Just Want to Make Love to You," were massively influential on The Band, the Rolling Stones, Led Zeppelin, and the Doors, to name a few. Waters was a personal hero of Levon Helm, who proudly produced 1975's *The Muddy Waters Woodstock Album* and even named his dog after him. Recommended: *The Best of Muddy Waters.*

Booker T. & the MG's

Helm was also highly enamored of Booker T. & the MG's, who he considered "the best band in the country" and hoped to someday join. As the house band for Memphis soul label Stax, the racially integrated group—leader and organist Booker T. Jones, guitarist Steve Cropper, bassist Donald "Duck" Dunn (who replaced Lewie Steinberg), and drummer Al Jackson Jr.—recorded and performed with such legendary vocalists as Otis Redding, Sam & Dave, Wilson Pickett, the Staple Singers, Eddie Floyd, and Albert King. And alongside their reputation as a top-notch backing unit, the MG's (named for producer Chips Moman's British sports car) were themselves makers of hit instrumentals like "Green Onions," "Time Is Tight," "Soul Limbo," and "Hip Hug-Her." Cropper's sidewinding, string-bending style is heard in Robertson's playing, and it's clear why Helm dug the group's skin-tight funk grooves. Although the drummer's dream of becoming an MG never panned out, he did enlist the group to play on his 1977 *RCO All-Stars* album. Recommended: *The Very Best of Booker T. & the MG's.*

The Carter Family

While Hank Williams is the genre's most influential solo artist, "the first family of country music" is the Carter Family. The original trio of singer A. P. Carter; his wife, autoharpist and singer Sara Carter; and his sister-in-law, guitarist and singer Maybelle Carter were the first vocal group to become country stars. In the 1920s and 1930s the trio cut hundreds of top-selling records, which influenced the subsequent generation of folk, country, and bluegrass musicians and were later rediscovered by rock players like The Band. What made the Carters exceptional were their pure, heartrending voices, which were the focus of their sound, unlike those of earlier country acts; A. P.'s penchant as a writer and song collector (many traditional tunes would have been lost without his efforts); and Maybelle's astounding, unique musicianship—by simultaneously playing the melody on her guitar's bass strings and the rhythm parts on its treble strings, she created a style that's still being imitated. Treasured Carter Family recordings include "Wildwood Flower," "Keep on the Sunny Side," "Wabash Cannonball," and "Can the Circle Be Unbroken." Recommended: *Wildwood Flower: 25 Country Classics.*

Sam Cooke

It's easy to hear why Rick Danko was so taken with Sam Cooke (1931–1964). There's certainly something of the soul pioneer's smooth, tender croon in Danko's on songs like "Christmas Must Be Tonight" and "The Unfaithful Servant." Yet another Mississippi-to-Chicago transplant, Cooke was the son of a Baptist minister and started singing in the choir of his father's church not long after he learned to speak. By his teens he was working in gospel groups, eventually joining the popular Soul Stirrers, which is where Danko first heard him. With the Soul Stirrers, Cooke became a star on the gospel circuit, but, in a move unheard of the time, he ultimately left the scene to pursue a career as a secular singer. His second solo single, 1957's "You Send Me," topped both the R&B and pop charts, establishing soul's sacred-secular crossover sound a year before Ray Charles's "What'd I Say." Other Cooke classics are "Chain Gang," "Shake," "Cupid," "Twistin' the Night Away," and the Danko showpiece "A Change Is Gonna Come." Recommended: *Portrait of a Legend: 1951–1964.*

Cannonball Adderley

From farther south—Florida, to be exact—came alto saxophonist Julian "Cannonball" Adderley (1928–1975). The Hawks caught an early-1964 Toronto gig by Adderley's sextet and were strongly affected, not just by his band's hard-swinging music, but also by its "cool and collected" demeanor and finely tailored look; soon after that event, the Hawks adopted a sharp "jazzster" style that led Danko to refer to 1964 as their "Cannonball period." Adderley was a major player in the development of hard bop and soul jazz, and his music's strongly blues-based sound appealed to listeners beyond the realm of straight jazz—a swath that included rock 'n' rollers like the Hawks. The '64 Cannonball Adderley Sextet included the leader's brother, trumpeter Nat Adderley, bassist Sam Jones, keyboardist Joe Zawinul, flutist and future Band acquaintance Charles Lloyd, and drummer Louis Hayes, whose restrained chops were key for Helm. Recommended: *The Very Best of Cannonball Adderley.*

Buddy Holly

Given his lasting effect on popular music, it's easy to forget that the career of Buddy Holly (1936–1959; born Charles Hardin Holley) lasted just eighteen months and that he was a mere twenty-two when a horrible plane crash took his life. But as his songs prove with every listen, Holly was the composer of some of rock 'n' roll's most enduring music, hits like "Peggy Sue," "That'll Be the Day," "Rave On," "Oh Boy!," "I'm Gonna Love You Too," "It's So Easy," and "Not Fade Away" (the last was a long-running highlight of Levon and the Hawks' sets). Born in Lubbock, Texas, singer-guitarist Holly was also a music business innovator, producing his own material and via his excellent group, the Crickets, introducing the now-common rock band format of two guitars, bass, and drums. Holly's guitar sound caught the ears of Robertson, who at age fourteen met the Texan and asked him how he got it from his amplifier. Holly replied that he'd simply blown a speaker in the amp and decided not to get it fixed. Recommended: *From the Original Master Tapes.*

Bobby "Blue" Bland

Singer Bobby "Blue" Bland (1930–2013; born Robert Calvert Brooks) was a godlike influence among up-and-coming 1960s blues/R&B-fixated musicians on both sides of the Atlantic. Born and raised in the Memphis area, Bland honed his torrid, tormented voice and sex-symbol mystique in gospel groups and the city's legendary Beale Street nightlife district. After a couple of singles for Chess and Modern, he signed with Duke Records, where he hit his stride in the late 1950s and early 1960s. For Duke, Bland cut deep, sweltering sides like "I Pity the Fool," "Turn On Your Love Light," and "Farther Up the Road," tracks that established his soul blues sound by pairing barbed electric guitar with swelling brass. The last two were bread and butter for the Hawks (see the Helm-sung outtake of the last song, retitled "Further On Up the Road," and the *Last Waltz* version with Eric Clapton). Bland's tough-but-tender voice is evident in that of Richard Manuel, who continued performing his "Share Your Love" long after its *Moondog Matinee* appearance. Recommended: *The Anthology*.

Lee Allen

Garth Hudson has credited "honkers and shouters"—slang for saxophonists and vocalists—with getting him into rock 'n' roll. One of his first heroes was Lee Allen (1927–1994), considered the archetypal rock 'n' roll/R&B saxophone honker by many. A key name on the 1950s New Orleans scene, Allen blew his mighty tenor on hits by Little Richard, Fats Domino, Lloyd Price, Smiley Lewis, Professor Longhair, Big Joe Turner, Amos Milburn, Band associate Bobby Charles, and others. The saxophonist also struck gold with his own instrumentals, most notably 1958's "Walkin' with Mr. Lee," an ebullient classic that features the piano work of Band comrade Allen Toussaint and defines the New Orleans sound the group channeled so well. In the 1970s and 1980s, Lee Allen recorded and performed with Dr. John, the Blasters, the Stray Cats, and the Rolling Stones. Other saxophonists whom Hudson has cited as influential include Coleman Hawkins ("Body and Soul"), Big Jay McNeely, Big Al Sears, Clifford Scott, Noble "Thin Man" Watts, Red Prysock, Sam "the Man" Taylor, Duke Ellington sidemen Ben Webster and Johnny Hodges, and King Curtis, who played on some of Ronnie Hawkins and the Hawks' early Roulette material. Recommended: *Walkin' with Mr. Lee* and *The Big Horn: The History of the Honkin' & Screamin' Saxophone*.

13

But He'll Go Down in the Shelter Late

The Basement Tapes

They're the Rosetta Stone of roots rock. The Basement Tapes, a set of recordings made by Bob Dylan and The Band in the Woodstock area in 1967, are perhaps the most mythologized recordings in the history of popular music. Rock critics have written whole books about them. Rock musicians of several generations have had their outlooks and music reshaped by them. And yet, paradoxically, the Basement Tapes are not, strictly speaking, rock at all. Mostly, they're a poorly recorded collection of obscure traditional songs; loose country, blues, folk, and pop covers; and sparse demo songs, many of which are hilariously bizarre. The better part of them were made in the cellar of a house in the middle of the woods by a bunch of guys with no thoughts of anyone else ever hearing their musical goofing around.

Some background. On July 29, 1966, Bob Dylan, we're told, had the Woodstock motorcycle accident that led to the cancelations of his upcoming world tour with the Hawks and all other appearances until further notice. But he still needed to work. He had a new family to support and he'd just bought a large house in town. And at the end of the day, he was a songwriter and a musician. Writing songs and playing music were not things he wanted to stop doing just because he wasn't making public appearances. Additionally, Albert Grossman had done well in placing Dylan's royalty-earning songs with Peter, Paul and Mary, the Byrds, and other artists, and Grossman was on him to write more songs, if only for that purpose.

Helm was back Down South and the other Hawks were hanging out in New York City, awaiting the now-scrapped Dylan tour. So what next, then? Robertson went up to Woodstock to help Dylan and Howard Alk with their film *Eat the Document*. Danko and Manuel visited in February 1967 to act in the movie, and Hudson soon followed. All of the men were smitten with the area. Its quiet stillness, easy small-town pace, and boundless natural beauty were the kind of deliverance they didn't even know they'd been missing during their loud, nonstop city and road life with Ronnie Hawkins and Dylan.

Early that spring, with Robertson and his girlfriend ensconced at Grossman's Woodstock estate, Danko, Manuel, and Hudson rented the house in western Saugerties known as Big Pink. There, they eased into a newfound scene of domestic calm, sharing in the household chores between hikes in the woods and football tossing in the backyard. They also began playing relaxed, mainly acoustic music on their own and with Robertson when he dropped by. Birds chirped, beards sprouted, and in the space of a few months, life went from a million screaming miles per hour to something reminiscent of a settler's homestead a hundred years before. And the group was loving it.

Itching to play and needing to placate Grossman with some song-plugger's demos, Dylan invited the four musicians over to jam and casually record in the "Red Room" of Hi Lo Ha. With Hudson manning a portable Ampex reel-to-reel, they began taping pretty much whatever they were doing—which was a lot. "We were doing seven, eight, ten, sometimes fifteen songs a day," recalls Hudson in *Million Dollar Bash*. "Some were old ballads and traditional songs, some were written by Bob, but others would be songs Bob made up as he went along. We'd play the melody and he'd sing a few words he'd written or else just mouth sounds or syllables."

However, for Dylan family life was still family life, and before long the reality of toddlers and toys running the house and other daily distractions dictated that the sessions be moved to the Saugerties basement that would give the recordings their name. Robertson and Dylan would drive over almost daily to Big Pink, where Dylan would write lyrics on a typewriter in the kitchen, take them downstairs, and set them to music with the others.

With Helm still absent, Manuel began playing drums. When the Arkansan came up to rejoin them in October 1967, he was amazed with Manuel's drumming abilities. He was also delighted to be able to switch off with Manuel and play mandolin, which hadn't had a place in the Hawks' or Dylan's electric rock 'n' roll but dovetailed perfectly with their new parlor-pickin' sound.

The musicians continued recording throughout the summer at Big Pink, where the bulk of the tapes were made, until vacating the premises in search of more living space. The operation was moved to Danko and Helm's new place on Wittenberg Road, where, after not quite a year of such activity, the

In 1975, to capitalize on the interest generated by the bootlegged Basement Tapes, Columbia Records released its "official" *The Basement Tapes*. While the Dylan-sung tracks on the Columbia version do come from the actual 1967 recordings, several of its Band-only performances were actually recorded later.   *Author's collection*

last of the recordings were made. When it was all over, there were dozens of rough-fidelity reels with well over a hundred songs and pieces of songs—unrealized sketches; reverent folk, country, and blues standards and doo-wop ditties; demented in-jokes like "See You Later Allen Ginsberg"; and embryonic renderings of eternal Dylan classics, like the two he wrote with Danko and Manuel, "This Wheel's on Fire" and "I Shall Be Released."

Recorded far from the neon explosion of the Summer of Love, the Basement Tapes, as they would come to be known, capture Dylan's most prolific songwriting period and a new beginning for his sidemen. Fourteen of the tapes' Hawks-backed Dylan originals were pressed onto demo acetates and sent to Grossman's clients, and several became hit covers: "The Mighty

Artist Bob Cato devised the surreal cover art of 1975's *The Basement Tapes*, (back cover shown here) basing many of the characters depicted in the photos on the ones mentioned in the double album's songs.   *Author's collection*

Quinn" for Manfred Mann; "This Wheel's on Fire" for Julie Driscoll, Brian Auger and the Trinity; "Too Much of Nothing" for Peter, Paul and Mary; and "You Ain't Goin' Nowhere" and "Nothing Was Delivered" for the Byrds. These demos were bootlegged and re-bootlegged and rumors ran rampant as fans dug for more unheard material by their reclusive sage and his cronies.

It's the Same Old Riddle: *The Basement Tapes* vs. the Basement Tapes

In 1975, Columbia Records bowed to demand and released the Dylan-approved, Robertson-supervised double album titled *The Basement Tapes*.

The gatefold jacket, designed by *Stage Fright* cover artist Bob Cato, features a photo of the whimsically costumed Dylan and The Band with a Fellini-ish circus of characters inspired by those in the songs—Quinn the Eskimo for "The Mighty Quinn," a woman whose tee-shirt reads MRS. HENRY for "Please Mrs. Henry." (The midget selling newspapers is likely some kind of a dig at Dwarf Music, the Grossman-controlled publishing company of Dylan's early material, with whom the singer had just resolved a lengthy dispute.)

The title of this "official" release is a bit of a misnomer. While the album's sixteen Dylan-sung songs do come from the actual 1967 Woodstock basement recordings, several of its eight Band-only songs, although written during that period, were actually recorded afterward and/or augmented with instrumental overdubs. Indeed, engineer Rob Fraboni, who worked on the album with Robertson, has stated that "Bessie Smith," "Don't Ya Tell Henry," and "Ain't No More Cane" were cut at the group's Shangri-La Studios in 1975. Even the "genuine" tracks, however, weren't the full, lost Dylan payload everyone had been waiting for, but instead were barely the tip of the goldmine. Miles of amazing material were still squirreled somewhere deeply away, where they would largely remain for decades, with only slivers leaking out here and there on bootlegs. In 2014, Columbia issued the walloping six-CD *The Basement Tapes Complete*, which bursts with 139 for-real, unenhanced, dirt-raw 1967 Basement Tapes songs that feature Dylan with The Band and come straight from Hudson's personal cache.

Questions of its "authenticity" aside, the 1975 Columbia *Basement Tapes* set is still an excellent listening experience, and The Band's tunes are a major reason why. Manuel's "Orange Juice Blues (Blues for Breakfast)," a *Big Pink* demo sonically embellished at Shangri-La, is a stroke of lounge-lizard R&B brilliance modeled on his main man, Ray Charles. The likewise libidinous "Yazoo Street Scandal," sung by Helm, was also cut at A&R Studios for *Big Pink* but left off the album. The ballad "Bessie Smith," written by Robertson and sung so sweetly by Danko, is a song that had been kicking around since the time of *The Band*, well after the Basement Tapes period, and Fraboni insists that the version on the 1975 *Basement Tapes* was newly recorded that year at Shangri-La (the same recording appears as a "1968" outtake on *A Musical History* and the 2000 *Cahoots* remaster). The traditional "Ain't No More Cane" (a.k.a. "Ain't No More Cane [On the Brazos]") is another 1975 recording, although one of a song the group had indeed been playing back in Big Pink (their marvelous versions with Dylan can be heard on *The Basement Tapes Complete*). Legitimately "basement" or not, this version of "Ain't No More Cane" is one of the group's most transcendent tracks,

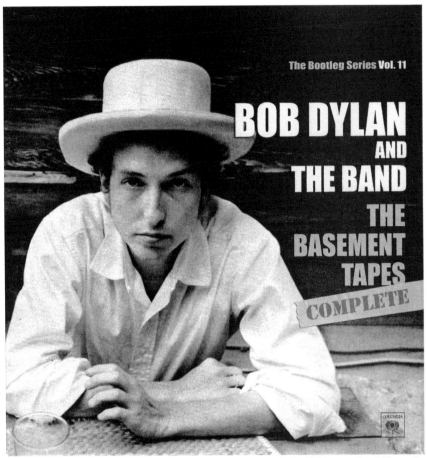

The *Basement Tapes Complete* box set released by Columbia in 2014 contains 139 tracks recorded by Bob Dylan and The Band in Woodstock and Saugerties during the informal 1967 sessions, many of them from previously unheard tapes in Garth Hudson's archives.
Author's collection

with Helm, Danko, and Manuel sharing in the lead vocals. The group had recorded the playful Robertson/Manuel song "Ruben Remus" twice in Woodstock, once at the failed 1967 Albert Grossman–produced sessions, and once as a *Big Pink* studio outtake; according to Rob Fraboni, the version on the 1975 album is the latter. "Don't Ya Tell Henry" and "Long Distance Operator" are two boisterous Dylan compositions. The Manuel-moaned "Long Distance Operator" predates even the Woodstock get-togethers, since Dylan had been performing it as early as 1965. The version on this album is a February 1968 *Big Pink* outtake. The only Band song here actually recorded in the basement of Big Pink in 1967 (although enhanced with overdubs) is the Manuel/Robertson composition "Katie's Been Gone." In the end, all of these songs are amazing no matter what their backstory, and the Dylan-sung songs on the set only served to make new myths about more hidden basement recordings.

So as fine a release as Columbia's *Basement Tapes* is, the case can be made that since it contains doctored and "false" recordings, it's not *really* the Basement Tapes. But then what is it, you ask, that makes the "real" Basement Tapes so significant?

Lo and Behold! Six Things That Make the Basement Tapes Important

When they were being made over the course of a few weeks in 1967, the Basement Tapes were nothing more than a duty to Dylan's manager and a series of rough reference exercises for the tapes' makers. An excuse for Dylan and his buddies to hang out, get buzzed, and have fun playing music. And when they were taping their casual sessions in Woodstock, any suggestion that what they were documenting would send out a subtle ripple and jostle music for generations to come would likely have elicited stoned laughter from the participants. These tapes were almost an afterthought, nothing that would ever be "important." But that's just what the Basement Tapes became. Here are are six reasons why.

The Sound of Dylan Influencing The Band

When the Hawks signed on with Bob Dylan in 1965, they were a hard-core rock 'n' roll band. Sure, several of them had loved country music when they were kids, but they'd left that "cornpone" stuff behind. For the Hawks, rockabilly and the raunchiest black R&B they could lay ears on had been the way. Folk music? Hadn't Dylan himself just publicly skewered that stiff old cow at Newport and roasted it on tour with the Hawks?

By his encouraging the group to goof around with him on songs like Hank Snow's "I Don't Hurt Anymore," Johnny Cash's "Big River," or Hank Williams's "You Win Again" and his own country-styled originals like "Nothing Was Delivered," Dylan reacquainted the Hawks with their country roots and recast the music in a new light that showed the hidden poetry in its noble simplicity. This key development carried over into The Band's pioneering of country rock with such songs as "Time to Kill" and "Rag Mama Rag." Perhaps even more revelatory to the five musicians was Dylan's introducing them to proper folk music via traditionals like "Bonnie Ship the Diamond" and "The Auld Triangle." Prior to this, they'd identified folk mainly with serious-toned singers like Dylan's ex, Joan Baez, and matching-shirted pop-folk acts like the Kingston Trio. But through Dylan the group picked up that these centuries-old songs and their descendants, pieces by Ian & Sylvia and Eric Von Schmidt, were in another way as powerful as anything by their rockabilly and R&B idols. The evidence for this is right there in folksy Band cuts like the high-seas-roving "Acadian Driftwood."

Dylan was also having a lyrical influence on Robertson, who had already soaked up the songwriter's epic-story style and penchant for biblical imagery via certain 1965–1966 songs; now Robertson was seeing such imagery created firsthand as a participant in the births of "Tears of Rage" and "This Wheel's on Fire." "The Weight" would not have come out of playing "Twist and Shout" in cold Canadian barrooms.

The Sound of The Band Influencing Dylan

The Band/Hawks were also leaving their musical mark on Dylan. He'd hired the group, of course, with the intention of helping to rip his music from the stunted trad-folk scene and drag it into the post–British Invasion present. Although he'd worked with bands on *Bringing It All Back Home*, *Highway 61 Revisited*, and *Blonde on Blonde*, those groups were made up of session players (the last album was cut in Nashville between dates with the Hawks but features only Robertson, who injects some boiling licks into one track, "Obviously 5 Believers"). Dylan hadn't worked with a steady band since his high school days and had developed his style as an unaccompanied solo acoustic performer. Working night after night on tour with the Hawks had reacquainted him with the feeling of playing as part of a collective that was able to think on its feet and move as one—which, after their many years on the road, the Hawks could do better than pretty much any band around.

His fruitful collaboration and comradery with the group led to their relaxed working relationship in Woodstock, setting the scene for him to try out song ideas that he wouldn't have attempted in the studio with the meter running (it's hard to picture him springing something like the gospel takeoff "Sign on the Cross" on a bunch of hired guns). Just as he'd reawakened the Hawks' interest in country music, their passion for early rock 'n' roll likely contributed to him revisiting the rock 'n' roll of his adolescence; hence the Basement Tapes' sense of youthful fun via an occasional Elvis or doo-wop cover.

And the wordy wordsmith was also being influenced by Robertson. "I played [Dylan] a ballad from the Impressions' *Keep On Pushing* album, 'I've Been Trying,' written by Curtis Mayfield," the guitarist told Barney Hoskyns. "I said [to Dylan], 'They're not saying anything much and this is killing me, and you're rambling on for an hour and you're losing me.'" Dylan apparently took this critique to heart, as the songs he wrote during the Basement Tapes are more compact and direct than his Beat-inspired odysseys of the preceding two years. Musically, the softer, acoustic-group style Dylan had developed together with The Band during their domestic Woodstock/Saugerties sessions shaped the sound of his next album, the pastoral *John Wesley Harding*, and to some degree, the one after that, the countrified *Nashville Skyline*.

The Sound of The Band Becoming The Band

Having survived Ronnie Hawkins's rock 'n' roll boot camp and the rigors of life as Levon and the Hawks and as Dylan's accomplices, in the Catskills the five musicians were suddenly free to work on their own material in a no-pressure environment. Playing into cheap microphones in Dylan's house and the acoustically challenging, cinder-block basement of Big Pink dictated that they listen more intently to each other to work out instrumental dynamics, and this, combined with the folk tunes Dylan was feeding them and their rustic, new surroundings, began to mold their music. "We would do it with [acoustic] guitar, mandolin, and Rick sometimes would just sing and maybe play along on a tambourine, and Garth would sometimes play accordion," recalled Robertson in the April 2005 issue of *Uncut* magazine. "Then, that instrumentation entered into other kinds of music."

The group began referencing the "stacked" vocal ensemble techniques of gospel soul influences like the Staple Singers and the Impressions. In his autobiography, Helm recalls the group's working up their rendition of "Ain't No More Cane" at this time as a transitional moment, in which he, Manuel, Robertson, and Danko each sang one of the four verses in turn and everyone joined voices to harmonize on the chorus, while Helm performed on mandolin, Manuel took up the drums, and Hudson played accordion. "With those multiple voices and jumbled instruments," Helm said, "we discovered our sound."

"Yazoo Street Scandal" is another pivotal Basement Tapes original. With Helm bawling over the top, the tune's shuffling, grease-dripping funk and

Southern imagery foretell "Up on Cripple Creek" and "The W.S. Walcott Medicine Show."

The First Rock Bootleg

One of Albert Grossman's acetates of the Dylan songs the singer and his friends had recorded during their subterranean sessions fell into the hands of Ken and Dub, a pair of enterprising, anonymous Los Angeles hippies. "Dylan is a heavy talent and he's got all those songs nobody's ever heard," one of them would tell *Rolling Stone* in 1969. "We thought we'd take it upon ourselves to make this music available."

And that was just what they did, taking seven songs from the disc to add to eighteen other rare Dylan tracks for a blank-labeled double LP they had pressed up in a plain white jacket and then sold, reportedly out of the trunk of a car, to L.A.-area record stores and head shops. The album, soon re-pressed with the rubber-stamped title *Great White Wonder*, started getting played on commercial FM radio by hip DJs. It got a glowing review in *Rolling Stone*, and before long it was itself being bootlegged by others. The murky mystique of the Woodstock Dylan/Band cuts not only fueled the rabid interest for more unheard Dylan material, but also led in quick succession to early clandestine LPs of material by the Beatles and the Rolling Stones and launched the entire bootleg industry.

The Birth of Lo-Fi

Today, it's very common for bands to record outside of a traditional recording studio. In fact, bands now frequently make entire albums in their rehearsal spaces or living rooms, and thanks to advances in recording technology, the fidelity is often superb. "Lo-fi" has gone from an aura of underground, cutting-edge coolness to a comparatively accepted aesthetic.

But such was not the case in 1967, when The Band and Dylan were recording on the fly using a low-tech, two-track Ampex 602 reel-to-reel recorder in the basement of Big Pink, with Garth Hudson juggling the engineering duties with playing the songs. This was at odds with the way records were then made. To make a record in the 1960s, you went into the clinical environment of a professional studio that was staffed by watch-watching, by-the-book worker bees. Of course, at the time Dylan and The Band weren't intending to make an album. They were just making rough demos of songs for Grossman to pimp out and playing for fun. But they found that the experience of recording in such a way—set up close together and moving at their own pace, not on the ticking clock of some stuffy, space-age studio—worked well. It fit their easy Woodstock pace of life and the handcrafted feel of the music they were making. So this was how The Band were now comfortable operating when they entered A&R Studios to begin recording *Music from Big Pink*. And it was why they quickly shot down that facility's method of isolating the players from each other and instead positioned themselves in a tight formation, with a minimum of acoustical separation, to cut the tracks as live as possible. For *The Band* and *Stage Fright* they took the concept even further, turning Sammy Davis Jr.'s pool house and the Woodstock Playhouse into ad hoc studios using gear they'd brought in. (Ultimately, their penchant for recording themselves would culminate with the construction of their own Shangri-La Studios.)

Not long after the release of *The Band*, other groups got it in their heads to make records this way as well; Led Zeppelin recorded parts of 1970's *Led Zeppelin III* at Bron-Yr-Aur Cottage in Wales, and that year the Rolling Stones used their new mobile recording studio to cut tracks for *Exile on Main St* at Mick Jagger's country estate and Nellcôte villa in France (the Stones were soon renting their rolling recording rig to Zeppelin, the Who, Deep Purple, and other artists). In the decades that followed, underground acts like R. Stevie Moore, Jandek, Sebadoh, and Pavement would embrace the kind of raw ambience and "imperfect" sound the Basement Tapes exemplified, helping to make the "lo-fi" (for "low-fidelity") approach a popular aesthetic in modern music. To any band today who decides to slow down and shack up with a portastudio, the Basement Tapes are your daddy. Make that granddaddy.

The "Old, Weird America" and the Birth of Americana

Writer Greil Marcus, a major vocal supporter of The Band, Bob Dylan, and the Basement Tapes, coined the phrase "the Old, Weird America" for the kind of esoteric, forgotten folk music Dylan was introducing his collaborators to in the parlors and cellars of Woodstock and Saugerties in 1967. Marcus wrote the liner notes for the 1975 *Basement Tapes* album and later penned a book named *The Old, Weird America*, which explores the sessions and their links to the pre–World War II recordings compiled on Harry Smith's influential 1952 *The Anthology of American Folk Music* (the book's title reprises that of an essay Marcus wrote for *The Anthology*'s 1997 reissue).

In his writings Marcus echoes Dylan's fascination with America's obscure, anonymously created, tradition-passed music by zeroing in on its inherent mystery and recasting it as a portal into the true history of American culture and a vessel of timeless truths. And of course, during the making of the Basement Tapes, prior to Marcus's observations, The Band had embraced this same new way of looking at old music. Many generations of roots rock and Americana acts modeled on The Band have since followed, and for these disciples the Basement Tapes will forever have a sacred place. They capture the exact moments when this revelation, this way of understanding and connecting with the always-living past, was hitting the five musicians—and the recordings' mysterious, long-shrouded allure doesn't hurt, either. The tapes created a consciousness that gave rise not only to the indie-Americana/alt-country scene, but also to the so-called New Weird America movement, which expands on the Basement Tapes' sensibility by fusing newer experimental styles with bedrock folk traditions.

14

Once I Climbed Up the Face of a Mountain

Band Landmarks in the Woodstock Area

E ven if you've never visited Woodstock, New York, it's obvious just from Elliott Landy's early photos of The Band: The relaxed pace and bucolic environs of the mountain town were nearly as responsible for shaping the group's sound as the earthy music they'd absorbed. But what may not be as clear to Band newcomers is that even before the arrival of Bob Dylan, the Hawks, and those who followed them there, the Woodstock area already had a long history in place as a supportive sanctuary for artists of all disciplines, musicians very much included. The area's close-but-not-too-close proximity to New York City continues to make it a relatively peaceful and easily commutable home base or weekend home for working Manhattan musicians, just as it was in early 1967 when the Hawks moved up from their (presumed) between-Dylan-tours digs in New York.

Sheltered by Overlook Mountain and other peaks and bordered by Echo Lake and the Ashokan Reservoir, the area was a favorite hunting spot and burial ground of the Esopus Indians. It was settled in around 1770 by Dutch farmers who'd been displaced from their previous home in what's now nearby Kingston by the encroaching English. Woodstock was formally established as a town in 1787, its agricultural economy augmented by gristmills, tanneries, bluestone quarries, woodcutters, and glassmakers. In the late 1800s, the town began its ongoing relationship with the art world by hosting painters of the Hudson River School movement. Boarding houses attracted groups of summering New Yorkers that included actors and circus people.

The early twentieth century brought the founding of the Byrdcliffe and Maverick art colonies and the Arts Student League of New York's summer painting school, as well as the permanent moves of many artists to the area. The concert festivals that the Maverick colony (started by breakaway Byrdcliffe founder Hervey White) began holding in 1915, along with the entertainment featured at the surrounding Catskills resorts in the Borscht Belt, helped create the climate that led to 1969's Woodstock Festival. (For those unaware, the three-day event, dubbed the Woodstock Music & Arts Fair, was *not* held here, although that was the original intention; it was moved by organizers an hour south to the town of Bethel at the behest of crowd-fearing Woodstock residents.) In addition to Helm—who made a point of "giving back" to the town he loved by playing at many local benefits during his final years—and his Band-mates, Woodstock has been home to such prominent personalities as composers John Cage, Henry Cowell, and Elmer Bernstein, comedian Henny Youngman, and actors Lee Marvin and Uma Thurman.

All the threads of the Woodstock backstory—the town's natural beauty, nearness to New York City, down-to-earth demeanor, and acceptance of artists and musicians—combined to make it just the right place, at just the right time, for the Hawks to redevelop their music and reemerge as The Band. And theirs is a story that continues to inspire musicians to forsake the insanity of modern urban life for a simpler existence in the woods, even if those woods exist only within the context of their music. In late-1960s/early-1970s Woodstock, everybody seemed to know everybody else, even across generations, which the nesting Hawks found refreshing after years spent playing sleazy dives. Simply put, without Woodstock and the lifestyle it offered them at the time, there may not have *been* a Band. "I don't think [The Band's first three albums] would have happened without it," Richard Manuel told the *Woodstock Times'* Ruth Albert Spencer in a 1985 interview. "I think this environment had a great deal to do with it."

This chapter covers some of the important sites related to The Band's halcyon Woodstock days.

I Ain't Got No Home: Woodstock Residences

The members of The Band and their close associates lived in several places during the group's early Woodstock period. Below are the major documented locations.

Big Pink

The best-known Band-related site, and one of the most famous spots in rock 'n' roll history, this pink-sided raised ranch in western Saugerties (just east of Woodstock) was built by a resident named Ottmar Gramms in 1952.

Woodstock Motel owner Bill Militello, who'd been putting up the newly arrived Hawks at his establishment, told Danko about the three-bedroom house at 2188 Stoll Road (today 56 Parnassus Lane) that was renting for $250 a month ($125, according to Helm) in early 1967. Danko, Hudson, and Manuel moved in while Robertson and his future wife, Dominique, shacked up elsewhere (see below).

Known locally as "Big Pink," the home became the combination clubhouse and musical incubator in whose cellar The Band and Dylan routinely got together to casually play. The rough, two-track recordings Hudson made of the spirited Big Pink hootenannies from April or possibly May 1967 to October of that year eventually emerged as the bulk of the Basement Tapes. Many of the original songs created by Dylan and The Band in the house—among them "I Shall Be Released" and "The Weight"—would be rerecorded elsewhere for *Music from Big Pink*. Several celebrated Band photos were shot by Elliott Landy at Big Pink, including the defining black-and-white image seen inside the LP cover.

In 1977, years after The Band's players had moved out, Big Pink was purchased by Michael Amitin, who rented it to classical music label and distributor Parnassus Records. In 1998 it was bought by Don and Sue LaSala, who run it as a bed and breakfast and have sustained its musical history by holding jam sessions in its fabled basement.

Byrdcliffe Arts Colony

On the southern slopes of Overlook Mountain, just outside the Woodstock town center, English industrialist and idealist Ralph Henry Whitehead, his wife Jane Byrd McCall, artist Bolton Brown, and writer Hervey White cofounded the Byrdcliffe Arts Colony in 1902. The three-hundred-acre community attracted artists, writers, musicians, and creative intellectuals to its grounds to exchange ideas, perform in its theater and barn venues, and work and live in its thirty-five rustic wooden studios and cabins. Although Whitehead's original self-sufficient utopian vision for the site went unrealized and the settlement was forced to sell off some of its property, a downsized version of Byrdcliffe still survives as the oldest operating Arts and Crafts–era artist colony in America. Some of the structures on what was originally Byrdcliffe land were built as traditional private homes, such as the ones where Dylan and Manuel lived during the Basement Tapes and early Band eras (see below). Byrdcliffe is open to visitors today for walking tours, performances, and exhibitions by its artists-in-residence.

Hi Lo Ha

Called "the jewel of the Byrdcliffe District" by a local realtor when it was offered for sale in 2014, Hi Lo Ha is on Camelot Road and was built in 1910 by the Stoehr family (its name is supposedly an amalgamation of the first two letters of Mrs. Stoehr's first name and those of her two daughters). Acquired by Bob Dylan and his new family in the summer of 1965 for $12,000 (the 2014 asking price was just under $3 million), the expansive Arts and Crafts–style estate—at the risk of this entry reading like a real estate listing—has glorious views and eleven lavish rooms. In a parlor of the house dubbed the Red Room, Dylan, Robertson, Danko, Manuel, and Hudson began meeting in late March 1967 to work out Dylan's new song ideas and play whatever music struck their collective mood. The reels that Hudson recorded on these near-daily occasions represent the start of the Basement Tapes period.

Thanks to the throngs of brazenly invasive fans who had discovered where their so-called spokesman was living, it wasn't long before Dylan moved on. In the spring of 1969 he and his family relocated to a more secluded farmhouse on Ohayo Mountain Road. Years later, Hi Lo Ha became the residence of Steely Dan's Donald Fagen.

Albert Grossman Estate

"The reason [Albert Grossman] first came to Woodstock was because my wife Shirley was told about a fabulous house that was available but cost $50,000, and Albert was the only person we could think of amongst our friends who could afford that then," artist Milton Glaser told the *Woodstock Times* in 2011. "Afterwards, Shirley managed to find a house for Dylan. You could say the future of Woodstock was set by these two events." Indeed, and they set the future of The Band as well, as those events prompted the Hawks' coming to town to be nearer to their musical employer and their soon-to-be manager.

Grossman and his wife, Sally, moved into this 1914-built home at 18 Striebel Road in the spring of 1964 (the road is named for the house's former owner, *Dixie Dugan* cartoonist John Striebel). The manager's clients were frequent long-term guests—Grossman liked to keep an eye on his artists—some of them living in rooms in the main house and some in the outbuildings located on the property. Robbie and his wife-to-be, Dominique (a journalist he'd met in Canada in 1965 while touring with Dylan), took a cabin here before ultimately finding their own place close by (see below).

Much later, author Neil Gaiman and his musician/performance artist wife, Amanda Palmer, lived in the home.

Robbie Robertson House

Robbie and Dominique Robertson moved from their temporary residence on Grossman's estate into this old, red farmhouse on Ricks Road in Woodstock. The property also has an outbuilding in which the group rehearsed.

Rick Danko/Levon Helm House

Not long after Helm arrived, the three-bedroom Big Pink began to feel a bit cramped. So Helm, Danko, Hudson, and Manuel decided to pair off into new dwellings. Once again, it was Danko who found the house, this one on Wittenberg Road just southwest of Grossman's and Robertson's homes. (Years later the property's driveway was rerouted to the adjacent West Ohayo Mountain Road, changing the home's physical address.) Known as the Cabot house, it had belonged to industrial designer Petra Cabot. Besides accommodating the rhythm section, the house served as the third and final Basement Tapes recording site. Elliott Landy's famous "Civil War" picture of the group was taken in the front yard. It was in 1968, on the serpentine, highly hazardous Ohayo Mountain Road, that the "a little too drunk, a little too high" Danko had the serious car accident that put him in traction and held up The Band's debut tour.

Garth Hudson/Richard Manuel House

With Danko and Helm and their makeshift studio ensconced on Wittenberg Road, the odd couple of the intensely cerebral Hudson and the withdrawn, self-medicating Manuel holed up in this house on Spencer Road (off Ohayo Mountain Road and above the Ashokan Reservoir; apparently road manager Bill Avis lived there as well). Previously one of the homes of the eccentric local artist Clarence Schmidt, who appears in *Eat the Document*, it was taken over by Woodstock transplant Van Morrison once Hudson and Manuel had left.

Richard Manuel House

Manuel briefly resided in this white clapboard house on Bellows Lane, which is just off Lower Byrdcliffe Road. The still-unpaved road is named for the home's original occupant, Ashcan School painter George Bellows, who lived there in the 1920s. Manuel wrote "Whispering Pines" here.

Shufelt-Fallon House

After he moved out of the Wittenberg Road house he'd shared with Helm (see above), Danko rented this house on West Hurley-Zena Road, which had been used as a post office in the early 1900s. Elliott Landy's Brown Album back-cover image of The Band crammed into the basement with their instruments was taken here, and the group would sometimes rehearse upstairs (there's a shot inside the LP's gatefold cover of Robertson and Helm jamming in one the rooms).

I Can Hear Something Callin' on Me: Other Recording Sites

Besides Big Pink and the other spots where the Basement Tapes were made, there were more locations where The Band recorded. Here are the three most significant.

Woodstock Playhouse

Located at 103 Mill Hill Road, this six-hundred-seat theater was where The Band recorded *Stage Fright* in June 1970. One of the seminal Sound-Out festivals (see below), this one featuring Richie Havens, Mothers of Invention keyboardist Don Preston, and others, took place here in 1968. The original 1938 structure in which *Stage Fright* was made was destroyed by fire in 1988 (arson was suspected) but the theater was later rebuilt. Besides holding concerts by Band friends like Noel Paul Stookey, Larry Campbell, Peter Yarrow, and Happy Traum, the reopened playhouse hosted performances by Levon Helm. When Helm passed away in 2012, approximately two thousand wake attendees were bussed from the site's parking lot to pay their last respects at his home/studio.

Bearsville Sound Studio/Albert Grossman Compound

The hamlet of Bearsville, in which Albert Grossman lived, was where he chose to build the self-contained headquarters of his entertainment empire. (The area's appellation is an Americanization of the surname of early settler and shopkeeper Christian Baeher; coincidentally, Grossman's nickname was "the Bear.") The centerpiece of the compound was the state-of-the-art Bearsville Sound Studio (commonly called Bearsville Studios) on Speare Road, which encompassed two separate recording facilities, Studios A and B. Construction on the complex began in 1969 and The Band was the first act to record there, cutting *Cahoots* in Studio B in early 1971; Bearsville was also where the live tapes of December 1971's Palladium shows were mixed down for *Rock of Ages.* An annex studio with residential suites called Turtle Creek was later opened in a converted barn on nearby Ricks Road (the Rolling Stones rehearsed there in 1978). Other artists who recorded at the various Bearsville facilities, many for Grossman's Bearsville Records label, include Janis Joplin, Bonnie Raitt, Randy VanWarmer ("Just When I Needed You Most"), Paul Butterfield, the New York Dolls, Foghat, John Sebastian, R.E.M., Phish, NRBQ, Alice Cooper, Foreigner, Peter Tosh, Patti Smith, the Dave Matthews Band, XTC, and others.

The epicurean Grossman also opened two restaurants on the creek-side former Peterson Farm at the intersection of Route 212 and Wittenberg Road: the tony Bear Café, where The Band reportedly ate almost every night for years, and the more casual Little Bear. On this site, Grossman client-artist and *Stage Fright* engineer Todd Rundgren also opened Utopia Video Studios in the building that now houses local broadcaster Radio Woodstock (Rundgren's Utopia Sound recording studio was in neighboring Mink Hollow). After Grossman's 1986 death (his memorial is on the property), the 240-seat Bearsville Theater he'd envisioned was completed by his widow. The Band played there in 1993.

Levon Helm Studios

Affectionately dubbed "the Barn" by its owner, this large, weathered-wood manse at 160 Plochmann Lane was built by Helm to be his home and recording studio in 1975 and rebuilt after it burned down in 1991. One of the first artists to record here was Muddy Waters, for 1975's Grammy-winning and

Helm-produced *The Muddy Waters Woodstock Album*, and among the other albums made in the stone-and-log-walled studio are The Band's *High on the Hog*, *Jubilation*, and *Jericho* and Helm's own *Dirt Farmer* and *Electric Dirt*. As of 2016, the Barn still holds the weekly Midnight Ramble sessions that the drummer began hosting there in 2003, which draw attendees from around the world to hear the crack Midnight Ramble Band and visiting guests like Los Lobos, Graham Nash, Jackson Browne, and others.

When the Music's Hot and You Might Have to Stand: Clubs and Cafés

Nature wasn't the only thing that attracted the Hawks to Woodstock. The town's small but healthy music scene was certainly part of the draw, and of course it blossomed during The Band's tenure. Here are some of the area's popular live venues.

Deanie's

For The Band and their fellow 1960s/'70s Woodstock scenesters, Deanie's bar and restaurant was the center of the local nightlife. "Known From Coast To Coast," according to its sign, the rambling structure at 109 Mill Hill Road was built as a boarding house by Civil War veteran Aaron Risely and had several lives (one as Ulster County's first gay bar, the Townhouse) before Allen "Deanie" Elwyn, who was descended from a family of pioneering local hoteliers, made it the new location for an eatery he'd begun in a converted trolley car. For years the bistro had a cocktail pianist, Odell "Flo" Scism, and reportedly drew a straighter early-evening crowd for its great dinners (the trout was caught right from a nearby stream). But it was also a center of jam sessions and late-night debauchery when Danko, Helm, Manuel, Paul Butterfield, and other rowdies were holding court and downing "Go Fasters" (two shots vodka, one shot cherry brandy, and a lemon wedge, filled out with club soda or 7-Up).

A fire in the late '70s saw Deanie's move up the road, but by most accounts the new location lacked the quality and atmosphere of its predecessor. The Band-era Deanie's site, at the intersection of Mill Hill Road and Route 375 (a.k.a. Levon Helm Memorial Boulevard), now houses another restaurant, Cucina.

Café Espresso

Originally called the Nook, this small, two-story building at the corner of Tinker Street and Tannery Brook Road was reopened by Bernard Paturel and his wife, Mary Lou, in 1962 as the Café Espresso. Its cozy (about fifty seats), street-level room quickly became the crucible of the modern Woodstock music scene when its booking agent, Woodstock Folk Festival cofounder Billy Faier, began hiring folk artists like Odetta, Joan Baez, and, in his first forays to the town, Bob Dylan, who wrote songs for *Another Side of Bob Dylan* and *Bringing It All Back Home* while staying in the "White Room" above the bohemian café. From those lucky enough to have been there, legends abound of closed-door, after-hours song swaps at the Espresso featuring Dylan, Baez, Odetta, Phil Ochs, and others. The Hawks were Espresso habitués—Danko loved to play checkers there—and the coffee-house continued to host live music in its later incarnation as the Tinker Street Café, once Paturel had moved on to manage the Bear Café (see above). Today, this site is the Woodstock Center for Photography.

The Joyous Lake

Opened in 1971, this storied nightery on Mill Hill Road was the wildly partying center of Woodstock's live music scene for nearly a decade and the site of the first performance by the reunited Band. Over the years, Band members played "the Lake" in various permutations, and big-name acts like the Rolling Stones did "secret" shows here to try out new material when they were recording or rehearsing at Bearsville Studios. The wood-lined bar and restaurant also presented the likes of Talking Heads, Phish, Charles Mingus, Who bassist John Entwistle, Rolling Stones guitarist Mick Taylor, Muddy Waters, Taj Mahal, Bonnie Raitt, Pat Metheny, and Bo Diddley, who taped a live album here in 1977. The club was remade as a disco in 1978 but soon reverted to a live music space before finally closing down. New owners briefly reopened it in the 2000s.

The Getaway Inn

In the 1980s, Danko, Manuel, and Helm and their friends regularly played at this roadhouse on Route 212 in Saugerties. Two of the 1985 solo dates Manuel did at the venue (now the eatery New World Home Cooking) were released on CD.

Sled Hill Café

Another well-remembered Woodstock live music spot, this tiny coffee shop, bar, and macrobiotic restaurant opened in 1964 and saw sets and spontaneous jams by townies like Tim Hardin, Van Morrison, Paul Butterfield, Mountain's Leslie West, and, naturally, various Band personnel. The café was a major documented hangout of the group's resident wild men—Helm, Danko, and Manuel (neither Robertson nor Hudson went out much, it seems).

More Band Haunts and Hangouts

As we've seen, for several decades Woodstock was abuzz with establishments that offered The Band and their cronies opportunities to down some drinks, grab a bite, shoot the shit, and pick some tunes. Besides the live-music joints mentioned above, in town there was the Purple Elephant Café, the Brass Rail, and Rose's Cantina; the Whitewater Depot was in nearby Mount Tremper. "The Watering Troff [on Tinker Street, later called Country Pie] was where I first laid eyes on Garth and Richard when I first visited town," says Tim Moore. "Breakfasts were at Duey's [52 Mill Hill Road] and the café at the Millstream Motel. Almost everyone came there—Van Morrison, The Band guys, Paul Butterfield, and Fred Neil were pretty much regulars at around ten-thirty or eleven." In the 1980s, Kingston had Uncle Willy's, the beloved site of shows by the reactivated Band, Danko and Manuel solo, Paul Butterfield, Happy Traum, and others (the bar closed and reopened later in another location).

Sleepin' Under the Stars: Other Key Woodstock Locations

In addition to the homes, recording sites, and music venues mentioned above, here are five other Band-associated local sites fans should know about.

Overlook Mountain

Tall enough that it was used as a navigation guide by early European sailors on the Hudson River, the breathtaking Overlook Mountain was also, according to historian Alf Evers's book *Woodstock: History of an American Town*, likely "a home to spirits and an entrance to the sky" for Native Americans. Composed of limestone bedrock formed by ice-age glaciers, Overlook is the southernmost summit of the Catskill Escarpment. A hike to its peak boasts incredible, boundless panoramas of the town below and hundreds of miles all around that can be heightened, literally, by ascending the staircase of its 1937 fire observation tower. An inspirational place for nature-loving writers like James Fenimore Cooper and Washington Irving and Hudson River School painters like Thomas Cole, it began drawing so many visitors that by 1823 a hotel, the opulent Catskill Mountain House, had been built on the mountain's eastern face to accommodate them (the hotel operated until 1941; today its ghostly ruins stand as a popular trailside attraction).

The stirring sight of Overlook, which hovers in the western vista above Big Pink's 3.9-acre lot, inspired The Band as well. Manuel, in particular, was moved by the mountain, composing "In a Station" about it. Perhaps the song's title and opening line allude to the depot of the long-defunct Otis Elevated Railway, which shuttled guests up the mountainside to the hotel in the early twentieth century.

John Joy Road

The intersection of this thoroughfare and Zena Road was the site of the front-cover group photo on The Band's second album. The road is named for farmer John Joy, whose son, handyman and stonemason Charlie Joy, worked for Albert Grossman and can be seen standing behind Bob Dylan on the cover of his 1967 album *John Wesley Harding*.

Sound-Out Fields

Also known as the Woodstock Sound Festival, the Woodstock Sound-Outs were a series of outdoor music festivals held from 1967 to 1970 that directly inspired local promoter Michael Lang to stage the better-known 1969 festival that shares the town's name. Conceived by Sled Hill Café manager John "Jocko" Moffitt, the early Sound-Outs were held near the intersection of Route 212 and Glasco Turnpike, on a farm just over the town line in Saugerties. At first, the informal concerts featured mainly local players like Tim Hardin, the Blues Magoos, Major Wiley, Billy Batson, and Richie Havens. But soon word spread about their unique vibe and beautiful open-air setting (one event was held indoors, at the Woodstock Playhouse), and the promoters began adding such internationally known acts as Procol Harum, the Soft Machine, and the Flying Burrito Brothers. While The Band aren't known to have performed at the Sound-Outs, they regularly attended them.

The Woodstock Sound-Out festivals, held in the town of Saugerties, directly inspired the better-known 1969 Woodstock Festival.   *Courtesy of Harold Swart*

Woodstock Village Green

The geographical nexus of the Town of Woodstock, this small grassy plot has long held concerts by area and visiting musicians, including several famous shows by Helm and his bands. The green was also the site where, at the drummer's behest, his hero Muddy Waters was presented with the key to the town (as depicted on the cover of *The Muddy Waters Woodstock Album*). In 2011, when Band friends Happy Traum and his brother Artie were recognized here for their contributions to Woodstock culture, Helm chauffeured Artie's widow, Beverly Traum, and Happy to the event in a Camaro convertible.

Woodstock Cemetery

This suitably peaceful country cemetery, accessible from Rock City Road in the center of Woodstock, is the final resting place of Rick Danko and Levon Helm, who are buried close together. Some notation from The Band's "Life Is a Carnival" is printed on the wall behind Helm's grave. (Richard Manuel is entombed in Avondale Cemetery in his hometown of Stratford, Ontario, Canada.)

15

If the Good Times Get You Through

Woodstock Musicians and Figures of the 1960s and 1970s

It's hard to imagine a time in Woodstock when the town and its environs weren't flourishing with music. In the spring and summer especially, music just seems to flow like the post-winter mountain runoff that fills the burbling creeks and brooks of the Catskills. Cover bands play the handful of local bars on weekends, coffee joints host open mics and folksingers, and bigger indie and classic rock acts visit the Bearsville Theater. Crusty steampunks strum banjos at the summer flea market as graying, ponytailed hippies beat their bongos on the village green. And thanks in part to the local fund-raising concerts Levon Helm played, the town's high school continues its music and arts programs.

Even before the early-1960s arrival of the folk musicians who led The Band and Bob Dylan to Woodstock, there was a music scene long in place. The Maverick chamber concert series, which clocked its one hundredth summer in 2015, attracted composers like Aaron Copland, Benjamin Britten, and John Cage. But with the town being thrust onto the world stage by its links to the Woodstock Festival, Dylan's residency, and the success of The Band's early albums, the scene swelled even further, and it has been growing and changing ever since. For a sense of The Band's community, here are some of the other musicians and figures with whom the group shared the hills, hollows, and hamlets of Woodstock.

Eric Andersen

Known for penning two of the most enduring standards of the modern folk era, "Thirsty Boots" and "Violets of Dawn," Pittsburgh-born singer-songwriter Eric Andersen made his name during the early 1960s in the coffeehouses of Massachusetts, San Francisco, and Greenwich Village before coming to Woodstock in the mid-1970s. The poetic, tender-voiced Andersen's most cherished albums are 1966's acoustic *'Bout Changes & Things* (not to be confused with the following year's electric *'Bout Changes & Things, Take 2*) and 1972's epic *Blue River*. The only solo acoustic act on 1970's Festival Express tour with The Band and others, he later recorded bonus tracks with Rick Danko and Garth Hudson for his unearthed 1972 album *Stages: The Lost Album* and formed a trio with Danko and Norwegian singer Jonas Fjeld.

Elizabeth Barraclough

Managed by Albert Grossman, this New Mexico–reared singer-songwriter cut two albums for the svengali's Bearsville label and had a low-level hit with her 1978 single "Covered Up in Aces." Barraclough was the longtime girlfriend of Band buddy Paul Butterfield and sometimes performed with Danko, Helm, Manuel, and Hudson.

The Bauls of Bengal

Easily the most exotic act in Albert Grossman's stable, the Bauls of Bengal were a family of immigrant gypsy street musicians the manager had met while visiting India. Two of them, brothers Luxman and Purna Das, can be seen standing with handyman Charlie Joy behind Bob Dylan on the cover of Dylan's *John Wesley Harding*. Tapes that Hudson recorded of the troupe playing in the basement of Big Pink were later released as *Bengali Bauls at Big Pink*, and Purna plays on Hudson's 2001 album *The Sea to the North*. Director Howard Alk's 1971 documentary *Luxman Baul's Movie* features narration by Band comrade Sally Grossman.

The Blues Magoos

These garage rock legends were headliners at the Woodstock Sound-Outs in 1968 and dominated both the local and Greenwich Village club scenes of the day. The Bronx-born quintet was formed by singer-guitarist "Peppy" Castro and organist-singer Ralph Scala in 1964; lead guitarist Michael Esposito joined in 1965. Their 1966 single "We Ain't Got Nothin' Yet" was a worldwide smash, and the title of their debut album, *Psychedelic Lollipop*, was one of rock's first commercial usages of the term "psychedelic." The Magoos wore pulsating, electrically lit suits onstage, toured with the Who and Herman's Hermits, and have influenced acts ranging from Pink Floyd to the Dead Kennedys. The band broke up in 1970 but was re-formed by Castro and Scala in 2008. Scala's wife, guitarist Beki Brindle, played with Danko, Manuel, and others.

Paul Butterfield

One of the most important figures in the evolution of modern blues and blues rock, fiery harmonica player and vocalist Paul Butterfield stands close behind Bob Dylan and The Band on the list of iconic Woodstock musicians. As he sang in the title refrain of his most famous track, Butterfield was born

With the Paul Butterfield Blues Band, singer and harmonica player Paul Butterfield helped take authentic electric blues from the gritty barrooms of Southside Chicago to a much wider audience. A close friend of The Band and a client of their manager Albert Grossman, Butterfield lived for years in Woodstock, where he collaborated and socialized with the group and other musicians.   *Getty Images*

in Chicago. There, he fell in love with electric blues via performances by Muddy Waters, Howlin' Wolf, Little Walter, and other local immortals. In 1963 he formed the interracial Paul Butterfield Blues Band, which included legendary guitarist Mike Bloomfield and brought electric Chicago blues to a new generation of young enthusiasts; Bloomfield and other band members backed Bob Dylan for his controversial "electric" set at 1965's Newport Folk Festival.

After making six albums for Elektra and performing at the 1969 Woodstock festival, Butterfield, who'd met the Hawks in Chicago years before, broke up his band and moved to town. He formed a new group, Paul Butterfield's Better Days, and became a regular collaborator with The Band. In *The Last Waltz*, the blues harpist can be seen tearing it up on "Mystery Train" and backing Muddy Waters with the group. He played on 1975's Helm-produced *The Muddy Waters Woodstock Album* and appears on the drummer's 1977 *RCO All-Stars* album. Butterfield cut two solo LPs for Bearsville (1976's *Put It in Your Ear* features Levon Helm and Garth Hudson) and toured with Rick Danko in 1979 and with Danko and Richard Manuel in the early 1980s. He died of a heroin overdose in 1987.

Cindy Cashdollar

This Grammy-winning steel guitar virtuoso is one of the few well-known Woodstock musicians who were actually born in the town, where she honed her formidable western swing/bluegrass/roots-rock chops while jamming with Danko, Helm's Woodstock All-Stars, and others. Cashdollar spent twenty-three years in Austin, Texas, eight of them as a member of Lone Star legends Asleep at the Wheel, before returning to her hometown. She's also toured and performed with Leon Redbone, Ryan Adams, and her fellow erstwhile Woodstockers Bob Dylan and Van Morrison.

Cat Mother & the All-Night Newsboys

Like the Blues Magoos, these guys were a New York band who moved up to the Woodstock area and performed at the Sound-Outs. The proto–country rock outfit was handled by Jimi Hendrix's manager, Michael Jeffery, and opened several times for the guitarist. Hendrix produced their debut album, 1969's *The Street Giveth and the Street Taketh Away*, which includes their sole hit, the 1950s medley "Good Old Rock 'n' Roll." Cat Mother supported The Band at the Fillmore East in 1969, and their violinist, Larry Packer, performed with The Band at the Last Waltz and on 1996's *High on the Hog*.

Bobby Charles

As the author of such iconic early rock 'n' roll/R&B hits as "See You Later, Alligator" (Bill Haley and His Comets), "Walkin' to New Orleans" (Fats Domino), and "(I Don't Know Why) But I Do" (Clarence "Frogman" Henry) and a recording artist for the Chess and Imperial labels in the 1950s, Bobby Charles (born Robert Guidry) was already a familiar figure to The Band when he came to Woodstock from his native Louisiana in 1971. Not long after his arrival, the swamp pop pioneer met up with Albert Grossman, who signed him to Bearsville Records for a fantastic self-titled album featuring Danko, Helm, Hudson, and producer John Simon. Charles sang his "Down South in New Orleans" with The Band and Dr. John at the Last Waltz (the performance, which is on the soundtrack, was cut from the film but can be found on YouTube) and appears on 1998's *Jubilation*. In 2010 he died of cancer, aged seventy.

Colwell-Winfield Blues Band

Another early headliner at the Woodstock Sound-Outs, the Colwell-Winfield Blues Band moved to the area from Boston following a tour opening for Led Zeppelin to promote their lone studio album, 1968's *Cold Wind Blues*. After they'd shared the bill with Van Morrison at one of the festivals, the singer hired some of the members for his backing band.

Karen Dalton

With one of the most hauntingly ragged voices in American music, folk blues singer Karen Dalton arrived on the Greenwich Village scene from her native Oklahoma in the early 1960s. Bob Dylan was an instant fan, admiring her Billie Holiday-esque vocal delivery and way with a banjo or a twelve-string guitar. Like Dylan, Dalton had ended up in Woodstock by the late 1960s. She made one album in 1969 for Capitol, *It's So Hard to Tell Who's Going to Love You the Best*, and one in 1971 for Woodstock Festival promoter Michael Lang's Just Sunshine label, *In My Own Time*. The sophomore set includes *Music from Big Pink/The Band* producer John Simon and later Band member Richard Bell on keyboards. Reportedly, the shelved Manuel/Robertson *Big Pink* track "Katie's Been Gone" is a paean to Dalton, its title inspired by her sublime version of the traditional "Katie Cruel." The singer, who never recorded any original material, battled stage fright and addiction, dropping out of music before succumbing to AIDS in 1993.

The Fabulous Rhinestones

Formed in 1971, the Fabulous Rhinestones featured ex–Electric Flag bassist Harvey Brooks, who'd played alongside Robertson and Helm at Bob Dylan's fateful 1965 Forest Hills and Hollywood Bowl concerts; also in the band were ex–Illinois Speed Press guitarist Kal David and ex-Buckinghams guitarist, keyboardist, and saxophonist Marty Grebb. The latter joined Danko's early solo group and coauthored songs that appear on The Band's 1990s albums *Jericho* and *High on the Hog*. Grebb also reportedly wrote and demoed songs with Richard Manuel during the 1980s, although as of this writing the tapes remain unheard.

Joe Forno

The proprietor of the local retail institution Colonial Pharmacy, Joe Forno seemed to know everybody in Woodstock and was liked by the majority of them. He was also the town judge who presided over a 1968 case involving Helm and Manuel; while driving drunk, the two had wrecked their cars within minutes of each other on Route 212 and then scuffled with the attending police officers. "All of 'em went in front of my dad that night," the justice's son, Joe Forno Jr., told the *Woodstock Times*. "He didn't know them, it was one of their first days in town. He told me the fine was 250 bucks. And he refused to take Albert Grossman's check, he didn't know who he was. We knew then he could handle authority. But he later became good friends with Albert and the guys in The Band." Indeed, Helm wrote that the elder Forno, who died in 2011, later became a personal mentor. In the 1980s and '90s, Joe Forno Jr. served as the reunited Band's manager.

Amy Fradon and Leslie Ritter

Still active on the scene today, the angelic harmony vocal duo of Amy Fradon and Leslie Ritter frequently performed with fellow Woodstockers like Todd Rundgren, John Sebastian, Happy and Artie Traum, and Rick Danko, who played on Fradon's 2000 album *Passion Angel* (her 2002 album *Small Town News* contains "Silver Wings," a loving tribute to the departed bassist).

Hamlet

Hamlet was The Band's dog. The large, black, curly-haired mutt had originally belonged to Bob Dylan, who gave him to Danko after he'd proven himself a bit too snippy around Dylan's young kids. Hamlet can be seen in several photos of the group taken by Elliott Landy during the Big Pink period.

Tim Hardin

Called America's "greatest living songwriter" by no less than Bob Dylan, Tim Hardin was the author of such constantly covered classics as "If I Were a Carpenter," "Reason to Believe," "How Can We Hang On to a Dream," and other songs that were hits for Bobby Darin, Johnny Cash and June Carter, and Rod Stewart. But besides being an exalted composer and a rivetingly sensitive, jazz-inflected folksinger, Hardin, an Oregonian who came to Woodstock via the Greenwich Village scene, was the archetypal troubled troubadour: a demons-dogged heroin addict/alcoholic who self-sabotaged his career repeatedly. He was on the bill at the 1969 Woodstock festival and was part of the gang of regular revelers and living-room jammers at the Spencer Road house shared by Manuel and Hudson. The influential singer-songwriter lost his battle with drugs in 1980 while living in Los Angeles.

Richie Havens

Forever known for his gripping, visceral performance of "Freedom" in the concert film *Woodstock*, Richie Havens, another Grossman-managed artist, and The Band were friends and mutual musical admirers who frequently shared bills. One of the native Brooklyn singer's trademarks was his singular way of interpreting the songs of others; his 1971 cover of the Beatles' "Here Comes the Sun" was a huge hit, and his version of "The Night They Drove Old Dixie Down" from the same era is likewise memorable. In 2010, three years before he passed away from cancer, Havens performed "The Weight" with the Levon Helm Band at the Newport Folk Festival.

Jimi Hendrix

Although Jimi Hendrix's music is worlds away from The Band's and there are no stories of him ever jamming with any of the guys (picture that!), he was a big fan of the group: In March 1968, he recorded a pre–*Big Pink* version of "Tears of Rage" in his hotel room after learning the song from a publisher's dub of the Basement Tapes (it can be found on the 2010 box set *West Coast Seattle Boy*). Mike Jeffery, the guitar god's second manager, had been living in Woodstock for two years when he rented the eight-bedroom Ashokan House estate to his newly signed charge following the June 1969 breakup of the original Jimi Hendrix Experience. And as the world knows, like The Band, the guitarist played for a rather large audience at Yasgur's Farm that August. By the following spring, Hendrix had left for England; by the following September, he'd left the planet.

John Herald

In 1959, John Herald (vocals, guitar) formed the bluegrass trio the Greenbriar Boys with his fellow New Yorkers Bob Yellin (banjo) and Eric Weissberg (fiddle, mandolin, banjo; Weissberg later found fame with "Dueling Banjos" from the 1972 film *Deliverance*). The group was massively influential on the Greenwich Village folk scene in the early 1960s, making successful albums for folk labels Vanguard and Elektra and packing Gerde's Folk City, where new kid in town Bob Dylan opened for and sang with them. Like many of his Village folkie peers, by the early 1970s Herald had ended up in the Woodstock area. There, he performed solo, led his own band, and was a member of the Woodstock Mountains Revue (see below). Herald's songs were performed by Linda Ronstadt, Maria Muldaur, Joan Baez, and Peter, Paul and Mary. He died at age sixty-five of an apparent suicide in 2005.

Howard Johnson

One of the top tuba players of his generation, Alabama-born Howard Johnson began his association with The Band when arranger Allen Toussaint tapped him for the horn section of the *Rock of Ages* and Last Waltz concerts. Also a master of baritone sax, bass clarinet, trumpet, and various reed instruments, he first rose to prominence on the early-1960s New York jazz scene. Johnson has worked with many big names in the rock and pop worlds (John Lennon, James Taylor, Taj Mahal); released albums under his own name and with the multiple-tuba-dominated group Gravity; led the house band of TV's *Saturday Night Live* during the 1970s; and appeared on the reactivated Band's 1998 album *High on the Hog*. A favorite sideman of

Helm, he served in the Levon Helm Band and Levon Helm and the Barn Burners.

Tim Moore

Singer-songwriter Tim Moore grew up in Philadelphia, where he played drums in Todd Rundgren's first band, Woody's Truck Stop. As a staff song-writer and session guitarist for Philly soul producers Thom Bell and the Gamble and Huff team, he met fellow staff writer Daryl Hall (later of Hall & Oates) and the two soon formed a band called Gulliver. The pair took a weekend trip to Woodstock around this time, and when Gulliver disbanded Moore moved up. He cut five albums for Asylum Records, the best known being 1975's *Behind the Eyes*, which includes "Rock 'n' Roll Love Letter" (later a hit for the Bay City Rollers). Moore jammed with the Rolling Stones and Peter Tosh at their 1978 Bearsville rehearsals, and his songs have been recorded by Eric Andersen, Richie Havens, Etta James, Art Garfunkel, and others.

Van Morrison

Irish rock's greatest poet lived in Woodstock for barely two years, but the bucolic spot made a deep impression on him, and his tenure in the town—along with those of Dylan, The Band, and Jimi Hendrix—cemented its reputation as a hip hub of music. The soulful singer became besotted with Woodstock during his first visit, in July 1968, and moved into the Spencer Road house formerly occupied by Hudson and Manuel with his new girl-friend, Janet Planet, in early 1969. Morrison played at that summer's Woodstock Sound-Out, befriended and jammed with The Band, and fre-quented the local clubs. By early 1971, however, the Belfast Cowboy, as he would come to be known via his drinking buddy Manuel's lyrical prodding in their tanked-up duet on *Cahoots* track "4% Pantomime," had split for the next hippie haven of Marin County, California.

Maria Muldaur

Before she hit with the smooth pop of 1974's "Midnight at the Oasis," Maria Muldaur (born Maria D'Amato) had begun her career in the early-1960s folk scene of her native Greenwich Village with the Even Dozen Jug Band (which also featured her fellow future Woodstocker John Sebastian; see below). In

1963 she joined the Jim Kweskin Jug Band, where she met her husband of several years, singer/multi-instrumentalist/composer Geoff Muldaur. While living in Woodstock during the early 1970s Maria became friends with The Band and played in the all-star Woodstock Mountains Revue. After relocating to the West Coast she returned to the area to perform with Helm at his Midnight Ramble events.

Van Morrison lived in Woodstock from 1969 to 1971, in a house once occupied by Garth Hudson and Richard Manuel. Perhaps "Van the Man's" most famous collaboration with the group, other than his appearance with them in *The Last Waltz*, is "4% Pantomime," his duet with Manuel on 1971's *Cahoots*.   *Getty Images*

Fred Neil

Doomed, deep-voiced cult folksinger Fred Neil is best known through others' interpretations of his songs. The most famous example is Harry Nilsson's version of "Everybody's Talkin'," which appeared on the *Midnight Cowboy* soundtrack, but other instances include "The Other Side of This Life" (recorded by the Animals, the Jefferson Airplane, and others) and "The Dolphins" (recorded by Dion, Tim Buckley, and Linda Ronstadt). The latter tune foreshadowed Neil's eventual rededicating his career from performing to working for the protection of dolphins in the wild.

Neil made one album in a duo with Vince Martin, *Tear Down the Walls* (1964), and four acclaimed discs of his own: *Bleecker & MacDougal* (1965), *Fred Neil* (1966), *Sessions* (1967), and *The Other Side of This Life* (1971). A former staff songwriter at the Brill Building, Neil moved to Woodstock in the late 1960s and became a jamming and drugging buddy of several Band members and their entourage. It's been said that The Band's "Stage Fright" was written about Neil, a notoriously reluctant performer, but this seems unlikely, as Robertson had plenty of grist for that tune within his own group. Neil eventually moved to Florida, where he died of skin cancer in 2011.

Bonnie Raitt

The daughter of stage musical star John Raitt, this vocalist and bottleneck-guitar queen attended high school in nearby Poughkeepsie. She started playing guitar at age twelve and discovered the blues early on, dropping out of college in Boston to play at local folk and blues clubs. By 1971 she had signed to Warner Bros. and become a familiar face around Woodstock, recording 1972's *Give It Up* at Bearsville Sound Studios. Manuel contributes harmony vocals on 1982's *Green Light* and Helm does the same on 1994's *Longing in Their Hearts*. Robertson jammed with Raitt at her 2000 Rock and Roll Hall of Fame induction, and to honor Helm's passing she was part of a star-studded rendering of "The Weight" at the 2013 Americana Awards.

Todd Rundgren

Soon to become a major artist in his own right, singer-songwriter and multi-instrumentalist Todd Rundgren was the up-and-coming recording engineer who worked on *Stage Fright*. Previously, the Philadelphia-area-born Rundgren had played with blues rockers Woody's Truck Stop and psychedelic/garage quartet the Nazz. He made his solo debut with *Runt* in 1970, the year he became an in-house producer/engineer for Bearsville Records, and during his ongoing solo career has explored pop, psychedelia, soft rock, soul, glam, art rock, and hard rock, as well progressive rock with the band Utopia. As a producer, he's overseen recordings by Janis Joplin, the Paul Butterfield Blues Band, Badfinger, Grand Funk Railroad, Hall & Oates, the New York Dolls, Meat Loaf, the Patti Smith Group, XTC, and others.

John Sebastian

The leader of the Lovin' Spoonful, whose rollicking, good-time hits like "Do You Believe in Magic," "Daydream," "Summer in the City," and "You Didn't Have to Be So Nice" helped define 1960s pop, singer-songwriter John Sebastian has lived in Woodstock for several decades. He was a familiar visitor beforehand, moving to town permanently after his notable solo acoustic set at the 1969 Woodstock festival. Sebastian grew up in Greenwich Village and began performing during the early days of the folk revival. He made one album with the Even Dozen Jug Band in 1964 and played with future Mamas and Papas members Cass Elliot and Denny Doherty in the short-lived folk rock group the Mugwumps. He and ex-Mugwumps guitarist Zal Yanovsky formed the Lovin' Spoonful in 1965; after the Spoonful broke up in 1968, Sebastian, who'd also worked as a session musician—he played bass on Bob Dylan's *Bringing It All Back Home* and harmonica on the Doors' "Roadhouse Blues"—turned solo, striking gold with the 1975 hit theme for TV's *Welcome Back, Kotter.*

Libby Titus

Our second Woodstock-born figure, singer-songwriter and actress Libby Titus (née Irene Jurist), was introduced to Levon Helm in the summer of 1968 via local novelist Mason Hoffenberg (1958's *Candy*). Titus was a waitress at Tinker Street's Café Espresso before splitting in 1965 for New York, where she had a son with her first husband, author Barry Titus. She returned to Woodstock when the marriage fell apart and met Helm, with whom she began a passionate, tempestuous relationship that lasted for much of the 1970s and produced a daughter, musician Amy Helm.

Titus has released two self-titled albums. The second, from 1977, features guest playing by Garth Hudson and coproducer Robbie Robertson. She has sung backup vocals for The Band and others, acted in films, and written songs with Burt Bacharach. Her own songs have been recorded by Linda Ronstadt, Bonnie Raitt, and Carly Simon. After splitting up with Levon Helm in 1976, Titus was Dr. John's girlfriend for several years. She eventually married Steely Dan's Donald Fagen.

Happy and Artie Traum

The tradition-toting conscience of the Woodstock music community, singer-songwriters Happy and Artie Traum first became good friends and pickin' partners with The Band during the Big Pink days. The brothers grew up in the Bronx, where Happy (born Harry Peter Traum) fell in love with American folk music via the early-1960s folk revival and took up banjo and guitar. He attended the "hootenannies" in Washington Square and Greenwich Village nightclubs, learned instrumental styles from Pete Seeger and blues great Brownie McGee, and cut the first recorded versions of "Blowin' in the Wind" and "Don't Think Twice, It's All Right" with his group the New World Singers. In 1963 he duetted with Bob Dylan on "Let Me Die in My Footsteps," one of Dylan's earliest recordings; he joined Dylan again in 1971 to sing harmony and play on a new version of "I Shall Be Released" and two other songs for *Bob Dylan's Greatest Hits, Vol. II.*

Artie picked up the guitar at a young age as well, following his older brother to Woodstock when Happy and his family moved there in 1966. The siblings were in the short-lived rock band Children of Paradise before concentrating on their duo act, which quickly became the toast of East Coast folk and signed a management deal with Albert Grossman. After making two acclaimed albums on Capitol, the Traums each recorded solo albums on which Band members appear (also see their 1994 "reunion" album *The Test of Time*), collaborated with other musicians, and were integral in starting the long-running Woodstock Mountains Revue. They continued to record and perform together over the years until Artie died of lung cancer in 2008. Happy released his seventh solo album, *Just for the Love of It*, in 2015.

Woodstock Mountains Revue

The Woodstock Mountains Revue was a loose, ever-changing collective of folk/roots-oriented Woodstock-area musicians that existed from the early 1970s through the early 1980s and recorded five albums of mainly traditional material (the first, 1972's *Music Among Friends*, was made under the group name Mud Acres). In addition to core founders Happy and Artie

Traum, lineups have included Paul Butterfield, Eric Andersen, Maria Muldaur, John Sebastian, Cindy Cashdollar, John Herald, banjoist Bill Keith, guitarists Rory Block, Bernie Leadon, and Arlen Roth, bassist Roly Salley, singer-songwriters Paul Siebel and Pat Alger, future Levon Helm sideman Larry Campbell, and many more.

Peter Yarrow

One-third of the Albert Grossman–assembled folk trio Peter, Paul and Mary, singer, guitarist, and activist Peter Yarrow was born in New York City but spent much of his childhood in his mother's cabin in Woodstock (where he let his friend Bob Dylan crash before Albert Grossman lived in town). With Peter, Paul and Mary, Yarrow recorded such massively selling early-1960s hits as "If I Had a Hammer," "Puff (The Magic Dragon)," "Leaving on a Jet Plane," and the Dylan breakthrough "Blowin' in the Wind."

It was Yarrow who lured John Simon to Woodstock in 1967 to work on *You Are What You Eat* and then got the Hawks to back Tiny Tim on its soundtrack, which led to the group meeting their soon-to-be producer. When the Hawks and Dylan were recording the Basement Tapes, Yarrow lent them some of Peter, Paul and Mary's audio gear for the sessions. Although their hits dried up with the end of the 1960s, Peter, Paul and Mary continued to tour and record until Mary's death in 2009.

The Trees Are So High: Other Woodstock Neighbors

By the early 1970s, you couldn't bump into a tree in Woodstock without shaking loose a whole nest of city-fleeing musicians. A small list of The Band's other creative neighbors at the time should mention jazz legend Charles Mingus, folksingers Jackson C. Frank and John and Beverley Martyn, singer-songwriters Tom Rapp (of Pearls Before Swine) and Jackie Lomax, and raga-folk guitarist Peter Walker, who recorded a live album at Helm's house in 1970. Other active bands included Children of God, Fear Itself, the Bummers, and Holy Moses, who featured Band crony Billy Batson and were slated to sign a Grossman/Danko production deal that ultimately fell through.

16

Could There Be Someone Among This Crowd

Ten Top Rock Acts Who Rethought Their Own Art After Hearing The Band

When it appeared in 1968, the subtle *Music from Big Pink* made an inversely seismic impression on the rock landscape. Many of the most high-profile, commercially successful names in the music world suddenly awoke from the psychedelic stupor of the preceding two years to feel hollow in the face of their lofty artistic excesses. It was like the secret key to making truly meaningful music had been right there in the soil beneath their feet the whole time. After The Band's arrival, musicians were inspired to reconnect with the Earth via the group's rich amalgam of American music. Here are ten of the day's leading examples.

The Beatles

The Beatles, who'd done more than anyone to popularize psychedelia with 1967's *Sgt. Pepper's Lonely Hearts Club Band*, were among The Band's earliest boosters and emulators. Parts of 1969's *Abbey Road* show The Band's influence creeping in ("Carry That Weight," indeed), but it's most audible in the gospel and roots rock of 1970's *Let It Be*, which was recorded in early 1969 when *Music from Big Pink* was fresh in the Fabs' ears. Paul McCartney would channel *Big Pink*'s and *The Band*'s organic vibes and the cabin jams of the Basement Tapes when he made *McCartney*, his home-recorded solo debut, in 1970. In the press Ringo Starr remarked how the recorded sound of Levon Helm's drums had inspired him—not knowing that Helm had in fact

Bob Dylan painted the cover of The Band's 1968 debut, *Music from Big Pink*.

Author's collection

based much of his damped-down sound on that of the Beatle himself (for all of The Band's being decidedly *un*psychedelic, *Sgt. Pepper's* was one of the few contemporary records they *had* been listening to). But of the four Beatles, George Harrison was The Band's most outspoken fan, calling them "the best band in the universe" and referencing their style across his solo career, starting with tracks on 1970's autumnal *All Things Must Pass*.

Eric Clapton

When Eric Clapton introduced The Band in 1992 at Bob Dylan's 30th Anniversary Concert Celebration, he remarked that *Music from Big Pink* "changed my life." Of all the cases of superstars who were affected by hearing The Band, Clapton's is, indeed, the most legendarily dramatic. In 1968, the guitarist, then in the enormously popular Cream, got hold of an advance tape of *Big Pink*. He took the tape on tour with him and listened reverently to it every night after playing virtuosic, high-volume—and, to him, by then unfulfilling—acid jams with Cream. He was blown away by and envious of The Band's ageless, unpretentious style, songwriting excellence, and tasteful musicianship.

Convinced of where he now wanted to go musically, Clapton broke up Cream and headed to Woodstock to meet The Band and try to join them. Awestruck, he was too shy to ask, so instead he formed the short-lived, similarly subdued-sounding Blind Faith before going onto the likewise downhome Delaney & Bonnie and Derek and the Dominos. Elements of The Band's music, especially Richard Manuel's song's, are clear throughout Clapton's solo work. In addition to appearances by all The Band's members, his 1976 album *No Reason to Cry* features guitarist Jesse Ed Davis, who had been inspired to play by seeing Robertson in Ronnie Hawkins and the Hawks.

Fairport Convention

Famous for launching the career of guitar genius and singer-songwriter Richard Thompson, British legends Fairport Convention did for their country's traditional music what The Band did for America's—and it was The Band that inspired them to do it. The Fairports were an American-styled folk rock band when they recorded a version of the Basement Tapes' "Million Dollar Bash," learned from one of Grossman's demo acetates. But after regrouping in the wake of a 1969 van crash that killed drummer Martin Lamble and Thompson's girlfriend, they focused instead on their own country's musical heritage and recorded that year's essential *Liege and Lief.*

"We were knocked flat by [*Music from Big Pink*]," recalled bassist Ashley Hutchings for *Uncut* in 2005. "It drew on so many different kinds of music. It really hammered home the very brave statement that old music can be new. A lot of people, even people of high stature, were in awe of [The Band]. Because these guys meant business. They weren't kids who'd come up with a few riffs. They had the authority of your grandad. And even Mick Jagger had to respond to that."

The Rolling Stones

Which Jagger and his bandmates certainly did. In late 1967, the Rolling Stones were riding the psychedelic wave with the aberrant *Their Satanic Majesties Request*. The Band's debut was released in July 1968, and by that March the Stones had shifted away from psychedelia and were making the sparse, acoustic-laced roots return *Beggars Banquet*, which was closely trailed by 1969's even rootsier *Let It Bleed*. Being devout blues disciples, the Stones had picked up on The Band's clear, sure knowledge of that idiom, and although the country influence that would crop up in the Stones' music is more directly due to their associations with the Flying Burrito Brothers' Gram Parsons, the country touches in The Band's output certainly held sway with them as well. Stones guitarists Keith Richards and Ron Wood both became close friends and jamming buddies of The Band.

The Grateful Dead

By 1970 the Grateful Dead had traded the long, strange trips of *Anthem of the Sun*, *Aoxomoxoa*, and *Live/Dead* for the easy, earthy winds of *Workingman's Dead* and *American Beauty*. Although the comparatively compact, folk-based music on the latter two LPs wasn't entirely foreign to the Grateful Dead—they'd begun as a jug band in the early 1960s—The Band's first two albums helped steer them back to their formative blues, country, and bluegrass influences. And the Canadian/American quintet's thematic focus was key for the Dead as well. "The [lyrical] direction [Robbie Robertson] went with The Band was one of the things that made me think of conceiving *Workingman's Dead*," Dead lyricist Robert Hunter told *Guitar World* in 2013. "I took it and moved it to the West, which is an area I'm familiar with . . . regional but not the South, because everyone was going back to the South for inspiration at that time." Live, the Dead would maintain their epically exploratory ways, but their later studio songwriting style stems more from their post-Band, country-rock bag than their earlier psychedelia.

Pink Floyd

Another band of psychedelic explorers impacted by The Band was Pink Floyd. On the surface, it may be difficult to square the British experimentalists' avant-garde space rock with *Music from Big Pink*'s songs about farms and frontier families. Yet bassist and vocalist Roger Waters has been emphatic about the Floyd's artistic debt to that album. "That one record changed everything for me," Waters told the *Dallas Morning News* in 2008. "After *Sgt. Pepper*, it's the most influential record in the history of rock 'n' roll. It affected Pink Floyd deeply, deeply, deeply. Philosophically, other albums may have been more important, like Lennon's first solo album. But sonically, the way the record's constructed, I think *Music from Big Pink* is fundamental to everything that happened after it." And almost twenty-five years after its release, Waters was still enamored with The Band, inviting them to perform at his 1990 Berlin performance of Pink Floyd's *The Wall*.

The Who

As with their above English brethren, one might think of the hard-rocking Who as being far removed from the influence of The Band's down-to-earth style. But as with those same British acts, think again. First off, the Who's mod roots are in the same R&B sources that make up a major segment of The Band's background. Pete Townshend, their main songwriter (and, like Robbie Robertson, the group's guitarist), being the conceptualist behind *The Who Sell Out* and *Tommy*, must have appreciated *The Band*'s cohesive "old America" leitmotif. The Who are known for their lyrical critiques of the music business and their place within it, so *Stage Fright*'s themes struck a chord with them as well (front man Roger Daltrey has cited "Stage Fright" as a favorite track). Perhaps the most overtly Band-influenced Who songs are on 1975's *The Who by Numbers*: the Danko-ish ballad "However Much I Booze" and the Cajun/country "Squeeze Box."

Led Zeppelin

The Who's heaviest rivals, and fellow Band followers, were the leading arena-rock powerhouse of the 1970s, Led Zeppelin. The quartet was formed by ex-Yardbirds guitarist Jimmy Page in 1968, the same year *Music from Big Pink* came out, and like the members of the Who, Page and his bandmates—singer Robert Plant, bassist John Paul Jones, and drummer John Bonham—had also been strongly shaped by much of the same blues, soul, and R&B artists beloved of The Band. They also picked up on the bluegrass and folk in The Band's sound, bending the influence of those elements back to the folk music of their homeland. Mandolin is a key component of acoustic Led Zeppelin tunes like "The Battle of Evermore" and "Black Country Woman," but it was Helm who had truly pioneered the use of that instrument in rock music; since *The Band* was the album all the hippest British musicians were listening to in 1969, it's very likely that Zep's mandolin use was inspired by Helm's. The British quartet reportedly covered "Chest Fever" early on, and their version, with Hudson-esque organ by Jones, is said to have eventually mutated into *Led Zeppelin*'s "Your Time Is Gonna Come."

Elton John

Rock's archetypal piano-pop balladeer, Elton John, and his songwriting partner, lyricist Bernie Taupin, openly replicated The Band's dust-bowl atmospherics on John's stardom-establishing early albums. His third LP, 1970's *Tumbleweed Connection*, most boldly references the group, with its country-gospel vocals, sepia-toned cover art, and old-time themes ("Burn Down the Mission" shares more with "Caledonia Mission" than just a word in its title). Although John's voice is closer in range to Danko's, it's hard not to think of the introspective Manuel throughout the ivory-tinkling Englishman's other early LPs. Helm's influence is prominent as well; see "Elderberry Wine" from 1973's *Don't Shoot Me I'm Only the Piano Player* ("Strawberry Wine," anyone?). The singer even named a song in the drummer's honor, "Levon," from 1971's *Madman Across the Water.*

Van Morrison

It's no accident Van Morrison was drawn to Woodstock and became a great friend and collaborator of The Band. With his band Them, he'd been through the mill of hard touring and pop-business machinations, as had the onetime Hawks, and was likewise seeking a calmer existence. Although his landmark, transitional November 1968 album *Astral Weeks* is more jazz-based and impressionistic than that summer's *Music from Big Pink*, its mellow vibes aren't that far removed from *Big Pink* cuts like "In a Station" or "Lonesome Suzie." The group's country soul influence is strongly detectable on the albums that followed, 1970's *Moondance* and *His Band and the Street Choir*, 1971's *Tupelo Honey*, 1972's *Saint Dominic's Preview*, and 1973's *Hard Nose the Highway*, and on snatches of 1973's *Veedon Fleece.*

Turn On Your Power: Others Who Were Influenced

At the same time as The Band's early albums were impressing the acts above, there were legions of notable up-and-coming artists also under their spell. In addition to establishing the Americana genre, the group's influence fostered several 1970s subgenres worth a mention. One is the laid-back country rock pioneered concurrently on the West Coast by the Flying Burrito Brothers and sanitized into AM gold by the Eagles, Jackson Browne, and Linda Ronstadt. Another is a sound now recognized as country funk, a swampy, soul-hillbilly hybrid exemplified by Band comrade Bobby Charles's eponymous 1972 album and likewise explored by the unknowns and big names heard on the Light in the Attic label's *Country Funk: 1969–1974* and *Country Funk II: 1967–1975* compilations (standout cuts include tracks by Tony Joe White and Mac Davis, and Jackie DeShannon's reverential version of "The Weight").

Along with the same 1950s R&B that the Hawks had purveyed, The Band was also a major influence on the mid-'70s British pub rock scene. Pub rock was a back-to-basics reaction against rock's move into arena-driven pomposity that paved the way for U.K. punk and launched the careers of professed Band fans Graham Parker, Elvis Costello, and Nick Lowe. Parker, who named his band the Rumour in a possible nod to the *Stage Fright* track, eventually settled in Woodstock, where he gigged with Rick Danko and recorded with Garth Hudson. Costello, who has named Danko his "absolute hero" as a vocalist, made 2006's *The River in Reverse* with Band arranger Allen Toussaint and guested with Levon Helm's Midnight Ramble Band. "I always thought The Band were the most convincing white band doing music based on deep soul," Costello told Barney Hoskyns. "They kind of invented their own version of it, almost by accident."

Lowe's early outfit Brinsley Schwarz was heavily modeled on The Band. "When *Music from Big Pink* came out, it was just so completely different from everything else at the time," Lowe told me in 2013. "When The Band played Wembley Stadium in 1974, they rehearsed at the farm we were all living on. We were just in awe. They left some empty bottles of Grand Marnier behind—which we saved on a shelf, as a shrine."

17

You'll See What They See Right Now

Photographer Elliott Landy

When most of us think of what The Band looked like, we think of the five grizzled frontiersmen in the stark images photographer Elliott Landy created for the covers of their first two LPs. The pictures have a feel that matches the music, showing the musicians who made that music looking exactly like you'd expect them to look. Nearly as well known for his similarly iconic photos that adorn Bob Dylan's *Nashville Skyline* and Van Morrison's *Moondance*, Landy was born in 1942 and grew up in New York. Besides having his photos featured on the covers of many prestigious magazines, he's published several books of his work. One of the most serendipitously perfect pairings of visuals and sonics ever to occur in the commercial recording medium, the uncanny union of Landy's lens and the time-tripping attitude of The Band's music was crucial to establishing the group's identity.

We Pointed You the Way to Go

In 1959 Landy graduated from the Bronx High School of Science, where his career in photography began rather inauspiciously. "I enrolled in the camera club, and the teacher who led it told everyone to bring in a list of all the cameras and lenses our families had at home," he says. "But all mine had was a [cheap Kodak] Brownie. I felt like I wasn't qualified enough to be there and thought, 'This is not for me.' I didn't pick up a camera for seven years after that."

When he did pick one up again, though, it was with the conviction to chronicle what few others were documenting. "I began wanting to stop the Vietnam War, and I tried to think of a way I could help do that," says Landy. "There were demonstrations going on against the war, but they weren't getting a lot of attention. There'd be, maybe, three inches of coverage in the *New York Times* and that was it. I started taking pictures at these protests that were going on. I went to the Associated Press and the big magazines, but nobody was interested in publishing them." His quest eventually led him to the radical hippie scene's burgeoning underground newspapers,

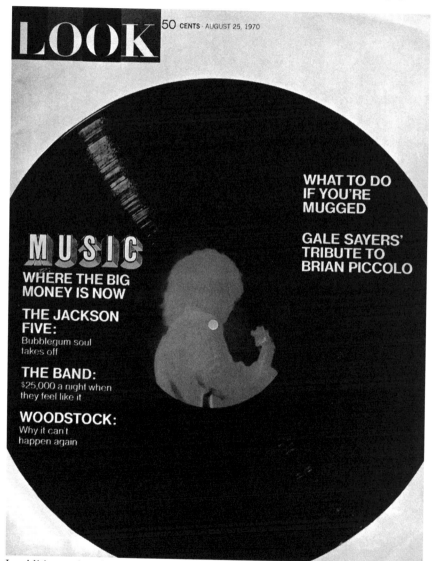

In addition to shooting the group for the classic covers of their first two albums, Elliott Landy photographed the quintet in Los Angeles for a spread in the August 1970 issue of *Look* magazine. (The cover montage seen here, not of a Band member, was created by Richard Alcorn and Dan J. McCoy.)

Author's collection

including the *West Side News* and the *Rat*. He soon became the photo editor at the latter, for whom he shot dramatic scenes of the era's heated antiwar and pro–civil rights demonstrations.

"Most of my education came from Lawrence Shustak, who was teaching at the Educational Alliance on the Lower East Side," says the photographer. "He was my mentor, and from him I learned the *attitude* of photography, more than just techniques." French street photographer Henri Cartier-Bresson was also inspirational. "With Cartier-Bresson, it was the total harmony of the composition that spoke to me," he enthuses. "His work is very simple but very emotional; it really creates a sense of universal experience." Landy's press pass allowed him access to movie industry events, where he began taking photos of screen celebrities like Marlene Dietrich, Darryl F. Zanuck, Elizabeth Taylor, and Richard Burton to sell to the mainstream press for extra income. But it also opened the door into another world.

Landy's credentials got him prime seats from Albert Grossman's office for the January 1968 Woody Guthrie memorial concert at Carnegie Hall starring Bob Dylan and the Hawks. The young photographer knew that getting shots of the elusive Dylan's long-awaited reemergence would be a major coup and he was, unsurprisingly, beyond thrilled. But when he got to the venue things didn't go so smoothly. "I walked up to the door with my date, carrying my cameras, and the guard stopped us, saying, 'No photos allowed,'" Landy says. "So I checked half my cameras and put half in my pockets and my lady friend's purse and we got back in line. I waited until Dylan came on and tried to shoot during the loud parts, because the camera I was using was pretty noisy." After being called out by one of Grossman's assistants, he managed to hand off the film to his companion before coming face to face with the singer's vehemently image-protective manager outside. "He started yelling at me, 'What are you doing taking pictures?' and I told him Bob Dylan's manager had said I could take pictures—at the time I didn't know *he* was Albert," says Landy. "Apparently, someone at this office had okayed it without telling him." After one of Grossman's henchmen had destroyed an unused decoy roll, the shaken photographer left with his date, the contraband film safe in her purse.

On March 6, 1968, after closing the book on the latest issue of the *Rat*, Landy was walking home and passed the Anderson Theater on Second Avenue. "The marquee said 'Country Joe and the Fish and Light Show,'" Landy recounts. "I wasn't sure what that was, but it sounded interesting. So I showed my press pass and they let me in." Inside, he was "hit by a barrage of color and sound" courtesy of the groundbreaking San Francisco psychedelic band and their accompanying light show. "The light artists were 'visual musicians,' manipulating the color projections along with the music; it was like they were another band behind the real band," says Landy. "I went up front with my camera and started to shoot."

Soon, he would be steadily immersed in documenting the exploding New York rock scene, photographing the likes of Jimi Hendrix, the Doors, the Who, and others at venues like the Fillmore East. "I loved taking pictures at concerts," he says. "To me, it was like advertising for the counterculture." A week after the Country Joe concert, he was back at the Anderson to photograph Big Brother and the Holding Company. Pleased with the results, he sent a few of the photos of Janis Joplin and her band to their manager Grossman's firm.

While shooting another Big Brother show, this one at West Eighth Street nightclub Generation (later to become Jimi Hendrix's Electric Lady Studios), Landy once again ran into Grossman. "He motioned me into a tiny room in the back of the club; I didn't have a clue what was happening next," he remembers. "He asked me if I was free that weekend to take some pictures in Toronto. I asked him of who and he told me, 'They're a new group, they don't have a name yet.' I said yes. Because Albert liked my work he was able to let go of what had happened between us at Carnegie Hall. He was being very gracious to me. That night, he also told me Dylan might be there for the picture. I felt my life going into high gear."

Went to the House That Brings a Smile

It turned out Dylan wouldn't be present for that particular picture, but there'd be other opportunities to photograph the Bard soon enough. Landy went over to meet Grossman's yet-to-be-named group at A&R Studios, where they were mixing the tracks for their first album. "The first time I heard The Band's music was the night I met Robbie Robertson and Garth Hudson to show them my photographs," Landy recalls. "After looking at my pictures in the hallway of the recording studio, Robbie took me into the mixing room and 'Chest Fever' was playing full blast through the studio speakers. It was really powerful, with Garth doing that long intro on the organ."

A few days later the Bronx-born shutterbug and producer John Simon had landed at the Toronto airport, they were picked up by his new subjects, "metaphorically blindfolded, since I had no idea where we were going," and driven ninety miles to the Danko family farm in Simcoe. There, on a sunny day, he took a wide-frame photo of the five young musicians and their

Photographer Elliott Landy was on hand to document The Band during the taping of their second album, in the pool house of a rented Hollywood estate. In this shot, producer John Simon leans over the mixing board as Garth Hudson assists with the engineering and Rick Danko, Robbie Robertson, and Levon Helm prepare to record. *Photo by Elliott Landy*

families—greying grandfathers in their hunting caps, wide-eyed, innocent grandchildren in their Sunday school best—all standing close together in front of a big red barn. Titled "Next of Kin," it would take up half of *Music from Big Pink*'s inside cover and send a powerful statement (unable to make the trip up from Arkansas, Helm's parents are seen in an insert shot). "The whole idea of the picture was totally unusual to me, because despite having a lot of relatives my whole issue at the time was to separate from my family," says Landy. "A lot of the 1960s were about rejecting old ways and family values and hating your family, all of that. But [the band members] were saying, 'We don't hate our families, we love them, they helped us get where we are today and we're grateful for them.'"

Then there was the matter of getting a portrait of the band alone. On Easter weekend, 1968, Landy drove up from New York and met the group at Big Pink. Over two sessions he shot rolls of them in the kitchen, around the house, and at several nearby wooded locations. But things just weren't clicking. "They said, 'These are good, but they aren't really what we're looking for,'" he says. One of the photos, taken of the five members' backs as they sit on a park bench next to the pond on the Big Pink property, seemed perfect, to Landy at least. "They wanted to stay almost 'anonymous' because they knew they didn't want to be locked into having a certain image or having to always play one certain kind of music—they didn't even want to have a name," he explains. "I felt then it really reflected the philosophy of who they were and what they were trying to do musically. But now I think it was a little too anonymous, perhaps." The image in question would eventually make it onto the covers of *Rolling Stone*'s August 1968 issue and The Band's 2000 *Greatest Hits* CD.

In May, Landy returned to Woodstock to try a third time. By then the group had moved out of Big Pink, and he was hanging out with Danko and Helm at their new digs on Wittenberg Road. "I'd gotten to know them more by then, and I saw how they had this 'old-timey' thing about them," says Landy. "I had a [Civil War photographer] Matthew Brady book, so I suggested we go for that look and they liked the idea. I looked at the form of Brady's pictures and thought, 'What is the mind space of the 1800s?' It was a big honor to be photographed in the 1800s. People took it very seriously and stood up straight and looked right at the camera, looking very dignified and standing very still because the film exposure was so slow then. We were sitting in the living room and I saw the perfect landscape, right outside the window. The Band guys were shy then, so to get them to liven up I asked a woman they knew who was there to take her clothes off. She did and danced around a little. They'd seen her without clothes on before, so it wasn't a big deal, but it made them laugh and I took a few pictures with her in them." Out of this relaxed shoot came the black-and-white "Civil War" photo of the group that appears inside *Music from Big Pink*'s gatefold, one of the most memorable images in rock 'n' roll. It was while working with The Band on *Big Pink* that Landy was introduced to Dylan, a connection that led to an exclusive *Saturday Evening Post* cover and that of *Nashville Skyline*. Later came Van Morrison's *Moondance* and other landmark albums.

Hey, Rainmaker, Can't You Hear the Call?

Every picture tells a story, the saying goes. But quite often the stories behind the making of the pictures are as interesting as the pictures themselves. Take Landy's iconic black-and-white photo adorning the front of The Band's second album. In the 1969 photo, standing left to right on Woodstock's then unpaved John Joy Road, the group stares blankly into the camera, looking raw and greasy. But that's not grease, it's rainwater. And it's likely the

Elliott Landy takes a rare self-portrait, circa 1969.

dampness wasn't coincidental. "I think we might have even been *looking* for rain," the lensman recalls. "I remember asking an art director I knew, 'Is there a way we can make it look like rain on them in a photo?' And the answer was no. Today, the technology exists that would allow you to do something like that, but back then it didn't." For Landy, however, the muddy tableau was a rare instance of him attempting to coax the proceedings. "I try to not manipulate people or things when I'm taking a picture," he explains. "The element of chance is very important. Of just going with the flow."

One memorable photo from the shoot shows Helm facing the other direction, a smiling Danko to his right. "They weren't happy about getting wet, and Levon, especially, didn't like posing for photos," says Landy about the rejected image. "He was probably bitching about it under his breath to Rick and making him laugh. We went over the pictures very carefully and I made eight-by-ten proofs to show the band, and everyone agreed on the one we ended up using for the cover." In a drier engagement, for the back cover Landy captured the musicians with acoustic instruments in the basement of Danko's home on West Hurley-Zena Road. The album's inside jacket shows the group in their rented Hollywood Hills pool-house-cum-recording-studio and Robertson and Helm rehearsing upstairs at Danko's house, along with several color shots from their 1969 Fillmore East shows.

Landy would snap the group on another muddy occasion when he served as the official photographer of the Woodstock music festival, but by the making of *Stage Fright* both he and the group had drifted apart. "I'd left Woodstock by then to live in Europe," he says. "I was turned off by what was going on the U.S., with Nixon and the Vietnam War, and I wanted to travel. And I'd found that I'd started thinking too much about how I was going to *sell* my pictures at the same time I was taking them. I was tired of the music business and wasn't interested in music photography anymore. I was much more interested in photographing my wife and new baby."

With Some People You Don't See the Whole Picture All at Once

Now the father of two, Landy would, however, work with The Band once again. In the 1990s he contributed live, studio, and outdoor images for the reunited group's *High on the Hog* and *Jericho* albums. When I spoke with him in 2015, he was preparing to launch LandyVision, an interactive smartphone video/music app that showcases his original work and enables users to create similar content in real time. He'd also just published *The Band Photographs: 1968–1969*, a lavish fine-art book of images culled from over twelve thousand photos of the original group.

"The guys in The Band were different from the other musicians I had been around," writes Landy in *Woodstock Vision*. "Even though they were young, hung out with the best of 'em, and did whatever 'irresponsible' things they wanted, there was a deep wisdom and maturity about them. They knew about life and about people. You couldn't fool them. They had been around and had seen it all with a really deep comprehension. I liked all of them a lot and felt really comfortable around them—like a kindred soul."

18

Passed Out Tickets Cautiously

Significant Band Concerts

By the time the Hawks had hooked up with Bob Dylan, they'd played hundreds of gigs and were already a well-oiled rock 'n' roll juggernaut. And of course, after they'd quietly gotten themselves together in Woodstock and become The Band, they would play hundreds more in settings that were generally nicer than the character-building, puke-and-switchblade joints of their earliest years. Below is a rundown of some of the most noteworthy concerts by the group.

Tony Marts Residency, Summer 1965

In their incarnation as Levon and the Hawks, the band was in residence for the summer of 1965 at a nightclub called Tony Marts. Located on the boardwalk in the New Jersey Shore town of Somers Point, Tony Marts booked the group to play what must've been a maddening schedule of near-constant—from noon to midnight—half-hour sets of covers for vacationing college students. Luckily, though, it was during this stint that the Hawks came to the attention of Bob Dylan, who was about to offer them what sounded like a much more interesting gig.

Forest Hills Tennis Stadium, August 28, 1965

And interesting it would be. This controversial concert in Queens, New York, was the live beginning of Dylan's association with the Hawks-cum-Band, although at this point only Robertson and Helm were present, complementing the singer's other sidemen, Al Kooper and Harvey Brooks. "Just keep playing," Dylan told the guys before they took the stage. "No matter how weird it gets." Weird it got and play they did, through the jeers and projectiles of the mainly rock 'n' roll–hating folkie audience. But when the smoke finally cleared, the signs were there that music history had been made. The Battle of Forest Hills had been won by the Minnesotan and his new mates—although Dylan himself seemed to be the only one who felt that way at the time, as even Helm and Robertson weren't so sure what to make of it all.

Austin Municipal Auditorium, September 24, 1965

This Austin, Texas, date began the historic 1965–1966 Dylan tour and served as the Hawks' live full-band debut with the singer. Although the rest of the tour would be a whirlwind freak show of loudly booing, aggressively intolerant crowds, the anomalous Austin audience and other Texans seemed to get where the music was going. "The Texas crowd loved Dylan's stuff, and so our first show as Bob Dylan with Levon and the Hawks was a smash," recalled Helm in his autobiography. "Weeks later, after a lot of booing had gone down elsewhere, Bob told me the Texas audience was the only one who'd understood what we were doing." So take that, New York.

Massey Hall, November 14, 1965

Unfortunately, this engagement with Dylan at the most esteemed concert venue in the quintet's old stomping ground of Toronto, one the group had likely been very much looking forward to, wasn't as warmly received as those in the Lone Star State. Enraged audience members threw pennies at the musicians, and a review in the *Toronto Star* trashed the show, singling out the Hawks as "a third-rate Yonge Street rock 'n' roll band." This all must've been quite a blow, and it likely cemented Helm's decision to quit a few weeks later. Thanks to yet another case of the small minds that plagued the tour, what should have been a triumphant return for these proud prodigal sons was instead—through no fault of the musicians—a debacle.

Manchester Free Trade Hall, May 17, 1966

With Helm now gone (until the group's 1967 Big Pink reunification), Mickey Jones was the deputized drummer when the Dylan/Hawks tour hit England. Along the tea-and-biscuits circuit they encountered ever-mounting resistance to Dylan's new sound. The hubbub reached a crescendo, literally, with this fabled standoff against the stuffies in Manchester's tony Free Trade

Hall—the occasion during which one concertgoer loudly decried Dylan as "Judas!" After Dylan's reply of "I don't believe you, you're a liar" came his directive to "Play it fucking loud!" And that was just what the Hawks did, launching into an extra-thunderous version of "Like a Rolling Stone." "It seemed like the louder the audience booed the louder it made us play," recalled Jones in the documentary *Down in the Flood*. For years, bootlegs of this concert circulated that erroneously identified it as one of the shows at London's Royal Albert Hall on May 26 or 27.

Carnegie Hall, January 20, 1968

Things had quieted down considerably by the time of this event, a Woody Guthrie memorial concert at Carnegie Hall. Marking the now semi-acoustic Dylan and the Hawks' first appearance since the singer's infamous motorcycle accident almost two years earlier, it also featured Helm back in the fold. They played only three songs—a rowdy "I Ain't Got No Home in This World Anymore," an understated "Dear Mrs. Roosevelt," and a boisterous "Grand Coulee Dam" —but despite the short set list (Pete Seeger, Joan Baez, Odetta, and others were also on the bill), the affair was critical. Not only was it the long-awaited reemergence of Dylan, it also showed the new side of his supposed electric terrorists and gave the public an early glimpse of what they'd been brewing up together in the basement of Big Pink.

Winterland Ballroom, April 17, 1969

This opening of a three-night stand at San Francisco's Winterland Ballroom was the group's first performance as The Band. It was not an encouraging debut. Two days before, Robertson had suddenly come down with a debilitating illness—possibly psychosomatic, thanks to anxiety brought on by high expectations in the wake of *Music from Big Pink*'s glowing press—that put the sold-out show in jeopardy. While the group sound-checked without him, the guitarist convalesced with a 103-degree fever in his Seal Rock Motel room as a hypnotist named Pierre Clement attempted, unsuccessfully, to rid him of the ailment.

The band, however, refused to cancel, although during the shambolic set they probably wished they had. Taking the stage four hours late, they were greeted with the patience-tried audience's loud catcalls and struggled to make it through seven songs, with Robertson propping himself up against Manuel's piano and Clement standing offstage gesturing at him and

The group's 1969 debut performances as The Band at San Francisco's Winterland Ballroom got off to a rocky start when Robbie Robertson was stricken with a 103-degree fever shortly before the show. The following week featured Led Zeppelin and Julie Driscoll, Brian Auger, and the Trinity, who had a U.K. hit with their version of "This Wheel's on Fire." *Author's collection*

shouting the magic command "Grow!" But there would be no growth that night, other than the growing discontent of the crowd. Finally, the five gave up and walked off, the attendees shouting more obscenities as they left. The next day, though, Robertson felt much better, and the April 18 and 19 shows were superb, if not as well attended. Four packed nights at New York's Fillmore East came next.

EVERY TUESDAY NIGHT
'THE SOUNDS OF THE CITY'
AUDITIONS · JAMS · GUEST PERFORMERS
$1.00 — 9 P.M. — 2 A.M. — $1.00

·∘APRIL❀	❀MAY∘·
APRIL 17·18·19 (NOT SUNDAY)	APRIL 24·25·26·27
THE BAND	LED ZEPPELIN
SONS OF CHAMPLIN	JULIE DRISCOLL·BRIAN
ACE OF CUPS	AUGER +THE TRINITY
··AT WINTERLAND··	THURS - SUN-FILLMORE WEST FRI - SAT - WINTERLAND
MAY 1·2·3·4	MAY 8·9·10·11
DEAD — PLANE	SANTANA
(DETAILS TO BE ANNOUNCED)	ALBERT KING
MONGO SANTAMARIA	ALBERT COLLINS

THE NOTORIOUS FILLMORE FINGERS BASKETBALL
TEAM HAS SCHEDULED A SERIES OF GAMES TO
BE HELD EACH TUESDAY EVENING, 7 P.M., PRIOR
TO THE AUDITION JAM SESSIONS. THESE GAMES
ARE OPEN TO THE PUBLIC WITH ADMISSION
INCLUDED IN THE REGULAR TUESDAY PRICE OF
ONE DOLLAR. ALSO INCLUDED: YELL LEADER,
FAR OUT CHEERS, POPCORN, AND SIX GORGEOUS
CHEERLEADERS IN LIVING FILLMORE COLORS.
NEW ADDITION TO THE MADNESS:
    THE LAST TUES. OF EACH MONTH BETWEEN
      THE AUDITIONS AND THE JAM -
    ··SQUARE DANCING··

OUR LOCATION: MARKET + VAN NESS
FOR INFORMATION: 431-4106

Toronto Pop Festival, June 22, 1969

The Toronto vindication the group had been seeking since their poorly received 1965 local show there with Dylan would not come, alas, with this slot at the opening night of the four-day Toronto Pop Festival at Varsity Stadium. Problems with the P.A.'s electronics early on got things off to a disastrous start. But this time, instead of Dylan's folkie-challenging music, what really doomed The Band with the press was their newfound casualness and restraint, which were taken to be aloofness; negative write-ups also called the act "too country." (The naysayers, however, would eat crow the following January, when the group revisited Massey Hall for an ecstatically applauded show.) Appearing at the festival the same night as The Band were Chuck Berry, Procol Harum, Steppenwolf, and Blood, Sweat & Tears. The occasion was the first time "Up on Cripple Creek" was played live.

Woodstock Music Festival, August 17, 1969

The Band played on the third and closing night of this, the mother of all rock festivals, in Bethel, New York. But for them it wasn't the love-in it seemed to be for everyone else. Arriving by helicopter from nearby Stewart Airport, the group was aghast at what looked, as Robertson told *Rolling Stone*, like "a ripped army of mud people." Paradoxically, the group, who actually lived in the town that the festival was named for, felt very much *not* at home. To the five, who were sober for the occasion, the idea of facing a throng of 400,000 largely stoned or tripping onlookers, the biggest audience ever at the time, must've been nerve-rattling.

Slotted between Ten Years After and Johnny Winter, The Band went on at 10:00 p.m., opened with a forceful "Chest Fever," and continued to play well. But the verdict is that their overall quieter set didn't connect as well with the teeming crowd as those by prior, apocalyptic acts like the Who, Sly and the Family Stone, and Janis Joplin. (Their appearance was filmed but not featured in the *Woodstock* documentary because, according to Robertson, they rejected director Michael Wadleigh's offer of a percentage of the movie profits in exchange for half their fee for the show; Manuel also commented that the shadowy footage didn't show all of them onstage at once, anyway.) Despite the eleven-song program's seemingly cool reception, it did elicit an encore, "Loving You Is Sweeter Than Ever," after which the five beat it back home through the mud as fast as they could.

Isle of Wight Festival, August 31, 1969

After Woodstock, The Band's next concert came two Sundays later, at another gigantic outdoor festival, this one on England's bucolic Isle of Wight. The show was their first overseas billing as The Band, and in addition to playing their own set they accompanied Bob Dylan, whom they hadn't played with since Carnegie Hall the year before. Technical problems pushed The Band's start time back almost two hours, which meant Dylan was also delayed and tension ensued. But in spite of the late kickoff, The Band won the irate punters over, playing most of *Music from Big Pink*, including the rarely performed, Robertson-sung "To Kingdom Come." And unlike at Woodstock or Toronto Pop, the more intimate acoustic numbers ("Ain't No More Cane," "Don't Ya Tell Henry") won them press accolades. The group's hour-plus set with Dylan was also a stunner, including mellow selections from *John Wesley Harding* and *Nashville Skyline* and howlers like "Highway 61" and "The Mighty Quinn." Also on the bill: Richie Havens, the Who, the Pretty Things, Free, Joe Cocker, the Moody Blues, and others. Taking notes in the front row: three Beatles and three Rolling Stones.

Academy of Music, December 28–31, 1971

Rock of Ages was taped during this magical four-night run at the now-gone opera house on New York's East Fourteenth Street. In their glorious first live performances with an Allen Toussaint–charted horn section, the group played like demons at the top of their game and left the audiences enraptured. This being the decadent 1970s, though, not everyone was there for the music. According to Saugerties resident Harold Swart, who went down to Manhattan to catch his famous neighbors on the first night, the men's room was a scene of surreal depravity. "People were puking and shooting up everywhere," Swart says. The final night, which Robertson has said yielded most of *Rock of Ages*, was New Year's Eve, for which The Band was joined by a surprise guest: Bob Dylan, who materialized out of another self-imposed exile to perform four off-the-cuff songs with the group. Quite a way to ring in 1972.

Watkins Glen, July 28, 1973

Officially called the Summer Jam at Watkins Glen, this three-way summit by The Band, the Grateful Dead, and the Allman Brothers Band dwarfed all previous records for concert attendance, attracting an estimated 600,000 to Watkins Glen raceway in upstate New York. When promoter Bill Graham first asked them to appear, the group was on break from performing and turned him down, but in the end the combination of the money and the proximity to their home was simply too good to pass up.

The four rare photos on this page and the following page show The Band performing at Monticello Raceway in upstate New York on September 5, 1971. *Photos by Harold Swart*

The sweltering summer show saw the premiere of a new song, "Endless Highway"; the tragic death of a surprise parachutist; and a torrential thunderstorm about thirty minutes into The Band's set that forced them to flee the stage. Fortified by whiskey shots, Hudson came back on to play an

extra-long "Genetic Method" until the rain relented and the others rejoined him to launch into "Chest Fever." "The Dead played first, during the day, and I remember them being boring and playing too long," says ex–Sonic Youth drummer Bob Bert, who camped out near the racetrack with a posse of high school friends. "The Allmans were way better, but The Band were perfect and really into it. I remember hearing that they enjoyed [the concert] so much they talked Dylan out of his hiatus to tour the following year."

Chicago Stadium, January 3, 1974

And the Dylan hiatus (his *Rock of Ages* appearance aside) was indeed broken with this, the first of two consecutive nights in Chicago that began the 1974 tour he co-headlined with The Band. Estimates put the audience at 18,500, and the concert served as a crucial test run for the players to figure out how they would pace the tour's following shows and get a grip on balancing Dylan's and The Band's material.

Wembley Stadium, September 14, 1974

This landmark London concert featured The Band, Joni Mitchell, Jesse Colin Young, and the headliners, Crosby, Stills, Nash & Young. The Band hadn't played the English city since their 1970 two-night engagement at the Royal Albert Hall. Reportedly, Manuel had been overindulging throughout this U.K. return visit and was not in a good way. With his voice shot and his drumming abilities questionable, the group had to find ways to compensate, so they spent an inordinate amount of time tuning up when they got onstage, and Robertson and Helm conversed throughout the performance, adjusting the set on the fly to concentrate on the songs they could pull off with the pianist as he was. Forced to skip Manuel's signature falsetto pieces (no "In a Station" or "Whispering Pines" this show), they also refrained from swapping instruments; for "The Weight," Hudson remained on organ instead of switching places with Manuel, as was usual, and none of the songs played featured Manuel on drums, which meant "Rag Mama Rag," their biggest U.K. hit, went unplayed (Manuel sat out the version of "Mystery Train" entirely). Nevertheless, the show was attended by somewhere between 72,000 and 80,000 people and is today remembered as a milestone of the 1970s concert era.

Winterland Ballroom, November 25, 1976

As Robertson tells it, the idea for this luminary-filled farewell show—the Last Waltz—was his. But according to producer Rob Fraboni, it was Danko who first suggested inviting some of The Band's famous friends to also perform at the grand send-off. In any event, the call went out to receptive superstar acquaintances Bob Dylan, Eric Clapton, Van Morrison, Neil Young, Joni Mitchell, Ringo Starr, Ronnie Wood, and Stephen Stills and some artists who represented various phases of the group's career and the genres they drew upon: Ronnie Hawkins (rockabilly), Paul Butterfield, Muddy Waters (blues), Emmylou Harris (country), the Staple Singers (gospel), Neil Diamond (Brill Building), Dr. John, and Bobby Charles (New Orleans jazz and R&B).

Five thousand concertgoers who'd snagged a $25 ticket (a hefty sum back then) to the Thanksgiving night event at San Francisco's Winterland Ballroom further reveled in the Allen Toussaint–arranged horn section, a holiday spread of several tons of specially catered food, a stage decorated with props from the San Francisco Opera's production of *La Traviata*, and intermission recitations by local poets Lawrence Ferlinghetti, Michael McClure, Diane Di Prima, Emmett Grogan, Lenore Kandel, Sweet William Fritsch, Robert Duncan, Dave Furano, Steve Gagne, and Freewheelin' Frank Reynolds.

The rest of The Band had been blindsided by Robertson's September announcement that he wanted to break up the group, but they nonetheless played the songs with a passion that belied—or, more accurately, channeled—their anguish. This is contagiously clear in both *The Last Waltz* and the unembellished black-and-white footage of the full four-and-a-half-hour concert viewable on YouTube. Another famous swan song would occur at Winterland two years hence, when the Sex Pistols imploded there.

The Roxy, March 1, 1978

Despite the fanfare of finality surrounding the Last Waltz, the glamorous occasion actually wasn't the last time the original Band played together. That happened during this solo gig by Rick Danko at the Roxy in Los Angeles, where the bass man was appearing to promote his self-titled 1977 debut album. Helm, Manuel, Hudson, and Robertson, who had all played on the disc, joined him onstage, unannounced, for a few songs during the late set. Their versions of "Stage Fright," "The Shape I'm In," and "The Weight" can be heard on the Danko bootleg CD *The Roxy, 1978* (Naughty Dog Records, 2009).

Joyous Lake, June 25, 1983

Helm had been touring with his old Arkansas buddies the Cate Brothers Band, and at this packed show at Woodstock's cozy Joyous Lake he, the Cates, and Paul Butterfield were joined by Danko, Hudson, and Manuel, making it the first time the four Band men had all played together on the same stage in five years. The quartet had actually decided to resurrect the group's name prior to the gig, which served as a warm-up for a tour that began with their first Canadian performance as The Band, on July 2, 1983, in Montreal. Their first official U.S. show as The Band that tour was on July 21 in San Jose, California.

Cheek to Cheek Lounge, March 3, 1986

The Band's sold-out booking at this nightclub in the Orlando, Florida, suburb of Winter Park saw Richard Manuel's last performances. After they'd played two sets to overjoyed audiences, the forty-two-year-old musician and father of two took his own life at the motel he and his bandmates were staying at. Reportedly, no one around him had sensed anything out of the ordinary about the pianist at the gig. But perhaps Helm had a premonition without realizing it. In *This Wheel's on Fire*, the drummer mentions how Manuel's rendition of Ray Charles's "You Don't Know Me" that night "made me want to cry."

Woodstock Festival, August 13, 1994

While The Band didn't have a great time at the first Woodstock Festival in 1969, they were nonetheless happy to be invited to play at its namesake, three-day, twenty-fifth anniversary festival. After all, it was being held literally right next door to the town of Woodstock, at Winston Farm in Saugerties, and Bob Dylan would also be performing. There was a handful of other veterans of the original fest—Santana, Joe Cocker, John Sebastian, Country Joe McDonald, Crosby, Stills & Nash—but most of the headliners were contemporary alternative and hard rock acts.

Unlike the 1969 edition, this incarnation was smaller (a mere 350,000) and much better organized, although the rain that hammered the site intermittently made the mud situation far worse than it had been at Yasgur's Farm. With Bruce Hornsby on piano and a brass section, The Band played on the festival's South Stage the second night and were joined for their set by Sebastian, McDonald, Roger McGuinn, Bob Weir, and Jefferson Airplane/Hot Tuna members Jorma Kaukonen and Jack Casady. An online account of the set says that part of the stage roof collapsed minutes before The Band went on, dumping water onto the monitor system, which knocked it out and prevented the musicians from hearing much of what they were playing. At a whopping thirty-two songs, their set may have been a tad long for the kids who'd come to see Green Day or Metallica, but with classics and surprises like the Rolling Stones' "(I Can't Get No) Satisfaction" (!) it must've pleased their parents.

19

Play Them One More Time for Me

Fifteen Rare Band Songs

D espite being one of the major recording acts of their day, The Band didn't really leave a lot of songs on the cutting room floor. When choosing the songs and takes for their albums, they generally chose well. Excluding the rare music they cut with Bob Dylan during the Basement Tapes period, there are a number of scarce Band tunes that remained in the vault for years until being released as bonus tracks on reissues, as well as a couple that remain unheard by most fans to this day. Here, we'll look at fifteen rare and rumored songs by The Band circa 1967–1977.

"Even If It's a Pig, Part Two"

A tape of this warped, completely atypical Big Pink basement piece reminded filmmaker and Hawks acquaintance Howard Alk of his associate John Simon's work on the similarly surreal Marshall MacLuhan album, *The Medium Is the Massage.* A multipart mini-suite nearly three minutes long, it features Danko on euphonium (or possibly trombone) and vocal, Manuel on tambourine and vocal, Hudson on baritone sax, and, bizarrely, Beat-poet spoken-word passages. "It was a very Dada-ish recording," Simon told Sid Griffin for *Million Dollar Bash.* "Not too musical, just nuts." It's yet to see an official release, although "Even If It's a Pig, Part One" has made it onto bootlegs.

"Upstairs, Downstairs"

A real mystery item from the early Big Pink days. Apparently, this obscure Manuel original was inspired by the working situation at the house; i.e., Dylan tapping out lyrics on a typewriter upstairs and then taking them down to the boys in the basement to set to music. As of this writing, the unheard "Upstairs, Downstairs" remains buried deep beneath the cellar floor, beyond the reaches of bootleggers. So far.

"Words and Numbers"

Another abandoned Manuel gem from that same Saugerties cellar, this sly, slinky blues killer can be heard on the box set *A Musical History*. Reportedly, the group let it go because it didn't fit the direction of the material that became *Music from Big Pink*. True enough, but they should have revisited it for one of their later albums. Its minor-key, evil-rhumba rhythm is addictive and Robertson's coiled-snake playing is some of his best. Manuel's lyrics— "Stick to your diet of fresh fruit juices / never indulge in self-abuses"—are painfully confessional.

"Endless Highway" (Studio Versions)

Although it debuted on vinyl via 1974's live album with Bob Dylan, *Before the Flood*, The Band had already recorded two studio versions of this strident rocker at Bearsville Sound Studios in 1972 between *Cahoots* and *Moondog Matinee*—one sung by Danko, the other by Manuel. In 1995, Capitol smeared the Danko version with prerecorded crowd noise for the phony *Live at Watkins Glen* before releasing the same track in its uncorrupted form on *A Musical History*. The earlier, Manuel-sung version is on the 2000 CD remaster of *Cahoots*.

"Poughkeepsie or Bust"

Alluded to by Sid Griffin in *Million Dollar Bash*, this uncompleted Robertson song exists on several Basement Tapes bootlegs as an instrumental simply called "Organ Riffs." Belying its bootlegger-affixed title, the recording is *not* a solo performance by Hudson but actually features the whole group.

"Even a Tomato"

Also an organ-dominated Basement Tapes–period track, this funky, nearly six-minute instrumental jam has Booker T. & the MG's–sounding soul sauce all over it. A reasonably clear transfer is on the bootleg Dylan CD *The Genuine Basement Tapes, Vol. 3*.

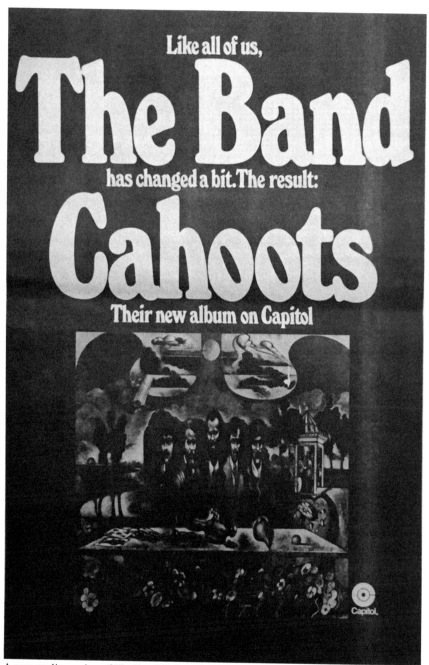

A rare studio version of "Endless Highway" recorded at the *Cahoots* sessions and featuring Richard Manuel on lead vocals, can be found on the 2000 Capitol CD remaster of the album.

Author's collection

"Get Up Jake" (Studio Version)

As with "Endless Highway," this song, which has Danko and Helm trading verses, appeared in live form on record long before its earlier, studio-recorded incarnation came out. Cut for *The Band*, it was ultimately left off that record for two reasons: (1) The group felt, quite rightly, that the addition of one more song would have made the album too long; and (2) the story in its lyrics, about a couple of countrified ferryboat operators, was too similar to that of the retiring sailor and Ragtime Willie in "Rockin' Chair," which is probably about right as well. Still, it's one of the group's best feel-good tunes, with a chorus that's impossible not to sing along to, which is probably why they decided to resurrect it for *Rock of Ages*. A mono mix of the studio version, cut among the Brown Album songs in Sammy Davis Jr.'s pool house, showed up as the B-side of "Ain't Got No Home" in 1973; the stereo mix emerged as a bonus track on the 2000 remaster of *The Band* and is included on 2005's *A Musical History*.

"Ferdinand the Imposter" (Garth Hudson recording)

One of The Band's best-known unknown songs, "Ferdinand the Imposter" circulated for years among collectors before finally getting its sanctioned debut on the 2000 *Music from Big Pink* CD remaster. There are two known recorded versions of the song: an incomplete studio take cut during the unsuccessful, pre–*Big Pink* demos produced by Albert Grossman; and this one, from the 1967 Hudson-engineered recordings in Saugerties. A minor-key folk rock number taped before Helm rejoined (Manuel, still learning drums then, provides the stiff beat), it has a plaintive vocal by Danko.

Although the parable style of Robertson's lyrics echoes the biblical-story approach he'd absorbed from Dylan, the namesake pretender in the song is undoubtedly a reference to Ferdinand Waldo Demara Jr., who made headlines after being outed for impersonating, among others, a ship's doctor, a prison warden, a psychologist, and a Benedictine monk. (Demara was portrayed by Tony Curtis in the 1961 film *The Great Impostor*, which is likely where movie maniac Robertson got the idea from.) The track is on disc one of *A Musical History*.

"Beautiful Thing"

On the same *Musical History* CD as the above version of "Ferdinand the Imposter" is this Richard Manuel song sketch. It was recorded in the fall of 1966 at photographer Barry Feinstein's Manhattan studio, where the group rehearsed while living in the city between their first Dylan tour and their upstate move. Sad, sparse, and true to its title, this short, raw tape has Manuel on hymnlike electric piano and Danko on bass, with the song's author intoning the still-wordless vocal melody. Nearly ten years later, Manuel and Danko completed the song and Eric Clapton sang it as the opening track of his Band-assisted album *No Reason to Cry*.

"Two Piano Song" (*Works*)

This odd instrumental is the only piece of music yet released from Robertson's grand, much-labored-over "unfinished symphony," *Works*. Inspired by the classical music of Polish avant-garde composer Krzysztof Penderecki, *Works* was intended to be a seamless suite about the American Indians that incorporated songs, instrumental music, storytelling, and spoken passages. Robertson toiled away on it from early 1972 into late 1973, occasionally trying out some of the music with his bandmates. But it never really clicked with them, and he himself found the sheer scale of such a compositional undertaking to be exhausting. The project was finally dropped as the group returned to more fun and familiar ground with *Moondog Matinee*.

"Two Piano Song," its title concocted after the fact, is a four-minute, twelve-second segment featuring, as one might surmise, two pianos (Robertson and Hudson), as well as drums (Helm), percussion (Manuel), bass, and cello (both Danko). As a song, it's more easy listening than rock (Robertson has even jokingly compared it to schmaltzy piano duo Ferrante and Teicher) and foretells 1977's similarly Muzaky "Islands." Hear this uncharacteristic sampling on disc four of *A Musical History*.

"Home Cookin'"

On disc five of *A Musical History* is this Rick Danko song, which has him and Robertson on guitars, Hudson on piano, Manuel on drums, and Helm on bass. An exceptional, country-inflected number, its rustic theme recalls the spirit of the Brown Album and parts of *Stage Fright*, but it was actually recorded later, at Shangri-La in 1976. The fact that it was passed over for inclusion on *Islands* in favor of filler like "Let the Night Fall" or "Right as Rain" is mystifying.

"(I Want to Be) The Rainmaker"

The earliest song sketches on *A Musical History* are two recordings made on a portable reel-to-reel machine in a Somers Point, New Jersey, hotel room when Levon and the Hawks were doing their 1965 Tony Marts residency. One is a demo of "The Stones I Throw (Will Free All Men)," whose final version is covered in chapter 10, and the other is this quirky curio. Written and sung by Robertson, the track features him on his acoustic accompanied by the handclaps and finger snaps of Manuel and Helm. In his liner notes, Robertson admits that the weird lyrics, about a boy who wants to make it rain all the time instead of becoming a shoemaker or an undertaker, were "probably drug induced."

In September 1975, Capitol issued "Twilight" as a U.K. single with "The Weight" as the B-side.   *Author's collection*

"You Don't Come Through"

Reworked from an earlier Basement Tapes–era sketch called "You Say You Love Me," this gorgeous Impressions homage by their documented devotee Robertson has soul man Manuel perfectly cast in the lead Curtis Mayfield vocal slot. Taped at Big Pink that quietly magical summer of 1967, it has the singer and Helm on tambourines (no drums), Danko on bass, and Robertson on acoustic but no Hudson (maybe he was focusing exclusively on his other role as Big Pink's house recording engineer).

"Working at the Canastas"

Attributed to Manuel, this laid-back, skeletal instrumental song sketch was recorded by the group at an October 24, 1968, session at Capitol's New York studios. It seems no words were written for it, which is why it sat in Capitol's cans until being used as the background music for the DVD menu of the *Musical History* box set. The light touch on the drums sounds more like Manuel than Helm, and there's barely any guitar on it, just a couple of bluesy licks near the beginning. But the tambourine and funeral-parlor organ give it that unmistakable Band-gospel feel.

"Bring It On Home to Me"

During the *Moondog Matinee* sessions, the group did more than thirty takes of this Sam Cooke classic sung by Danko, their biggest resident Cooke fan. Surprisingly, given that there exist great live versions of him singing it with the Hawks in the early 1960s, none of the attempts made at Bearsville Studios in 1973 were deemed acceptable. Perhaps, forced to choose between Cooke's "Bring It On Home to Me" or "A Change Is Gonna Come," they felt, as with the two Chuck Berry songs they cut during the same sessions, that one Cooke tune on the album was enough and simply went with the better performance. If that was the case, fair enough. But why, then, is the song not among the bonus tracks on the 2001 *Moondog Matinee* reissue or on *A Musical History*? More of Danko singing Sam Cooke? How bad could that possibly be? What say, vault keeper?

20

Just Another Whistle Stop

The Band's Official Live Albums

Other acts of the late 1960s and early 1970s released legendary live albums. Think of the Rolling Stones' *Get Yer Ya-Ya's Out*, the MC5's *Kick Out the Jams*, the Allman Brothers Band's *At Fillmore East*, the Who's *Live at Leeds*, or Jimi Hendrix's *Band of Gypsys*. The Band's *Rock of Ages* belongs on the same top shelf as all of these classics of the era, but it's not the only commercially released live album the group recorded. The wealth of *un*official live Band recordings is delved into later in the book, so here we'll discuss the group's over-the-counter, in-concert releases.

Bob Dylan Live 1966

Bootlegged for years as one or the other of Dylan and the Hawks' May 26 and 27, 1966, concerts at London's Royal Albert Hall, this recording actually comes from their May 17 appearance at Manchester Free Trade Hall. Columbia cleaned the sound up for legitimate release in 1998 as the fourth volume in its ongoing Bootleg Series of unearthed Dylan material. Disc one is devoted to Dylan's opening solo acoustic set, while disc two comprises one of the powerful, full-electric-band performances that created such firestorms of controversy at nearly every tour stop—indeed, this is the very document that captures the infamous cry of "Judas!" by one outraged, folk-traditionalist concertgoer.

Helm had taken his temporary leave by this point, and the drums are manned by Mickey Jones. The electric set tears open with "Tell Me, Momma" and dips into "I Don't Believe You (She Acts Like We Never Have Met)," all nasal yowls and harmonica squeals from Dylan over Hudson's carnival organ and Danko's unyielding bass. Robertson's bent, single-string accents sizzle and snake their way through "Baby, Let Me Follow You Down" and

"Leopard-Skin Pillbox Hat," while Manuel hammers his ivories hard and fills all the right spaces with barrelhouse touches not previously heard in the music halls of Merry Olde England. Six songs in, for the tuned-in or taunting souls who didn't flee the venue covering their ears, the vibe gets dark and doom-laden with the down-tempo "Ballad of a Thin Man"; Hudson's avant-garde filigree is cartoonishly strange on this one. The rousing rant "Like a Rolling Stone," stretched from its already daring six-minute-single length to eight unrelenting minutes of pure, iron-cast rock 'n' roll, ends this dramatic evening, the players going out with all guns blazing. After the last crescendo: the applause of the converted, the sound of amplifiers being switched off, and a stock recording of "God Bless America" wafting out of the P.A.

Rock of Ages

When The Band decided to record 1971's four year-ending shows at New York's Academy of Music for a projected double album, they wanted to do something they hadn't done before. But what? They weren't about to echo their acid rock rivals with side-long jazz odysseys. Nor did they want to merely re-create the studio versions of fan favorites, something critics had actually panned them for doing. Robertson hit on an idea. With the whole group still basking in the success of Allen Toussaint's horn chart for *Cahoots*' "Life Is a Carnival," how about hiring him to write arrangements for some of their songs?

Everyone loved the concept, so Toussaint wrote charts ahead of time and flew up to Woodstock in mid-December with the plan of fine-tuning them with the group and directing the horns at the rehearsals and concerts. Horribly, though, he discovered his suitcase with the arrangements had been lost at the airport. No matter. Sequestered in a Woodstock cabin with some music paper, a tape recorder, and plenty of hot tea, the New Orleans genius got to work writing new charts from scratch. After he emerged, a horn section of top New York jazzmen was assembled: Howard Johnson on tuba, euphonium, and baritone sax; Snooky Young on trumpet and flugelhorn; Joe Farrell on tenor and soprano saxes and English horn; Earl McIntyre on trombone; and J. D. Parran on alto sax and E-flat clarinet. Garth Hudson would take his usual tenor and soprano sax solos on "The W.S. Walcott Medicine Show" and "Unfaithful Servant." Band friends Mac Rebennack (a.k.a. Dr. John), Bobby Charles, and songwriter Doc Pomus gave their informed guidance on working with large R&B horn setups, but

Recorded with a full horn section at New York's Academy of Music, the electrifying *Rock of Ages* hit number six on the U.S. national charts.   *Author's collection*

with the shows coming up quickly, there wasn't much time to rehearse with this greatly expanded, and potentially convoluted, aggregation. After only one full-cast run-through, and with no guarantee their fans at the sold-out-in-advance dates would even accept the augmented lineup, The Band stepped onto the Academy stage for the December 28 opening show.

No one need have worried. *Rock of Ages*, released in August 1972, made *Rolling Stone*'s Album of the Year, went to number six on the national charts, and still ranks as one of rock's top live albums. From the moment the horn men come blaring in on the double LP's opener, The Band's grit-grinding version of the Holland-Dozier-Holland-penned "Don't Do It," it's clear how electrified the crowd—and the players themselves—are with the big, bold, brassy new live sound. Released by Capitol as a single, the track reached

The *Rock of Ages* track "Don't Do It" became The Band's final Top Forty single when it reached number thirty-four on the *Billboard* Hot 100 in 1972.   *Author's collection*

thirty-four on the *Billboard* Hot 100 chart, the second and final time The Band would make the Top Forty after 1969's "Up on Cripple Creek." According to Robertson, about 80 percent of the original release was taken from the final night. On songs such as "Rag Mama Rag," "Across the Great Divide," "Chest Fever," and especially "The Night They Drove Old Dixie Down," the fullness of the brass adds a sonic aura, burnishing the songs but never obscuring their essence or the playing of The Band's five members—it's as if the horns are the previously unseen spirit shadows of these songs, who've chosen to reveal themselves only for these shows.

They're not heard on all of the numbers, though: "The Weight," "Stage Fright," "This Wheel's on Fire," "The Shape I'm In," and the previously unreleased "Get Up Jake" are all hornless, as is Hudson's nearly eight-minute solo organ intro to "Chest Fever," which was officially dubbed "The

Genetic Method" (the title of an academic paper about tribal music he'd read) for the release of *Rock of Ages*. Taped during the final minutes of 1971, it includes snippets of "Auld Lang Syne." The album ends with Helm, the group, and the horns blaring out Chuck Willis's R&B blaster "(I Don't Want to) Hang Up My Rock and Roll Shoes."

Helm later said *Rock of Ages* was the most fun he had making a Band album, and Robertson concurred, telling Rob Bowman in the *Musical History* liner notes that playing with the horn section was "the greatest experience of our life." For reasons unknown, in 1980 Capitol reissued the original two-LP gatefold set as separate albums in near-identical covers.

Bob Dylan joined the group for four unrehearsed songs on the last night, the capper being an ecstatically received "Like a Rolling Stone." The second CD of the 2001 expanded *Rock of Ages* remaster includes the previously unheard Dylan tunes and six by The Band (sans horns) that were culled from the December 28, 29, and 30 shows. In 2013, Capitol released the four-CD/one-DVD *Live at the Academy of Music*, which features remixes by producer Bob Clearmountain and soundboard mixes remastered by Robbie's son Sebastian Robertson and adds nineteen previously unreleased tracks from across all four nights, all in a hardcover book package with extensive liner notes. The raw looseness of many of these unheard tracks, arguably, gives an even better sense of what it must've been like to be there (check out the tough version of "Strawberry Wine"). The first two CDs include one version of each of the songs played at the concerts, while the latter two feature the entire New Year's Eve show. The DVD includes film clips of the December 30 performances of "The W.S. Walcott Medicine Show" and "King Harvest (Has Surely Come)" and the New Year's Eve audio (in 5.1 Surround) set to photos from the night. A two-CD version includes only the deluxe set's first two discs of non–*Rock of Ages* material.

The Last Waltz

Since it's the audio document of a concert film, the soundtrack to *The Last Waltz* is assumed by many to be a live album. Not really. Yes, it's included here because it's not a standard studio album and it features the songs from the movie's Winterland performances by The Band and their guest singers. But it also includes the studio-recorded instrumental "Theme from the Last Waltz" and the MGM-soundstage-taped "The Last Waltz Suite."

And there's something else that potentially calls into question its live-album status: It's not totally live. "A lot of the performances, though they

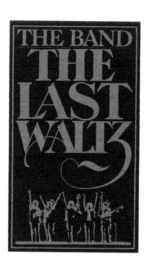

Most of the parts played by the musicians in The Band during the "live" performances on the *Last Waltz* soundtrack were re-recorded in the studio for the film and the three-LP set.   *Author's collection*

made the audience happy, needed to be fixed for the record," explains John Simon, the concert's music director and, with Rob Fraboni, the album's coproducer. "Rick's bass was generally out of tune, Richard hit a lot of [vocal] cracks, Garth always looked for opportunities to improve his parts, and Robbie was a perfectionist who wanted to fix his parts, too. In addition, the horns, mixed in the remote truck, were badly balanced. So [in the studio afterward] everyone redid their parts—except for Levon." (Some who were there have attributed the sloppy-sounding original performances to the large amounts of drugs being freely circulated backstage.) To be fair, it should be noted that many so-called live albums back then, and doubtlessly far more today, are doctored up via post-performance overdubbing.

But technically live or not, the *Last Waltz* soundtrack puts across the experience of that final concert and remains a generally joyful listen for many fans of the group and the film.

The first five sides of the sprawling 1978 triple album (reissued on double CD) have all of the songs from the film but add several that were left out: The Band doing "Life Is a Carnival"; "I Don't Believe You (She Acts Like We Never Have Met)" with Dylan; Manuel and Van Morrison's gorgeous duet on "Tura Lura Lural (That's an Irish Lullaby)" with John Simon on piano; and a great Cajun romp with Bobby Charles on "Down South in New Orleans," which features Hudson on accordion and Dr. John on guitar. Side six is devoted to the five-part "The Last Waltz Suite," which encompasses the performances of "The Weight" with the Staples and "Evangeline" with Emmylou Harris, the otherwise unavailable new originals "The Well" (sung by Danko) and "Out of the Blue" (a rare Robertson lead vocal), and the vocal-less "The Last Waltz Refrain."

Rhino's richly packaged and annotated four-CD 2002 *The Last Waltz* box set ups the original album's thirty tracks to sixty, all of them remixed by Robertson. The Band-only tunes include the concert versions of "The Weight," "This Wheel's on Fire," "Rag Mama Rag," "Acadian Driftwood," "The W.S. Walcott Medicine Show," a truncated "The Genetic Method/ Chest Fever," and the encore of "Don't Do It." The previously unreleased guest songs are a stomping "Caledonia" with Muddy Waters; Eric Clapton doing "All Our Past Times," a song he wrote with Danko; "Four Strong Winds" with Neil Young; Joni Mitchell's "Shadows and Light" and "Furry Sings the Blues"; and "Hazel" with Dylan. As in the movie and the original soundtrack, the running order is nothing like that of the actual event, as The Band played their own set before bringing their guests out (seek out the bootleg *The Complete Last Waltz* for a true sequential re-creation). Present on the fourth disc, along with the complete "Last Waltz Suite," are the star-heavy jams ("too many coked-up cooks in the kitchen" would be a good way to describe these two tracks); rehearsals of "King Harvest (Has Surely Come)," "Rag Mama Rag," and the songs sung by Morrison and Dr. John; and instrumental sketches for "The Well," "The Last Waltz Theme," and "The Last Waltz Refrain," which has a beautiful Hudson tenor sax solo. Robertson's remixes of the original soundtrack were issued as a double CD by Rhino, who, using the same remixes, also put out a 2003 limited-edition deluxe vinyl package signed by the guitarist that includes reproductions of an original event ticket, table placard, and concert poster plus other sundries. A DVD audio version appeared in 2002.

Live at Watkins Glen

Anyone who complains that the *Last Waltz* soundtrack isn't "live" enough to make it a legitimate live album is directed to this digital sham released by Capitol in 1995. Ostensibly a recording of the group's set at the 1973 Summer Jam at Watkins Glen festival, this ten-track album was apparently put together in the late 1970s or early 1980s using mainly previously unreleased material with canned crowd noise dubbed in.

Only Hudson's brilliant solo "Too Wet to Work" and the intuitively titled "Jam" come from the actual concert. The original "Endless Highway" and the version of Chuck Berry's "Back to Memphis" that opens the disc are *Cahoots/Moondog Matinee*–era studio outtakes; "Don't Ya Tell Henry" is the same one that's on 1975's *The Basement Tapes*; and the rest of the songs—"I Shall Be Released," "Loving You Is Sweeter Than Ever," "The Rumor," "Time to Kill," and "Up on Cripple Creek"—are the same six Academy of Music recordings that appear as bonus tracks on 2001's *Rock of Ages* remaster.

The Band's members have roundly disowned *Live at Watkins Glen*, stressing they were not involved with its release in any way. "Jam" (also found on the 2000 bootleg *Old Shoes*) isn't very interesting musically, and "Too Wet to Work" is available on the *Across the Great Divide* box set, so there's not much to recommend about this duplicitous disc.

21

Knockin' Lost John

A Profile of Producer John Simon

"I was the only one who was there for every minute, every note of the first two albums. That's saying something."

—John Simon

ohn Simon is dealing with a wily woodchuck when I arrive to interview him in the summer of 2015. "He chewed halfway through the garden fence," says the producer on the sunny deck of his unpainted-clapboard home near Woodstock. "So today I have to go out and borrow a trap." In this writer's mind, it's entirely Band-appropriate: Perhaps if it'd been forty-six or -seven years ago, when the group was working up the material for *The Band*, the pesky critter in Simon's yard would have shown up in one of their songs—another countrified character making a cameo via Robbie Robertson's backwater imaginings. Like Jack the dog in "The Weight."

Simon's involvement with The Band was as important to their initial success as that of their two more famous friends, Bob Dylan and Albert Grossman. Perhaps even more so. Because although their association with the Dylan-Grossman machine did get them notoriety and a record deal, it was the sympathetic sonic advising of Simon that so perfectly captured their sound for the whole world to hear. Not many other producers could have so successfully transitioned between *Big Pink*'s windswept panorama and *The Band*'s "little workshop" vibe. The group could easily have been stuck with a faceless, clueless, bow-tie-wearing staff producer who wanted to make them "current" by molding them into yet another bunch of wannabe Beatles. But in the brainy Simon the group recognized all the same sensibilities and musical references they shared among themselves; Robbie Robertson called him "the outside ear and opinion you could trust." There were many complicated reasons, of course, for The Band's musical decline after their first two LPs, but the lessened involvement of Simon helped set the scene for those dimishing returns.

Flashback to the Past

Simon was born in 1941 and raised in Norwalk, Connecticut, a coastal town known for its oyster harvesting. The classically schooled pianist and composer-arranger describes his New England upbringing as "apple pie. I remember marching in the Fourth of July parade as a kid, all of that small-town-Americana stuff." Hinting at his later studio work as an arranger and occasional horn player, it was the family's 78s of brass-band composer and conductor John Philip Sousa that Simon remembers being the first music to grab his ear. His father, a doctor, played the violin, and the younger Simon began learning piano at age four, accompanying his dad on classical pieces. "My folks were always listening to classical records," he recalls. "I started out learning Haydn, Mozart, and Beethoven. Then I slowly moved on to more

The 1971 debut album by The Band's early producer, John Simon, features Rick Danko, Garth Hudson, Richard Manuel, and other guest players.   *Author's collection*

complicated stuff, like Chopin and Brahms. But I didn't like to practice for practice's sake—I much preferred to be out playing ball with my friends."

A fascination with jazz came next, fueled by the recordings of Benny Goodman's epochal 1938 Carnegie Hall concert and saxophonist Gerry Mulligan's Quartet with trumpeter/vocalist Chet Baker. "What killed me about the Mulligan band was the leanness of the music," says Simon, who began writing songs in his preteen years. "After a while, I asked my parents if I could study music with someone who was *not* a classical pianist. So I started taking lessons from Ande Wuhrer, who taught me stride and boogie-woogie and coached me on improvisation. And he told me that whenever I was playing a job I should look for the people who walked on the dance floor in rhythm. He said, '*Those* are the people you should be playing to.'"

And pretty soon he was. While still a teenager, Simon wrote two stage musicals and led a succession of small jazz combos, composing some of their material and playing at local dances, strip clubs, lesbian bars, wherever there was work. "Ethnic weddings were the most fun," he says. "I got to learn a lot of Hungarian music, a lot of polkas." (The experience came in handy later, when Simon produced polka king Frankie Yankovic and worked with The Band on their arrangement of the Eastern European–flavored "Last Waltz Theme.")

Simon majored in music at Princeton, where he composed musicals for the university's Triangle Club, touring Army bases in Europe with one such production. He put together a band that made the finals of the elite Georgetown Intercollegiate Jazz Festival and studied with legendary serialist composer Milton Babbitt, and soon word of his abilities spread beyond campus. In his senior year, Simon was buttonholed by recruiters from two esteemed companies, both offering positions that paid the princely salary of $85 a week. "One was writing jingles for an advertising firm, the other was as a 'trainee' at Columbia Records," Simon says. "I wasn't sure what a trainee did, but Columbia sounded more interesting."

I Will Hear Every Word the Boss Man Say

At the label he was assigned to the Legacy department, working closely with Columbia president Goddard Lieberson on original-cast recordings of Broadway shows and a series of album/book sets of Civil War and cowboy songs. After moving over to an A&R/production position, one of his first projects was overseeing saxophonist Charles Lloyd's 1965 album *Of Course, Of Course*, which features Robbie Robertson on the track "Sun Dance." "Charles and Robbie and their pot dealer all lived in the same building, so that's how they knew each other," explains Simon, who doesn't recall much about his brief first encounter with the guesting guitarist. "Robbie was on the date because he was an excellent rock guitarist and made a good contrast to the other musicians, who were all really schooled, top-level jazz players."

It was Simon's production and arrangement work on the Brian Epstein–managed act the Cyrkle's 1966 single "Red Rubber Ball" (coauthored by Paul Simon; no relation), an instant U.S. number two hit that established the Connecticut kid in the eyes of his employers. In addition to a raise and "a new office, with a plant in it," he was given even freer artistic rein in Columbia's increasingly "wide-open" pop department.

The extent of his newfound freedom soon became apparent with Simon's production of 1967's *The Medium Is the Massage*, a weird audio verité album based on media theorist Marshall McLuhan's book of the same name. That year, Simon also took over the making of Leonard Cohen's debut. "Leonard told me he was going nuts in the Chelsea Hotel and needed a new producer," says Simon. The resulting album, *Songs of Leonard Cohen*, stands as one of the most beautiful and influential debuts of all time and is home to several of Cohen's greatest compositions: "Suzanne," "Sisters of Mercy," "So Long, Marianne," and "Hey, That's No Way to Say Goodbye."

Later in 1967, the young producer was brought in to help with another project that was already underway: Simon & Garfunkel's fourth album, *Bookends*. "Right away, it was total mind meld between the three of us," Simon recounts. Upon its April 1968 release, the disc shot to the top of the charts, staying at number one for seven weeks. Simon next helmed the sessions for *Child Is Father to the Man*, the smash initial album by organist/singer Al Kooper's pioneering jazz rock outfit Blood, Sweat & Tears. Kooper pointed out to Simon that he'd make more money if he gave up his staff slot at Columbia and became an independent producer. Simon seized on the advice and has been a freelancer ever since.

The Monterey Pop festival of June 1967 is remembered for its career-establishing performances by the Jimi Hendrix Experience, the Who, Otis Redding, Janis Joplin, and others. But another pivotal event occurred there—one that, although no one knew it at the time, would set off a chain of events that also changed the course of popular music: John Simon met Peter Yarrow of Peter, Paul and Mary, and the singer invited him to his hometown of Woodstock to coproduce the *You Are What You Eat* film and soundtrack (the latter contained "My Name Is Jack," a song Simon wrote that became a hit for Manfred Mann).

"I'd never seen an art colony or a town like Woodstock before," says Simon, who took up the offer. "It was very bohemian, very beatnik and permissive." He moved into a house with filmmaker Howard Alk to help edit the documentary. "One night while Howard and I were busily trying to make a movie out of those cans of film, there was this godawful bleating outside," recalls Simon. "We went to the window and there were four guys dressed in a halfhearted gesture toward Halloween, playing instruments with which they were apparently unfamiliar, serenading Howard because, I think, it was his birthday."

The four guys were Robertson, Manuel, Danko, and Hudson. "Howard had heard my zany Marshall McLuhan album and he had heard a tape that Richard, Rick, and Garth had recorded in their basement," says Simon. "It was entitled 'Even If It's a Pig, Part Two.' Like the McLuhan album, it was a crackpot production. So Howard thought we all would be a good match. He was right."

I Guess You Really Have to Stay

"In the fall of 1968, I returned to New York and soon I heard from Robbie Robertson," Simon recollects. "He told me what I already knew, because there'd been word about it around Woodstock: He and the other guys were hoping to make a record and they needed a producer. Robbie invited me back up to Woodstock to talk about going into the studio. So I went back up there and he took me directly to Big Pink. An indication that the writing was on the wall, that they indeed were going to make a record, was the arrival the day before of Levon Helm.

"Robbie proved to be a canny individual—as he has been since I've known him," Simon continues. "While he was checking me out as a potential partner, he told me about the music they'd been making. But it wasn't until my third trip up to Woodstock that he let me hear the songs that he and the others had taped on an old reel-to-reel in the basement of Big Pink. Of course I loved the material. The guys had a deep respect, bordering on reverence, for the roots of American music, stretching back from the music of their generation to rockabilly and early rock 'n' roll, to the bluegrass of Appalachia, the blues of the Mississippi Delta, and even Stephen Foster and popular music of the nineteenth century. And it seemed to me that they had a sort of unspoken commitment to be as good as they could, in order to earn a place as part of that tradition."

"What also struck me immediately was the fact that they had two really good singers in Rick and Richard—Levon's not on the original Basement Tapes—and I loved the color Garth brought to the songs, and of course Robbie's guitar playing," says Simon. "Levon was a little older, more venerable, but not any less crazy than the others. I'd never smoked so much dope before I started hanging out with those guys. It was a pleasant, joyous experience. They were fun guys and a big hit around Woodstock."

The producer and the musicians got to work on honing the material. "I felt like I was contributing as an equal partner with the members of the band," says Simon, "sometimes discussing the songs themselves with Robbie, but mostly attending to the arrangements." The preproduction would pay off when the group entered Simon's familiar workplace, Columbia's Studio A—now renamed A&R Studios—to record what was intended to be a demo. "*Never* had I achieved so much with a group in that studio in such a short time," he enthuses. "In one afternoon session, we recorded fully one-third of the album that was to become *Big Pink*. I played the rough tapes from the session for our friends, and Albert got so much confirmation as to the quality of the stuff from people he trusted like [Dylan sidekick] Bobby Neuwirth and Howard Alk and his wife, Jonesy, that he probably felt confident flying with a tape to L.A. He got us a deal. With Capitol Records. We were to fly out to L.A. to finish the album there, which was an excellent idea because winter was coming on in Woodstock and the prospect of Southern California sunshine seemed irresistible."

After "basking in the California sun" for nearly a month, Simon and the group completed recording *Music from Big Pink* at Capitol's Hollywood studios, returning to New York in the spring to mix the tracks. Simon also performs on the album, playing piano on "Caledonia Mission." "The guys could tell I really wanted to play on something, so they let me sit in," he remembers.

With the success of *Big Pink*, Grossman began sending Simon some of his other clients: the Hawks' old Toronto friend Gordon Lightfoot (1968's *Did She Mention My Name?*), the Electric Flag (1968's *An American Music Band*), and Big Brother and the Holding Company (1968's seminal *Cheap Thrills*). "[Big Brother] wanted to make a live album, and they were great live," says Simon, who would also produce Mama Cass's 1968 *Dream a Little Dream* album and tour with Taj Mahal. "But they made a lot of musical mistakes onstage, and on record mistakes are forever. So that's why it's a 'fake' live album, with studio performances and the crowd noise dubbed in."

Bum notes were less a worry with The Band, and when it came time to record album number two, Simon was looking forward to getting back in the studio with his pals. "We had stayed in pretty close contact since *Big Pink* was released, and now I was based in Woodstock," says Simon. "So moving ahead together with the follow-up album was a natural thing." He and Robertson had become closer friends—Simon and his former wife, Brooke, are the godparents of Robbie and Dominique's first child, Alexandra—and decamped to Hawaii, where the guitarist worked on new songs as Simon offered input.

The two next met the rest of the group in a rented Hollywood estate that once belonged to entertainer Sammy Davis Jr. The home's pool house had been soundproofed and recording equipment had been brought in and set up. "It would be an understatement to say that making this album was a lot of fun," says Simon about the relaxed atmosphere that yielded *The Band*, considered their best album by many—and one of the greatest in rock history. "As with the first album I was happy to be a contributor to the music beyond the producer's usual role of just saying, 'Okay, we're rolling. Take one.' There was no control room glass to frustrate conversation. We were all just in one big room, making music. I got to play the piano (on 'King Harvest [Has Surely Come]'), which I love to do." The producer-musician had essentially become the band's sixth member during the Brown Album sessions (which were completed in New York), also contributing self-taught tuba and various horns; he's even listed as such on the back cover, although Robertson rebuffed his queries to formally join.

Farewell to My Other Side, I'd Best Take It in Stride

Despite the wild success resulting from their working relationship with Simon, for their third album, *Stage Fright*, The Band chose to produce themselves with engineer Todd Rundgren. Simon did, however, stop by the record's legendarily tension-fraught spring 1970 sessions to offer advice (hence his "Special Thanks" on the cover). His own debut recording, 1971's plainly titled *John Simon's Album*, features guest work by, among others, Hudson, Danko, and Manuel; the track "Davey's on the Road Again," which the producer cowrote with Robertson, was the second of his songs to be covered by Manfred Mann (unfortunately, it didn't fare as well as "My Name Is Jack").

From that point, Simon and The Band would be largely out of each other's orbit for several years, as his former charges got on with their careers and he played on sessions by Eric Clapton, Howlin' Wolf, Dave Mason, and others; produced such artists as Seals & Crofts, John Martyn, John Sebastian, Jackie Lomax, and Bobby Charles; and waxed his second album, 1973's jazz-oriented *Journey*.

But in 1976 Simon got a call from Robertson asking him to be the music director for the Last Waltz concert. "The Band would be backing up all of these different artists—Neil Young, Joni Mitchell, Neil Diamond, Van Morrison, Dr. John, and everybody else—but, apart from Garth, they didn't read music," Simon says. "So I would have to explain to them, in their terms, what to play—what chords, what the format of the songs were, what notes made up particular lines in the arrangement, and so on." Using a system of hand signals, Simon rehearsed the players the week before the show at The Band's Zuma Beach studio, directing them in this way during the concert between playing piano for Morrison's and Diamond's numbers and apprising director Martin Scorsese of the arrangement highlights. "It was a heady time, everyone had a good time and seemed happy to be there," reminisces Simon. "All in all, the Last Waltz was a glorious, ambitious scheme and I applaud Robbie, Marty Scorsese, Bill Graham, and all the musicians and crew who pulled it off."

Since the Last Waltz, more production work has followed for Simon: Gil Evans's *Priestess*, David Sanborn's *Heart to Heart*, Steve Forbert's *Jackrabbit Slim*, and the *Best Little Whorehouse in Texas* original-cast album, among other recordings. So has the occasional solo album: 1992's acclaimed *Out on the Street* features Helm, Danko, and Hudson, while The Band's organist also appears on the 2000 Hoagy Carmichael tribute *Hoagyland*. In 1993, Simon returned to the Band fold to produce the reconstituted outfit's *Jericho*, playing on four songs.

Shockingly, Simon says he has gotten no royalties for his work on The Band's classic first two albums. "In 1976 I told Robbie I hadn't received any royalty checks or even an earnings statement for several years now," he says. "He said he'd look into it and get back to me. When he called back, lo and behold, over $60,000 owed to me had been discovered, but—and this is the huge 'but' that changed everything—he said that sales of those albums had fallen way back and they would like me to sign a paper agreeing to forgo any future royalties from the first two albums (for reasons of bookkeeping or some such) and that sales of the *Last Waltz* album were expected to be enormous, so I'd come out ahead. Well, that turned out to be wrong information. Sales from those first two albums continued to be steady and still are. I've brought this all up to Robbie a couple of times since and each time he disavowed any memory. I asked not for restitution of the considerable royalties I'd been denied, but just for royalties from that point forward.

John Simon produced *Jericho*, The Band's 1993 return album, which is commonly regarded as the latter-day group's best effort.
Author's collection

Robbie agreed that it was unfair, but still has not taken steps to change things. Of course, I have to take a lot of the blame myself. I was smoking too much pot at the time and should have been looking after my own interests."

So at the time, did Simon have any sense of the profundity of the music that he and The Band were making, that "The Weight" and "I Shall Be Released" would become, in essence, modern-day hymns? "Not at all," he says. "That was the beautiful thing about it. We were just smoking dope, making music, and listening to old stuff like Bill Monroe and Muddy Waters. But the music we were making did actually give me chills then, the same as it does now." Despite the sour royalties issue, the producer and pianist, who today regularly plays with his jazz trio in the Woodstock area, recalls the era fondly. "I'd bring it all back in a flash if I could," he beams. "It was a wonderful part of my life."

22

With My Very Best Friend

The Band's 1974 Reunion with Bob Dylan

By mid-1973, both The Band and Bob Dylan were on the ropes. Neither had released a commercially successful album since 1969. Of Dylan's last three, 1970's *New Morning* had generated mostly lukewarm reviews, and the same year's *Self Portrait* and the album of its left-overs, 1973's *Dylan*, were savaged by critics. For The Band, *Stage Fright* and *Cahoots* had been poorly received, while the live *Rock of Ages* was dismissed by many as a time-marker. With their records not selling well and fissures forming within the group, the quintet many called the world's greatest working rock 'n' roll band seemed about ready to fizzle out. But a mutual reprieve was right around the bend.

Dylan was now living in Malibu and had recently signed with David Geffen's new Asylum label. Geffen and promoter Bill Graham had pitched him on the idea of making a new album and doing a tour. The singer had turned his back on performing and knew he had to face up to going back out on the road to maintain his career, but he was less than comfortable with the concept. In his absence the rock audience had burgeoned to colossal levels, with major acts moving from headlining theaters to selling out stadiums. And he hadn't done a real tour since 1966, when his accompanists weren't yet The Band and stars in their own right.

Bob Dylan and The Band played Long Island's Nassau Coliseum on January 28 and 29, 1974. *Courtesy of Harold Swart*

Rare snapshot of The Band's appearance with Bob Dylan at Nassau Coliseum on January 28, 1974. It was the nineteenth stop on Tour '74.   *Courtesy of Harold Swart*

   With the group fresh from July's attendance-record-setting Watkins Glen festival and a successful two-night stand at New Jersey's Roosevelt Stadium, Dylan pumped them for details about the new realities of the road as he mulled the prospect of his reemergence. At his invitation, Robbie Robertson came to California to talk about The Band co-headlining a tour with him and playing on the new album he was to make for Asylum. Their old friend, the most famous pop musician in the world, was returning to the stage after eons in hiding, and he wanted them to be part of it? The quintet hadn't played with him since the 1971 New Year's Eve *Rock of Ages* concert, but they certainly didn't need much coaxing. By early fall, the rest of the group had moved out to Malibu with their families, and with Dylan they soon began daily, thirteen-hour rehearsals for the tour. *Moondog Matinee* was released in October but written off as another holding move by much of the press, raising the stakes for The Band to once again prove themselves on the road. In November, around a marathon practice schedule in preparation for the tour, work was started on *Planet Waves*, Dylan's first album of new material in four years—and his first and only studio album with The Band.

Key to the Highway: Tour '74

That month, the six-week, forty-show tour was announced with a full-page ad in the *New York Times* for mail-order tickets. Graham's FM Productions was bombarded with five million purchase applications for the 650,000 available seats, making Tour '74, as it was being called, the biggest live-entertainment event ever undertaken up to that point.

The tour began at Chicago Stadium on January 3 in front of a capacity crowd of 18,500. Surrounded onstage by a homey collection of prop living room furniture, the six musicians opened with the obscure, early Dylan tune "Hero Blues" and eased into a program that also included Band favorites "The Night They Drove Old Dixie Down," "Stage Fright," and "Share Your Love with Me." A fifteen-minute intermission was followed by a solo acoustic set by Dylan; The Band returned on their own to do "Life Is a Carnival," "The Shape I'm In," "When You Awake," and "Rag Mama Rag"; Dylan rejoined them for "Forever Young" and "Something There Is About You," from *Planet Waves* (which came out the following week), and "Like a Rolling Stone." For the encore, The Band did "The Weight" and then Dylan came back on with them for his "Most Likely You Go Your Way (And I'll Go Mine)." The remainder of the shows saw slight differences ("Hero Blues" was quickly dropped from the set), but this night basically established the template for the remaining shows on this tour by the most famous pairing in rock history. The grand procession wrapped up on Valentine's Day at the Los Angeles Forum.

Dylan hadn't approached the tour as a yawning musical nostalgia trip. Although during the winter outing he and The Band performed many of his best-known songs—"It Ain't Me Babe," "Blowin' in the Wind," "All Along the Watchtower"—they were given new arrangements and sung and played with a harder, heavier edge. The Band's basic sound was different, too, tastefully colored by Garth Hudson's new synthesizer, a Lowrey model called the String Symphonizer. The tour yielded the live double album *Before the Flood*, which appeared in June 1974 and sold extremely well. But even the considerable financial success of Tour '74 wasn't enough to keep Levon Helm or Dylan from later saying it was one long, passionless payday. But the excursion nevertheless seemed to energize the two parties creatively, as the following year they both delivered studio albums that were considered strong comebacks: Dylan with *Blood on the Tracks* and The Band with *Northern Lights—Southern Cross* (recorded in their newly built Shangri-La studio). Let's look at the two albums most closely associated with 1974's celebrated reunion.

Before the Flood was recorded in New York, Seattle, Oakland, and Los Angeles.

Author's collection

Planet Waves

Fast and loose. That that was the way Bob Dylan wanted to make this album. If living too close to the bustling entertainment capital of the world meant he couldn't make a record the way he'd last recorded with The Band, "with the windows open and a dog lying on the floor," as he told *Rolling Stone* the Basement Tapes had been made, then he wanted to make it casually and with a minimum of fuss. And so he and The Band pretty much did, cutting the meat of *Planet Waves*' tracks in only six sessions at Hollywood's Village Recorder. The record went gold through advance orders and hit number one on *Billboard*'s album chart. But when the final figures came in 1974 it had sold much less than had been anticipated: a comparatively modest 600,000 copies. Critical response was also subdued, with some writers shrugging it off as an unambitious collection of simple songs about domestic life.

But time has shown *Planet Waves* to be one of Dylan's most underrated records, a sparse set that balances the jaunty warmth of the Cajun accordion-seasoned opener "On a Night Like This," both a song of rekindled romance and a metaphor for this musical reunion, with the dark themes of disintegrating love in "Wedding Dress" and the harrowing "Dirge" (the latter featuring only the singer on piano and Robertson on gypsy-esque acoustic guitar). Also highlights are the two versions of Dylan's heartfelt blessing to his children, the instant classic "Forever Young"; one is a soothing lullaby, the other a lively country rocker. Interestingly, while a few *Planet Waves* songs (including a solo acoustic version of the outtake "Nobody 'Cept You") were played during the early shows of Tour '74, with the exception of "Forever Young" all of them were dropped in favor of older material. That song and the yearning "Hazel" would be performed by Dylan and The Band at the Last Waltz concert, the former supplying one of the film's most rousing segments. (Oddly, Richard Manuel's last name is misspelled as "Manual" in the scrawl—Dylan's, it's assumed—on the back cover.)

Before the Flood

Although *Planet Waves* was the album Dylan and The Band were ostensibly plugging on Tour '74, everyone involved knew the entire spectacle was really about the old stuff. That's what people were coming to hear, what they always come to hear. Not the songs from a record that isn't even out when the tour starts. And as mentioned above, the players essentially scuttled any plans of continuing to play new songs after only a few dates.

Asylum Records pulled "Most Likely You Go Your Way (And I'll Go Mine)" as the single from *Before the Flood*. The B-side is a Band-only performance of "Stage Fright."   *Author's collection*

So in a way it's not all that shocking that there are no songs from *Planet Waves*—not a single one—on the platinum-selling *Before the Flood*, which was taped at shows in New York, Seattle, Oakland, and Los Angeles. And admittedly, it's lamentable that four of the two-LP set's eight Band-only songs— "The Night They Drove Old Dixie Down," "The Weight," "The Shape I'm In," and "Stage Fright"—had already been performed on *Rock of Ages*, not to mention that, likely owing to excessive imbibing and fatigue, Manuel's and Danko's voices are plainly shot on the latter two; Manuel's vain attempt to re-summon his once-towering falsetto on "I Shall Be Released" is a hard blow to the heart. Helm, though, is robust and true on "Up on Cripple Creek," even if the song takes no unexpected turns. The vinyl debut of the spirited Danko vehicle "Endless Highway," though, is a welcome surprise. On the truckin' tune, which they'd premiered at Watkins Glen just the summer before, the group sounds decidedly amped up.

But the Dylan tunes, those with and without The Band, are really what's best about *Before the Flood*. The squalling Bard reinvigorates chestnuts like "Don't Think Twice, It's All Right," "Rainy Day Women #12 and 35," and, especially, "Like a Rolling Stone" with a bellowing force even he seems to be shocked by. Later on, he'd say his performances on the tour were nothing *but* force. But it is a force that is inspiring to hear. And judging by the more animated mood that pervades the following year's *Northern Lights—Southern Cross*, it seems that some of that force, at least momentarily, had rubbed off on The Band.

23

Forbidden Fruit

Twenty Essential Band Bootlegs

T hanks to their performances with Bob Dylan on the pirated Basement Tapes, The Band unwittingly helped usher in the explosion of bootleg albums that flourished alongside rock's stadium-level rise in the 1970s. As with other major acts of the era, surreptitiously made recordings of The Band's concerts and underground-circulated tapes of their studio-vault material have been pressed up discreetly on vinyl or CD, to be sold on the black market to eager fans for whom the official releases simply aren't enough. Many of these bootlegs have been, and continue to be, bootlegged themselves. If you bought this book, odds are that you, ahem, may have a *friend* with an interest in such, er, *exotic* items. Assuming that's the case, here are twenty of the most interesting Band recordings of dubious origin. But remember, you didn't hear it here.

Birth

Taken from an audience tape of the group's 1969 live debut as The Band at San Francisco's Winterland Ballroom, this historic, eight-song document comes from April 19, the final date of the three-night engagement. The sound is extremely muffled, but then again, it's sort of amazing the recording exists. "In a Station" is especially sweet, cutting through the low fidelity and hitting you right in the heart. Plus, there's a rare rendition of "To Kingdom Come" and the folk standard "Little Birds." Also issued as *From Winterland 69.*

Crossing the Great Divide

The title of this lavish three-CD set, which has been rebooted a few times, is very similar to Capitol's 1989 three-CD box, *Across the Great Divide*, so don't be confused. Although much of its content has since been rendered redundant via its appearing elsewhere (the Basement Tapes tracks and the three *Big Pink*–era demos are in clearer, remastered form on official Columbia Legacy and Capitol reissues), this is a nice-looking and overall okay-sounding career-spanning set. Disc one covers the Levon and the Hawks, Dylan and the Hawks, and Basement Tapes eras; disc two is *Big Pink* through *Rock of Ages*; and disc three covers the early 1970s, the 1974 tour with Dylan, the Last Waltz, and the reunited Band (the last includes Helm and Dylan doing "The Weight" at New York's Lone Star Café in 1988 and three 1991 *Jericho*-era demos). A release that was clearly put together with love—well, as much love as there can be from a bootlegger.

At Woodstock

This disc on the German Home(r) Entertainment Network label is of surprising sonic quality (likely taken from the unused *Woodstock* film feed) and includes The Band's entire set at the 1969 Woodstock festival, except for the encore of "Loving You Is Sweeter Than Ever." That track appears on an identically titled 2000 CD on the Wilcock label, which lacks this one's "I Shall Be Released" and "We Can Talk." "Where's Dylan?" yells some audience fool before Manuel and the group slip into a sublime "Tears of Rage."

Isle of Wight Festival 1969

"I hope country music goes down all right in the Isle of Wight," says Robertson before a goosebump-raising version of "Ain't No More Cane on the Brazos," track four of this decent-sounding audience recording of The Band's complete nine-song set at the August 1969 U.K. festival. The 2004 GSR label Bob Dylan bootleg titled, simply, *Isle of Wight* includes both The Band's set and their songs with him.

Live 1970

The first CD of this 2012 double-disc set reprises the oft-bootlegged mono audience recording of the July 10, 1970, show at the Hollywood Bowl, which, interestingly, had Miles Davis as the opener. But new to the world of Band collector's curios is the content of disc two: the group's January 1, 1970, concert at Queens College's Colden Auditorium in Flushing, New York. There's some tape hiss and crowd chatter and it's a more distant front-of-house source than the Hollywood Bowl tape, but rare it is. And the energy of the performances makes it very much worth seeking out.

Syria Mosque 1970

Most of this eighteen-track Japanese CD comes from a 1970 Dutch television film of the group's concert at Pittsburgh's Syria Mosque (footage of four songs appears on the *1969–1970* DVD mentioned elsewhere in this book). It appears to be a soundboard tape. The version of "Strawberry Wine" is particularly lusty.

Frankfurt, Germany

It seems that YouTube is the only place to find this twenty-two-song, audio-only document of the May 20, 1971, show at Frankfurt's massive Jahrhunderthalle. For an audience tape in the age of sketchy P.A. systems, the sound is full and remarkable, with stunning harmonies on "Rockin' Chair."

Royal Albert Rags

Another boot taken from a distantly seated ticketholder's tape, this one finds the five back at the Royal Albert Hall on June 2, 1971, for their first London appearance since playing the same venue with Dylan in 1966. One can sense the rapt attention in the house during "The Unfaithful Servant," and the closing version of "Slippin' and Slidin'" is fiercely propulsive.

In Central Park NYC 1971

For years, there were mostly incomplete versions of the June 30, 1971, concert at Central Park's Wollman Skating Rink in New York circulating (although there was a scarce early-'70s vinyl release that spread the entire show across an LP and a bonus seven-inch). When it appeared in 1997, the twenty-four-karat-gold audiophile *Central Park in the Dark* was deemed worth the wait by the faithful. But with that iteration having come and gone, *In Central Park NYC 1971*, on Italy's Rock Rare Collection Fetish label, is the most readily findable high-quality edition.

Ultrasonic Studios, Hempstead, NY 1971

These eleven tracks from the Long Island rehearsals for the December 1971 *Rock of Ages* concerts at New York's Academy of Music are in jaw-dropping clarity, and supposedly from the master reels. The vocals, horns, guitar, between-song banter, and general room sound are revelatory. The long-gone *Academy of Outtakes* double CD has most of these tracks, but it omits one of the two takes of "The W.S. Walcott Medicine Show" and both takes of "Rag Mama Rag"; all tracks also appear on *Watkins Glen Soundcheck 1973 & Ultrasonic Studios Hempstead NY 1971*, which may be easier to locate.

We Will Set You Free

Very listenable audience-sourced recording of the group's whole August 21, 1971, set for the Beggar's Banquet festival at Toronto's Borough of York Stadium (they headlined over Seatrain, Lee Michaels, Edgar Winter's White Trash, Sundance, and Sha Na Na). "Look Out Cleveland" really ripped that night.

Roosevelt Stadium (single CD version)

In 1973, The Band, then at the peak of their live popularity, played three consecutive nights (July 30–August 1) at Jersey City's Roosevelt Stadium. While there have been some so-so audience-recorded bootlegs of the shows (*Old Dixie*, *This Wheel's on Fire*, and a three-CD set also called *Roosevelt Stadium*) and a soundboard tape of their mediocre July 31 set (*Blue Highways*), it's this, the single-CD release of the August 1 set, that you'll want. A quality soundboard recording, it's further notable in that it contains an early version of "Endless Highway" (predating its official debut on *Before the Flood* the following year), more covers than was usual for one show ("Back to Memphis," "Share Your Love," "Don't Do It," "Loving You Is Sweeter Than Ever"; the version of "Saved" comes from the night before), and heated versions of "Life Is a Carnival," "Chest Fever," and other songs.

Carter Barron Amphitheater

The quintet's July 17, 1976, concert at the four-thousand-seat Carter Barron Amphitheater in Washington, D.C., has been booted multiple times, which certainly surprised no one, as it was aired live on the syndicated radio show *The King Biscuit Flower Hour*. On disc it's appeared as *Live USA*, *Ophelia*, *And*

THE BAND

CARTER BARRON AMPHITHEATER

WASHINGTON DC, JULY 17TH 1976

INCLUDES
DON'T DO IT
THE SHAPE I'M IN
IT MAKES NO DIFFERENCE
THE WEIGHT
KING HARVEST (HAS SURELY COME)

OPHELIA
TEARS OF RAGE
FORBIDDEN FRUIT
THIS WHEEL'S ON FIRE
THE NIGHT THEY DROVE
OLD DIXIE DOWN

The Band's July 17, 1976, concert at Washington, D.C.'s Carter Barron Amphitheater was aired on *The King Biscuit Flower Hour* and has been bootlegged repeatedly.

Author's collection

The Band Played On . . . Without Robbie Robertson, King Biscuit Flower Hour, Musical Legacy, and *Twilight in Concert.* The great sound and attractive packaging of this straightforwardly titled 2014 CD on the Keyhole label warrant a big thumbs-up, as do the liner notes, which reprint an article about the group from the March 1976 issue of *Crawdaddy* magazine. Also issued on vinyl by DOL Records in 2015 with the erroneous title *Live in Washington, DC August 16, 1976.*

Plays On

The guys must have hit the road immediately after packing up from the Carter Barron Amphitheater show, as the next night they had to be at the

Music Inn in Lenox, Massachusetts, where this good-quality double CD derives from. The four-hundred-mile trek would likely account for the lengthy stage introduction (a minute and a half of tuning; they must have been pretty out of it) that begins disc one. But once things get going, the group doesn't sound too tired at all, as the performances are animated and tight. Paul Butterfield and tuba man Howard Johnson sit in for the show-closing "Life Is a Carnival."

Palladium Circles

On September 18, 1976, when The Band played the opening night of New York's Palladium, the room would have looked very familiar to them—the venue was actually the reopened Academy of Music, where they had

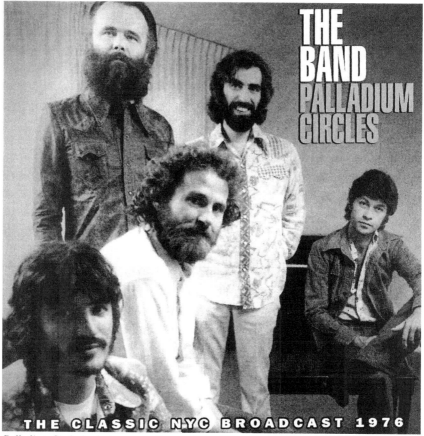

Palladium Circles includes a rare live version of "Acadian Driftwood."   *Author's collection*

recorded *Rock of Ages* four years earlier. Released in 2014, this seventy-eight-minute CD is taken from the same FM broadcast that begat the two-disc *A Night at the Palladium* and *Take a Load for Free* and leaves off those sets' "Forbidden Fruit" and some stage introductions. A rousing "Ophelia" kicks off the party, which also includes a version of the very rarely performed "Acadian Driftwood."

The Complete Last Waltz

Limited to three thousand copies, this extravagant 1995 four-CD set on the Cool Daddy imprint contains The Band's entire 1976 farewell concert at San Francisco's Winterland ballroom. Culled from soundboard and film sources (with a slight, unobtrusive hum on some tracks), it boasts seventeen cuts that didn't make the official live release, such as an impeccable "Georgia on My Mind," a horn-augmented "This Wheel's on Fire," and all of the guest-star appearances (no poets, though). It's packaged in a mini-binder with individual CD envelope sleeves, a thirty-six-page booklet of photos, liner notes, and other artwork, and even a facsimile of a Last Waltz welcome card. An identically titled four-CD-R version of the complete event released by the Hot Stuff label in 2006 comes completely from soundboard tapes (with none of the overdubbed performance repairs of the Warner Bros. soundtrack). Both of these sets command high prices on the collector's market, if you can find them.

After the Waltz

Also an exhaustive multidisc set, this six-CD-R compendium focuses on the post–Robbie Robertson years (1982–1996) and features performances by the retooled Band and various solo and combination appearances by Danko, Manuel, Hudson, and Helm. High points include Manuel's last solo concert (the Lone Star, New York, February 8, 1986) and guest spots by Emmylou Harris, Traffic's Dave Mason, David Hidalgo and Louie Perez of Los Lobos, and others.

And Then There Were Four

This super-crisp 2015 CD came from a radio broadcast of the freshly reunited Band at the University of Chicago's Mandel Hall. The show in the intimate, 750-capacity theater took place on November 6, 1983 (not July 2,

And Then There Were Four comes from a 1983 Chicago radio broadcast by the reunited Band. The sound quality is excellent.   *Author's collection*

as the back cover states), and should give pause to anyone who says The Band wasn't still a great live unit after Robertson left. Helm, Danko, Hudson, and Manuel are contagiously overjoyed to be playing live together again (here with the Cate Brothers Band) and the instrumental performances are excellent. Manuel struggles with his falsetto during "I Shall Be Released" and switches to a lower register, but Helm and especially Danko are in superb voice. In addition to the fine versions of the hits, there are unexpected versions of "Milk Cow Boogie" and "Java Blues," the latter from Danko's self-titled solo album. Also released as *The Weight: Live in Chicago 1983*.

Live in Tokyo 1983

This is a Dutch two-CD/one-DVD set of the Cate Brothers–era Band's September 2, 1983, Tokyo concert during the group's first visit to Japan. Once again, Manuel's voice is rough at times, but overall the show represents an enjoyable live representation of this edition of the group. On a version of the Louis Jordan hit "Caledonia," Helm steps out front to sing and blow some harp while Terry Cagle holds down the backbeat. "Hey, Garth, you know what my mama told me?" he says to Hudson. "She said, 'Boy, everybody's been talkin' about the way you and Caledonia's been hangin' out. You been staying up late, goin' down to that sushi bar, eatin' all o' that raw fish!'" One wonders what the Far Eastern audience made of such down-home repartee.

24

And He Got Caught in the Spotlight

The Last Waltz

f there's a better concert movie than *The Last Waltz*, it hasn't played outside of heaven yet. Martin Scorsese's larger-than-life 1978 document of The Band's 1976 farewell show at San Francisco's Winterland Ballroom is a dreamlike, two-hour journey through the final performance of one of the greatest bands of all time. It's also the fittingly grand finale for an entire era of popular culture, in which one of that epoch's principal acts, joined by a handpicked roster of their influential friends, fades gracefully away beneath dimming chandeliers. Even Levon Helm, who during its production was outraged with Robbie Robertson's decision to break up the group and considered the film a reminder of an unhappy time, eventually conceded, grudgingly, that it likely is the most beautiful concert movie ever made.

The Band spent a week preparing for the night they'd officially dubbed "the Last Waltz" at their studio/clubhouse Shangri-La with their old producer John Simon, who'd been appointed music director for the show. "It all went pretty smoothly," says Simon. "Each day, one or two of the guest artists would show up to rehearse their numbers. But the best rehearsal of all was the dress rehearsal in [Winterland]. I felt like a ringleader at a circus calling the shots for an audience of, basically, me. Each time we took a break, I'd run over to Marty Scorsese's hotel room to deliver the sequence of each song—who sang when, who played solos, et cetera." Using Simon's sequences, the director meticulously mapped out the camera cues for the performances.

The evening started with the Berkeley Promenade Orchestra playing classical waltzes for professional dancers. "When The Band finally went on I listened to the first songs from the soundboard in the hall, to make sure everyone there was hearing the balance as good as it could be," recalls

Simon, who at points also coached the musicians from the wings. "I went onstage to make sure all was okay with the horns. And that was a stroke of luck, because as Robbie was counting off their first song, I raised my hand to get him to stop because the sequence had been changed and the horns had the wrong song in front of them." According to Simon, Robertson wrote "The Last Waltz Theme" during the concert's intermission of readings by San Francisco poets and Simon himself ended up teaching the instrumental piece to the other players, on the spot.

The biblical drama behind the making of the film, the staging of the concert, and the sheer scale of the whole thing was as dramatic as the music itself. The stage's sumptuous set was conceived by famed production designer Boris Leven (*West Side Story*, *The Sound of Music*) using props from the San Francisco Opera's production of Verdi's *La Traviata*, and the lighting bathed the whole affair in a honey-toned glow. Yet although it remains an embarrassment of aural and filmic riches, *The Last Waltz* does have (admit it, Band fans) a few bothersome characteristics. Joni Mitchell's and Neil Diamond's star-powered, forced-fit sets feel out of place, their music having little to do with The Band's. Then there was the legendary cocaine use that went on throughout the production; infamously, thousands of dollars were spent in post-production using a process called rotoscoping to edit out coke residue seen hanging from Neil Young's nose. And there are those who have decried it as a pompous, self-mythologizing exercise, bisected with sycophantic Robertson close-ups and interviews, that ignores the audience. But even the most beautiful diamond has its flaws, and the gorgeously immortalized sum of *The Last Waltz*'s brilliant portions is easily greater than that of any difficult passages.

The Last Waltz is a veritable pageant of memorable moments. Every viewing yields new and previously passed-over pearls of transcendent performance, aesthetic delight, and poignant, lost-in-the-cracks genius. Here are ten favorite scenes.

Cutthroat

In the opening scene, Rick Danko, looking laid-back and cool in brown leather, is shooting pool in the hangout room of Shangri-La.

"Hey, Rick, what's the game?" Scorsese asks.

After racking up, the bassist glances distractedly at the camera. "Cutthroat," he replies.

The director prods him further. "What's the object?"

"The object is to keep your balls on the table," he answers, about to smoothly break the proceedings open with a crack of his cue, "and knock everybody else's off."

Danko appears oblivious to the metaphors. And why wouldn't he be? He was the genial lamb of intellectual innocence, not the symbolism-driven auteur Scorsese or his Bergman-buff apprentice, Robertson. But the parallels are right there: that of the group breaking up and scattering, and that of the take-no-prisoners, blow-every-other-band-off-the-stage philosophy they'd perfected under Ronnie Hawkins.

"Don't Do It"

"The beginning of the beginning of the end of the beginning," says Robertson during the film when Scorsese asks him what its concert represented to him. Although Scorsese placed the unplanned encore of "Don't Do It" at the front of the movie as an allusion to the guitarist's answer—the night's actual first song was "Up on Cripple Creek"—their interpretation of the Marvin Gaye hit makes a gripping starter here, just as it does on *Rock of Ages*. And besides the poetic set-list reshuffling, there's another metaphor at play: on one level the song's narrator is begging his lover not to break his heart, but in this context it can also be seen as a plea for the group not to break up. Going for broke, the fivesome just *kills* "Don't Do It," the very last song the original Band would formally play together live. Propelled by Helm's desperate vocal, it feels like it's about to go crashing off the rails at any moment. Which of course it never does. Next stop: The ages.

The Hawk Takes Flight

"Whoo! Big time, Bill! Big time!"

For raw, rocking power, it's hard to beat the rollicking reunion of Ronnie Hawkins and his onetime boys for their 1963 signature hit "Who Do You Love." Mugging it up between Danko and Robertson with trademark lewdness, Hawkins prowls 'n' growls amid the group's grinding, unrelenting crunch. He takes off his hat to comically fan Robertson's fiery fingers on the scorching solo. Hudson interjects with some squiggly stabs—"Take it easy, Garth, doncha gimme no lip!" the Hawk hollers playfully toward the organist's corner. This is one of the few points of the night where Helm seems genuinely joyful, happy as a hog to be back behind his old boss.

"The Weight"

It's so very hard to pick a favorite *Last Waltz* scene, but for this repeat viewer the version of "The Weight" with the Staple Singers is the one. There was certainly no better guest choice to represent the gospel ingredient of The Band's alchemical Americana on film than the Staples, whose multipart singing style had been an incalculable influence on the group since their earliest days. The Band played the song on their own at Winterland and filmed this loving rendition with the familial foursome at an MGM Studios soundstage in Hollywood the following year. As usual, Helm's hardscrabble voice takes the first verse. But then comes Mavis Staples's emphatic, goosebump-inducing exhortations on the second, followed by the slow-'n'-low-voiced patriarch Pops Staples. Up next is the animated Danko's quavering passage about Crazy Chester and finally the coda, sung by all, with a heart-stopping vocal flourish to fade things out. Chills.

Lesson from Levon

As mentioned above, Helm had his reasons for not being in the best of moods during the making of the movie. But being the consummate professional, he never let his misgivings get in the way of delivering superb performances onstage—and offstage as well. During the interviews, the tension could get thick between him and Scorsese, who was often the needling source of the drummer's discontent. But here, Helm, God bless him, doesn't step away from doing the group and their music justice. He drawls about the formative parts of his Southern youth—W.S. Walcott's Rabbit's Foot Minstrels; the saucy, salacious midnight rambles; the pre–Chuck Berry duck walks; the geographically specific merging of country, bluegrass, blues, rhythm, and show music that, "if it dances," becomes "something else." "What's it called?" Scorsese inquires. Keeping a twinkle in his eyes and cracking a grin that's as warm as it is patience-tested, Helm replies: "Rock 'n' roll." No wonder he became such a damn fine actor. Despite the awkwardness of the situation, it's clear Helm still believed that The Band was bigger than the sum of its parts. And here he reminds us that the group is also part of a continuum that's even bigger than that.

"The Night They Drove Old Dixie Down"

Yes, hands down one of The Band's greatest songs and an expected inclusion in the show. But the version here takes on added, if you will, weight. A song about the last stand of Southern pride in the wake of the Confederacy's defeat, on this particular night it's quite obviously a metaphor for the last stand of The Band itself. With stoic somberness the Allen Toussaint–charted horns begin, burnishing the epic tragedy of both the song's subject and the palpable emotions of the occasion. You feel the shattered frustration in Helm's fusillade rolls and especially in his vocal: *How did we get to this point? Why, dear Lord, must this be the end?* An eerie coincidence: The opulent chandeliers hanging overhead were used in *Gone with the Wind*. And watch the back of the stage during the first chorus. Something makes the curtains ripple for a few seconds—like battle flags, waved defiantly but ultimately in vain. Helm wrote that it's perhaps the best live performance the group ever gave of the song, and that's very easily believed.

Clapton Comes Undone

With The Band being an act that "changed his life," there was no way Eric Clapton was going to pass up the group's final go-round. Slowhand made the scene with "All Our Past Times," a song he cowrote with Danko (left out of the movie), before launching into "Further On Up the Road," the Bobby "Blue" Bland chestnut that had been in the Hawks' repertoire as well as his own. But about forty seconds into the song, the front end of Clapton's hastily fastened strap pops off, causing the stunned Englishman to stop soloing and partially drop his Stratocaster (it sounds like he drops an F-bomb in there as well). There's a split second where everyone freezes, looking shocked. And then, as if everything had been planned, Robertson picks the baton right up, leaping into the opening with a burning solo that seamlessly completes the one Clapton had begun. The two rival gunslingers then proceed to shoot it out, the band cooking around them with machinelike precision. Absolute magic. And there were cameras there to catch it.

Muddy Moves the House

It was thanks only to Helm's Southern stubbornness that his hero Muddy Waters stayed in the picture. During the show's lead-up, Robertson and his fellow organizers had suddenly decided they needed more time for Neil Diamond and the other "contemporary" guests and asked Helm to take the blues god off the bill. Enraged, the drummer threatened to quit then and there if Waters wasn't kept firmly in place (reportedly, Ronnie Hawkins was also nearly a victim of such machinations). Luckily for us, Helm got his way, and the intense, unremitting pounding of Muddy's classic "Mannish Boy" made it in. Backed by The Band with Paul Butterfield on harp and Waters's guitarist Bob Margolin, the sixty-three-year-old legend shudders, leers, points accusingly, and snarls with pure sexual bravado—"I'm a *mannnnnn!*" If the grinning Robertson had had any reservations about keeping the Chicago icon on board, they've evaporated, and the evening's energy takes a quantum leap. Shockingly, the song almost went undocumented: All of the cameramen save for László Kovács, the Hungarian-born cinematographer of *Easy Rider* and *Five Easy Pieces*, had stopped to reload, and it was his lone lens that captured this incredible moment. Not seen: a proudly beaming Waters kissing Helm on the forehead after the song.

Van Brings the Caravan

As torrid as "Mannish Boy" is, it's the appearance of Van Morrison that kicks things into high gear—literally. Although his turn at the mic is closely preceded by some great Band songs and Paul Butterfield's wailing on a funky "Mystery Train," we've also just suffered through the excruciating Joni Mitchell and Neil Diamond numbers. But turn on your electric light. Turn up your radio. Because here comes the Belfast Cowboy, stealing the night with his glitter-spangled maroon suit and whisky-keg voice on "Caravan," from his Woodstock-period album *Moondance*. Morrison's on a mission to turn this train around, and oh how he does. The brass section explodes from behind on the *Na, na, na-na! Na, na, na!* refrain as he punches the air and high-kicks his way across the front of the stage, stirring the crowd to a screaming frenzy and wringing out every last ounce of his Irish soul until he's dizzy and spent. "Van the man!" shouts Robertson as the singer exits stage right, coining the singer's famous nickname right before our disbelieving ears and eyes.

Dylan Delivers!

The Bard giveth, and the Bard very nearly taketh away. To finance the massive undertaking of making the film, Scorsese and Robertson had turned to Mo Ostin, the president of Warner Bros. Records. Ostin, who had been trying to lure The Band away from Capitol to his label, offered to advance them $1.5 million toward the movie—but *only* if Bob Dylan was in it. Dylan agreed and arrived in San Francisco the week of the concert to rehearse, but he decided backstage at Winterland, about fifteen minutes before he

The Last Waltz is considered by many to be the most beautiful concert movie ever made. This original lobby card for the 1978 theatrical release depicts the ensemble performance of "I Shall Be Released." Left to right: Dr. John, Neil Diamond, Joni Mitchell, Neil Young, Rick Danko, Van Morrison, Bob Dylan, and Robbie Robertson. *Author's collection*

was due to sing with The Band, that, well, he just wasn't that into it. Part of his reasoning, he said, was that *The Last Waltz* would be competing with *Renaldo and Clara*, the forthcoming film about his 1975 Rolling Thunder Revue tour. This, unsurprisingly, sent pretty much everyone into a panic.

After some tense negotiations, show promoter Bill Graham got the okay to shoot only Dylan's last two songs. The mid-'60s Dylan/Hawks staple "Baby, Let Me Follow You Down" and the *Planet Waves* ballad "Hazel" were played with the cameras off; with them back on, we're treated to the bearded, pimp-hatted Dylan leading the boys through another tender *Planet Waves* track, "Forever Young"; a spontaneous, roaring reprise of "Baby, Let Me Follow You Down"; and the arm-waving, all-star finale of "I Shall Be Released" with singers Clapton, Joni Mitchell, Dr. John, Neil Young, Neil Diamond, Paul Butterfield, Ronnie Hawkins, and Bobby Charles plus Ringo Starr on second drum kit and Ron Wood on guitar. It's a truly triumphant ending, especially with the knowledge that, mere minutes before, it was looking like *The Last Waltz* would be lost.

25

Music in the Air, I Hear It Everywhere

Box Sets and Best-Ofs

T he Band isn't the easiest act to anthologize. Many of their best songs are scattered across their later albums, but it's generally agreed that their greatest material is concentrated on the first two. And *Music from Big Pink* and *The Band* are so flawless as complete works that, really, they're best experienced just as they are. It feels sacrilegious to isolate and tear out tracks and reassemble them elsewhere, like yanking brothers and sisters apart and jamming them together with their cousins. Even the subsequent, spottier records have their own narrative and flow, representing a certain period in the group's evolution, and should really be viewed through that lens.

But maybe another way to think of such an unthinkable idea, at least when it comes to being forced to choose songs for a "best-of" compilation, is this: There's always a place for a great mixtape. Mixtapes are usually composed of songs by several artists, but what could be better than a mixtape of *only* great songs by The Band? Maybe you're doing a long drive and you'd like to hear one of the better *Cahoots* or *Islands* cuts but aren't in the mood to suffer through the lesser ones. A well-programmed anthology is the perfect solution. And if you leave the programming to someone else, the existential crisis is *their* dilemma, not yours. Problem solved. No guilt.

There are many Band anthologies on the market. Below are the best of the best-ofs. And for those hard-core fans who want a deeper immersion and more music than a single album can supply, here also are the most-recommended multidisc box sets.

The Shape I'm In

Annotated by *Across the Great Divide* author Barney Hoskyns, this is arguably the best single-CD Band survey currently available. Some may chide the compilers for not including anything from *Islands*, but in terms of overall listenability the track list is tight and plays much like one of The Band's live shows, kicking off with the title rocker, unfurling the audience favorites, and tearing down the house at the end with "Don't Do It."

Greatest Hits

The next-best single-disc anthology out there in 2016 is this eighteen-track comp sourced from the early-2000s remasters of The Band's Capitol albums. The expected tunes from *Music from Big Pink* and *The Band* are here, and the later titles are well represented.

The Best of The Band

Released by Capitol in 1976, this single album is the first-ever Band anthology and contains their best-known songs: "The Weight," "Up on Cripple Creek," and "The Night They Drove Old Dixie Down," as well as "Twilight," which had previously only been out as a single. The British version replaces the U.S. version's "Tears of Rage," "It Makes No Difference," and "Don't Do It" with "Time to Kill," "I Shall Be Released," "Ain't Got No Home," and their U.K. hit "Rag Mama Rag." The 1994 Australian import adds nine tracks to the U.S. and U.K.'s eleven.

The Best of The Band, Volume II

A handy way to check out the reunited Band's music, this 1999 Rhino Records compilation pulls tracks from their three 1990s albums, *Jericho*, *High on the Hog*, and *Jubilation*. Reissued with different artwork by Pyramid Media in 2013.

Anthology

First issued by Capitol in 1978 as a double album—likely to cash in on that year's release of *The Last Waltz*; the cover art is vaguely similar to the Warner Bros. soundtrack—this set was reissued as two separate volumes in 1980 and 1982. Twenty big songs on each disc, roughly in chronological order. The 1978 edition has liner notes by rock scribe Robert Palmer.

The two-LP *Anthology* was originally released by Capitol in 1978; the label later issued the two discs as separate volumes.   *Author's collection*

A Musical History

The mother lode. Bound in a beautifully illustrated hardcover book with extensive, album-by-album liner notes by Band scholar Rob Bowman (some of which overlap with his notes for The Band's single-disc remasters), this 2005 five-CD/one-DVD set overseen by Robbie Robertson covers all eras of the original group's career, from their beginnings with Ronnie Hawkins through their work with Dylan, their 1968–1977 albums, and right up to *The Last Waltz*. It's not for the casual fan, but serious Bandophiles will find it essential. Among its 102 well-chosen and rare tracks are a staggering 32 previously unreleased cuts that include revelatory outtakes, live songs, alternate versions, demos, and song sketches. The DVD contains footage from the 1970 Capitol promo film of the group rehearsing in Woodstock and live clips from 1970's Festival Express tour, 1971's *Rock of Ages* Academy of Music concerts, 1974's Wembley Stadium concert, and 1976's *Saturday*

Night Live appearance. *The Best of A Musical History* samples nineteen tracks from the full set and is available as a single CD or a CD/DVD combo (the DVD has five clips from the box).

To Kingdom Come

This 1989 double CD (or triple LP) makes an excellent compromise between any of the single-disc compendiums and the box sets. With twenty-eight tracks, it offers a solid overview of the crucial years and includes the not-often-anthologized "4% Pantomime" and "Knockin' Lost John."

The Collection

This fourteen-song 2007 Dutch compilation is interesting in that instead of centering on *Music from Big Pink* and *The Band*, as most Band best-ofs do, it focuses mainly on the later Capitol albums.

The Moon Struck One

Kind of a cool concept, although not as an introduction. This fourteen-cut Dutch compilation is comprised only of songs sung by Richard Manuel. No rarities or surprises, but if you've ever dreamed of a Manuel-vocals-only Band mixtape, your prayers have been answered.

Across the Great Divide

Until the advent of *A Musical History*, this three-CD, fifty-six-track 1994 set was the definitive Band box. Discs one and two are selections from the studio albums. Disc three has cuts from the 1975 *Basement Tapes*, *The Last Waltz*, and the fake *Live at Watkins Glen* CD plus some rarities, most of which have since appeared as bonus tracks on the 2000/2001 remasters and/or *A Musical History* (some exceptions: a raw Levon and the Hawks version of "Honky Tonk" taken from the *Live 1964* bootleg, a walloping "Slippin' and Slidin'" from a 1970 St. Louis show, and Manuel crooning a beautiful "She Knows" live in 1986, which was later tacked onto *High on the Hog*). *The Best of Across the Great Divide* samples sixteen cuts from the set.

The Millennium Collection: 20th Century Masters

This is a streamlined, ten-song hit list mainly pulled from the first three albums, although "It Makes No Difference" is here from *Northern Lights—Southern Cross*. Also released as *10 Great Songs*.

Capitol Rarities 1968–1977

This thirty-three-track 2015 CD rounds up all the bonus tracks that appeared on the 2000/2001 remasters of the Capitol albums. It's an affordable no-brainer if you already have the original albums and don't want to rebuy them just to get the extras.

Collected

Released in the Netherlands by Universal Music, *Collected* is a four-disc set that opens with the 1965 Canadian Squires/Levon and the Hawks rarity "Leave Me Alone" and moves into a couple of Basement Tapes tunes before continuing on into disc two with material from The Band's 1960s and 1970s albums, including "When You Awake" live with Bob Dylan from *Before the Flood*; the song sketch of "Twilight" is on *A Musical History*. Disc three is made up of assorted solo/side project tracks and songs by the 1990s Band, while the fourth disc is a DVD of a live Band tribute concert by Dutch musicians.

Three of a Kind

This 2011 set was produced by Capitol for sale exclusively at Levon Helm's Midnight Ramble events, although copies do sometimes come up for sale online. It boxes up *Music from Big Pink*, *The Band*, and *Stage Fright* (no bonus tracks), each in a standard jewel case.

The Capitol Albums: 1968–1977

If you need to upgrade those worn vintage LPs, this lush 2015 vinyl box set from Universal Music contains 180-gram pressings of all of The Band's classic Capitol albums, including the double *Rock of Ages*, with their original artwork.

26

That's the Stuff You Gotta Watch

The Band on Film

T here have been many movie and television projects that have involved or focused on The Band as a group and as individuals, either as documentary subjects, actors, narrators, or musical contributors. In this chapter, we'll cast our eyes on some of the fivesome's notable big- and small-screen endeavors.

You Shoulda Seen What I Just Heard: Documentaries and Music Films

Naturally, we'll want to look at the concert and music-oriented programs first. Below is a rundown of the best-known—and most obscure—musical entries in The Band's filmography.

The Last Waltz (1978)

Martin Scorsese's opulent document of the original Band's guest-heavy parting concert is surveyed on other pages of this tome. But of course it still belongs right here, at the top of this listing of Band-oriented films. In addition to the two-hour film itself, the 2002 Special Edition DVD of *The Last Waltz* includes previously unseen footage of the all-star, end-of-show jam, a featurette with Robertson and the director about the making of the film, plus theatrical trailers, audio commentaries, and a photo gallery. A 2008 Japanese double DVD adds a piece on cinematographer Lázsló Kovács. *The Last Waltz Celebration*, a Japanese bootleg triple DVD, recreates the full live concert by editing together songs from the official film and independently shot black-and-white segments (the entire black-and-white live film was bootlegged in 2006 as *The Lost Waltz*).

Ain't in It for My Health: A Film About Levon Helm (2010)

The essential bookend to *The Last Waltz*. An antidote to the sometimes glitzy tendencies of Scorsese's opus, this far more personal film is a powerful portrait of the drummer, capturing his tough-as-nails spirit as well as his moments of vulnerability and his warm humor and generosity. Directed by Jacob Hatley, it tells the tense-but-triumphant tale of Helm's life and music while intimately detailing his struggle with throat cancer, the regaining of his voice, and the making of his stunning 2007 album, *Dirt Farmer*. Mostly filmed at Helm's famed Barn home/recording studio in Woodstock (where the director also lived for much of the shooting), it follows him from his TV room to the doctor, the stage, and points between, with cameos by friends Billy Bob Thornton, Chris Robinson (Black Crowes), and Rick's wife, Elizabeth Danko. "This sense of mortality was present from the beginning," Hatley told *Rolling Stone*. "He was not going to go quietly into the night."

Only Half Way Home (2008)

Hatley also directed this twenty-minute short inspired by the music of *Dirt Farmer*. Great scenes of Helm reconnecting with his youth while driving a tractor and chewing the fat with local farmers, playing with his band in a wood-lined tavern, and acting masterfully in some dramatic vignettes. Find it on YouTube.

The Authorized Videography (1995)

Released concurrently with The Band's 1995–1996 tour, this one-hour documentary is narrated by Harry Dean Stanton and features interviews with the then-surviving members and with associates like Ronnie Hawkins, Eric Clapton, George Harrison, and others. It's a little cardboard-ish, and producer Mark Hall doesn't have the flow (or the budget) of a Scorsese, but it does a decent job of running down The Band's basic story, from the Hawks era to their performance at the 1992 gala celebrating Bob Dylan's thirtieth anniversary as a recording artist. There are some sticking points: When the recording of *The Band* in Sammy Davis Jr.'s pool house is being discussed, it's actually the 1970 Capitol promo clip of the five playing at Robertson's Woodstock studio that's shown, and the fact that Helm quit the 1965 Dylan tour isn't mentioned. Unlike *The Last Waltz*, Helm is much more the focus here, and his reminiscences about Arkansas music and how he created the drum patterns on The Band's songs are fascinating.

Classic Albums: The Band (1997)

Even though it focuses chiefly on one era of the group—the making of *The Band*—this is the best-made non–*Last Waltz* Band doc. Directed by Bob Smeaton (*The Beatles Anthology, Festival Express*) for the BBC's *Classic Albums* series, it's an excellent portal into what made The Band and their music so distinct. A scene-setting lead-up explains the group's origins as the Hawks and their mid-sixties union with Dylan, and *The Band* is examined track by track, with Robertson, Helm, and Danko telling the stories behind the tunes and demonstrating their inner workings (Hudson's his characteristically amiable-but-untalkative self). Some key moments: Helm and producer John Simon listening to the original reels in the studio, using the mixing board faders to single out the vocals and instruments; Robertson at a piano re-creating the way he quietly composed "The Night They Drove Old Dixie Down" as his newborn son slept; and Danko's heart-melting solo acoustic renditions of "The Unfaithful Servant" and "When You Awake." Commentators include Eric Clapton, George Harrison, road manager Jonathan Taplin, Elton John lyricist Bernie Taupin, Elliott Landy, writers Barney Hoskyns and Greil Marcus, and others.

Festival Express (2003)

As great as their live performances are in the glossy *The Last Waltz*, the three songs in *Festival Express* may add up to the most gripping and true-to-life cinematic representation of the group at the height of their live powers. In 1970, promoters Ken Walker and Thor Eaton set up Festival Express, a five-day summer concert tour co-headlined by Janis Joplin, The Band, and the Grateful Dead that crossed Canada by rail. The Band is seen careening through "Slippin' and Slidin'," a lovely version of "The Weight," and, with Manuel in spectacular voice, an especially touching "I Shall Be Released." Other peaks include the onboard jams, in particular Danko, Joplin, and Jerry Garcia's sloshing-drunk rendition of "Ain't No More Cane on the Brazos" (there's also a blues jam by Danko and Buddy Guy). Likewise appearing on the 2014 two-DVD issue are Ian & Sylvia and Great Speckled Bird, the Flying Burrito Brothers, Eric Andersen, Delaney & Bonnie, and more. Another Japanese bootleg, 2005's *Festival Express Outtakes*, is devoted to live Band tour footage left out of the documentary.

Eat the Document (1972)

Assembled from film shot on the Bob Dylan/Hawks 1966 U.K. tour, this surreal, Dylan-produced documentary was not released to theaters and has never officially come out on VHS or DVD, but bootlegs abound. In addition to scenes of backstage drug-taking and the singer and Robertson working on new songs in hotel rooms, the fifty-two-minute color film has great footage of audience-tension-fraught performances—including the moment of the infamous "Judas!" cry at Manchester Free Trade Hall.

Easy Rider (1969)

The studio recording of "The Weight" would subsequently be used in many movies, but never to as great effect as it first was, during Peter Fonda and Dennis Hopper's desert chopper ride in this counterculture classic. The Band opted not to lease the song for the soundtrack album, so instead the LP contains a carbon-copy version by the Los Angeles group Smith.

Woodstock Diaries (2002) / Woodstock: The Music (2001) / Woodstock: The Lost Performances (1991)

The Band's set at the 1969 Woodstock festival was filmed but doesn't appear in Michael Wadleigh's monumental 1970 documentary named for the event. Part of the reason for this is that the group didn't feel their performance was up to snuff. Of the ten songs they played, the only one to appear on VHS or DVD is "The Weight," which is indeed marred by Robertson's off-pitch vocals and distracting incidental exclamations (in *This Wheel's on Fire*, Helm implies that the group usually preferred to mask Robertson's vocal shortcomings by keeping his stage mic turned off). That tune is found on each of these compilations, all of which round up various performances by other acts that were omitted from the better-known *Woodstock*. However, a YouTube quest yields a devastatingly fine rendition of "Tears of Rage" whose quality matches anything in the proper film. Hopefully, the entire set will eventually make it out.

Down in the Flood (2012)

British documentary about the collaborations between Bob Dylan and The Band, stretching from the 1965 and 1966 tours to the Basement Tapes period, the 1974 tour, and their sporadic later relationship. Interviewed are Garth Hudson, John Simon, Ronnie Hawkins, authors Barney Hoskyns, Sid Griffin, and Anthony DeCurtis, and Helm's replacement on the '66 tour, Mickey Jones. It has the stuffy feel characteristic of other DVDs on the Sexy Intellectual label, but it's informative, nonetheless.

World Tour 1966: The Home Movies (2002)

Mickey Jones brought his 8mm movie camera on the road while he was briefly backing up Dylan as a Hawk. The *World Tour 1966* DVD tenuously strings together ninety minutes of his silent, color film (generic, Dylan-ish music has been dubbed in) of the musicians on and off stage, and mainly features Jones's commentary. For hard-core Band buffs only.

1969–1970 (2006)

This bootleg on the Hook & Jab imprint contains six songs by Dylan and The Band at 1969's Isle of Wight festival shot in grainy black-and-white from right in front of the stage ("The Weight" is the sole Band-only tune) and four songs from The Band's 1970 concert at Pittsburgh's Syria Mosque, which were in filmed in professional color for Dutch television. The DVD opens with three 1969 solo Dylan tunes on U.S. TV.

You Are What You Eat (1968)

Directed by Barry Feinstein (*Monterey Pop*), this flower-power freak-out flick features music supervised by John Simon and the film's producer, Peter Yarrow. A certain group of Big Pink denizens back bizarro Tiny Tim for two songs heard in the movie, which also stars Frank Zappa, David Crosby, and Paul Butterfield.

The Band in Woodstock (1970)

Filmed in the outbuilding that was converted to a rehearsal studio on Robertson's property, this Capitol Records promo for *The Band* shows the group performing "King Harvest (Has Surely Come)" and "Up on Cripple Creek" in front of floor-to-ceiling windows on a sunny Woodstock day, with Robertson playing an Epiphone electric hollow body instead of his standard Fender Telecaster or Stratocaster. Both songs can be glimpsed on YouTube and in various docs, but only "King Harvest" is on The Band's *A Musical History* box set DVD.

Casino Arena, 1976

This fantastic-sounding black-and-white video of the group's full July 7, 1976, concert (sixteen songs) in Asbury Park, New Jersey, has yet to see an official DVD release. A shame, that. Because even though Manuel's voice is gruff, there's an occasional spike of stage feedback, and the raw, sometimes dim footage lacks *The Last Waltz*'s flash and overdubs, it seems like this is what the group *really* sounded like during their mid-1970s live zenith. And it's astonishing. Watch it on YouTube.

Saturday Night Live (1976)

The Band famously performed the night before Halloween on the NBC comedy/variety show *Saturday Night Live* in 1976. Most musical acts only did two songs on the show, but perhaps in light of the group's looming farewell, *SNL*'s producers allotted them four numbers: "Life Is a Carnival," "Stage Fright," "Georgia on My Mind," and "The Night They Drove Old Dixie Down." The last song appears on the five-DVD *Saturday Night Live: 25 Years of Music, Vol. 1*; the others are on *A Musical History* (see above). Helm returned with his RCO All-Stars to perform on the show in 1977, as did a solo Robertson in 1988.

The Old Grey Whistle Test (1977)

In 1977, BBC music show *The Old Grey Whistle Test* took a field trip to Albert Grossman's Bearsville complex for a special devoted to the acts on his label. Presented are interviews and performances by Foghat, Jesse Winchester, Elizabeth Barraclough, Mountain's Corky Laing, Todd Rundgren's Utopia, and Paul Butterfield, whose band features Helm on drums, Dr. John on keyboard, and David Sanborn on sax. Grossman holds court outside the Bearsville Theater, and there are scenes of the recording studio's interior. Check YouTube.

Robbie Robertson: Going Home (1998) / Robbie Robertson: A Retrospective (1994)

These are essentially two different versions of the same Disney Channel documentary on Robertson that originally aired in 1994. Surveyed are his life with and without The Band, his live and studio solo work, and The Band's induction into the Rock and Roll Hall of Fame. Interviewees include Eric Clapton, Martin Scorsese, Daniel Lanois, and others.

Rick Danko's Electric Bass Techniques (1987) / Levon Helm on Drums and Drumming (1992)

The bassist and drummer made these insightful instructional tapes (now out on DVD and instant download) for friend Happy Traum's Homespun Music label. Both are available from the Homespun website.

No Direction Home (2005)

Nearly three decades after *The Last Waltz*, Martin Scorsese reunited with Bob Dylan for this superb account of the Bard's early life and career. As with *Chronicles*, Dylan's eminently readable autobiography, the story cuts off with the singer's 1966 self-exile, so there aren't any scenes of the Isle of Wight show or his 1974 tour with The Band. But recurring throughout is the incredible 1966 U.K. color concert footage shot by D. A. Pennebaker during the making of *Eat the Document*.

AIRS (2004)

A DVD of dubious Asian origin, this perplexingly titled release pairs a tight 1978 set by Danko and his band on PBS's *Soundstage* (mainly tunes from his first solo album; the version of "Sip the Wine" is truly majestic) with the April 18, 1980, musical appearance by Helm and actress Sissy Spacek on NBC's *Midnight Special* to promote *Coal Miner's Daughter* (the show is interspersed with clips from the movie).

Live in Tokyo 1983 (2011)

This is a visually poor bootleg DVD transfer of a bootleg VHS tape (*Japan Tour*) of the group's September 2, 1983, Tokyo concert during their first tour of Japan. It's also available as part of *Live in Tokyo 1983*, a two-CD/one-DVD set.

"Red Hot + Country" (1994)

Helm performs "Caledonia" and "The Weight" with John Hiatt and others in the fifth episode of AIDS awareness group the Red Hot Organization's 1990s television performance series.

The Road (1995)

One installment of the short-lived live music TV show *The Road* focused on the 1990s-era Band. Featured in the program are live clips from two Illinois concerts and interviews with the veteran members and Jim Weider, Randy Ciarlante, and Richard Bell.

VH1's Behind the Music: Robbie Robertson (1998)

The guitarist was the subject of the thirty-third episode of the VH1 network's popular exposé-style series.

The First Waltz (1999)

This concert film documents a live tribute to *The Last Waltz* at a Chicago benefit revue for homeless teens. Guest of honor Rick Danko shares the stage with Smashing Pumpkins front man Billy Corgan, Cheap Trick guitarist Rick Nielsen, Ivan Neville, the Mekons' Jon Langford, Alejandro Escovedo, bluesmen Lonnie Brooks and Sir Mack Rice, and others. Danko gets the spotlight on "It Makes No Difference" and "Book Faded Brown," and the entire cast joins in for the finale of "The Weight."

Yonge Street: Toronto Rock & Roll Stories (2011)

This award-winning, three-part Canadian TV series about Toronto's early rock 'n' roll scene was coproduced by Jan Haust (*The Basement Tapes Complete*). Naturally, Ronnie Hawkins and Robbie Robertson get much face time, and they and other musicians and scenesters discuss the Hawks' central role on the city's main musical artery during its golden age as a musical hub.

SCTV Volume 1 Network 90 (2004)

Levon Helm acts in a sketch and performs "Sweet Peach Georgia Wine" and Eddie Cochran's "Summertime Blues" with the Cate Brothers in a 1981 episode of the crazed Canadian comedy program *SCTV* that appears on this five-DVD set.

Ed Sullivan's Rock 'n' Roll Classics (2005)

This three-DVD box set includes The Band's November 2, 1969, performance of "Up on Cripple Creek" on CBS's long-running *The Ed Sullivan Show*. Hands are shaken with the famously stiff host after they play.

The Band Is Back (2003) / Reunion Concert (1983)

Released in Canada, the U.S., and Australia under alternate titles, this film captures the just-reunited group (Cate Brothers era) at Vancouver's Queen Elizabeth Theatre in 1983. Includes interviews with Danko, Helm, and Manuel and a backstage blues jam by Helm and Hudson.

Japan Tour (year unknown)

Lengthy (two hours), professionally taped document of the group's Tokyo concert on the 1983 reunion tour. This was one of The Band's first Japanese shows and the crowd is clearly pleased, but the performance feels somewhat rote overall. Also released as *Live in Tokyo*.

Live at the New Orleans Jazz Festival (1996/1998)

Much better is this appearance by the Weider/Ciarlante/Bell edition at the 1994 New Orleans Jazz Festival, which is intercut with interviews. Manuel is missed, of course, but the group is energized and visibly having fun. Weider wields his axe mightily, and it's a rare treat watching Helm play bass on "Crazy Mama" while Danko strums guitar. On the track listing, "It Makes No Difference" is erroneously titled "The Sun Don't Shine Anymore."

Making a Noise: A Native American Musical Journey (1999)

This PBS documentary on Native American music examines Robbie Robertson's artistic exploration of his indigenous heritage and his collaborations with other Native American musicians.

Ultimate Collection (2005)

Another Japanese boot, this one is composed mainly of 1980s and '90s TV appearances by The Band and solo members. It also includes color footage of the group's November 1, 1970, concert at Pittsburgh's Syria Mosque.

This Country's Rockin' (year unknown) / Let It ROCK! (1995)

Both of these titles center on Ronnie Hawkins and feature music by his renowned onetime Hawks. *This Country's Rockin'* has the new Band on a 1989 bill with Hawkins at the Silverdome in Pontiac, Michigan. *Let It ROCK!* depicts the Hawk's sixtieth birthday concert in 1995 and sees The Band in the company of Jerry Lee Lewis, Carl Perkins, and other well-wishers.

Hail! Hail! Rock 'n' Roll! (1987)

The occasion of another rock 'n' roller's sixtieth birthday, that of the legendary Chuck Berry, is celebrated in this acclaimed biography/concert flick. Also on screen are compere Keith Richards, Eric Clapton, Bruce Springsteen, Bo Diddley, Jerry Lee Lewis, Little Richard, Roy Orbison, the Everly Brothers, and others. But cut from the final version is an amazing and touching scene in which Berry pores over his scrapbooks with Robbie Robertson, who also accompanies the father of rock 'n' roll on acoustic guitar while he recites poetry. It's found among the extras on the DVD.

Ringo Starr and His All-Starr Band (1990)

This release catches Danko, Helm, and Hudson in the former Beatle's traveling supergroup in 1989, along the way slipping some Band favorites in between Starr's Fab Four and solo hits and songs by his other sidemen, Dr. John, Joe Walsh, and Billy Preston.

The Wall Live in Berlin (2003)

In 1990, Danko, Helm, and Hudson were once again part of an all-star project when Pink Floyd's Roger Waters enlisted them to help perform his group's album *The Wall* in Germany. (The full Band performed on the bill separately.) Hudson plays accordion on several songs with Waters, and he, Danko, and Helm accompany Waters and Van Morrison on "Comfortably Numb" and Sinead O'Connor on "Mother."

Live at Loreley (2001)

Better filed under "The Stuff You *Don't Wanna* Watch" is this DVD of a concert at the Loreley outdoor amphitheater in St. Goarshausen, Germany, on The Band's 1996 *High on the Hog* tour. Originally shown on the TV show *Rockpalast*, it depicts the group playing to a thinner-than-usual, poncho-clad audience on a gray, rainy day (not the most inspiring conditions), and Danko, looking very unhealthy and very out of it, is plainly struggling, his troubles mirrored in the faces of his bandmates. The group had just come off a string of disastrous shows in England and Ireland that had seen the bassist unable to complete the sets. The end was clearly nigh.

The Midnight Ramble Sessions, Volume 1 (2005) / The Midnight Ramble Sessions, Volume 2 (2005) / Ramble at the Ryman (2011)

These three releases chart the return of Levon Helm at the height of the cherished Midnight Ramble events at his Woodstock home, which provides the setting for the first two DVDs. Helm was going through a tough spot with his throat cancer during the making of *Volume 1* (which includes a CD of the show as well), so Little Sammy Davis handles the lead vocals in addition to playing harmonica on a set of blues covers. With *Volume 2*, Helm's voice is back (check the fierce version of "Don't Ya Tell Henry"), along with a bigger band and visitors Dr. John and Chuck Berry pianist Johnnie Johnson. First broadcast on PBS, *Ramble at the Ryman* takes the show on the road for a sold-out night in 2008 at Nashville country music temple the Ryman Auditorium. The program includes some appropriate old-time country chestnuts ("No Depression in Heaven," "Deep Elem Blues") and guests Buddy Miller, Sheryl Crow, John Hiatt, and mandolinist Sam Bush.

Eric Clapton's Crossroads Guitar Festival 2013 (2013)

Robertson was among the Slowhand-picked six-stringers filmed live at this two-day concert to benefit the Englishman's Crossroads drug-treatment center. He and E.C.'s band jam on "Who Do You Love."

Bob Dylan 30th Anniversary Concert Celebration (2014)

This is Sony Legacy's star-filled chronicle of the 1992 Madison Square Garden concert celebrating Dylan's third decade of record-making. The Band plays "When I Paint My Masterpiece" and joins the assembled multitude for the finale of "Knockin' on Heaven's Door." Sadly, Robertson didn't make the scene, presumably because of the bad blood between him and Helm.

Love for Levon (2013)

This two-DVD/two-CD set immortalizes the 2013 concert at the Izod Center in New Jersey to honor Helm's memory while raising funds to keep his Woodstock home in his family's control and ensure that its Midnight Rambles would continue. Performing mainly Band and solo Helm songs is a celestial body of musical luminaries that includes Garth Hudson, Roger Waters, Gregg Allman, Mavis Staples, Lucinda Williams, Jakob Dylan, John Mayer, My Morning Jacket, Phish's Mike Gordon, Allen Toussaint, Joan Osborne, Jorma Kaukonen, and many more. Most are backed by either the Levon Helm Band and their horn section or the specially assembled All Star Band, which features drummer Kenny Aronoff and bassist Don Was.

Something Like You Ain't Never Seen: Band Members in Dramatic and Narrative Roles

There have been other rock groups with members who've crossed over into movie and TV work, but few have explored that world as extensively as The Band. With Elvis and the Beatles, it was about matinee idolatry and management-driven branding. With The Band, it was a case of the members taking advantage of their unique personalities and images to find honest work.

For Robertson, it was also a natural extension of his fascination with film. Yet for all his leading-man good looks and cinematic aspirations, the guitarist's acting and screenwriting efforts have met with only limited success. Instead, he's found his niche as a soundtrack composer and curator par excellence, writing, recording, and selecting outside music for a still-growing list of films, many of them overseen by his friend Martin Scorsese. For *Raging Bull* (1980), he enlisted Hudson and Manuel to perform incidental music; his other notable soundtracks include *The King of Comedy* (1983), *The Color of Money* (1986), *The Departed* (2006), *Shutter Island* (2010), and *The Wolf of Wall Street* (2013).

Although the others gave it a go themselves, it was Helm who turned out to be The Band's most prolific actor. A natural talent, he starred in over a dozen films, usually playing some kind of wizened down-home yokel, and in episodes of the television series *Midnight Caller* and *Seven Brides for Seven Brothers* (he played an itinerant country singer in the latter). Helm also occasionally worked as a film narrator, something Robertson has done as well, as did Danko (the bassist recorded an unused voiceover for the 1979 Who documentary *The Kids Are Alright*).

Carny (1980)

Robertson cowrote and stars in this drama about a pair of carnival hustlers named Frankie and Patch (played by Gary Busey and Robertson, respectively) who hook up with an adventure-seeking small-town waitress named Donna (Jodie Foster). The film tanked, but it marked Robertson's first foray into soundtrack work. The *Carny* soundtrack, recorded with Dr. John and Randall Bramblett and including a rare Robertson vocal on Fats Domino's "The Fat Man," is worth seeking out.

Coal Miner's Daughter (1980)

In his very first dramatic role, Helm gives an utterly convincing performance as Ted Webb, the father of Loretta Lynn, for this biopic about the country music icon. Coached by actor Tommy Lee Jones (who plays Lynn's husband), Helm was reportedly considered for an Academy Award for his work in the film. "In the end it wasn't a big transition because I've been around people like the Webbs all my life," Helm explains in *This Wheel's on Fire*. "Add the basic formality to people that makes life in the South a bit more pleasant, and that was the character."

Levon Helm recorded a version of the Bill Monroe bluegrass classic "Blue Moon of Kentucky" for the soundtrack of the 1980 film *Coal Miner's Daughter.*

Author's collection

Eliza's Horoscope (1975)

Band fan Tommy Lee Jones, here in his first starring role, plays a political radical in this tortuous, Bergman-wannabe film about a woman who meets up with a mysterious astrologer. Richard Manuel, wine glass constantly in hand, portrays a character known simply as the Bearded Composer. According to director Gordon Sheppard, The Band, via Robertson, had agreed to do the soundtrack but ultimately backed out. Barney Hoskyns cites Robertson's prioritizing of his *Works* project as the reason given.

The Right Stuff (1983)

Next to his part in *Coal Miner's Daughter*, Helm's portrayal of Major Jack Ridley in this saga of the original Mercury 7 astronauts stands as his most acclaimed role. In his autobiography, Helm recalls having an awkward moment when the real-life General Chuck Yeager, who is played in the film by Sam Shepard, stumbled upon him and Shepard sharing a joint off set. The film won eleven Oscars, including Best Picture.

Richard Manuel stars in the 1975 low-budget art film *Eliza's Horoscope.*
Author's collection

The Dollmaker (1984)

Helm plays a factory worker named Clovis, opposite Jane Fonda, in this made-for-TV movie about the lives of a transplanted Kentucky family during World War II.

Best Revenge (1984)

This thriller about an American tourist in Spain who's forced to take part in a multimillion-dollar drug deal features Helm as the lead character, Bo. The soundtrack, composed by prog rocker Keith Emerson, has Helm singing and Hudson playing accordion on the track "Straight Between the Eyes."

Smooth Talk (1985)

Turkey Scratch's favorite son is seen on screen once again, this time in the supporting role of Harry in a Joyce Carol Oates–scripted coming-of-age thriller starring Treat Williams, Mary Kay Place, and a teenage Laura Dern.

Man Outside (1986)

All of the members of The Band, save Robertson, have bit parts in this low-budget crime drama shot in Arkansas. Helm plays the local sheriff, Danko plays the father of a kidnapped/molested boy, Manuel plays a vigilante seeking justice for the crime, and Hudson fittingly plays an enigmatic hermit. But beware: The not easily found film has been described as unwatchably bad.

End of the Line (1987)

Another Arkansas production, this comedy follows the exploits of railroad company employees who steal a locomotive to protest the railway's closing. It stars Kevin Bacon, Wilford Brimley, Sarah Vowell in her first film role, and, as Leo Pickett, Levon Helm, whose dialogue about "catfish hoggin'" is the movie's saving grace.

Elvis '56 (1987)

Helm narrates this one-hour documentary about the life of Elvis Presley during the pivotal year of 1956, when he shot from Sun Records to international stardom.

Staying Together (1989)

An '80s comedy about three Southern brothers who pull together when their father decides to sell the family's chicken restaurant, *Staying Together* includes Helm in another minor role and features his Woodstock All-Stars on the soundtrack.

The Crossing Guard (1995)

Robertson has a small role (a character named Roger) in this Sean Penn–directed drama about a father who plots to kill the man who took his daughter's life in a hit-and-run accident. Jack Nicholson, David Morse, and Angelica Huston are the main stars.

Feeling Minnesota (1996)

Helm references his gospel roots to play a Bible salesman in this hit black comedy starring Keanu Reeves and Cameron Diaz.

Great Drives (1996)

The percussionist narrated an episode of this defunct PBS series that explored the sights, people, and culture along famous American roads. He's seen piloting a classic car down U.S. Highway 61 from Memphis to New Orleans, checking out blues, country, gospel, and jazz musicians en route.

Fire Down Below (1997)

Helm is a Southern reverend in this Steven Seagal shoot-'em-up set in the hills of Kentucky. There's a fleeting scene of him singing and playing guitar at a church picnic. Kris Kristofferson and Harry Dean Stanton are in it as well.

The Adventures of Sebastian Cole (1998)

Helm didn't have to travel far to act in this coming-of-age comedy, which was filmed in lush Dutchess County, just across the Hudson River from Woodstock.

The Three Burials of Melquiades Estrada (2005)

Tommy Lee Jones reached out again to Helm to star in this highly rated crime flick about a ranch hand (Jones) who kidnaps a border patrolman to help bring a murdered friend's body to Mexico for burial. Helm plays a blind, desert-dwelling old man they meet along the way.

Shooter (2007)

In this tellingly titled action yarn, Mark Wahlberg is a former Army sniper on the run after being framed for an assassination attempt on the president. Once again, Levon plays another crusty old character the protagonist befriends while hiding out, in this case a legendary Tennessee gunsmith named Mr. Rate.

In the Electric Mist (2009)

Helm's last acting role reunited him with Tommy Lee Jones in this mystery about a New Orleans detective investigating some murders and a corrupt businessman. He plays the ghostly Confederate general John Bell Hood, whom Jones's character encounters one spooky evening in the bayou. The night they drove old Dixie down, indeed.

A Sea of Green (2014)

Garth Hudson was cast as a minor character named "the Cultivator" in this, to be kind, extremely amateurish indie action film about a marijuana dealer.

27

(I Don't Want to) Hang Up My Rock and Roll Shoes

The Band Reunites (1983–1999)

While it had been Robbie Robertson's idea to break up The Band in 1976, it was an idea no one else in the group ever quite understood, least of all Levon Helm. In his later years, as he cursed Robertson for claiming the majority of The Band's songwriting credits—and royalties—the drummer would shake his head at Robertson's pushing what was one of the best bands of its day off a cliff, seemingly because he had developed aspirations in the film world.

On the other hand, the group had hit a wall. Their last few albums, even the critically exalted *Northern Lights—Southern Cross*, hadn't sold well. There was much internal bickering over royalty distribution and fulfilling their contract with Capitol versus continuing to shoot their wad via one-offs for Columbia with Bob Dylan. Neither of the group's other major writers, Rick Danko and Richard Manuel, was contributing songs, which put the weight, as it were, on Robertson. And although Helm had since beaten the heroin addiction he'd dealt with around the time of the *Stage Fright* sessions, Danko and Manuel were spiraling downward with drug and alcohol addiction—especially Manuel, who was putting away eight bottles of Grand Marnier a day in his Malibu beach house with the curtains closed (perhaps "putting away" isn't the best phrase; there were over 2,000 empties in the house when he vacated it in 1976).

Maybe just taking a break while the afflicted members got whatever help they needed could have saved the original Band. Robertson, though, was resolved to pack it in, a decision he underscored in a grand and very public fashion as the driving force behind the Last Waltz. But although they didn't exactly know it when they played the final note and walked off the

Winterland stage that night, taking a break from playing together as The Band was exactly what they were doing. *Most* of them, that is.

As Robertson made his niche in Hollywood, his former bandmates struggled to keep afloat with side work, solo albums (Danko and Helm), occasional collaborations with others and among themselves (Danko/Manuel and Danko/Helm acoustic tours, Danko/Manuel/Hudson trio dates, Hudson and Manuel playing on Robertson's soundtracks for *Raging Bull* and *The Color of Money*), and non-musical endeavors that included Helm's acting career. But the reality was that The Band, as Helm had long maintained, was bigger than all of them—a brand name that would bring far more people out to shows than any of them did as solo artists or in small groupings. And although Robertson was otherwise occupied, the remaining four still loved playing together and loved playing the Band songs that millions of people still loved to hear.

According to Helm, Manuel had dried out by the early 1980s and had been talking to him about a Band reunion almost from the instant they'd finished their San Francisco send-off, saying he'd always thought they were just taking a "vacation." And, seven years after the *Last Waltz*, the vacation ended when he, Helm, Danko, and Hudson decided to revive The Band—without Robertson. Danko called to invite him, but Robertson declined, giving the four his blessing but saying he wasn't about to play in a reunited Band after the finality of the Last Waltz. That was fine with Helm, who remained bitter about the guitarist's dominance of the songwriting credits and hadn't wanted to ask him anyway. But just who, exactly, would attempt to fill the shoes of the legendary guitarist of one of the most influential bands of all time when they reunited in 1983?

Volcano, I'm About to Blow: Kicking Off with the Cate Brothers and Jim Weider (1983–1986)

In the beginning of the reunion, those shoes were filled by a quartet: the Cate Brothers Band, led by the guitarist Earl Cate and keyboardist Ernie Cate and also including bassist Ron Eoff and drummer Terry Cagle, Helm's nephew. Helm had briefly played with the Arkansas-based Cates in 1966, when he was back home after leaving the Dylan/Hawks tour, and had toured with them in Canada and the U.S. in 1981. Originally, the idea had been for the masterful Earl to come in as Robertson's replacement, but since the Cates were a family band it didn't seem right to break them up, so the first lineup of the revived Band swelled to become an eight-piece. After their June 25 warm-up show at the Joyous Lake in Woodstock, the octet played a sold-out tour (with the Cate Brothers Band opening and joined mid-flight each night by Helm, Danko, Hudson, and Manuel) of Canadian theaters with a week in the U.S. before making the group's first visit to Japan. The Japanese jaunt was incredibly successful, with sold-out shows in Tokyo, Osaka, Sapporo, Nagoya, and other cities (sushi lover Helm must have been in high heaven). For the next two years, the expanded Band continued to tour theaters and large clubs in North America on their own and played to 33,000 as the opener for the Grateful Dead at Syracuse's Carrier Dome in 1983.

(**EMA·TELSTAR**)

```
ITINERARY THE BAND

July 2, 1984

EMA representative:  TOMMY AHLEN


Monday, July 2        Depart Oslo, flight SK 482           11.10
                      Arrive Stockholm                     12.05

                      Hotel:  Strand
                      Address:  Nybrokajen 9 ·
                      Phone:  08-22 29 00
                      Telex:  10504

                      CONCERT AT GRÖNA LUND, STOCKHOLM      20.00

                      Address:  Allmänna gränd
                      Phone:  08-67 01 85ext 130

                      Equipment get in                     08.00
                      Doors open                           14.00
                      Curfew                               21.39

Tuesday, July 3       Hotel:  Strand

Wednesday, July 4     Depart Stockholm                     t.b.a.
```

No bokningsnummer. 0086

The group mainly performed in the U.S. and Canada in 1984 but still found time for overseas shows. This tour itinerary sheet contains scheduling information for a concert in Stockholm, Sweden.

Author's collection

Guitarist Jim Weider was born and raised in Woodstock, where he'd played with high school groups and singer-songwriters, and had idolized The Band. "They were the hometown band, and I was really proud of that," Weider says. "There were pieces of Woodstock in their music. I still remember working in a stereo store when Garth brought in a copy of *Music from Big Pink*, which had just come out. The owner put it on and turned it all the way up, and I was just blown away. There was this feeling about The Band, that their music was about the common man, and that attracted me. Plus, [in The Band's music] there was rock 'n' roll, country, blues, the whole history of American music. Everything I loved." Weider left town in the early 1970s for freelance playing in Nashville and Atlanta, but by the beginning of the next decade was back in Woodstock, where he was soon performing with Manuel, Artie Traum, and Helm's band the Woodstock All-Stars.

The Band embarked on a summer 1985 tour opening for Crosby, Stills & Nash, but midway through it became clear that the eight-piece lineup was no longer economically sustainable. The Cates were sent home and Weider was summoned to take their place as the group reverted to a quintet. "I was in my early thirties, and it changed my life," recalls the guitarist. "They were one of my favorite bands. But, knowing them as well, it was just an incredible honor to be asked. We went right into the studio to cut some tracks not long after I joined, but 'Country Boy' [on 1993's *Jericho*] was the only one that ever came out from that session." The group continued to tour tirelessly, playing auditoriums, state fairs, and clubs like New York's Lone Star Café, the site of some celebrated gigs. But all of that came to a halt in the early hours of March 4, 1986, when Richard Manuel hanged himself in his hotel bathroom following a show at the Cheek to Cheek Lounge in Winter Park, Florida.

Too Soon Gone: The Band's Final Years (1986–1999)

Hard as it no doubt was, in the week after Manuel's funeral and memorial services The Band's remaining members threw themselves back into their work. "We went out as a four-piece for a little bit," says Weider. "It was definitely difficult. But sometimes when you lose somebody it's almost better to go out and play instead of sitting around. Like Levon always said, 'Music is a healer.'" So the shaken group edged its way back onto the healing highway, filling out their sound for several dates with ex–Beach Boys guitarist and singer Blondie Chaplin, who also doubled on drums. Early Hawks guitarist Fred Carter Jr. even joined for a few shows in 1987. In 1988, Terry Cagle took Helm's place on drums for an Australian tour that featured Danko, Hudson, Blondie

Chaplin, New Riders of the Purple Sage pedal steel guitarist Buddy Cage, and Woodstock blues harpist Sredni Vollmer, who would continue to augment the group over the next few years. Ironically, Stan Szelest, who Manuel had replaced in the Hawks back in 1961, reemerged to take the piano bench.

Things looked promising when the quintet of Helm, Danko, Hudson, Weider, and Szelest signed to Sony in 1990 and recorded an album with singer-songwriter Jules Shear, who contributed lead vocals and several songs. But, citing the declining record sales of acts of The Band's vintage, the label dumped the group without releasing the record, a blow compounded by Szelest's January 1991 death from a heart attack. (In another cruelly ironic twist, the sessions included "Too Soon Gone," Szelest and Helm's tribute to Manuel and the recently departed Paul Butterfield, and Shear's "Tombstone, Tombstone"; the full unreleased album was bootlegged in 2005 as *Tombstone*.)

Randy Ciarlante, Helm's fellow drummer in the Woodstock All-Stars and a powerhouse singer and occasional bassist, was added to the lineup during the 1990 Sony sessions. "I guess Levon wanted to start branching out a little bit and get involved with the mandolin and the harp, play some bass and some rhythm guitar and what have you," Ciarlante told Band fanzine *Jawbone* in 1997. "He wanted me to play the drums so he could break away and do that stuff. I think that was probably the original reason I got in in the first place." Whatever the reason Helm pushed for Ciarlante's inclusion, it paid off in performance: The drummer's R&B-schooled voice meshed well with the others', and when he played his full kit side-by-side with Helm's it brought a new and dazzling, cross-rhythmic element to the group. Szelest's replacement turned out to be a major coup: Billy Preston, who'd famously played with both the Beatles and the Rolling Stones and had several hits of his own in the 1970s ("Nothing Leaves Nothing," "Will It Go Round in Circles"). But the funk icon lasted just one gig with The Band, an August 3, 1991, benefit for the Woodstock Youth Center, before he was arrested for the sexual assault of a teenage boy in California and insurance fraud related to a home fire. Next to bravely take The Band's seemingly cursed piano slot was another Ronnie Hawkins and the Hawks alumnus: Toronto-born Richard Bell, who'd played with Hawkins in the late 1960s before joining Janis Joplin's Full Tilt Boogie Band.

With the lineup now settled as the sextet of Helm, Danko, Hudson, Weider, Ciarlante, and Bell, The Band made their long-awaited studio comeback with 1993's *Jericho*; *High on the Hog* and *Jubilation* followed. Although none of the records came close to the sales of any of their Capitol-era albums, The Band remained a hard-working, consistent, fan-pleasing draw on the large-theater circuit—until 1999, when the shock of Danko's death brought the nearly forty-five-year career of one of music's finest groups to a close.

"The Band's songs are some of the most deep-rooted songs in American music, like history books themselves," says Weider, who, in addition to leading his own Project Percolator and releasing solo albums, would go on to perform with Ciarlante in Band-repertory outfit The Weight. "They're songs that will live on forever."

Listen to the Serenade: The Reunited Band's Albums

There are those who have decried The Band for getting back together without Robertson, saying they merely became a bar band. But those people don't know, or forget, that The Band *began* as a bar band. None of them, Robertson included, joined Ronnie Hawkins and the Hawks with any expectations of playing to teeming masses of humanity in football stadiums. That level of stardom simply didn't exist in the late 1950s and early 1960s. They signed on because they wanted to play wild rock 'n' roll to happy dancers in bars, party a bit, see the country, and, in the words of Hawkins himself, "get more pussy than Frank Sinatra" (the reserved Hudson probably left that part out when he told his parents he was joining the group as their music teacher).

Of course, Robertson's ambitions eventually grew and took him in directions away from the bandstand. But the others remained, simply, musicians who needed to work and who loved playing music more than just about anything else. Through all they'd endured—stadiums and stardom, drugs and booze, births and deaths, car wrecks, music industry rip-offs, the fires that had destroyed Helm's (1991) and Hudson's (1978) homes—playing music was all they'd ever known. And while it's undeniable that the quality of The Band's 1990s albums, whose songs are mostly composed by outside writers, doesn't approach *Music from Big Pink* or *The Band*, they have their bright spots nonetheless.

Jericho

Nineteen ninety-three's *Jericho*, on the Nashville indie label Pyramid, has the most bright spots. The fluorescent Peter Max cover painting of Big Pink makes it plain that the group intended to rekindle the magic of their early Woodstock years. Although it admittedly falls short of that formidable goal,

The Band's final lineup of (left to right) Rick Danko, Richard Bell, Garth Hudson, Randy Ciarlante, Jim Weider, and Levon Helm played the Fox Theatre in Boulder, Colorado, in 1996.
Author's collection

it's certainly a more rewarding listen than the original Band's mish-mash-mush 1977 contract-fulfiller, *Islands*. And in an attempt to reconnect with their glorious *Music from Big Pink*/Brown Album era the group made a logical choice in bringing back their old ally John Simon as a coproducer.

The set opens with "Remedy," a dance-friendly tune sung by Helm and written by Weider and Canadian singer-songwriter Colin Linden; further highlights include the "Dixie Down"-ish miner's dirge "The Caves of Jericho" and group's zydeco love letter to their newfound Far Eastern fans, "Move to Japan." There are some well-chosen covers here as well: blues tunes by Muddy Waters and Willie Dixon; Bob Dylan's "Blind Willie McTell," featuring a haunting Danko vocal and New Orleans blues piano great Champion Jack Dupree; and the album's top performance, Bruce Springsteen's "Atlantic City" with Helm on lead vocal and mandolin. It's impossible, though, to discuss *Jericho* without mentioning its two most bittersweet tracks: "Too Soon Gone," the tribute to Richard Manuel cowritten by Jules Shear and the recently departed Szelest and vocalized by Danko, and "Country Boy," a chilling live 1985 performance sung by Manuel himself.

High on the Hog

Broadly speaking, the songs on 1996's *High on the Hog* aren't as well selected as the ones on *Jericho*, although there are some adventurous choices, the foremost being female R&B vocal group En Vogue's 1992 hit "Free Your Mind." The opener, "Stand Up," sung by Helm, is a funk tune with hilariously clever lyrics about erectile dysfunction. Unfortunately, its musical generic-ness can't be saved by even its large horn section and Jew's-harp overdub (or is that Garth's "Cripple Creek" clavinet?). This is a number that must have gotten the group's hard-drinking, die-hard audience up and dancing, but it falls flat on disc. The same can be said of the slow, horn-heavy blues "Back to Memphis," which isn't the Chuck Berry tune The Band recorded as a *Moondog Matinee* outtake but, rather, a song by Southern

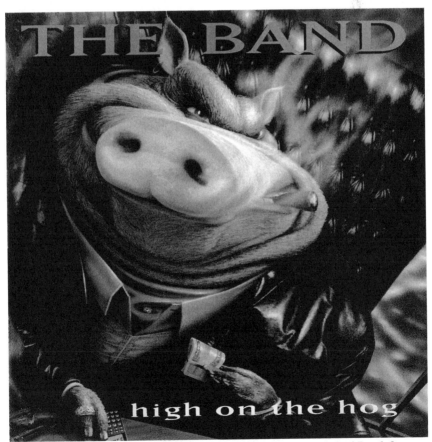

Nineteen-ninety-six's *High on the Hog*, the second album by the reunited Band, features a posthumous appearance of Richard Manuel singing "She Knows."   *Author's collection*

rockers the Kentucky Headhunters. Helm plays bass and Danko sings lead on J. J. Cale's "Crazy Mama," which has some searing slide by Weider. There are two Dylan covers this time around, a reprise of *Planet Waves*' "Forever Young" and the Ciarlante-sung "I Must Love You Too Much," which rocks hard and beats out the Shear/Szelest R&B belter "The High Price of Love" as the album's most animated cut. Champion Jack Dupree returns from *Jericho* to sing the Bo Diddley-ish "Ramble Jungle," and the ghost of Richard Manuel reappears via a tear-tugging live version of "She Knows" taped weeks before his death.

Jubilation

The Band's tenth and final album was apparently a difficult one to make. "I felt bad for Levon because he really wasn't feeling good when we were

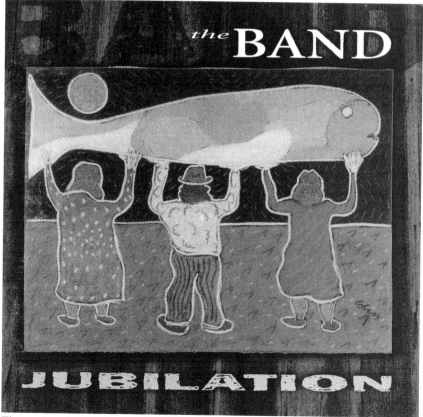

The sessions for The Band's last album, 1998's *Jubilation*, were plagued by the onset of Helm's throat cancer.

Author's collection

making it," says Weider about the drummer, who at the time had recently begun his ordeal with throat cancer. "So I wasn't as proud of that album as I was the other two." And it's indeed clear that Helm, who would later regain some of his voice after treatment, is struggling with his vocals on some tracks. But at times this works in the songs' favor, as Helm's not-goin'-down-without-a-fight orneriness brings a patina that's unique to this album; see the emotional "Don't Wait" and the gritty Allen Toussaint song "You See Me." Eric Clapton guests on guitar on "Last Train to Memphis" and another guest, singer-songwriter John Hiatt, takes the lead vocal spot on his "Bound by Love." "White Cadillac" pays tribute to the original group's rockabilly guru, Ronnie Hawkins, and the album closes out with Hudson's soothing instrumental "French Girls." But it's the opener, the beautiful "Book Faded Brown," that's the shiniest gem. Sung by Danko and written by Paul Jost, this touching, reflective ballad is the bassist's best vocal performance since "It Makes No Difference."

28

He Played Out His Heart Just the Time to Pass

Solo Albums

It might seem surprising that the original members of The Band, a superstar act of their day, didn't go on to release a lot of solo albums after their breakup. Excluding bootlegs, live releases, and side projects, as of 2016, forty years after the Last Waltz, there existed between the five musicians a grand total of fourteen official studio albums. By comparison, their four friends in the Beatles had put out almost sixty. But knowing even a tiny bit about the personalities of The Band, the difference between the two groups' levels of solo output isn't so shocking, really. John Lennon, Paul McCartney, and George Harrison had all been highly productive songwriters within the Beatles (even Ringo wrote a couple of tunes) and continued to be after their 1970 split. Richard Manuel and Rick Danko wrote or cowrote some fantastic songs during their too-short lives, but they were never as prolific as Robbie Robertson, who is known as the writer of the vast majority of The Band's songs. After the group's breakup he became much more devoted to his film music work than his career as a solo musician, and his former accomplices mainly worked as sidemen or session players and simply didn't write or record much under their own names. Below, we'll examine the handful of extant solo albums by The Band's founders, several of which may be unfamiliar to fans.

Rick Danko

The bassist's solo legacy is slim but bookended with two fairly solid studio albums.

Rick Danko's self-titled 1977 debut was the first solo album released by a Band member.
Author's collection

Rick Danko

Although it would be the only proper solo album he would make during his lifetime, Danko's self-titled 1977 set for Arista was actually the first solo release by a Band member. Recorded at Shangri-La Studios, it features guest appearances by all four of Danko's former bandmates and his brother Terry Danko on drums, as well as Eric Clapton ("New Mexicoe"), Ronnie Wood ("What a Town"), Blondie Chaplin, and Tex-Mex legend Doug Sahm. Although a couple of the songs were solely written by Danko (including the gorgeous, glistening "Sip the Wine," which he plays a tape of for Martin Scorsese during an interview segment in *The Last Waltz*), most were cowritten with Bobby Charles or Emmett Grogan. Despite its being, overall, a linear, slightly funky effort that never quite takes off, "Sip the Wine" and the appropriately energetic "Java Blues" make the album a worthy purchase.

Danko/Fjeld/Andersen / Ridin' on the Blinds

Danko formed a trio with folk singer Eric Andersen and Norwegian singer-songwriter Jonas Fjeld after the three hit it off at a spur-of-the-moment Woodstock show. The group toured Norway soon after and recorded a quiet, self-titled 1991 album that has them accompanied by Scandinavian musicians and includes appearances by Garth Hudson on accordion. The opener, "Driftin' Away," was cowritten by Danko, Andersen, and Elizabeth Danko, Rick's wife. The rest of the tracks are Andersen or Andersen/Fjeld compositions and folk and R&B covers. (*One More Shot*, a 2001 double CD, reissues *Danko/Fjeld/Andersen* and adds a live disc.) *Ridin' on the Blinds*, from 1994, has a nice Danko re-rendering of The Band's "Twilight" and the Danko/Andersen tunes "All Creation" and "Keep This Love Alive."

Times Like These

Assembled a year after Danko's death, mostly from scattered 1990s studio dates, *Times Like These* shows the singer was still in fairly fine voice right up to the end. Backed by Professor Louie and the Crowmatix, he croons some favorite covers—Sam Cooke's "Chain Gang," the Grateful Dead's "Ripple," Fats Domino's "Let the Four Winds Blow" live with Helm on harmonica—and, in a move of poetic programming, revisits "All Our

Past Times," his 1976 collaborative piece with Eric Clapton. Danko also returns to his Big Pink days, with Garth Hudson on gypsy accordion, for an acoustic, flamenco-ish "This Wheel's on Fire" that is perhaps even more haunting than the famous 1968 version. Listening to these recordings, one gets the overwhelming sense that Danko somehow knew his life was nearly done. Which makes them all the more poignant. A 2002 Japanese memorial release adds 1999's *Live on Breeze Hill*.

Live Albums

A number of official and bootleg CDs starring the bassist alone and with collaborators have circulated. These include the solo *In Concert* (1997), *Live on Breeze Hill* (1999), *At Dylan's Café* (2009), *Live at the Tin Angel* (2011), and *Live at the Iron Horse* (2011). *Live at O'Toole's Tavern* (2009) and *Live at Uncle Willy's* (2011) are with Manuel and *Live at the Lone Star* (2011) is with Manuel and Paul Butterfield.

Robbie Robertson

Roberton's solo discography represents an adventurous departure from the music of The Band.

Robbie Robertson

Robbie Robertson waited more than a decade after The Band's dissolution to unveil his first solo album. A lot had changed in the rock world since 1976, and it's clear that in the making of his most acclaimed album, 1987's *Robbie Robertson*, the guitarist was challenging himself and striving hard not to trade on his past with The Band. His ambitious nature, after all, was a major aspect of what pushed The Band to create the epic songs they're so well known for. Listening to his long-anticipated return, however, some may feel he was being *too* ambitious, trying too hard with producer Daniel Lanois to make lush, "big" music that would compete for 1980s relevancy with radio acts like Peter Gabriel and U2 (both of whom appear on the album). But strip away the plush sheen and '80s drum sound and there are some decent numbers here, such as the Bryan Ferry-ish "Somewhere Down the Crazy River" and the aching "Broken Arrow." The lead track, "Fallen Angel," is a tribute to the recently departed Manuel.

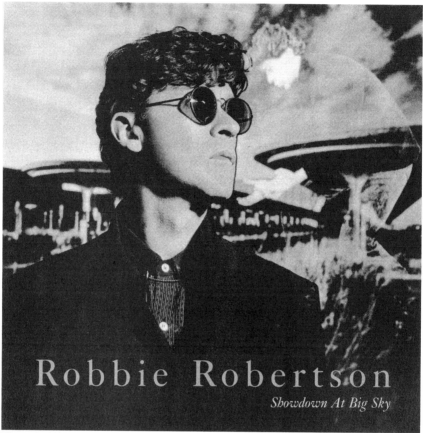

The epic "Showdown at Big Sky" is one of the cuts from Robbie Robertson's 1987 solo debut that was issued as a single.

Storyville

Across his four solo albums to date, Robertson has never directly revisited the roots rock of The Band. But with 1991's *Storyville*, another outsized opus, he does hint back to the historical-concept angle of *The Band*. Loosely set in New Orleans's fabled, turn-of-the-century red light district of Storyville, the ten-song album includes guest work by Aaron and Art Neville, members of the Meters, and other Crescent City greats, as well as horn arrangements by iconic producer and band leader Wardell Quezergue. "Go Back to Your Woods" was cowritten with pianist Bruce Hornsby.

Music for the Native Americans

In 1994, Robertson reached back to his Mohawk heritage for inspiration on *Music for the Native Americans*, which features a collective dubbed the Red Road Ensemble. Again, the content points toward the percolating, world-music-textured, electronic-programmed style of Peter Gabriel, bringing to mind the former Genesis front man's soundtrack to Martin Scorsese's *The Last Temptation of Christ*. Many of the musicians on the mostly instrumental album are of Native American lineage as well, including country pop singer Rita Coolidge and Robertson's son Sebastian (drums on "Golden Feather") and daughter Delphine (background vocals on "Coyote Dance").

Contact from the Underworld of Red Boy

As one might guess from its title, 1998's *Contact from the Underworld of Red Boy* continues the guitarist's reconnection with his Native American

A "Hot New Remix" of Robertson's "Showdown at Big Sky" was released to radio stations.   *Author's collection*

background and the plight of his people (imprisoned activist Leonard Peltier phones in his vocals, literally, on "Sacrifice"). This time around, Robertson brought in techno producer/DJ Howie B and dance music remixer Marius de Vries. He sprinkles in some bluesy guitar here and there and brings his parched vocals to a few cuts.

How to Become Clairvoyant

Robertson retained de Vries as the coproducer of this, his first album in the nearly fifteen years after *Red Boy*. The 2011 disc sees him swapping the indigenous-American themes and techno beats of his last two records for a collection of songs that trace the story of his life. The opener, "Straight Down the Line," and "When the Night Was Young" chronicle his wild times with Ronnie Hawkins and the Hawks, while "This Is Where I Get Off" seems to address the breakup of The Band. Guest players include Steve Winwood, Eric Clapton, Tom Morello, Trent Reznor, and pedal steel virtuoso Robert Randolph. Maintaining the extravagant atmosphere Robertson sought with his previous four albums, the sound can feel exaggerated and distant. It's a long way from the basement of Big Pink, that's for sure.

Levon Helm

Compared to that of the other members, Helm's solo discography is generally considered the most satisfying by Band fans.

Levon Helm and the RCO All-Stars

Helm signed to ABC Records and pulled out all the stops for this 1977 debut by his RCO All-Stars, a world-beating dream band that included Dr. John, Paul Butterfield, Hawks guitarist Fred Carter Jr., most of Booker T. & the MG's, and a giant horn section; Robertson and Hudson make studio appearances as well. Produced at Shangri-La and Helm's newly built studio in Woodstock, the record's big-band blues and R&B offers few sonic surprises. But as a brassy, danceable tour de force, it squarely hits its intended target. Dr. John/Mac Rebennack contributes a couple of compositions, but the only Helm writing credit is "Blues So Bad," a collaboration with Henry Glover.

Levon Helm

The drummer returned in 1978 with this eponymous sophomore LP, which was partially taped at Alabama's famed Muscle Shoals Sound Studios. Booker T. & the MG's guitarist Steve Cropper and bassist Donald "Duck" Dunn are back after their RCO All-Stars stint, and Helm's past and future collaborators Earl and Ernie Cate sing backups on their original "Standing on a Mountaintop." Produced by Dunn, the album does include some of Helm's stock-in-trade New Orleans funk (Allen Toussaint's "Play Something Sweet [Brickyard Blues]," Al Green's "Take Me to the River"), but it's less than satisfying in that the good songs are outweighed by unsuitable, middle-of-the-road filler like the Gerry Goffin/Barry Goldberg soft-rock mewler "Audience for My Pain" and the opening power ballad "Ain't No Way to Forget You."

American Son

Better is 1980's *American Son*, recorded the year before, during the Nashville sessions that yielded Helm's fine version of "Blue Moon of Kentucky" for the *Coal Miner's Daughter* soundtrack (the performance also appeared as a single, backed by a cover of Lee Dorsey's "Working in the Coal Mine"). Fred Carter Jr. produced and plays guitar on the album, which is generally more in the country rock mode than the previous two recordings (no horn section here); two of the tracks, "Watermelon Time in Georgia" and "Nashville Wimmin," are by Country Music Hall of Fame songwriter Harlan Howard. Still, there is a bit of lively Levon funk on *American Son*; check "Sweet Peach Georgia Wine" and the "Cripple Creek"–like "Hurricane," with its Garth-ish Jew's-harp licks.

Levon Helm

No, that's not a misprint. The singing drummer's fourth album, released in 1982, shares the self-referencing title of his second. And the similarities between the two albums don't end there. Once again, the recordings took place in Muscle Shoals with "Duck" Dunn producing and playing alongside Steve Cropper. And once again the proceedings begin with an indistinct contemporary pop rock song that doesn't fit Helm's voice or demeanor ("You Can't Win Them All") and are filled out mostly with unmemorable tunes by freelance songsmiths. The Hawks-era cover staples "Money" and "Willie and the Hand Jive" could have been opportunities to roll tape and simply capture the percussionist doing what he did so naturally, but instead they're subsumed by "modern," disco-pandering bombast. What Helm needed were ears who truly *got* who he was, what he did best and liked to do—and knew how to best capture those things with the right songs, in the right setting.

Dirt Farmer

It took twenty-five years, but Helm finally found those ears. Right under his very nose, so to speak. Recorded at his own studio, 2007's shockingly great

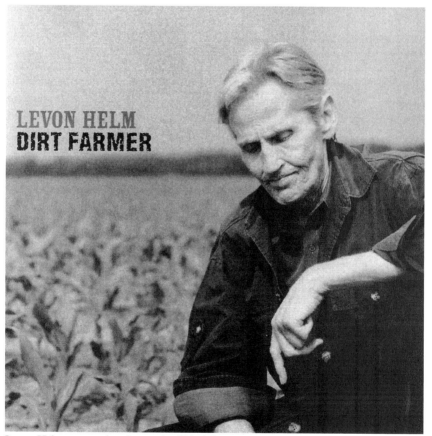

Levon Helm returned to the music of his Arkansas youth for the 2007 album *Dirt Farmer*, winning a Grammy for Best Traditional Folk Album.   *Author's collection*

Dirt Farmer was coproduced by his guitarist Larry Campbell and daughter Amy Helm, who encouraged her father to return to some of the traditional songs he'd sung with his family as a boy on their Arkansas farm. Cut mostly live after his 1998 throat cancer surgery and multiple radiation treatments, the sessions offset his weathered-but-right voice with perfectly pure acoustic instrumentation—resonator guitar, accordion, fiddle, mandolin, pump organ, piano, wood-y drums—on evergreens like "False Hearted Lover Blues," "Poor Old Dirt Farmer," the Carter Family's "Single Girl, Married Girl," and the lonesome "Little Birds," whose harmony structure had made it a key, influential tune in The Band's early repertoire. But there are breathtaking newer songs as well: Paul Kennerley's humorous "Got Me a Woman" (with Amy on drums) and Buddy and Julie Miller's plaintive "Wide River to Cross." The winner of a Grammy for Best Traditional Folk Album, the time-defying *Dirt Farmer* fulfills, at last, Helm's promise as a solo artist and is considered by many to be the best post-Band album from any of the group's members.

Electric Dirt

On the other hand, there are those who feel more strongly about the 2009 follow-up, the tellingly named *Electric Dirt*. Which is difficult to argue with. Also produced by Campbell, this richly rewarding record—which also won a Grammy, for Best Americana Album—has its share of delicious acoustic tracks, too (Happy Traum's "Golden Bird," the Stanley Brothers' "White Dove"). But it generally leans toward a fuller sound, one seasoned with tasteful electric guitar and embraced by Allen Toussaint's and Steve Bernstein's arrangements for the Levon Helm Band's five-piece horn section. The Campbell/Helm composition "Growin' Trade" updates the preceding album's "Poor Old Dirt Farmer" to tell the story of a planter who falls on hard times and is forced to replace his generations-old crops with marijuana, while the Staple Singers' "Move Along Train" exemplifies the strong gospel flavors heard elsewhere among the tracks. Sadly, this would be Helm's last studio album. But what a fine way to go out.

Ties That Bind: The Best of Levon Helm (1975–1996)

This two-disc set on Australia's Raven label rounds up the best tracks from Helm's post–original Band/pre–*Dirt Farmer* years.

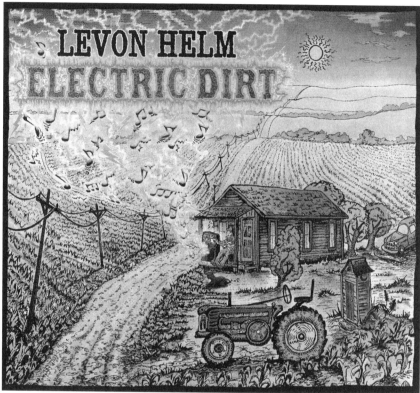

With 2009's *Electric Dirt*, Helm picked up a second Grammy, this time for Best Americana Album. As the title indicates, the disc builds on the acoustic-based sound of 2007's *Dirt Farmer* by adding more electric instrumentation.   *Author's collection*

Levon Helm and the RCO All-Stars Live

After a *Saturday Night Live* appearance by the RCO All-Stars, Helm was hospitalized for kidney stones and other fatigue-related ailments just before the group's planned fifty-date debut U.S. tour. Once he'd recovered, the large, expensive-to-maintain band managed to do some dates before disintegrating, including the 1977 New Year's Eve show at New York's Palladium heard on this 2006 release. It's a sweltering set, opening with a driving version of "Ain't That a Lot of Love" that edges out the one The Band did for *Islands* and closing with a swinging take of the Lead Belly–identified "Goodnight Irene." "Ophelia" is exceptionally electric, Butterfield wails on his signature "Born in Chicago," and Dr. John growls out a funky adaptation of Muddy Waters's "Got My Mojo Workin'." A party it is.

Garth Hudson

After and during The Band's existence, Hudson made his mark as the group's busiest freelance player. Although light, his solo resume is rewarding and reflects his experimental and classical leanings.

Music for Our Lady Queen of the Angels

Composed and recorded by Hudson in 1980 as incidental music for an art installation by sculptor Tony Duquette, this is easily the most unusual item in the Band members' combined solo catalog. A suite of six atmospheric soundscapes, it recalls the ambient, experimental recordings of Brian Eno and interweaves recordings of croaking frogs and chirping birds with church organ and poetic recitations by actor Charlton Heston. Interesting stuff, but not something to reach for when you're in the mood for "The Weight" again. Originally on cassette and reissued on CD in 2005.

The Sea to the North

Hudson sounds like he had a field day making this, his first proper solo album, which came out in 2001. A predominantly instrumental work (his wife, Maude, does contribute some vocals) that straddles improvisational jazz, psychedelia, rock, classical, Middle Eastern, and experimental styles, it's just the kind of labyrinthine aural journey one would expect from the man who gave us "The Genetic Method." There's a wild trip through the Grateful Dead's "Dark Star," and Helm is among the guest players.

Live at the Wolf

This 2005 CD of a 2002 show by Garth and Maude Hudson at the London, Ontario, Public Library's Wolf Performance Hall includes versions of "The Weight" and "It Makes No Difference" as well as Bob Dylan's "Blind Willie McTell."

Richard Manuel

Alas, Richard Manuel never got around to making a solo album before he committed suicide in 1986. But bootlegs and after-the-fact releases exist.

Whispering Pines: Live at the Getaway 1985

This is the best to emerge so far. Recorded just a few months before his death, *Whispering Pines* is a recording of a solo concert Manuel did at the Saugerties venue the Getaway. Bootlegged for years on cassette, it was issued in 2002 on CD in Japan by Dreamsville Records, with bonus tracks in 2005 by Canadian imprint Other People's Music, and in 2007 by Dutch label Corazong. Manuel's voice is well-worn, but it's fascinating to hear the way he adapted Band songs like "King Harvest" and "The Shape I'm In" to a solo-piano setting, and he's joined on others by Danko, Jim Weider, and blues harpist Sredni Vollmer. That night's rendition of "She Knows" is particularly devastating.

29

We Can Take In a Jamboree

The Band as Guest Musicians

R obbie Robertson, Levon Helm, Rick Danko, Garth Hudson, and Richard Manuel have played on hundreds of records by other artists. Here are twenty of their most notable extracurricular appearances.

Todd Rundgren, *Runt* (1970)

Danko and Helm appear on "Once Burned," a track on Rundgren's solo debut.

John Simon, *John Simon's Album* (1971)

The first solo album by The Band's erstwhile producer features Danko on bass, Manuel on drums, and Hudson on soprano sax. His *Out on the Street*, from 1992, has Danko on vocals, Helm on drums, and Hudson on synth and accordion.

Ringo Starr, *Ringo* (1973)

Helm (mandolin), Danko (violin), Robertson (guitar), and Hudson (accordion) grace the ditty "Sunshine Life for Me (Sail Away Raymond)" on this third solo effort by the Beatles drummer. In 1989, Danko and Helm toured as members of Ringo Starr's All-Starr Band.

Joni Mitchell, *Court and Spark* (1974)

"Raised on Robbery," off side two of this album by Robertson's fellow Toronto-transplant and West Coast neighbor, is marked by his characteristically cooking guitar.

Neil Young, *On the Beach* (1974)

Helm drums on "See the Sky About to Rain" and "Revolution Blues," the latter also featuring Danko on bass and David Crosby on guitar. Helm also plays on 1980's *Hawks and Doves*.

Carly Simon, *Hotcakes* (1974)

Robertson plays on this album's Top Ten cover of Inez and Charlie Foxx's "Mockingbird," sung by Simon and James Taylor.

The Barbarians, "Moulty" (1966)

According to Victor "Moulty" Moulton, the singing, hook-handed drummer of Massachusetts garage band the Barbarians, Robertson, Hudson, Danko, and Manuel backed him in the studio on this 1966 regional hit single.

Hirth Martinez, *Hirth from Earth* (1975)

Robertson produced and played on eccentric California singer-songwriter Martinez's debut, a record that also features organ by Hudson. John Simon produced Martinez's *Big Bright Street* (1977), which has Hudson on accordion.

Eric Clapton, *No Reason to Cry* (1976)

All five members perform on this album by the omnipresent English singer and guitarist. The eleven-song set was recorded at the group's Shangri-La Studios.

Leonard Cohen, *Recent Songs* (1979)

Hudson plays keyboards and accordion on "Our Lady of Solitude" and "The Gypsy's Wife."

Members of The Band perform on garage rock greats the Barbarians' 1966 single "Moulty."

Author's collection

Various Artists, *The Legend of Jesse James* (1980)

Helm was a natural to be cast as a vocalist alongside Johnny Cash in this concept album about a post–Civil War outlaw. Emmylou Harris and Charlie Daniels appear as well.

Willie Nelson/Webb Pierce, *In the Jailhouse Now* (1982)

Manuel plays piano on the title track of this summit by two of country music's all-time kings.

The Call, *Modern Romans* (1983)

Hudson had already played on the self-titled 1982 debut by this California new wave outfit when he returned for the follow-up, *Modern Romans*, which contains the MTV smash "The Walls Came Down." He also played on 1984's *Scene Beyond Dreams*; Robertson is on 1986's *Reconciled*.

Tom Petty and the Heartbreakers, *Southern Accents* (1985)

Coproduced by Robertson and Dave Stewart, the sixth LP by these long-running rockers boasts the vocal harmonies of Manuel and the keyboards of Hudson.

Marianne Faithfull, *Strange Weather* (1987)

The '60s pop singer turned Brechtian chanteuse tapped Hudson as her accordionist for this sparse, torchy masterpiece. He and Dr. John also appear on Faithfull's live *Blazing Away* from 1990.

The Chili Brothers, *Empty Bottles* (1988)

Rick Danko sings lead on three tracks of this album by Massachusetts bar band the Chili Brothers, who backed him on live solo dates. Late-period Band accompanists Buddy Cage and Sredni Vollmer are also heard.

Camper Van Beethoven, *Key Lime Pie* (1989)

Hudson adds his touch to this full-length by the 1980s college radio stalwarts; "Interlude" is basically him warming up on a pump organ in the studio.

Rufus Wainwright, *Want One* (2003)

Helm guests on drums on "14th Street" from this Great American Songbook–schooled singer-songwriter's *Want One* album and on "The One You Love," from its follow-up, *Want Two*. Both albums were recorded at Bearsville Studios. Hudson plays on Rufus's sister Martha Wainwright's self-titled 2005 debut.

Norah Jones, *Feels Like Home* (2004)

Helm drums and Hudson plays keyboards on "What Am I to You" from the internationally successful jazz-pop vocalist's third album.

Neko Case, *Fox Confessor Brings the Flood* (2006)

Session king Hudson lays down organ on four tracks of this acclaimed recording by the Canadian alt-country songstress, a project that also includes their mutual friends the Sadies.

30

Where Do We Go from Here?

The Musical Legacy of The Band

In The Band's footsteps came acts who parlayed their rusticated style into variants ranging from agile country funk (Little Feat) to blue-collar, R&B-based rock (Bruce Springsteen and the E Street Band), stripped-back, acoustic folk-blues roots (Hot Tuna), and slicked-up, M.O.R. imitations (the Eagles). But even today, decades after the quintet were at their height, their songs continue to inspire players to pick up their instruments and draw upon the enduring roots of American music—and, like a group formerly called the Hawks once did, to make that music their own. Here are some notable recent acts that follow in the dusty trail of The Band.

The Jayhawks

With their lush harmonies and sweetly mournful songwriting, this sumptuous Minneapolis alt-country outfit soared high atop the 1990s early Americana wave. Recommended: *Hollywood Town Hall*.

Wilco/Son Volt

These two groups were formed from the ashes of Uncle Tupelo, who pioneered the "No Depression" alt-country sound (the subgenre got its name from Uncle Tupelo's 1990 album). Wilco, led by singer-guitarist Jeff Tweedy, moved from a rootsy style to more experimental realms. Recommended: *Yankee Hotel Foxtrot*. Son Volt is helmed by singer-guitarist Jay Farrar and has maintained a more traditional approach. Recommended: *Trace*.

Mumford & Sons

With Elton John, Mavis Staples, and others, these popular British indie folk rockers paid tribute to Levon Helm with a version of "The Weight" at the 2013 Grammy Awards. Leader Marcus Mumford also performs with Elvis Costello and others in the New Basement Tapes, a project that sets unearthed Basement Tapes–era Bob Dylan lyrics to original music. Recommended: *Sigh No More.*

Los Lobos

Los Lobos could be called The Band of the barrio. Formed in East L.A. in 1973, the five-piece group fuses rock with country, blues, Tex-Mex, folk, R&B, and traditional Mexican and Spanish music. Helm played on their 1990 album *The Neighborhood*, and they've played at his Midnight Ramble events. Recommended: *Wolf Tracks: The Best of Los Lobos.*

The Sadies

Founded in 1994 by brothers Dallas and Travis Good, this phenomenal Toronto garage/punk/country/surf/rockabilly/all-that-good-stuff quartet are fanatical fans—they even cover the Hawks'/Canadian Squires' "Leave Me Alone," among numerous Band songs. Garth Hudson has performed and recorded with them. Recommended: *Favourite Colours.*

The Avett Brothers

Another brotherly act, this one was formed in 2000 and centers on siblings Scott and Seth Avett. Their early records are steeped in acoustic folk and bluegrass, but their later efforts, produced by hitmaker Rick Rubin (the Black Crowes), are in a more rocking, Band vein.

Blue Rodeo

At The Band's 1989 Canadian Music Hall of Fame induction ceremony, this long-running native pop country-rock quintet backed Robertson, Danko, and Hudson on a version of—what else?—"The Weight." Recommended: *Outskirts.*

The Palace Brothers

Led by singer-songwriter Will Oldham, this Kentucky collective debuted in the early 1990s with a hushed, beautifully sad, lo-fi folk sound that conjures the spirits of the Basement Tapes and *Music from Big Pink* for a new generation. An actor as well as a musician, Oldham starred in 1987's *Matewan*, whose dramatization of 1930s Southern labor union struggles dovetails with some of The Band's lyrical themes. He has also recorded under his own name and as Palace Songs, Palace Music, and Bonnie "Prince" Billy. Recommended: *There Is No-One What Will Take Care of You.*

The Gourds

To make their tenth studio album, Austin, Texas, staples the Gourds went straight to the hearth of Helm, recording 2011's Larry Campbell–produced *Old Mad Joy* at Levon Helm Studios. Also recommended: *Ghosts of Hallelujah.*

Counting Crows

While well known for 1993's inescapable, Van Morrison-esque hit "Mr. Jones," these alt-pop stalwarts are up-front about their debts to The Band; see 2002's "If I Could Give All My Love (Richard Manuel Is Dead)." Recommended: *Hard Candy.*

Robyn Hitchcock

The Soft Boys main man credits the marginalized *Stage Fright*, rather than *Music from Big Pink* or *The Band*, as the Band album that made him a fan—such a fan that in 2015 the whimsical British songsmith performed the entire album live with the Sadies as his backup band. Recommended: *I Often Dream of Trains.*

Fleet Foxes

Much of this heavily bearded, harmony-rich Northwestern U.S. band's style is traceable to English folk, but the bucolic side of The Band is evident in their sound as well. Recommended: *Fleet Foxes.*

Led by founding singer and guitarist Robin Pecknold (seated at far left), Seattle band Fleet Foxes blend English folk with Band-style Americana.   *Getty Images*

Lord Huron

Lord Huron's leader, singer-songwriter Ben Schneider, made no bones about who his idols were when he named his group's L.A. recording facility Whispering Pines Studio. Recommended: *Strange Trails.*

Nick Cave and the Bad Seeds

It may seem a stretch to include the dark poet of post-punk and his group here. But Cave's lyrical fascination with the Southern Gothic literature of

William Faulkner and Flannery O'Connor echoes Robertson's, and the Bad Seeds' piano/organ combination is pure Manuel/Hudson. Recommended: *Let Love In*.

The Waco Brothers

Like Cave and crew, Jon Langford and his band the Mekons also came out of the late-'70s punk explosion. After the Mekons had begun working country influences into their scrappy style, Langford launched side project the Waco Brothers to more fully explore his Americana appetite. The results play like The Band filtered through the Clash. Recommended: *Cowboy in Flames*.

The Waterboys

From across the pond as well, the Waterboys have at times leaned toward arena pomp. But their key albums *Fishermen's Blues* (1988) and *Room to Roam* (1990), both full of panoramic, folk-based songs and shimmering with fiddles and mandolins, do for traditional Celtic music what The Band did for older American styles. Recommended: *Fishermen's Blues*.

Dawes

The spell of The Band is unmistakable on the earnest-but-easygoing records of this West Coast unit. Lead singer Taylor Goldsmith's voice floats somewhere between those of Danko and Jackson Browne. Recommended: *North Hills*.

Old 97's

These sidewinding country-rockers began in Dallas in 1993, but leader Rhett Miller would later spend time in the Hudson Valley soaking up the vibes of The Band. It shows on the Old 97's albums and in his solo output. Recommended: *Too Far to Care*.

Railroad Earth

Juggernauts of the jam-band circuit, Railroad Earth cross rock with bluegrass, folk, Celtic, and improvisational jazz elements—but never at the expense of their great songs. Recommended: *Elko*.

The Low Anthem

Neo-folk traditionalists the Low Anthem spent the winter of 2010 recording their third album in a crumbling former pasta sauce factory in their hometown of Providence, Rhode Island. The Bolognaise Tapes, perhaps? Recommended: *Smart Flesh*.

Over by the Wildwood: The Band's Woodstock Heirs

More than a decade after The Band called it quits, the Woodstock area they knew as home still teems with their local musical peers and descendants. Let's meet a few.

Amy Helm

Singer-songwriter and mandolinist Amy Helm is, of course, literally a Band descendant, being the daughter of Levon Helm. In the early 2000s, she cofounded the gospel-bluegrass-country quintet Ollabelle. Between playing in her father's band on the road and at his Midnight Ramble sessions, she recorded her long-awaited debut, 2015's *Didn't It Rain*. Amy currently performs with her band the Handsome Strangers.

Larry Campbell and Teresa Williams

Likewise linked closely to Levon Helm are the husband-and-wife duo of guitarist, fiddler, and singer Larry Campbell and singer and guitarist Teresa Williams, who were both integral to the drummer's late-period bands. Campbell, who produced Helm's final albums, *Dirt Farmer* and *Electric Dirt*, had toured for seven years with Bob Dylan before the couple settled in Woodstock.

Mike and Ruthy

Another husband-and-wife act, folk-rockers Mike and Ruthy, a.k.a singer-guitarist Michael Merenda and singer-violinist Ruth Ungar, met as members of New York band the Mammals. Ruth is the daughter of renowned Hudson Valley fiddler Jay Ungar of the likewise married twosome Jay Ungar and Molly Mason (the creators of the music for Ken Burns's documentary *The Civil War*). The Mike and Ruthy Band's 2015 album *Bright as You Can* features the song "The Ghost of Richard Manuel," which should tell you something about the duo's approach.

The Felice Brothers

The pride of Palenville, New York, a microscopic hamlet just up the road from Big Pink, the Felice Brothers have channeled the vagabond ethos of the Hawks and the ramshackle sound of the Brown Album–era Band more strongly than just about any act of the early 2000s. The group formed around the nucleus of Ian, James, and Simone Felice and went from busking on the Manhattan streets to headlining sold-out international tours and releasing critically acclaimed albums. Simone Felice later went solo.

Steve Earle

For a spell in the 2010s rock-driven country singer-songwriter, actor, and folk activist Steve Earle lived in Woodstock, where he befriended and began performing with Levon Helm. The drummer recorded Earle's "The Mountain" for *Dirt Farmer* and there are clips of Earle singing the song with Helm's band on YouTube.

Mercury Rev

The music of neo-psychedelic rockers Mercury Rev isn't audibly descended from the elemental styles that inform The Band's. But much of their cosmic sound is imbued with a similar emotional essence. "When we were writing [acclaimed 1998 album] *Deserter's Songs*, it struck us that some of the intangibles in it were from listening to The Band," singer Jonathan Donohue explained to *Uncut*. "So rather than beat around the bush, we gave them a call." Thus, Helm and Hudson make guest appearances on *Deserter's Songs*; Danko had agreed to play on the follow-up, *All Is Dream*, but passed away before the sessions.

Professor Louie and the Crowmatix

The hardest-working band in Woodstock, Professor Louie and the Crowmatix are led by keyboardist Aaron "Professor Louie" Hurwitz, who produced The Band's three 1990s studio albums. With the Crowmatix, Hurwitz worked with Danko, Helm, and Hudson on numerous solo recording projects and live performances.

Tom Pacheco

In addition to recording many of his own albums, singer-songwriter Tom Pacheco coauthored tunes with Helm and Danko for The Band's *Jubilation* album and contributed two numbers to Danko's *Times Like These.* Jim Weider produced Pacheco's albums *Rebel Spring*, *The Last American Songwriter: Bare Bones II*, and *Woodstock Winter*, which features The Band's bassist and drummer.

The Wood Brothers

Our list's last band of brothers is the acoustic duo of singer and guitarist Oliver Wood and bassist Chris Wood, the latter a founding member of jazz-funk trio Medeski, Martin and Wood. It's not difficult to picture the austere songs on 2008's *Loaded* wafting out of Big Pink in 1967.

Connor Kennedy

The Band's Woodstock legacy is in good, strong hands with this young blues-rock guitarist and singer-songwriter, who leads his own groups and has worked with Amy Helm and others (check YouTube for the two performing our heroes' "Christmas Must Be Tonight"). Kennedy grew up in the area attending the Midnight Rambles at Levon Helm's barn. "It really was the most musically important time of my life," the guitarist, who eventually performed there himself, told the Kingston *Daily Freeman* in 2013. "It influenced the kind of music I like. Levon and The Band raised music to a whole new level."

Selected Bibliography

The following list does not reflect all of the sources used in the research for this book, but it includes the ones that proved to be the most useful in my work.

Books

Editors of *Rolling Stone* magazine. *Knockin' on Dylan's Door: On the Road '74.* New York: Pocket Books, 1974.

Finkelstein, Bernie. *True North.* Toronto: McLelland & Stewart, 2012.

Goodman, Fred. *The Mansion on the Hill: Dylan, Young, Geffen, Springsteen and the Head-On Collision of Rock and Commerce.* New York: Vintage Books, 1998.

Griffin, Sid. *Million Dollar Bash: Bob Dylan, The Band, and the Basement Tapes.* London: Jawbone Press, 2007.

Hajdu, David. *Positively Fourth Street: The Lives and Times of Joan Baez, Bob Dylan, Mimi Baez Fariña, and Richard Fariña.* New York: Farrar, Straus and Giroux, 2001.

Harris, Craig. *The Band: Pioneers of Americana Music.* New York: Rowman & Littlefield, 2014.

Hawkins, Ronnie, with Peter Goddard. *Ronnie Hawkins: Last of the Good Ol' Boys.* Toronto: Stoddart, 1989.

Helm, Levon, with Stephen Davis. *This Wheel's on Fire: Levon Helm and the Story of The Band.* Chicago: Chicago Review Press, 1993.

Hoskyns, Barney. *Across the Great Divide: The Band and America.* Milwaukee, WI: Hal Leonard, 1993.

Jennings, Nicholas. *Before the Gold Rush.* Toronto: Viking, 1997.

Landy, Elliott. *The Band Photographs: 1968–1969.* Montclair, NJ: Backbeat Books, 2015.

———. *Woodstock Vision: The Spirit of a Generation.* New York: Backbeat Books, 2009.

LaRaia, Paul. *The Levon Helm Midnight Ramble.* New York: Backbeat Books, 2009.

Malanowski, Jamie. *The Book of Levon: The Trials and Triumphs of Levon Helm.* Amazon Digital Publishing/Bolt Books, 2014.

Marcus, Greil. *Mystery Train: Images of America in Rock 'n' Roll Music*. New York: E.P. Dutton, 1975.

——. *The Old, Weird America: The World of Bob Dylan's Basement Tapes*. New York: Picador, 2009.

Maynard-Reed, Pedrito. *Diverse Worship: African-American, Caribbean & Hispanic Perspectives*. Downers Grove, IL: InterVarsity Press, 2000.

Mersereau, Bob. *The History of Canadian Rock 'n' Roll*. Montclair, NJ: Backbeat Books, 2015.

Niven, John. *Music from Big Pink*. New York: Continuum, 2005.

Palmer, Robert. *Blues & Chaos: The Music Writing of Robert Palmer*. New York: Scribner, 2009.

Robertson, Robbie, with Jim Guerinot, Sebastian Robertson, and Jared Levine. *Legends, Icons & Rebels: Music That Changed the World*. Toronto: Tundra Books, 2013.

Robertson, Sebastian. *Rock & Roll Highway: The Robbie Robertson Story*. New York: Henry Holt and Company, 2014.

Schneider, Jason. *Whispering Pines: The Northern Roots of American Music from Hank Snow to The Band*. Toronto: ECW Press, 2009.

Smart, Paul. *Rock & Woodstock*. Fleischmanns, NY: Purple Mountain Press, 1994.

Articles

Browne, David. "Dylan's Accidental Masterpiece." *Rolling Stone*, November 20, 2014.

Hasted, Nick. "To Kingdome Come." *Uncut*, April 2005.

Poppy, John. "The Band: Music from Home." *Look*, August 25, 1970.

Liner Notes

Bowman, Rob. *The Band: A Musical History* box set. Capitol Records, 2005.

——. *Music from Big Pink*, *The Band*, *Stage Fright*, *Rock of Ages*, *Moondog Matinee*, *Northern Lights—Southern Cross*, and *Islands* CD remasters. Capitol Records, 2000–2001.

Griffin, Sid, Clinton Heylin, and Jan Haust. *Bob Dylan and The Band: The Basement Tapes Complete*. Columbia Records, 2014.

Websites

http://theband.hiof.no/
http://www.thebandofficial.com/
http://www.geocities.jp/hideki_wtnb/bandcontents.html

Index

THE FAQ SERIES

Nirvana FAQ
by John D. Luerssen
Backbeat Books
9781617134500.................... $24.99

Pink Floyd FAQ
by Stuart Shea
Backbeat Books
9780879309503....................$19.99

Elvis Films FAQ
by Paul Simpson
Applause Books
9781557838582.................... $24.99

Elvis Music FAQ
by Mike Eder
Backbeat Books
9781617130496.................... $24.99

Pearl Jam FAQ
*by Bernard M. Corbett and
Thomas Edward Harkins*
Backbeat Books
9781617136122...........................$19.99

Prog Rock FAQ
by Will Romano
Backbeat Books
9781617135873...................... $24.99

Pro Wrestling FAQ
by Brian Solomon
Backbeat Books
9781617135996...................... $29.99

**The Rocky Horror
Picture Show FAQ**
by Dave Thompson
Applause Books
9781495007477 ....$19.99

Rush FAQ
by Max Mobley
Backbeat Books
9781617134517 ....$19.99

Saturday Night Live FAQ
by Stephen Tropiano
Applause Books
9781557839510..................... $24.99

Seinfeld FAQ
by Nicholas Nigro
Applause Books
9781557838575.................... $24.99

Sherlock Holmes FAQ
by Dave Thompson
Applause Books
9781480331495.................... $24.99

The Smiths FAQ
by John D. Luerssen
Backbeat Books
9781480394490.................. $24.99

Soccer FAQ
by Dave Thompson
Backbeat Books
9781617135989...................... $24.99

The Sound of Music FAQ
by Barry Monush
Applause Books
9781480360433................... $27.99

South Park FAQ
by Dave Thompson
Applause Books
9781480350649.................. $24.99

Bruce Springsteen FAQ
by John D. Luerssen
Backbeat Books
9781617130939.......................$22.99

Star Trek FAQ
(Unofficial and Unauthorized)
by Mark Clark
Applause Books
9781557837929.....................$19.99

Star Trek FAQ 2.0
(Unofficial and Unauthorized)
by Mark Clark
Applause Books
9781557837936.....................$22.99

Star Wars FAQ
by Mark Clark
Applause Books
978480360181 .... $24.99

Quentin Tarantino FAQ
by Dale Sherman
Applause Books
9781480355880 .... $24.99

Three Stooges FAQ
by David J. Hogan
Applause Books
9781557837882....................$22.99

TV Finales FAQ
*by Stephen Tropiano and
Holly Van Buren*
Applause Books
9781480391444 ....$19.99

The Twilight Zone FAQ
by Dave Thompson
Applause Books
9781480396180 ....$19.99

Twin Peaks FAQ
*by David Bushman and
Arthur Smith*
Applause Books
9781495015861.......................$19.99

The Who FAQ
by Mike Segretto
Backbeat Books
9781480361034 .... $24.99

The Wizard of Oz FAQ
by David J. Hogan
Applause Books
9781480350625 .... $24.99

The X-Files FAQ
by John Kenneth Muir
Applause Books
9781480369740................... $24.99

Neil Young FAQ
by Glen Boyd
Backbeat Books
9781617130373.......................$19.99

Frank Zappa FAQ
by John Corcelli
Backbeat Books
9781617136030......................$19.99

HAL•LEONARD®
PERFORMING ARTS
PUBLISHING GROUP

FAQ.halleonardbooks.com

0316